PRAISE FOR

Happy City

"Charles Montgomery's message is simple: If we're going to save the world, we must first be happier, and that means creating happier cities. *Happy City* isn't just a book about urban design written for urban professionals; it's for everyone who's ever wondered if their city could be a better place, and what they can do about it."   —Jarrett Walker, author of
Human Transit

"A brilliant, entertaining, and vital book. Charles Montgomery deftly leads us from our misplaced focus on money, cars, and stuff to consider what makes us truly happy. Then everything changes—the way we live, work, and play in humanity's major habitat, the city."
—David Suzuki, host of CBC's *The Nature of Things* and
cofounder of the David Suzuki Foundation

"What makes *Happy City* such an instructive book is that it first describes the pathologies distressing big cities, globally, and then outlines the solutions that can offer a cure."   —Robert Collison, *The Toronto Star*

"[An] ambitious cross-disciplinary and prescriptive book."
—Tom Vanderbilt, *Columbia Journalism Review*

"I thought I already lived in a happy city: New York. But Charles Montgomery reveals how much happier all of us—kids and adults—can be if we only reconsider what actually contributes to the good life. Suddenly I'm thinking of all the ways we can make millions of people happier. What a great book!"   —Lenore Skenazy, author of *Free-Range Kids*

"[Charles Montgomery] builds a convincing case for a new metric of success. The best way to judge a city is not through its median income or soaring architecture, he suggests, but through the happiness of those who live there."   —Diane Brady, *Bloomsberg Businessweek*

"A great book." —Brian Hines, *Willamette Live*

"In a word, *wow*. I thought I had it all figured out, but this is something I was missing. In echoing all the great economic, health, and environmental mandates for walkable cities, I had mostly sidestepped the concept of happiness, thinking it too intangible to discuss in a compelling way. Thank goodness Charles Montgomery has had the guts and the skill to correct my error with this fascinating and entertaining book."
—Jeff Speck, author of *Walkable City*

"I read *Happy City* with surprise and delight. Finally, a book that reveals to a broad audience the essence of what it takes to make a city that promotes health and happiness." —Suzanne H. Crowhurst Lennard, LivableCities.org

"Charles Montgomery's *Happy City* is a gutsy examination of the neuroscience and psychology behind urban well-being and a guide for making our cities happier. If bike-able burbs and amenable, shoppable, walkable neighborhoods sound too good to be true, give *Happy City* a chance to change your mind." —James S. Russell, author of *The Agile City*

ELIZABETH BORNE

CHARLES MONTGOMERY

Happy City

Charles Montgomery is an award-winning journalist and urban engagement specialist, and the author of *The Shark God*, which won the 2005 Charles Taylor Prize for Literary Non-Fiction under its Canadian title, *The Last Heathen*. Find him at www.charlesmontgomery.ca and www.thehappycity.com.

Happy
City

TRANSFORMING

OUR LIVES

THROUGH

URBAN DESIGN

CHARLES MONTGOMERY

FARRAR, STRAUS AND GIROUX | NEW YORK

Farrar, Straus and Giroux
18 West 18th Street, New York 10011

Grateful acknowledgment is made for permission to reprint a haiku from Honku:
The Zen Antidote to Road Rage by Aaron Naparstek, copyright © 2003
by Villard Books. Reprinted by permission of Aaron Naparstek.

The Library of Congress has cataloged the hardcover edition as follows:
Montgomery, Charles, 1968–
Happy city : transforming our lives through urban design / Charles Montgomery. —
First edition.
    pages   cm
Includes bibliographical references.
ISBN 978-0-374-16823-0 (hardback) — ISBN 978-1-4299-6953-6 (ebook)
    1. City planning—Psychological aspects.   2. Urban beautification—Psychological
aspects.   3. City dwellers—Psychology.   4. Environmental psychology.   I. Title.

HT166 .M5865 2013
307.1'216—dc23

2013022587

Paperback ISBN: 978-0-374-53488-2

Farrar, Straus and Giroux books may be purchased for educational, business, or
promotional use. For information on bulk purchases, please contact the Macmillan
Corporate and Premium Sales Department at 1-800-221-7945, extension 5442, or
write to specialmarkets@macmillan.com.

www.fsgbooks.com
www.twitter.com/fsgbooks • www.facebook.com/fsgbooks

15   17   19   20   18   16   14

BRITISH COLUMBIA
ARTS COUNCIL
An agency of the Province of British Columbia

We acknowledge the support of the Canada Council for the Arts, which last year
invested $157 million to bring the arts to Canadians throughout the country.

Nous remercions le Conseil des arts du Canada de son soutien. L'an dernier,
le Conseil a investi 157 millions de dollars pour mettre de l'art dans la vie des
Canadiennes et des Canadiens de tout le pays.

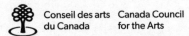

Conseil des arts   Canada Council
du Canada   for the Arts

Contents

Happy City

1. The Mayor of Happy

There is a myth, sometimes widespread, that a person
need only do inner work, in order to be alive like this; that a
man is entirely responsible for his own problems; and that
to cure himself, he need only change himself . . . The fact
is, a person is so far formed by his surroundings, that his
state of harmony depends entirely on his harmony with his
surroundings.

—Christopher Alexander,
The Timeless Way of Building

I chased the politician through the bowels of a dull cement office
block on the edge of a twelve-lane freeway. Everything about him
suggested urgency. He hollered with the hurried fervor of a preacher.
He wore the kind of close-trimmed beard favored by men who don't
like to waste time shaving. He jogged through the building's basement
parking deck in a long-legged canter, like a center forward charging
for a long pass.

Two bodyguards trotted behind him, their pistols jostling in hol-
sters. There was nothing remarkable about that, given his profession—
and his locale. Enrique Peñalosa was a perennial politician on yet
another campaign, and this was Bogotá, a city with a spectacular reputation for kidnappings and assassination. What was unusual was
this: Peñalosa didn't climb into the armored SUV typical of most
public figures in Colombia. Instead, he hopped on a knobby-tired
mountain bike and quickly cranked his way up a ramp into the sear-
ing Andean sunlight. Then he was off, jumping curbs and potholes,
riding one-handed, weaving across the pavement, and barking into

his cell phone while his pin-striped trousers flapped in the breeze. His bodyguards, a photographer, and I all pedaled madly behind, like a throng of teenagers in the wake of a rock star.

A few years earlier, this ride would have been a radical and—in the opinion of many Bogotanos—suicidal act. If you wanted to be assaulted, asphyxiated by exhaust, or run over, Bogotá's streets were the place to be. But now it was 2007, and Peñalosa insisted that things had changed. We would be safe. The city had gotten happier, thanks to his plan. *Happier*—that was the word he used over and over again, as though he owned it.

Young women giggled as he passed. Overall-clad laborers waved.

"Mayor! Mayor!" a few of them shouted in Spanish, though it had been six years since Peñalosa had held that job, and his campaign to regain it had barely begun. He waved back with his phone hand.

"Buenos días, hermosa!" he said to the girls.

"¿Cómo le va?" he answered the men.

"Hola, amigo!" he offered to anyone who looked his way.

"We're living an experiment," he finally yelled back at me as he pocketed his cell phone. "We might not be able to fix the economy. We might not be able to make everyone as rich as Americans. But we can design the city to give people dignity, to make them *feel* rich. The city can make them happier."

There it was, the declaration I have seen bring tears to so many eyes with its promise of urban revolution and redemption.

It's been six years since my ride with the Mayor of Happy, but the memory has remained with me, as vivid as the Andean sun. That was the day the journey began.

You may never have heard of Enrique Peñalosa. You may not have been among the crowds that gave him a hero's welcome in New York, Los Angeles, Singapore, Lagos, or Mexico City over the last decade. You may never have seen him raise his arms like an evangelist or holler his philosophy over the noise of a hundred idling car engines. But his grand experiment and his even grander rhetoric inspire an urbanist fervor wherever he goes. Peñalosa has become one of the central figures in a movement that is changing the structure and soul of cities around the world.

I first saw Peñalosa work his rhetorical magic back in the spring of 2006. The United Nations had just announced that some day in the following months, one more child would be born in an urban hospital or a migrant would stumble into a metropolitan shantytown, and from that moment on, more than half the world's people would be living in cities. Hundreds of millions more were on their way. By 2030 almost five billion of us will be urban. That spring, Habitat, the UN's agency for human settlements, called thousands of mayors, engineers, bureaucrats, and do-gooders together for the World Urban Forum. The delegates met in a harborside convention center in Vancouver to figure out how to save the world's exploding cities from disaster.

The world had little inkling of the great recession slouching on the horizon, yet the prognosis was bleak. The problem? On the one hand, cities were pumping out most of the world's pollution and 80 percent of humanity's greenhouse gas emissions. On the other, all predictions suggested that cities were going to be slammed by the effects of climate change, from heat waves and water scarcity to waves of migrants running from droughts, floods, and water wars. The experts agreed that cities would bear more than three-quarters of the cost of adapting to global warming. They would be short on energy, tax revenue, and jobs. There seemed to be no way they were going to be able to help citizens meet the goals of security and prosperity that urbanization had always seemed to promise. The gathering was sobering.

But the mood changed when Peñalosa took the podium. He told the mayors that there was hope, that the great migration was not a threat—no!—it was a tremendous opportunity to reinvent urban life. As poor cities doubled or tripled in size, they could avoid the mistakes that rich cities had made. They could offer their citizens lives that were better, stronger, freer, and more joyful than those offered by most cities of the day. But to accomplish this, they would have to completely rethink their beliefs about what cities are for. They would have to let go of a century of thought about city building. They would have to let go of some of their dreams.

To make his point, Peñalosa told a story.

Toward the end of the twentieth century, Bogotá had become a truly horrible place to live—one of the very worst on earth. Overwhelmed with refugees; seared by a decades-old civil war and sporadic terrorism in the form of grenades and firebombs (deadly "explosive potatoes" being the most common means of attack); and hobbled by traffic, pollution, poverty, and dysfunction, the Colombian capital was regarded both at home and abroad as a living hell.

When Peñalosa ran for the mayor's seat back in 1997, he refused to make the promises doled out by so many politicians. He was not going to make everyone richer. Forget the dream of becoming as wealthy as Americans: it would take generations to catch up to the gringos, even if the urban economy caught fire and burned blue for a century. The dream of riches, Peñalosa complained, served only to make Bogotans feel bad.

"If we defined our success just in terms of income per capita, we would have to accept ourselves as second- or third-rate societies—as a bunch of *losers*," he said. No, the city needed a new goal. Peñalosa promised neither a car in every garage nor a socialist revolution. His promise was simple. He was going to make Bogotans happier.

"And what are our needs for happiness?" he asked. "We need to walk, just as birds need to fly. We need to be around other people. We need beauty. We need contact with nature. And most of all, we need not to be excluded. We need to feel some sort of equality."

Ironically, in giving up the chase for the American dream, Peñalosa was invoking a goal set out in the American Constitution: by pursuing a different kind of happiness, Bogotans, despite their relatively meager paychecks, really could beat the gringos.

These days, the world is not lacking for happiness gurus. Some insist that spiritual practice is the answer. Others tell us that we must simply ask the universe for prosperity, that we can get closer to God by getting richer, and get richer by inching closer to God. But Peñalosa did not call for mass counseling or religious indoctrination or state-funded courses in positive psychology. He did not preach the law of attraction or the tenets of transformative wealth. This was a gospel of transformative urbanism. The city itself could be a device for happiness. Life could be improved, even amid economic doldrums, by changing the shapes and systems that defined urban existence.

Peñalosa attributed an almost transcendent power to a certain kind of urbanity. "Most things that people buy in stores give them a lot of satisfaction the moment they buy them," Peñalosa told me.

"But after a few days, that satisfaction decreases, and months later, it completely melts away. But great public space is a kind of magical good. It never ceases to yield happiness. It's almost happiness itself." The humble sidewalk, the park, the bike path, and the bus were suddenly elevated to the psycho-spiritual realm.

Peñalosa insisted that like most cities, Bogotá had been left deeply wounded by the twentieth century's dual urban legacy: First, the city had been gradually reoriented around private automobiles. Second, public spaces and resources had largely been privatized. Cars and mobile vendors took over public plazas and sidewalks. People had walled or fenced in what were once public parks. In an age where even most of the poor had televisions, common civic space was disregarded and degraded.

This reorganization was both unfair—only one in five families even owned a car—and cruel. Urban residents had been denied the opportunity to enjoy the city's simplest daily pleasures: walking on convivial streets; sitting around in public; talking; gazing at grass, water, falling leaves, and other people. And playing: children had largely disappeared from Bogotá's streets—not because of the fear of gunfire or abduction, but because the streets had been rendered dangerous by sheer speed. When any parent shouted, "Watch out!" everyone in Bogotá knew that a child was in danger of being run over. So Peñalosa's first and most defining act as mayor was to declare war: not on crime or drugs or poverty, but on private cars.

"A city can be friendly to people or it can be friendly to cars, but it can't be both," he announced.

He then threw out the city's ambitious highway expansion plan and instead poured his budget into hundreds of miles of bike paths; a vast new chain of parks and pedestrian plazas; and a network of new libraries, schools, and day-care centers. He built the city's first rapid transit system, using buses instead of trains. He hiked gas taxes and banned drivers from commuting by car more than three times a week. I'll discuss the details later, but the thing to understand here is that this program redesigned the experience of city living for millions of people, and it was an utter rejection of the philosophies that have guided city builders around the world for more than half a century. It was the opposite of the city that North American laws, habits, the real estate industry, financing arrangements, and development ideologies have favored. In particular, it was the opposite of the vision that millions of middle-class people around the world have chased to suburbia.

In the third year of his term Peñalosa challenged Bogotans to participate in an experiment, a *día sin carro*. As of dawn on February 24, 2000, all private cars were banned from city streets for the day. More than eight hundred thousand vehicles sat still that Thursday. Buses were jam-packed and taxis hard to come by, but hundreds of thousands of people followed Peñalosa's example and hit the streets under their own steam, walking, cycling, skating to work and school.

It was the first day in four years that nobody was killed in traffic. Hospital admissions fell by almost a third. The toxic haze over the city thinned. People still got to work, and schools reported normal attendance. Bogotans enjoyed the day so much that they voted to make it a yearly affair, and to ban all private cars during rush hour *every day* by 2015. People told pollsters that they were more optimistic about city life than they had been in years.

Peñalosa recounts this story with all the fervor of Martin Luther King on the Washington Mall, and with similar effect. I saw three thousand people at the World Urban Forum leap up from their chairs and cheer in response. UN statisticians brought their hands together despite themselves. Indian economists beamed and loosened their ties. Senegalese delegates shook and danced in their carnival-colored wraps. Mexican architects whistled. My heart beat faster, too. Peñalosa seemed to be affirming what so many urban thinkers are sure of, but very rarely have the guts or the audacity to say. The city is a means to a way of life. It can be a reflection of all our best selves. It can be whatever we want it to be.

It can change, and change dramatically.

The Movement

Is urban design really powerful enough to make or break happiness? The question deserves consideration because the happy city message is taking root around the world. Since Peñalosa's three-year term in office—consecutive terms are illegal in Colombia—delegations from dozens of cities have landed in Bogotá to study its transformation.

Peñalosa and his younger brother, Guillermo, the city's former parks manager, were called to advise cities on every continent. While the elder proselytized from Shanghai to Jakarta to Lagos, the younger hit Guadalajara, Mexico City, and Toronto. While Guillermo whipped up hundreds of activists in Portland, Enrique was urging planners in Los Angeles to let traffic become so unbearable that drivers simply abandoned their cars. In 2006 Enrique Peñalosa was the talk of Manhattan after he announced to crowds of gridlock-obsessed New Yorkers they should ban vehicles entirely from Broadway. Three years later, the impossible vision began to come to life around Times Square. The happy city had gone global.

The Peñalosa brothers are far from alone in the happy city crusade. The movement has its roots in the antimodernist foment of the 1960s and has gradually drawn architects, neighborhood activists, public health experts, transportation engineers, network theorists, and politicians into a battle for the shape and soul of cities—a confrontation that is finally reaching critical mass. They have torn down freeways in Seoul and San Francisco and Milwaukee. They have experimented with the height, shape, and facades of buildings. They have turned the black top of suburban shopping malls into mini-villages. They have reconfigured entire towns to better suit children. They have torn down backyard fences and reclaimed neighborhood intersections. They are reorganizing the systems that hold cities together and rewriting the rules that dictate the shapes and functions of our buildings. Some of these people aren't even aware that they are part of the same movement, but together they are aiming a wrecking ball at many of the places we have spent the last half century building.

Peñalosa insists that the unhappiest cities in the world, the ones perfectly calibrated to turn wealth into hardship, are not the seething metropolises of Africa or South America. "The most dynamic economies of the twentieth century produced the most miserable cities of all," Peñalosa told me over the roar of traffic in Bogotá. "I'm talking about the U.S., of course—Atlanta, Phoenix, Miami, cities totally dominated by private cars."

For most Americans, the claim that prosperity and the cherished automobile propelled wealthy cities away from happiness is practically heresy. It is one thing for a Colombian politician to offer advice to the world's poor, but it is quite another for him to suggest that the world's most powerful nation should be taking design criticism born on the potholed byways of South America. If Peñalosa is right, then not only have generations of planners, engineers, politicians, and land developers been mistaken, but millions of us have taken a wrong turn on the road to the good life.

But then again, over the last few decades, prosperity and well-being in America have followed completely different trajectories.

The Happiness Paradox

If one was to judge by sheer wealth, the last half century should have been an ecstatically happy time for people in the United States and other rich nations such as Canada, Japan, and Great Britain. Riches were piled upon riches. By the turn of the century, Americans traveled more, ate more, bought more, used more space, and threw away more stuff than ever before. More people than ever got to live the dream of having their own detached home. The stock of cars—and bedrooms and toilets—far surpassed the number of humans who used them.* It was an age of unprecedented bounty and growth, at least until the great recession of 2008 stuck a needle into the balloon of optimism and easy credit.

And yet the boom decades of the late twentieth century were not accompanied by a boom in happiness. Surveys show that people's assessment of their own well-being in the United States pretty much flatlined during that time. It was the same with citizens in Japan and the United Kingdom. Canada fared only slightly better. China, the new star of supercharged GDP growth, is providing yet more evidence of a paradox. Between 1999 and 2010, a decade in which average pur-

---

*Americans used to get by with one bathroom. Now half of households have two or more. In 1950 there was one car for every three Americans. By 2011 there were almost enough motor vehicles to put every man, woman, and drooling baby behind a wheel. In 2010 Americans racked up more than double the highway miles than in 1960. They flew ten times as far in airplanes. Their new homes offered more than three times as much square footage for each inhabitant. The wealth explosion was even reflected in landfills: in 2010 the average person produced nearly four and a half pounds of garbage every day—a 60 percent jump from 1960.

chasing power in China grew more than threefold, people's ratings of their own life satisfaction stalled, according to Gallup polls (although urbanized Chinese were happier than their rural cousins).

In the final decades of the last century, Americans increasingly complained of personal problems. By 2005 clinical depression was three to ten times as common as it was two generations ago. By 2010, one in ten Americans reported that they suffered from depression. Six to eight times as many college students experienced depression in 2007 as they did in 1938. Although this may be partly due to cultural factors—it's now more acceptable to talk about depression—objective mental health statistics are not encouraging. High school and college students—the easiest group to survey—climbed higher and higher on what mental health researchers cheerily call the Paranoia, Hysteria, Hypochondriasis, and Depression scales. One in ten Americans is taking antidepressants.

Analysis from free-market think tanks such as the Cato Institute assures us that "high levels of economic freedom and high average incomes are among the strongest correlates of subjective well-being," which is to say that being rich and free should make us happier. So why wasn't the half-century surge in wealth accompanied by a surge in happiness? What was counteracting the effect of all that money?

Some psychologists point to the phenomenon dubbed the "hedonic treadmill": the natural human tendency to shift our expectations along with our changing fortunes. The treadmill theory suggests that the richer you get, the more you compare yourself to other rich people and the faster the wheel of desire spins beneath your feet, so that you end up feeling as though you haven't made any progress. Others blame the growing income gap, and the realization by millions of middle-class Americans that they were falling farther behind the richest members of society, especially during the last two decades. There is some explanatory truth in both of these theories, but economists have crunched the survey numbers and concluded that they only partially explain that widening gap between material and emotional wealth.

Consider this: The decades-long expansion in the American economy paralleled the migration of society from the country to cities, and from cities to the in-between world of sprawl. Since 1940, almost all urban growth has actually been *sub*urban. In the decade before the big bust of 2008, the economy was driven to a large extent by the boundless cul-de-sac-ing, tract housing, and big-box power centering of the landscape at the urban fringe. For a time, it was impossible to separate growth from suburbanization. They were the same thing. More people than ever got exactly what they thought they wanted. Everything we have come to believe about the good life would suggest that this suburban boom was good for happiness. Why didn't it work? And why was faith in this model so quick to evaporate? The urban shake-up that began with the mortgage crisis in 2008 hit the newest, shiniest, most sprawling parts of the American city the hardest.

Peñalosa's argument was that too many rich societies have used their wealth in ways that exacerbate urban problems rather than solve them. Could this help explain the happiness paradox?

It's certainly a good time to consider the idea, now that tens of thousands of freshly paved cul-de-sacs across the United States have passed six springs without sprouting new homes. From the United States to Ireland to Spain, communities on the edge of suburban sprawl, that most American of forms, have yet to regain their pre-crash value. The future of cities is uncertain.

We have reached a rare moment in history where societies and markets appear to be teetering between the status quo and a radical change in the way we live and the way we design our lives in cities. For the first time in nine decades, census data in 2010/2011 showed that major American cities experienced more growth than their suburbs. It's too early to tell if this is a complete turning of the tide of urban dispersal. Many forces are at play, from the lingering housing market slowdown and high unemployment to historically low population mobility. But other forces are systemic and powerful enough to permanently alter the course of urban history.

First is a reckoning on energy. It will probably never again be inexpensive to fill a gas tank. There is too little easy oil left in the ground, and there are too many people competing for it. The same goes for other nonrenewable forms of energy and raw materials. The sprawl city requires cheap energy, cheap land, and cheap materials, and the days of cheap are over. Another force is a truth acknowledged by every sober, informed observer: cities are contributing to the crisis of climate change. If we are going to avoid the cataclysmic effects of global warming, we must find more efficient ways to build and live. Of course it is not at all certain that a rush back to urban density will produce better lives than did suburban dispersal.

But the happy city theory presents an alluring possibility.

If a poor and broken city such as Bogotá can be reconfigured to produce more joy, then surely it's possible to apply happy city principles to the wounds of wealthy places. And if more extravagant, private, polluting, and energy-hungry communities have failed to deliver on happiness, then the search for a happier city might well be expected to reveal a greener, more resilient city, a place that saves the world while saving our own lives. If there was a science behind it, presumably that science could also be used to show how all of us might renovate good feelings in our communities.

Of course, Peñalosa's rhetoric is not science; it raises as many questions as it answers. Its inspirational qualities do not constitute proof of the city's power to make or break happiness, any more than the Beatles' "All You Need Is Love" is proof that all you really do need is love. To test the idea, you would have to decide what you meant by happiness, and you would need a way to measure it. You would have to understand how a road, a bus, a park, or a building might contribute to good feelings. You would have to tabulate the psychological effects of driving in traffic, or catching the eye of a stranger on the sidewalk, or pausing in a pocket park, or of feeling crowded or lonely, or of the simple feeling that the city you live in is a good or bad place. You would have to go beyond politics and philosophy to find a map of the ingredients of happiness, if it exists at all.

The cheers in that Vancouver ballroom echoed in my ears for the five years I spent charting the intersection of urban design and the so-called science of happiness. The quest led me to some of the world's greatest and most miserable streets. It led me through the labyrinths of neuroscience and behavioral economics. I found clues in paving stones, on rail lines, and on roller coasters, in architecture, in the stories of strangers who shared their lives with me, and in my own urban experiments. I will share that search with you, and its hopeful message, in the rest of this book.

One memory from early in the journey has stuck with me, perhaps because it carries both the sweetness and the subjective slipperiness of the happiness we sometimes find in cities.

It occurred on the afternoon that I chased Enrique Peñalosa through the streets of Bogotá. Just as he had insisted on that first ride, our cycle across what was once one of the most infamous of cities was a breeze. The streets were virtually empty of cars. Nearly a million of them had stayed home that morning. Yes, it was *el día sin carro*, the car-free experiment that had grown into a yearly ritual.

At first the streets felt slightly eerie, like landscapes from a post-apocalyptic *Twilight Zone* episode. All the rumble and roar of the city quieted. Gradually we expanded into the space left by the cars. I let go of my fear. It was as though an immense tension had been lifted from Bogotá, as though the city could finally shake out its exhaustion and breathe. The sky was a piercing blue. The air was clear.

Peñalosa, who was running for reelection, needed to be seen out on his bicycle that day. He stumped compulsively, hollering that same *"Cómo le va"* at anyone who appeared to recognize him. But this did not explain his haste or his quickening pace as we traversed the north end of the city toward the Andean foothills. He stopped answering his phone. He stopped answering my questions. He ignored the whimpers of the photographer who crashed his bicycle on the curb ahead of him. He gripped his handlebars with both hands, stood up, and muscled into his pedals. It was all I could do to keep up with him, block after block, until we arrived at a compound ringed by a high iron fence. Peñalosa dismounted, breathing hard.

Boys in crisp white shirts and matching uniforms poured through a gate. One of them, a bright-eyed ten-year-old, pushed a miniature version of Peñalosa's own bicycle through the crowd. Peñalosa reached out, and suddenly I understood his haste. The guy had been rushing to pick up his son from school, as other parents were doing that very moment all up and down the time zone. Millions of mini-vans, motorbikes, hatchbacks, and buses were congregating outside schools from Toronto to Tampa at this very moment—the same ritual, the same drumming of steering wheels, the same stop and go, the same corralling and ferrying of children. Only here, in the heart of one of the meanest, poorest cities in the hemisphere, father and son would roll away from the school gate for a carefree ride across the metropolis. This was an unthinkable act in most modern cities. It

The Mayor of Happy
Enrique Peñalosa in Bogotá, 2007 (Andrés Felipe Jara Moreno, Fundación por el País Que Queremos)

was also a demonstration of Peñalosa's urban revolution, a terrific photo op for the happy city.

"Look," he yelled to me, waving his cell phone toward the bicycles that flooded around us. "Can you imagine if we designed the entire city for children?"

We followed a wide avenue that had indeed filled with children, as well as suited businessmen, young ladies in short skirts, apron-clad ice-cream men pushing refrigerated tricycles, and vendors selling sweet arepas from pushcart ovens. They did seem happy. And Peñalosa's son was safe—not because of those bodyguards, but because he could travel freely, even veer that bike wildly off course without fear of being struck by a speeding automobile. As the sun fell and the Andes caught fire, we arced our way along the wide-open avenues, then west along a highway built just for bicycles. The kid raced ahead. Peñalosa let go of his impulse to campaign. He followed his son, laughing, and the bodyguards huffed and pedaled hard to catch up, and Juan, the photographer, wobbled behind on his bent rims.

At that point I wasn't sure about Peñalosa's ideology. Who was to say that one way of moving was better than another? How could anyone know enough about the needs of the human soul to prescribe the ideal city for happiness?

But for a moment I forgot my questions. I let my handlebars go, raised my arms in the air in the cooling breeze, and remembered my own childhood of country roads, afterschool wanderings, lazy rides, and pure freedom. I felt fine. The city was mine.

2. The City Has Always Been a Happiness Project

> The question of the purpose of human life has been raised countless times; it has never yet received a satisfactory answer and perhaps does not admit of one . . . We will therefore turn to the less ambitious question of what men show by their behavior to be the purpose and intention of their lives. What do they demand of life and wish to achieve in it? The answer to this can hardly be in doubt. They strive after happiness; they want to become happy and to remain so.
> —Sigmund Freud, *Civilization and Its Discontents*

> Whatever creates or increases happiness or some part of happiness, we ought to do; whatever destroys or hampers happiness, or gives rise to its opposite, we ought not to do.
> —Aristotle, *Rhetoric*

If you wandered into the city-state of Athens a little over twenty-four hundred years ago, you would invariably find your way to the agora, a broad plaza filled with market stalls and lined by the Athenian governing council's meeting chambers, law courts, marbled temples, altars to gods, and statues of heroes. It was a glorious place, simultaneously stately and messy with commerce. If you pushed your way through the crowds of shoppers and vendors, you might have encountered a bearded gentleman holding philosophical court on the veranda of one of the great halls at the agora's edge. This is where Socrates regularly pummeled his fellow citizens with questions that challenged them to see the world anew. "Do not all men desire happiness? Or is this just a ridiculous question?" Socrates famously asked one interlocutor. Receiving the answer most of us would give, he continued, "Well then, since all of us desire happiness, how can we be happy? That is the next question."

If we are going to figure out if cities can be reconfigured to boost happiness, we actually need to start one question earlier: What, exactly, do we mean by happiness? This was a question of public preoccupation in Athens, and it has occupied the minds of philosophers, gurus, shysters, and, yes, city builders ever since. Even though most of us believe that happiness exists and that it is worth pursuing, its dimensions and character seem always just out of reach. Is happiness simply contentment or the opposite of misery? Even straightforward definitions feel subjective: A monk might measure it differently than a banker or a nurse or an architect would. Some people find no greater bliss than in flirting on the Champs-Élysées. Others find it grilling hot dogs in the privacy of a secluded backyard.

One thing is certain: we all translate our own ideas of happiness into form. It happens when you landscape your garden or choose where to live. It happens when you buy a car. It happens when a CEO contemplates the form of a new skyscraper headquarters or when a master architect lays out a grand scheme for social housing. It happens when planners, politicians, and community boards wrestle over roads, zoning laws, and monuments. It is impossible to separate the life and design of a city from the attempt to understand happiness, to experience it, and to build it for society. The search shapes cities, and cities shape the search in return.

This was especially true in Athens. From the middle of the fifth century A.D., the Greeks gave the idea of human happiness a privileged place among goals. Although only a small fraction of the Athenian population actually enjoyed the rights of citizenship, those who did experienced enough wealth, leisure time, and freedom to spend a lot of time arguing about the good life. It was wrapped around a concept they called *eudaimonia*, which can be translated literally as "to be inhabited or accompanied by a good *daimon*, or guiding spirit," though it's best understood as a state of human flourishing. Each philosopher argued for a slightly different version of it, but after a few decades of debate Aristotle summed up the emerging view thus: everyone pretty much agreed that good fortune, health, friends, power, and material wealth all contributed to that blessed state of *eudaimonia.* But these private assets were not quite enough, not even in a city-state where citizens could experience all of life's hedonistic possibilities. Existing for pleasure alone was a vulgar state befitting animals, he argued. A man could achieve pure happiness only by reaching the height of his potential, and that meant not just thinking virtuously but behaving virtuously too.

Meanwhile, civic and personal well-being were intimately linked.* The polis, the city-state, was a shared project that Athenians cared for with almost religious fervor. The city was more than a machine for delivering everyday needs; it was a concept that bound together Athenian culture, politics, mores, and history. Its citizens were like hands on the deck of a ship, Aristotle noted, with a common duty to propel it forward. In fact, he argued that the polis was the only vehicle through which a man could really achieve *eudaimonia.* Anyone who did not concern himself with public life was himself less than whole.

The relationship between these ideas and the design of the city in which they grew was striking. The Athenians sought the patronage of their gods—they maintained a neighborhood of stone palaces for Athena and other members of the Greek pantheon on the flat hilltop of the Acropolis—but the Athenian sense of personal agency and civic spirit was reflected in architectures closer to the earth. Just beneath the Acropolis, any citizen—that is, a free male born in the city—could have his say on civic policy at the speakers' platform that was cut into the side of the Pnyx Hill. There was enough room for a gathering of twenty thousand citizens in this natural amphitheater, a staggering embodiment of the new principle of equal speech. The *eudaimonia* debate raged at the academies of Plato, Aristotle, and Epicurus, but it always returned to the agora, whose openness at the heart of the city-state was not a demonstration of executive power, as it is in so many modern plazas, but an invitation to participate in the life of the polis.

It is hard to say whether these open architectures nudged Athenians toward a more civic philosophy or whether it was philosophy

---

*Even the Hedonists, despite their modern caricature as wine-sodden party animals, believed that the greatest pleasures were to be found in virtuous acts. Still, most thinkers at the time agreed that the fully virtuous life was so rare that if you achieved it, you were probably already a god.

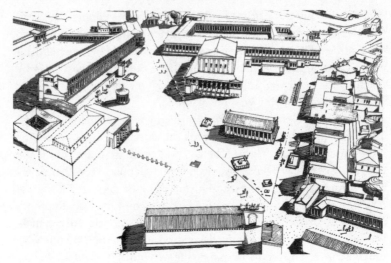

The Agora

The Greek philosophy of the good life was built right into the heart of Athens. Surrounded by temples, monuments, law courts, and government meeting chambers, the agora was a truly public place where commercial goods and ideas were traded freely. (Robert Laddish, All Rights Reserved, www.laddish.net)

itself that produced architecture. But together they seemed to demand that virtuous citizens infuse public gathering places with potent, even dangerous vitality. Of course, even in classical Athens, there were limits. Socrates challenged his agora audiences' thinking about the role of the gods so relentlessly that he was sentenced to death for corrupting Athenian youth. The tension between free speech, shared space, and civic stability has continued to inform urban design ever since.

Shape-Shifting

As philosophies about happiness shift, so does urban form. The Romans, like the Athenians, were so deeply attached to their city that Rome itself was a spiritual project. Civic pride drove heroic feats of engineering and architecture—from aqueducts, highways, sewers, and massive ports to muscular temples and basilicas—which helped

Rome grow into the world's first megacity, with a peak population of more than one million.* As Rome grew fat on the fruits of its vast empire, its citizens adopted a new god of happiness. In 44 B.C. Julius Caesar approved construction of a temple to Felicitas, the god of pleasure, fortune, and fertility, not far from the Curia Hostilia, the meeting place of the Senate.

But when it came to city building, the Roman elite increasingly focused on creating monuments to their own glory. The Campus Martius, Rome's public district, became a cluttered treasure box of spectacular imperial structures, almost all of them turned inward, with scant means to move between them. In contrast to the roads linking Rome to its empire, streets in the Campus Martius were pathetically underdesigned, narrow, and scarce. The two public avenues, the Via Sacra and the Via Nova, were barely sixteen feet wide. Emperor after emperor squeezed his own ever-larger forum into the district, but most failed to orient these structures into an overall city plan. The architectural ambition—and expense—became more and more outrageous. After conquering the Transylvanian region of Dacia around A.D. 106, the Emperor Trajan had to auction off fifty thousand Dacian prisoners in order to pay for a 115-foot marble column wrapped in a spiral frieze portraying his battles.

Private glory trumped public good. For every marbled *domus*, there were twenty-six blocks of cramped tenements. Although Julius Caesar tried to rationalize these slums by imposing height limits and fire regulations, life among the tenements was harsh. The narrow streets were filled with refuse, and the noise was constant. Entire apartment buildings collapsed with frequency. As faith in and affection for the city withered, public architecture and spectacle were put to work to placate the increasingly rebellious lower classes. Massive baths, shopping opportunities (including Trajan's five-story *mercato*, the world's first mall), bloody gladiator battles, circuses, and displays of exotic animals were the tools of distraction.

*The Roman sense of discipline and control was manifest in the orthogonal road grids laid down as garrison towns on three continents and as far north as Scotland. It may not have been linked to a philosophy of happiness per se, but the security provided by the Roman Empire undoubtedly led to prosperity and well-being across its territories for centuries.

Where the Athenian philosophers had championed the spiritual life of the polis, the Romans gradually came to be disgusted by city life. Rome's greatest poet, Horace, fantasized about returning to a simple farming existence.* Foreshadowing a twentieth-century trend, the patrician elite retreated to their villas in the countryside or on the Bay of Naples.

As the Roman Empire declined, urban well-being across Europe was reduced to the essentials of security and survival. Happiness, if you could call it that, came to be embodied by two architectures. In the early Middle Ages, no city could survive without walls. But just as essential was the cathedral, which made an entirely unique promise regarding happiness.

Like cities since the beginning of urbanity, Christian and Muslim communities in the former Roman territories positioned their sacred architecture at the heart of urban life. Islam forbade representations of the sacred image, but the Christian church embodied its faith story in form. The cathedral's footprint in the shape of the cross alluded specifically to the suffering of Christ. But inside, architecture offered a means to transcend worldly pain. Medieval churches made use of high walls and vaulted ceilings so that every visitor would have a personal experience of the Ascension. Even today, if you stand inside Paris's Notre Dame Cathedral, your eye will inevitably be drawn higher and higher until it reaches an inner roof above the nave. As Richard Sennett once pointed out, it is a journey all the way to the base of heaven. The message is clear: happiness awaits in the afterlife, not here on earth.

But the medieval church carried with it another message: that the anchor of the city, the place that gave it meaning and connected it to heaven, was public. Often churches were surrounded with open space delineating the shift from secular to sacred. Here, in the shadows of the church, is where babies were abandoned and plague victims tolerated. Here is where you could beg for help if you were desperate. At

---

*Horace wrote:
Happy the man who, free from cares,
like men of old still works
his father's fields with his own oxen,
encumbered by no debt.

the heart of the city—the transition zone between earth and heaven—
was a promise of empathy.

Feeling All Right

Happiness, as expressed in philosophy and architecture, has always
been a tug-of-war between earthly needs and transcendent hopes,
between private pleasures and public goods. For centuries, Europeans put their faith in heavenly salvation. That changed in the Age of
Enlightenment. A boom in wealth, leisure time, and longevity convinced eighteenth-century thinkers that happiness was both a natural
and widely attainable state here on earth. Governments were obligated to promote happiness for everyone. Sure enough, in the fledgling
United States, the Founding Fathers declared that God had endowed
men with the unalienable right to pursue it.

But this happiness was nothing like the *eudaimonia* of ancient
Greece.

The English social reformer Jeremy Bentham encapsulated the
new approach to the concept in his principle of utility: since happiness was really just the sum of pleasure minus pain, he said, the best
policy for governments and individuals on any given question could
be determined by a straightforward act of mathematics, so as to maximize the former and minimize the latter. The obvious problem was
figuring out how to measure the two.

Scholars of the Enlightenment liked nothing more than to take
a scientific approach to social problems. Bentham was a man of his
time, so he devised a complex set of tables called the felicific calculus, which gauged the amount of pleasure or pain any action was
likely to cause. By adding up what he called "utils," the calculus could
be used to determine the utility of repealing laws against usury, or
investing in new infrastructure, or even architectural designs.*

---

*Bentham made his own infamous foray into architecture, providing a chilling
warning about the limits of weaving social goals into design. The Panopticon was a
jail in which a circle of stacked cells faced inward toward a central guard tower. The
windows of that tower would be shaded, so prisoners would have to assume they
were always being watched. This sense of godlike omnipresence, he argued, would
not only save money on prison guards but would also reform inmates' morals. He

But feelings stubbornly refused to submit to Bentham's score sheet. He found it impossible to neatly calibrate the pleasure to be had from, say, a good meal, an act of kindness, or the sound of a piano, and he was therefore at a loss to find numbers to insert into equations that might produce the right prescriptions for living.

Regardless of the difficulty of measuring happiness, people still attempted to incorporate it into the architectures of the day. In London, Jonathan Tyers, an erstwhile leather merchant, transformed the walled Vauxhall Gardens south of the Thames into a leafy, pay-per-visit wonderland of outdoor portraits in rococo style, hanging lanterns, open-air concerts, and spectacle. The Prince of Wales visited, but so did anyone who could scrape up the modest one-shilling admission. Egalitarian hedonism ruled. Tightrope walkers entertained crowds of thousands, fireworks exploded, and mothers searched the garden's verdant nooks for misbehaving daughters.

In France, Enlightenment ideals flowed through the public realm, through politics, and into revolution. The rulers of the Old Regime tightly censored print publications, so people traded news and gossip in parks, gardens, and cafés. When he inherited the sprawling Palais-Royal in Paris, Louis Philippe II, head of the House of Orléans and a supporter of the egalitarian ideals of Rousseau, threw open the gates to the complex's lush private gardens and arcades. The Palais-Royal became a public entertainment complex populated by bookshops, salons, and refreshment cafés. It was a nexus of hedonic diversion, but also of philosophical and political foment. In the messy realm where public life, leisure, and politics collide, enlightened talk in the Palais-Royal about the right for all to enjoy happiness contributed to a revolution that would eventually see Louis Philippe II lose his head.

---

hoped the design could be adopted for hospitals, sanitariums, and even schools. In a letter to a friend, he imagined a school where "all play, all chattering—in short, all distraction of every kind—is effectually banished by the central and covered situation of the master, seconded by partitions or screens between the scholars." Bentham reasoned that under the gaze of their master and isolated from their friends, children would begin to internalize the gaze of their master, thus relieving them of the tension between their passion for play and their fear of punishment. Architecture, guided by science, would determine both the thought and behavior of its occupants.

**Vauxhall Gardens—The Grand Walk, c. 1751,
by Giovanni Antonio Canal**
*During the Enlightenment, London's premier pleasure garden, with its leafy
promenades and performance pavilions, was a nexus of egalitarian hedonism,
at a price even the masses could afford.* (From the Compton Verney Collection)

Moral Renovations

Since the Enlightenment, architectural and city planning movements
have increasingly promised to nurture the mind and soul of society.
Members of the City Beautiful movement were explicit in their assur-
ances. Daniel Burnham, designer of the 1893 World's Columbian
Exposition in Chicago, proclaimed that beauty itself could reform
society and conjure new virtue from citizens. His showpiece was a
model city of gleaming white Beaux Arts monuments scoured clean
of any signs of poverty. For the rest of central Chicago, Burnham
proposed a City Beautiful: an overlay of grand avenues and elegant
buildings that would restore to the city "a lost visual and aesthetic
harmony, thereby creating the physical prerequisite for the emer-
gence of a harmonious social order." (He was much less clear about
how the plan would provide for the poor who would be displaced to
make room for the newly decorated city. Within weeks of the closing

of the spectacular Columbian Exposition, thousands of workers were left unemployed and homeless, shut out of the now-empty hotels built for the Fair. Arsonists set fire to the fair's remaining buildings.)

That faith in the power of architectural metaphor later found life on the far end of the political spectrum. Joseph Stalin's reconstructions of postwar Eastern Europe in the style known as socialist realism were designed to exude power, optimism, and enough public elegance to assure people that they had made a collective status leap. You can still see remnants of that vision on Berlin's Karl-Marx-Allee. The boulevard is so wide (almost 300 feet) that it feels completely empty without a full-on military parade. Its edges are populated with offices and once-elegant workers' apartments whose facades, with their architectural ceramics, cupolaed towers, and statues helped them earn the descriptive moniker "wedding cake" half a century ago. If one ignores his sinister record, a walk down the boulevard might have one accepting Stalin's proclamation: "Life has improved, my friends, life has become more cheerful. And when life is cheerful, it is easier to work hard."

Others have tried to engineer the good society through sheer architectural efficiency. "Human happiness already exists expressed in terms of numbers, of mathematics, of properly calculated designs, plans in which the cities can already be seen!" declared the Swiss-French architect Le Corbusier, the high priest of the modern movement that emerged in Europe between the wars. In 1925 Le Corbusier proposed bulldozing much of the Right Bank in Paris and replacing the ancient neighborhoods of the Marais with a grid of superblocks on which would be arranged a series of identical sixty-story cruciform towers. That plan was never carried out, but Le Corbusier's ideas were widely embraced by socialist governments, which used the modernist's historically pristine approach to exert their new ideals on a grand scale across Europe.

Some modern reformers argued that the secret to happiness was to escape the city altogether. English reformers led by Ebenezer Howard planned utopian towns around train stations in the countryside.* In America, the advent of the automobile prompted innova-

---

*Robert Pemberton, a wealthy pupil of Jeremy Bentham's, was convinced that the sharp-angled geometries of buildings and streets of old cities led to vice and mental

tors from Henry Ford to Frank Lloyd Wright to declare that liberation lay at the end of a highway. Private automobiles would free people to escape the central city to build their own self-sufficient compounds in a new kind of urban-rural utopia. In Wright's planned Broadacre City, citizens would drive their own cars to all the means of production, distribution, self-improvement, and recreation that would be within minutes of their miniature homesteads. "Why should not he, the poor wage-slave, go forward, not backward, to his native birthright?" Wright wrote. "Go to the good ground and grow his family in a free city." Together, technology and dispersal would produce true freedom, democracy, and self-sufficiency.

The pursuit of happiness has never delivered anything like Wright's Broadacre City. Instead, it has led millions of people to detached houses with modest lawns—houses purchased with loans from huge financial institutions—far from employment, in the landscape now commonly known as suburban sprawl. This, the most common urban form in North America, has some roots in the American notions of independence and freedom that Wright espoused. But those roots go deeper, tapping into a particular way of thinking about happiness and the common good that reaches all the way back to the Enlightenment.

Buying Happiness

After Jeremy Bentham and his followers failed in their attempts to measure happiness, early economists seized on Bentham's concept of utility, but they cleverly reduced his felicific calculus to something they could actually count. They could not measure pleasure or pain. They could not add up virtuous action or good health or long life or pleasant feelings. What they could measure was money and our

---

illness. He proposed building a Happy Colony in New Zealand, which would consist of a twenty-thousand-acre settlement of concentric agricultural circles around a core of colleges, workshops, and plazas decorated with gigantic celestial maps. By adopting the circular patterns he observed in the cosmos, Pemberton was sure the design would lead to the "perfection and happiness" of its colonists. His vision went unrealized.

Broadacre City
A vision of extreme dispersal by Frank Lloyd Wright. The architect believed that highways—and, apparently, new flying machines—would set urbanites free to inhabit and work on their own autonomous plots in the countryside.
(Courtesy of the Frank Lloyd Wright Foundation Archives [The Museum of Modern Art | Avery Architectural & Fine Arts Library, Columbia University, New York], © Frank Lloyd Wright Foundation, Scottsdale, AZ)

decisions about how to spend it, so they substituted purchasing power for utility.

In his *Inquiry into the Nature and Causes of the Wealth of Nations*, Bentham's contemporary Adam Smith warned that it was a deception to believe that wealth and comfort alone would bring happiness. But this didn't stop his followers or the governments they advised from relying on the crude measures of income when measuring human progress over the next two centuries. As long as economic numbers grew, economists insisted that life was getting better and people were getting happier. Under this peculiar analysis, our estimation of well-being is actually inflated by divorces, car crashes, and wars, as long as those calamities produce new spending on goods and services.

The first tract suburbs were grand acts of entrepreneurism by bold, self-interested developers. And their product—detached single-family homes on their own yards—promised newcomers a world of privatized comforts. The innovation precipitated a powerful new economic engine: as people moved from inner cities to detached homes in increasingly distant sprawl, they bought furniture and appliances to fill those homes, and cars to move between increasingly disconnected destinations.

The market economist's case for suburban sprawl goes like this: if you can judge what makes people happy by observing how they spend their money, then the fact that so many people have purchased detached homes in urban sprawl is proof that it leads to happiness. As writers such as Robert Bruegmann and Joel Kotkin have argued, sprawl fulfills American's *preferences* for privacy, mobility, and detachment from the problems of high-density environments. By this way of thinking, sprawl reflects every individual's natural-born right to maximize utility.

But this interpretation ignores a few inconvenient truths. First, as I will explore in this book, our preferences—the things we buy, the places we choose to live—do not always maximize our happiness in the long run. Second, sprawl, as an urban form, was laid out, massively subsidized, and legally mandated long before anyone actually decided to buy a house there. It is as much the result of zoning, legislation, and lobbying as a crowded city block. It did not occur naturally. It was *designed*.

How are we to judge the happy prescriptions of the city builders and citizens who came before us and now work among us? Does the detached suburban home really make its owners more independent and free? Did the democratic gathering spaces of ancient Athens really help lead the Greeks any closer to *eudaimonia*? Do perfectly straight highways produce more feelings of freedom than narrow, winding roads? Can beautiful architecture lead us to a shared sense of optimism? Which of the high-minded schemes of the great city builders have actually produced more of the pleasurable feelings Jeremy Bentham called "hedons"? Does Enrique Peñalosa—or anyone else who promises happier design—have a leg to stand on?

These questions take us all the way back to Socrates: What is happiness, really? Now is a great time to take another stab at defining it, because during the decades that the suburban project accelerated, a network of psychologists, brain scientists, and economists devoted themselves to the study of the subject that intrigued the Greeks, stumped the Enlightenment scholars, and provided fodder for those who design cities to this day.

A Science of Happiness

In the early 1990s the University of Wisconsin psychologist Richard Davidson attempted to isolate the sources of positive and negative feelings in the human brain. Doctors have long noticed that people with damage to the front left side of their brain (the left prefrontal cortex) sometimes, and quite suddenly, lose their sense of enjoyment in life. In this, Davidson saw a clue to the neuroscience of happiness. He attached electroencephalogram (EEG) monitor caps—which measure electrical activity—to the scalps of volunteers and then showed them short film clips designed to elicit either happiness and amusement or disgust. He found that the happy clips—say, of smiling babies—produced more activity in the left prefrontal region of his volunteers' brains, while images of deformed infants activated the right prefrontal region. Those brains were offering up a map of feelings.

Later, Davidson surveyed his volunteers on their feelings and then slid them, one by one, into a functional magnetic resonance imaging machine. (fMRI machines map activity in the brain by tracking levels of blood oxygenation, which are revealed in varying levels of magnetism.) He found that people who claimed to be happy tended to have more blood flowing to that left prefrontal region than to the right side. In another study, researchers got people to rate and record their mood every twenty minutes during the workday and give blood samples every two hours. The worse people rated their own moods, the higher the concentrations of cortisol (the hormone most associated with stress and anxiety) were in their blood.

These and scores of similar experiments in the past couple of decades have produced an insight that might seem intuitive, but which we had no way of proving until recently: if you want to gauge how happy people are, just ask them.* Most people who tell researchers they are happy are not only telling the truth but are right.

This may not seem surprising. After all, most of us are pretty sure if we are happy or not. But these revelations refuted the classic tenet of economics: the assumption that only our purchasing decisions can truly reveal what makes us happy. Now economists and psychologists can use surveys to see how huge numbers of people are feeling, taking us one step closer to fulfilling Bentham's dream of figuring out what it is that makes people feel good or bad.

That project found its modern-day champion in the Princeton psychology professor Daniel Kahneman, the only noneconomist who has ever won a Nobel Prize in Economics.

Rather than modeling human decisions and satisfaction through simplified mathematical equations—as economists had done for decades—Kahneman and his colleagues conducted experiments to see what made life pleasant or unpleasant for people in the real world. They called their new science "hedonic psychology." Much like Bentham, they argued that the best way to judge happiness was to conduct a thorough account of life's good and bad moments. One of Kahneman's early studies established a link between happiness and urban life. He asked more than nine hundred working women in Texas to divide the previous day up into episodes, like scenes in a movie, and then to describe everything they did and how they felt at the time. Of all the ways they passed their days, having sex made the women happiest of all, with socializing coming a close second. What made them least happy? Commuting to work.

A purely hedonic approach to urban happiness would determine how the city affects our mood, then would boost the good stuff and stamp out the bad. Environmental psychology has found plenty of raw material for such a task. Researchers have proved, for example, that we are bothered by snakes, spiders, sharp edges, loud, unpredictable

---

*Other studies have shown that people who say they are happy are more likely to be rated as happy by friends, more likely to respond to requests for help, less likely to be absent from work, less likely to get into arguments, and less likely to sign up for psychological counseling. They live longer and get high scores on mental health assessments.

noises, darkness, and dead-end alleys, but we enjoy novelty, soft edges, nice scents, gentle surprises, and pleasant memories.

There is a place that has sought to deliver these things, in part by blotting out any sign of the discomforts and ugliness of the modern city. If you have kids, chances are they have begged you to take them there. Officially branded "The Happiest Place on Earth" when it opened its gates in 1955, Disneyland was conceived as a pay-per-visit alternative to the freeways and sprawl that were just beginning to dominate Southern California.

Inside Disneyland, even today, every architectural detail, every view, every transportation experience, every sensation—right down to the texture of the pavement and the scent of the air—was designed with the express purpose of tipping the hedonic scale. Cinderella's Castle, a reminder of childhood fantasies, marks the center of the perfect universe. A lush garden or forest is always just around the corner. The stomach-churning spins and drops of Space Mountain last just long enough to give riders a shared experience of danger, but not long enough for induced stress hormones to start compromising our immune systems. It's no accident that every Disneyland visit begins and ends with a walk along Main Street U.S.A., a parade of cartoon-cute shops and unhurried bustle that simulates the perfect small town that films, television, and the Disney entertainment machine itself have imprinted on all our memories. By turning the spigot on those memories, Disneyland can give you the sense that you have come home, no matter where in the world you grew up. It is a lovely feeling for all but the most diligent skeptic.

If ephemeral pleasures are all there is to happiness, then Disneyland really would be the happiest city on earth. Architects and town planners have copied its forms in shopping centers, downtowns, and neighborhoods around the world. Neuroscientists marvel at the virtuosity of its designs (and I'll explain some of its successes later in this book). But like Disney's films, the happiness of Disneyland requires a suspension of disbelief. You must pretend along with cheery shopkeepers and mascots whose job title—"cast member"—belies a contractual obligation to maintain their smiles. You must not ponder the hard work and grit of daily life that are hidden so skillfully behind Main Street U.S.A.'s facades and the berm that separates the park from the sprawl of Southern California. When the street artist Banksy propped an inflatable Guantánamo Bay detainee inside the park, Disneyland's trains actually ground to a halt so that the site could be cleansed of the offending reference to real life. Any interruption of the cheery choreography is a threat to this carefully crafted hedonic machine.

We are left with the question of authenticity: If you're happy, does reality matter? The philosopher Robert Nozick once challenged people to imagine an "experience machine" that would sink occupants into a lifelong dream, something like a coma state, in which neuropsychologists could stimulate their brains, simulating the most wonderful pleasures imaginable. Nozick argued that plugging into the machine would be a kind of suicide. He predicted that most people would opt for a life that was less pleasant, but one that involved real challenges, real striving, real pleasure and pain.

Even if it were possible to live out one's life in Disneyland, a eudaimonic approach would surely require seeing past Disney's consumable facades, acknowledging the struggles of the cast members who play its character roles, and engaging with the urban systems that support the experience machine. Disneyland and its visitors contribute to the traffic and urban blight that awaits beyond its berms. You cannot separate one pleasurable moment from the system that created it, or your own role in creating that system. The question then is, how can real designs in real places infuse life with the sensual and sensory pleasures we often pay to experience? Should they even try?

Beyond the Hedonic City

Our rejection of the experience machine carries us back to the deeper notion of happiness for which the Greeks argued. So does the evidence from the emerging field of happiness economics, where Kahneman's peers have tried to understand what influences the happiness of entire societies, drawing on data produced by census reports and polls such as the massive World Values Survey and the Gallup World Poll. These surveys don't simply measure *affect*, or people's relative cheeriness in the moment. They ask how people feel about their entire life.* The hope is to distill *eudaimonia* down to a number that can be compared with just about any variable, from income to unemployment to the length of our commutes and the number of friends we have, and then to understand all the ingredients that combine to create life satisfaction.†

These surveys are fueling a revolution in economics, partly because they contest the power of massive advances in spending power to make societies happier. After countries reach the standard of living that many first world countries hit around 1960, happiness and gross national product stop following the same trajectory.‡ Income matters, of course, but it is only part of the story.

It's true that if you live in a poor country, getting richer goes hand in hand with getting happier. This makes sense. You are unlikely to say you are happy when you cannot offer food, shelter, and security to your children. But in the world's rich countries, working harder to earn more money gets less effective once you've passed the average income mark. After that, each extra dollar delivers proportionately less satisfaction.

If money isn't everything, what is the full recipe for happiness? Adam Smith's followers in classical economics have never produced a plausible answer, but the surveys offer a few. People who are well educated rate their happiness higher than those who aren't. Employed people are happier than unemployed people—even in European states where generous welfare policies insulate citizens from the most destructive effects of unemployment.

---

*Some surveys ask people to mark where they think they stand on a ladder representing a progression from the worst possible life to the best possible life. Other surveys stick with: "In general, how happy would you say that you are—very happy, fairly happy, or not very happy."

†If you were to ask one or two people about their happiness and their life, you might not learn so much. People are bound to make mistakes when answering subjective questions. They might be influenced by weather, last night's football game, or the jerk who cut them off on the way home from work. But when surveys test thousands of people, the sheer numbers crowd out the errors that creep into individual self-reports. With big enough sample numbers, the surveys point at the economic and social conditions that go along with societal happiness.

‡In the United States, subjective well-being plummeted during the 2008 recession. But it returned to prerecession levels by 2010, long before the economy recovered, according to the Gallup Organization.

Life satisfaction is strongly influenced by location.* People in small towns are generally happier than people who live in big cities. People who live next to the ocean report being happier than those who don't. Living under the flight path of commuter jets is terrible for happiness. Persistent wind is bad, too. But we do not always respond logically to environmental stimulus. Living near garbage dumps seems to make people much less happy than living near toxic waste sites, presumably because they can smell the dump but not the toxic threat. The devil you know is harder on happiness than the devil you don't, at least in the short term.

Self-reported happiness correlates with a lot of things that money cannot buy. Leisure time and shorter commutes are good. So is good health (although *feeling* healthy is more important than actually *being* healthy, and that feeling may have more to do with the quality of your friendships than with your medical plan). Believing in some kind of God helps. But so does just showing up at a church or temple—whether you believe or not—and so does participation in volunteer groups that have nothing to do with religion. The environment we live in really does matter. Public health officers working with the London borough of Greenwich compared conditions in council housing estates (subsidized housing) with all kinds of environmental

---

*In a groundbreaking 2009 study, economists mined more than a million survey responses to create the first life-satisfaction ranking for U.S. states. They compared their results with an earlier study that ranked quality of life using such objective data as weather, wind speed, length of coastline, national parks, hazardous-waste sites, commuting times, violent crime, air quality, local taxes, local spending on education and highways, and cost of living.

The life satisfaction and quality-of-life rankings matched up. (This seems only logical, but it was a big deal for the happiness economists. It offered some of the first empirical evidence that people's rankings of their own life satisfaction match up with real-world conditions usually associated with quality of life. When thousands of people are miserable, they tend to have good reasons for it.) But the study also suggested that Americans might be getting their real estate decisions wrong on a massive scale. After all, New York and California, states with some of the highest real estate prices—suggesting that people really, really want to live there—were flopping around at the bottom of the American happiness barrel, at dead last and forty-sixth, respectively.

"Bargains in life are usually found outside the spotlight," noted Professor Andrew Oswald, coauthor of the study. "It seems that exactly the same is true of the best places to live."

factors, and they found, not surprisingly, that mold in apartments dragged people's happiness down much more than, say, street conditions or dog poop on the sidewalks.

But Carol Ryff, a developmental psychologist who collaborated with Richard Davidson at the University of Wisconsin, argues that such lists still don't get us close enough to a definition of the good life that Aristotle would endorse. Indeed, she bristles at the mere mention of the word *happiness*.

"Aristotle offered us the image of a cow in the field, contentedly chewing its cud. He was absolutely clear that this is not what *eudaimonia* is about! It's about getting up every day and working very hard toward goals that make your life meaningful, sometimes in ways that are not at all conducive to short-term contentment," Ryff told me. "In fact, it may not be about contentment at all. It's about the realization of talent and potential, and the feeling that you are able to make the most of your abilities in life."

Ryff came to this conclusion after conducting a unique experiment to test her point. First she created a checklist that included measures of well-being from the most respected psychologists of the last century. Her all-star *eudaimonia* checklist is worth listing. It includes:

- Self-acceptance, or how well you know and regard yourself
- Environmental mastery—your ability to navigate and thrive in the world
- Positive relations with others
- Personal growth throughout life
- Sense of meaning and purpose
- Feelings of autonomy and independence

That list might seem as if it were ripped from a daytime talk show, but Ryff found physiological evidence for its power. She surveyed a group of women between sixty and ninety years old who rated themselves on each element of psychological well-being, then checked those results against their health. Women with high scores for Ryff's markers of psychological well-being were much healthier than those with low scores. They had better resistance to arthritis and diabetes. They had less cortisol in their saliva, which meant not only that they were less stressed out, but that they were at lower risk for cardiovascular and other diseases. They slept longer and more deeply.

Psychologists have long connected feelings of happiness to good health. But Ryff's study demonstrated the synergistic power of living a meaningful, challenging, and connected life—exactly the kind that the Greeks championed and built in Athens. A bit of heroic struggle can be good for you.

Ryff calls this ideal state "challenged thriving." It's one reason why some people chase their dreams amid the grit, noise, chaos, and expense of big cities such as New York, when they could have enjoyed a bigger home, more leisure time, and shorter work hours back home in Akron. It's why, after a few days of soaking up the saltwater vistas and mild air at her place on Orcas Island in Washington State, Ryff itches to return to the challenges of her laboratory on the snow-blown campus of the University of Wisconsin.

The city is not merely a repository of pleasures. It is the stage on which we fight our battles, where we act out the drama of our own lives. It can enhance or corrode our ability to cope with everyday challenges. It can steal our autonomy or give us the freedom to thrive. It can offer a navigable environment, or it can create a series of impossible gauntlets that wear us down daily. The messages encoded in architecture and systems can foster a sense of mastery or helplessness. The good city should be measured not only by its distractions and amenities but also by how it affects this everyday drama of survival, work, and meaning.

What Matters Most

Of all of these, the most important psychological effect of the city is the way in which it moderates our relationships with other people. This last concern is so powerful and so central to personal and societal well-being that researchers who study it become positively evangelical. Economist John Helliwell is a case in point. The University of British Columbia professor emeritus has distinguished himself in decades of research on quantitative macroeconomics, monetary policy, and international trade. But since his late-career conversion to happiness economics, Helliwell prefers to introduce himself as

Aristotle's research assistant, and he tends to begin his lectures with a sing-along version of the children's song "The More We Get Together, the Happier We'll Be." He has evidence to back that song up; and cities, countries, and the United Nations are listening.

Helliwell and his team have run several iterations of the World Values Survey and the Gallup World Poll through their statistical grinders and have found that when it comes to life satisfaction, relationships with other people beat income, hands down. For example, these polls asked people if they had a friend or relative to count on when needed. Just going from being friendless to having one friend or family member to confide in had the same effect on life satisfaction as a tripling of income.

Economists love to turn relationships into numbers. Helliwell produced this: if 10 percent more people thought they had someone to count on in life, it would have a greater effect on national life satisfaction than giving everyone a 50 percent raise. But it is not only our close relationships that count. Our trust in neighbors, police, governments, and even total strangers has a huge influence on happiness—again, much more than income does.

Imagine that you dropped your wallet somewhere on your street. What are the chances you would get it back if a neighbor found it? A stranger? A police officer? Your answer to that simple question is a proxy for a whole list of metrics related to the quality of your relationship with family, friends, neighbors, and the society around you.

In fact, ask enough people the wallet question, and you can predict the happiness of cities. Helliwell had it inserted into various Canadian surveys, and he found that cities where people believed they'd get their wallets back always scored highest for life satisfaction. It was the same with neighborhoods within those cities. Trust was the key, and it mattered far more than income: three of Canada's biggest, richest cities—Calgary, Toronto, and Vancouver—were among the least trusting and also among the least happy. St. John's, a rocky outpost and the capital of perennially poor Newfoundland, was near the top of trust and happiness lists. Meanwhile, citizens of the country where people trust their neighbors, strangers, and even their government the most—the Danes—consistently come out on or near the top of happiness polls. A similar lesson appears over and over again in psychology, behavioral economics, and public health. Happiness is a house with many rooms, but at its core is a hearth around which we gather with family, friends, the community, and sometimes even strangers to find the best part of ourselves.

As it happens, we are hardwired to trust one another, in spite of our natural wariness of strangers. Economics once put this down to sheer self-interest: the more we trust one another, the more we can maximize utility by, say, cutting more ambitious deals to trade goods or services. But Paul Zak, an economist working out of a lab at Southern California's Claremont Graduate University, found much deeper, physiological processes at work when he took a neuroscientist's approach to trust. A man even cheerier than John Helliwell, Zak set up various games in which anonymous participants would trade money back and forth with strangers. Traditional economics tells us that each player will do what it takes to walk away with as much money as possible. That's how the economic man of their theories should behave. But it is not how Zak's volunteers treated one another. Zak found that most of them were generous with one another, even when it would not lend to financial reward. They were choosing altruism over profit. Intrigued, he took samples of their blood. Remarkably, Zak found that the blood of players who engaged in cooperative, trusting exchanges was awash with the molecule oxytocin.

Oxytocin is most commonly known as the hormone that washes through women when they give birth and breast-feed. Released by the pituitary gland in the hypothalamus region of the brain, it is a neurotransmitter whose first task is to tell receptors in the pleasure centers of the brain that it's time to feel what we typically describe as "warm and fuzzy." Its happy message travels down into the chest along the vagus nerve, where it can slow the heart to a more languid pace. It produces a feeling of heightened calm that can last a few seconds or as long as twenty minutes. As long as you have it, you are more likely to trust other people. You are more likely to cooperate and pay forward favors of generosity and kindness. The oxytocin studies point to a dynamic, generative quality in societal trust. The molecule is both an incentive and a reward for altruism. Not only does it feel good to experience positive social signs from others— smiles, handshakes, opened doors, bargains kept, and cooperative merging in traffic—but it feels good to reinforce those feelings of trust among both friends and strangers. It works best of all when we do it face-to-face: in the kitchen, over a fence, on the sidewalk, in the agora. Distance and geometry matter, as we will see.

The Tug-of-War

It's important here to acknowledge the implications of this physiological aspect of trust. Ever since Charles Darwin pondered the self-sacrifice committed by certain honeybees (who die in the attempt to remove their barbed stingers from the skin of an intruder), evolutionary biologists have marveled at evidence of what most of us might call altruism in particular species.* Animals that live in groups are more successful when they cooperate with one another. The consensus seems to be that such cooperation is more than just a habit. The urge is woven into the genetic code of species from bees, wasps, and termites all the way to apes and, yes, humans, the most social animals on the planet. The oxytocin effect is physiological proof. Of course this is what philosophers and spiritual leaders have been saying all along. For all the weight that proponents of classical economics place on selfishness, Adam Smith himself grasped the duality of human need. In his other great treatise, *The Theory of Moral Sentiments*, Smith argued that human conscience comes from social relationships, and that the natural empathy produced by being among other people is an essential part of well-being and should guide our actions. The father of economics was more Athenian than his modern followers admit.

Although humans are certainly not as helpless in the face of instincts as honeybees, each of us benefits when some of us subsume

---

*Why, Darwin wondered in *On the Origin of Species*, would a honeybee sacrifice its own life for the sake of the hive? The answer, he proposed, was that the sting might be useful to the community as a whole. If the altruistic bee did not survive, it would at least in its own death help ensure the survival of its relatives. Biologists continue to argue about whether cooperation is driven by a family-level genetic imperative or a broader model which holds that communities do better when individuals sacrifice themselves for the benefit of the wider group—or both. The debate was recently renewed by the biologist E. O. Wilson, who argued in favor of group selection over kin selection—essentially saying that evolutionary forces act not just on the level of individuals, but at the level of social groups.

private goals for the sake of the community, and everyone benefits when *everyone* cooperates. As the oxytocin studies illustrate, our brains reward us for working well together. At the same time, the drive by each of us to promote our own interests creates a dynamism and wealth that can overflow through the city. We all embody the tension between selfishness and altruism.

This ambiguity is written into the fabric of cities. The Greeks strove for individual achievement and protected their families in walled homes while championing the polis in the agora. Rome rose as its wealth was poured into the common good of aqueducts and roads, then declined as it was hoarded in private villas and palaces. Paris's most glorious public gardens were built for the enjoyment of a ruling elite but now provide hedonic delights for all. The high modernists of the last century used architecture like an ethical bulldozer, pushing communities toward a symbolic, forced, and not-always-convivial closeness. The late great urbanist Jane Jacobs argued that the streets of 1960s Greenwich Village were made friendly and safe specifically because they were shared by many people. On the other end of the spectrum, millions of Americans have pursued a private version of happiness to detached structures far from any hint of what the Greeks would have called an agora.

The balance shifts back and forth with philosophy, politics, and technology. It exists in the relationship between private and public resources and landscapes. It lives in the ways we use conspicuous architectures to set ourselves apart. It exists in the height of walls, the distances between our homes, and even the means and velocities of our travels.

The pursuit of urban happiness demands that we acknowledge the real needs embodied in this tension and find a way to balance their contradictions.

But we should never forget this fact: even though the modern cosmopolitan city makes it easier than ever for individuals to retreat from neighbors and strangers, the greatest of human satisfactions lies in working and playing cooperatively with other people. No matter how much we cherish privacy and solitude, strong, positive relationships are the foundation of happiness. The city is ultimately a shared project, like Aristotle's polis, a place where we can fashion a common good that we simply cannot build alone.

This sense of a shared future matters now more than ever. Evidence is mounting that the global ecosystems that support human life are in danger. This crisis calls for the kinds of sacrifice we make only when our sense of trust and shared fate is cranked way up. As the economist Jeremy Rifkin has suggested, the circle of empathy must be widened beyond the household, beyond communities and even nations, so that we care enough about other species, ecosystems, and the planet itself to save them from destruction. A temporary happiness, or one built on a debt of misery deferred to future generations, is as false as the cheery sensation inside Robert Nozick's experience machine.

It is not certain that we can all make the leap to universal empathy, but what is clear is this: as a social project, the city challenges us not just to live together but to thrive together, by understanding that our fate is a shared one.

Happy City: A Job Description

Just as each of us will choose our own path toward the good life, we will probably never agree on a single definition of happiness. It can't be summed up by the number of things we produce or buy, nor by any magical felicific calculus. But the firing synapses of our brains, the chemistry of our blood, and the statistical heft of our collected choices and opinions do offer a map that approximates the wisdom of philosophers. These things confirm that most people, in most places, have the same basic needs and most of the same desires. They tell us truths we already know in our gut, but which we have too rarely acknowledged. They suggest that there is wisdom in the mountain kingdom of Bhutan's adoption of gross national happiness as a measure of progress rather than gross national product, and in the decision by policy makers around the world, including the governments of Great Britain, France, and Thailand and cities such as Seattle, to pay attention to new measures of well-being that include not just how much citizens earn, but how we feel. The truths of happiness science should also lead us to accept that Enrique Peñalosa and his fellow travelers are right: cities must be regarded as more than engines of wealth; they must be viewed as systems that should be shaped to improve human well-being.

I propose a basic recipe for urban happiness drawn from the insights of philosophers, psychologists, brain scientists, and happiness economists. What should a city accomplish after it meets our basic needs of food, shelter, and security?

- The city should strive to maximize joy and minimize hardship.
- It should lead us toward health rather than sickness.
- It should offer us real freedom to live, move, and build our lives as we wish.
- It should build resilience against economic or environmental shocks.
- It should be fair in the way it apportions space, services, mobility, joys, hardships, and costs.
- Most of all, it should enable us to build and strengthen the bonds between friends, families, and strangers that give life meaning, bonds that represent the city's greatest achievement and opportunity.
- The city that acknowledges and celebrates our common fate, that opens doors to empathy and cooperation, will help us tackle the great challenges of this century.

None of these goals are radical. The challenge now is to see just how the shapes and systems of our cities contribute to meeting them. How are today's cities performing? How would we build differently, and live differently, if we could chart the connection between the designs of our cities and the map of happiness? What would we change if we could?

It is audacious to believe that the city might build happiness just by changing its shape.

But it is foolish not to chase the thought, because around the world, and especially amid the sprawlscapes of modern North America, the evidence shows that cities do indeed design our lives.

3. The (Broken) Social Scene

He who is unable to live in society, or who has no need
because he is sufficient for himself, must be either a beast
or a god.

—Aristotle, *Politics*

If someone asked you to draw a picture of a city, what would it look
like? Would you sketch a forest of tall buildings and monuments?
Would there be taxis, bicycles, buses, or subways? Would there be
streets crowded with shops, and lots of people walking on sidewalks,
in parks, or on plazas? If you drew any combination of these things,
most people who saw your picture would know that they were looking at a city. This is curious because the majority of Americans (and,
increasingly, people in other countries) live in places that just don't
look like that picture.

Most of us do not live near anything like a traditional downtown
or near any architecture that might appear in the design magazines
that supposedly follow the latest trends. We do not live in the sooty
slums of the industrial revolution, nor do we live in the spacious
Manhattan apartments inhabited by TV characters who can't possibly afford them. The pursuit of domestic comforts has led us to a
landscape that is unique in history but ubiquitous in geography, and
increasingly familiar around the world.

Anyone serious about exploring how modern cities influence
happiness has got to start by looking clearly at the landscape to which
we have devoted the vast majority of our resources over the last half
century. I found my guide to that place in a parking lot in Stockton,
California, in sprawl's worst season.

Cesar Dias, a fast-talking, chubby-cheeked deal maker, was a Realtor with Stockton's Approved Real Estate Group. He was the kind of guy who could see the upside of just about any bad news, including the mortgage crisis that was then sweeping the country. At the time, San Joaquin County, a collection of farm towns turned commuter havens a couple of hours east of San Francisco, was California's foreclosure capital. In 2007, more people had lost their homes in Stockton, the county seat, than anywhere else in the nation except Detroit. Dias had rented a couple of minibuses, shrink-wrapped them in images of smiling homebuyers, and invited the world to come scavenge the county for deeply discounted pieces of the American dream.

One sunny Saturday I joined Dias as he and the other sales guys herded a few dozen potential buyers onto a pair of buses. There were soda and chips for everyone and, apparently, deals galore. Dias took pains to convince us all to see the mortgage crisis as a fantastic opportunity: a moment of vulnerability as the housing market showed a crack in its armor of optimism.

We left Stockton's desiccated downtown, climbed the on-ramp to Interstate 5, cruised above an archipelago of industrial parks and power centers, and soon emerged into a pastiche of artificial lakes, golf courses, and wide, silent streets whose names evoked the landscapes they had buried: Brookside, Golden Oak, Pine Meadow. The van slowed wherever burnt lawns and unkempt gardens revealed the opportunity of bank foreclosures. The tour hit a dozen houses in three hours. The bus vibrated with a euphoric sense of good fortune and urgency. "*Vámonos!*" Dias would shout each time the convoy pulled up to a FOR SALE sign. "It's a half-price sale!"

Cheered on, the group would sprint over the lawn and charge into the open maw of the next stucco-fronted home. We dashed from room to room, upstairs and down, taking phone shots of damaged drywall, checking carpets, and knocking on the moldings of faux-Victorian fireplaces.

At one point the crowd filed into a house (an "executive home," according to Dias's flyer) in the managed community of Spanos Park East. Three-car garage. Grand foyer. Formal dining room. Plantation shutters. It was a fine place—but Dias wasn't impressed. I found him standing outside, scowling at the front lawn. The grass had been left unkempt and unwatered for months. It was the color of a bale of straw.

"The bank should have come by and sprayed this," he said.

"You mean watered it?" I asked.

"No, sprayed it green. *Painted* it," he said, exasperated but dead serious. There were so many bank-owned homes for sale in Stockton that any blemish threatened to suck the air right out of an already-deflated price. Banks and sellers needed to keep up appearances, to convince people that this American dream was coming back to life.

Dias called his enterprise the Repo Home Tour, but it was much more than that. This was a journey to the frontier of the world's biggest-ever experiment in city building. Three-quarters of all U.S. construction in the last three decades has looked like the terrain we were traversing.

The development pattern is elegantly simple: Over here are the residential zones, generally distinguished by detached homes, broad lawns, and wide, curving streets, each zone anchored by an elementary school. Over there are the commercial districts, or power centers, where national retailers occupy warehouse-size boxes clustered like islands in dark oceans of parking. And over there are the office and industrial parks, with their own ample surface car-storage zones. All of these distinct urban units are connected by high-speed freeways and arterial roads so generous that they have obliterated the once-meaningful metric of proximity. They loop around the various distilled districts, skirt the old city center, and shoot across farms and mountains until they pierce the heart of the nearest metropolis. Distance is reduced to abstraction. Home is simultaneously far from and close to everything else, depending on the number of cars on the road at any moment. Through the windows of a tour bus on a sunny Saturday morning, life in this landscape appeared perfectly ordered.

Observers of this particular way of organizing cities have tried to name it. When our great-grandparents first moved to residential enclaves outside the city core, we called such places suburbs. When suburbs began to scatter beyond the urban edge, some called them exurbs. When, in the 1980s, downtown businesses seemed to be moving en masse to freeway-fed business parks and megamalls, *Washington Post* reporter Joel Garreau dubbed these new agglomerations "edge cities." But urban life has now been stretched to such an extent that suburbia, exurbia, and edge cities together form a distinct system that has transformed the way that entire city-regions function. This is the system that some have come to call sprawl. I will call it the dispersed city, for the characteristic that defines almost every aspect of it.

While the world's architectural critics and so-called thought leaders tend to focus their attention on iconic structures and rare designs, the journey to the happy city must begin out here, in the landscape of the infinitely repeated form, on the plains of dispersal. For every new urban plaza, starchitect-designed tower, or sleek new light-rail network, there are a hundred thousand cul-de-sacs out in the dispersed city. This is the environment that, more than any other, defines how Americans and millions of people in wealthy cities across the globe move, live, work, play, and perceive the world, and how millions more will live if cities return to the trajectory they were on before the crash. If you are going to talk about the modern city, you have to begin out here, at the edge of the urban blast radius.

These neighborhoods accomplish several historic feats: They take up more space per person, and they are more expensive to build and operate than any urban form ever constructed. They require more roads for every resident, and more water pipes, more sewers—more power cables, utility wiring, sidewalks, signposts, and landscaping. They cost more for municipalities to maintain. They cost more to protect with emergency services. They pollute more and pour more carbon into the atmosphere. In short, the dispersed city is the most expensive, resource-intense, land-gobbling, polluting way of living ever built. Anyone with any faith in the human ability to make good decisions about our well-being would expect that this massive investment in dispersal has enabled healthier, safer, more resilient, and more joyful lives. Given how many millions have chosen to call it home, you would expect that the dispersed city would produce greater happiness. But good cheer was in short supply that spring in San Joaquin County.

Dias, like so many Americans, believed that the hardship and instability of the foreclosure crisis was ephemeral, a kind of temporary madness sparked by greedy bankers and their now-infamous predatory lending practices. Many of Dias's own clients had fallen for subprime mortgage offers in the boom years. Now that those people were gone—nobody in the tour really wanted to talk about *where* they had gone or who they were—Stockton was bound for a comeback. The hard times were over. These edge neighborhoods would perk up once low house prices attracted a new set of residents better able to pay for them. My fellow Repo tourists certainly subscribed to this view. They were calculating their offers even before we got back to the office.

But there is a flaw in this optimistic logic. It ignores the role of the urban system itself. A fuller accounting leads right back to the map of the dispersed city. Instability was designed right into the exurbs of San Joaquin County.

Imagine you lived, say, along the gentle curve of Erickson Circle in Weston Ranch, a collection of several hundred modest 2,500-square-foot homes just off I-5, south of Stockton. (In a five-minute cruise through this neighborhood, I counted two dozen FOR SALE signs and half a dozen dejected-looking families loading their beds and chairs and big-screen TVs into rented moving trucks.*) If you wanted to pick up some milk, you would drive to the closest grocery store, which would be the Food 4 Less, about two miles away. If you wanted to work out, that would be five-odd miles to the In-Shape Health Club, just off Highway 4. Your kids could walk to school, but the nearest community swimming pool would be six miles away, and the happening mall, Park West Place, would be twelve miles north on I-5. As for work, if you were like your neighbors, you would commute sixty miles to San Francisco, a distance that translated into a four-hour round-trip on bad days. This journey would not make you unique: the majority of Weston Ranch's boom-time buyers were commuters escaping high home prices in the Bay Area. At the time, Weston Ranchers had a stronger relationship with a distant metropolis than they did with their own city.

It was this distance, as much as climbing mortgage rates, that broke the commuter's back. After holding steady for nearly fifteen years, gas prices doubled between 2004 and late 2006 to past $3 per gallon, then spiked to more than $4 in the summer of 2008. Suddenly the folks who commuted to the Bay Area from San Joaquin County were forking out more than $800 for fuel each month—for some, more than a quarter of their wages, and in many cases, more than people were spending on their mortgages. Families with kids, who

---

*At the time, there was a higher percentage of bank-owned homes in Weston Ranch than in any other neighborhood in the country.

were bound to even more mandatory road miles, were in the most trouble of all.

It was the same in dispersed neighborhoods all across the country. Moving to the edge committed real estate migrants to a massive, sustained investment in automobiles and fuel. The average exurban family needs at least one more car than do families who live close to where they work, shop, study, and play. That family also spends twice as much just getting around in order to meet its daily needs. It's very, very hard for people in the dispersed environment to cut back on driving. This is one reason that by 2011, the average family of four spent more on transportation than on taxes and health care combined. (It's also a reason that the farther a house was from a vibrant city center, the more likely it was to experience foreclosure during the crash, the deeper its price collapsed, the less likely that price has bounced back since, and the less analysts now expect it to be worth in the future.*)

So from a purely economic perspective, the newest parts of the dispersed city flunk the resilience test. Investing in a detached home on the urban edge is like gambling on oil futures and global geopolitics. Of course this fragility is not just an economic problem. It's also a social problem. When people lose their homes, local relationships get severed and holes are torn in the lives of families and neighborhoods. These stories have been recounted in heart-wrenching detail in popular media over the last few years, so I will not dwell on them. The more fascinating and telling story, in my opinion, involves the foreclosure era's survivors: people who scored amazing deals on dream homes on the urban edge and still live there today. After spending time with them, I do not envy their hot deals at all. Their travails serve as a warning about the social costs of distance and the dangers of rebooting the sprawl machine.

---

*By 2011, nearly three-quarters of the homes in the 18th Congressional District, which includes Stockton, were "underwater," or worth less than their mortgages. Indeed, across the country, "metropolitan areas with the weakest core neighborhoods had the highest levels of foreclosures."

A 2012 report by the Demand Institute predicts that, even though housing prices will continue to recover for the next few years, prices will be weighed down by the weakest segment of the market: sparsely populated outer communities with low walkability and access to amenities.

The Stretched Life

Take Randy Strausser, a hardworking and relatively prosperous resident of the dispersed city who won the foreclosure sweepstakes. Randy and his wife, Julie, bought a California-style ranch house in Mountain House, a partially finished exurban development south of Stockton, in 2007, when the market was tanking. At the time, Mountain House was just behind Weston Ranch in foreclosures. This was great news for the Straussers. They paid half of what some of their neighbors had paid for their places. The house seemed perfect: It had high-end fixtures, high-efficiency heating and air-conditioning, and a private fenced garden. It looked out on a green belt with a creek. According to the American dream narrative of the Repo Tour, Randy should have been an extremely happy man when I met him a couple of years later.

But he was not, and his unhappiness speaks to the dispersed city's power to fundamentally reorder social and family life. If you accept the key message from happiness science, which is that absolutely nothing matters more than our relationships with other people, it is a story worth exploring.

Part of Randy's problem was that, like a quarter of the people in San Joaquin County, he worked over the hills in San Jose. In fact, his was a family of long-distance commuters. At dawn on any given weekday, Randy; his septuagenarian mother, Nancy; and his daughter, Kim, would all be out on the highway, often driving alone from their respective homes, crossing two mountain ranges and speeding past half a dozen municipalities to their jobs in the Bay Area, each racking up more than 120 miles round-trip. Randy gave the highway three or four hours a day, in addition to the trips he made for his job as a heating and air-conditioning specialist. With housing prices still sky-high near San Francisco, this was what one had to do to live in a detached home in a "good" community.

One evening I hopped into the passenger seat of Randy's Ford Ranger as he left his business park office. The sun was just setting over San Francisco Bay as we made the long merge from Route 101 to Interstate 680. The stacked overpasses of the interchange arced in silhouette across a glowing sky. Randy ignored the sunset in order to focus on that first merge. He stretched his fingers and tightened them around the wheel, adjusted the Bluetooth in his ear, eyed the tail-lights converging on the 680, and described his typical day.

Smack the alarm off at 4:15 a.m. Shower. No breakfast. Hit the highway at five to beat the traffic. Arrive by 6:15 a.m. Eat at work. Try to be back on I-680 by 5:30 p.m. It was harder to beat the rush in the afternoons. He was lucky to get to his front door by 7:30. No coffee on the drive, no talk radio—those just made him angry, and he wanted to control his anger in order to respond rationally to the pressures of the freeway.

"But coming home to your place in Mountain House, that's the payoff," I offered declaratively as we flew past the office parks of Pleasanton, forty minutes in, almost halfway home.

He shook his head. On bad traffic days, when Randy got home, he would grab a hose and water the garden until he calmed down. Then he'd hop onto the elliptical trainer to straighten out his aching back. On really bad days, when the drive calcified his fatigue and frustration, Randy drove another twenty minutes to the World Gym over in Tracy. Not slowing down for chitchat with the gym crowd, he would crank the Van Halen on his old Walkman and sweat out his aggression. Then it was back home for a shower and bed.

For now, we will forget Randy's road-induced back pain. We will put aside his irritation with other drivers and his general bitterness at having to spend so much time on the highway. (After all, not everyone minds a long commute. Randy's mother, Nancy, told me she enjoyed the two-hour drive to Menlo Park, near Palo Alto, in her gold Lexus.) It was Randy's relationships with the people around him that were hurt most by his long-distance life.

Randy disliked his neighborhood intensely. He couldn't wait to get out of Mountain House. The problem had nothing to do with the aesthetics of the place. It was still as pristine and manicured as the day he and his wife moved in. It was the people who bothered him. He did not know, like, or particularly trust his neighbors. I asked him economist John Helliwell's trust question: What were the chances that he'd get his wallet back if he happened to drop it on his street?

"I'd never see it again!" he said with a laugh. "Look, shortly after we moved in, we were burglarized. The police were the first to say we'd never see any of our stuff ever again. This happens constantly out here. Everybody turns their head away. Nobody looks out for each other."

Lost wallet return rate

83%

25%

People's estimation of
chance that a stranger
would return their wallet.

Percentage of actual
wallets returned by strangers
in experiment.

We Can Trust Other People More Than We Think

Survey respondents rate the likelihood of a stranger returning their lost wallet at only about 25 percent. But an experiment in Toronto found that among real strangers, the likelihood of return was better than 80 percent. (Scott Keck, with data from Helliwell, John, and Shun Wang, "Trust and Well-Being," working paper, Cambridge, MA: National Bureau of Economic Research, 2010)

Had Mountain House attracted a particularly untrustworthy demographic? Probably not. Randy's mistrust actually points to the tricky twist in that lost-wallet question: your level of faith in getting your wallet back has almost nothing to do with the actual rate of wallet losses and returns in your community. The numbers are independent, just as most people's perception of safety has more to do with the plentitude of graffiti than the density of purse snatchers. Most people's response to the wallet question ends up having as much to do with the quality and frequency of their social interactions as it does with the actual trustworthiness of other people, Helliwell told me.* We may live among noble, honest, wallet-returning people, yet

*When the *Toronto Star* newspaper decided to test trustworthiness by scattering wallets around Toronto, citizens proved that they were much more trustworthy than anyone imagined: while Torontonians told national surveyors that strangers would return lost wallets only about a quarter of the time, the *Star* experiment saw more than 80 percent of wallets returned. This is remarkable, considering that the return of a wallet requires more than just honesty or the absence of corruption. The

if we do not experience positive social interactions with them, we are unlikely to build those bonds of trust.

Randy complained that his neighbors didn't keep an eye on one another's homes. They didn't chat on the sidewalks. They didn't get to know one another.

But how would they? The urban system gave them few opportunities. There were some five thousand people living in partially finished Mountain House, but there were virtually no jobs and no services beyond a little library, a couple of schools, and a small convenience store. Most of the adults drove out of Mountain House before dawn and returned after dark, cruising, one by one, into their garages and closing the doors behind them. The only people left during the day were the kids. So Randy's lack of trust in his neighbors was at least partly artificially induced. In stretching his daily routine, the city had sucked much of the spectrum of casual social contact right out of the neighborhood.

This is not a local phenomenon, nor is it a trivial matter.

The Social Deficit and the City

Just before the crash of 2008 a team of Italian economists led by Stefano Bartolini tried to account for that seemingly inexplicable gap between rising income and flatlining happiness in the United States, using the statistical method known as regression analysis.* The Italians tried removing various components of economic and social data from their models, and they found that the only factor powerful enough to hold down people's self-reported happiness in the face of all that wealth was the country's declining social capital—the social

---

wallet finder must go out of her way to perform an act of kindness for a complete stranger. This confirms what social scientists learn over and over again: our fellow citizens are more likely to return wallets, more likely to help strangers, and much less likely to rob, cheat, mug, or kill us or each other than most of us think.

*This involves adding or removing independent variables from the statistical recipe to see how they affect an outcome. It's a bit like figuring out the secret recipe for a soup you tasted at a restaurant. Back in your own kitchen, you try various combinations of spices until you finally replicate that taste.

networks and interactions that keep us connected with others. It was even more corrosive than the income gap between rich and poor.

A healthy social network looks like the root mass of a tree. From the most important relationships at the heart of the network, thinner roots stretch out to contacts of different strength and intensity. Most people's root networks are contracting, closing in on themselves, circling more and more tightly around spouses, partners, parents, and kids. These are our most important relationships, but every arborist knows that a tree with a small root-ball is more likely to fall over when the wind blows.

The sociologist Robert Putnam warned back in 2000 that these networks of lighter relationships had been dwindling for decades. The trend has continued. People are increasingly solitary. In 1985 the typical American reported having three people he could confide in about important matters. By 2004 his network had shrunk to two, and it hasn't bounced back since. Almost half the population say they have no one, or just one person, in whom they can confide. Considering that this included close family members, it reflects a stunning decline in social connection. Other surveys show that people are losing ties with their neighborhoods and their communities. They are less likely to say they trust other people and institutions. They don't invite friends over for dinner or participate in social or volunteer groups as they did decades ago. Like Randy Strausser, most Americans simply don't know their neighbors anymore. Even family bonds are being strained. By 2004 less than 30 percent of American families ate together every night. All of these conditions are exacerbated by dispersal, as I will explain. But first, a reminder of why they constitute a happiness disaster.

As much as we complain about other people, there is nothing worse for mental health than a social desert. A study of Swiss cities found that psychotic disorders, including schizophrenia, are most common in neighborhoods with the thinnest social networks. Social isolation just may be the greatest environmental hazard of city living— worse than noise, pollution, or even crowding. The more connected we are with family and community, the less likely we are to experience colds, heart attacks, strokes, cancer, and depression. Simple friendships with other people in one's neighborhood are some of the best salves for stress during hard economic times—in fact, sociologists have found that when adults keep these friendships, their kids are better insulated from the effects of their parents' stress. Connected people sleep better at night. They are more able to tackle adversity. They live longer. They consistently report being happier.

There are many reasons for America's shrinking social support networks: marriages aren't lasting as long as they used to, people work longer hours, and they move frequently (the bank-enforced exodus during the mortgage crisis didn't help). But there is a clear connection between this social deficit and the shape of cities. A Swedish study found that people who endure more than a forty-five-minute commute were 40 percent more likely to divorce.* People who live in monofunctional, car-dependent neighborhoods outside of urban centers are much less trusting of other people than people who live in walkable neighborhoods where housing is mixed with shops, services, and places to work. They are also much less likely to know their neighbors. They are less likely to get involved with social groups and even less likely to participate in politics. They don't answer petitions, don't attend rallies, and don't join political parties or social advocacy groups. Citizens of sprawl are actually less likely to know the names of their elected representatives than people who live in more connected places.†

---

*The 2011 study by Erika Sandow found that long commutes create conflict on the home front: when one member of a couple takes on a longer commute, his spouse ends up taking on more responsibilities at home and is more likely to take part-time or lower-paying employment. Even in enlightened Sweden, the partner making the sacrifice is usually the woman.

†Living in dispersal correlates with a shocking retreat from public life, according to extensive analysis of the Social Capital Community Benchmark Survey of nearly thirty thousand people begun in 2000. It is hard to pinpoint the origin of this retreat. It may be because people in the dispersed city have invested so heavily in private comfort that they feel insulated from the problems of the rest of the world. It may be that sprawl has attracted people who are naturally less interested in engaging with the world, socially or politically. These are both possible, but evidence suggests that the spatial landscape matters. Sociologists point out that the suburbs have done an efficient job of sorting people into communities where they will be surrounded by people of the same socioeconomic status. Meanwhile, the architectures of sprawl inhibit political activity that requires face-to-face interaction. It is not that sprawl makes political activity impossible, but by privatizing gathering space and dispersing human activity, sprawl makes political gathering less likely. Where would you go for a

This matters not only because political engagement is a civic duty, and not just because it is one more contributor to well-being. (Which, by the way, it is: we tend to be happier when we feel involved in the decisions that affect us.) It matters because cities need us to reach out to one another as never before. A few years after convincing the world of the value of social capital, the sociologist Robert Putnam produced evidence that the ethnic diversity that is increasingly defining major cities is linked with lower levels of social trust. This is a sad and dangerous state of affairs. Trust is the bedrock on which cities grow and thrive. Modern metropolitan cities depend on our ability to think beyond the family and tribe and to trust the people who look, dress, and act nothing like us to treat us fairly, to honor commitments and contracts, to consider our well-being along with their own, and, most of all, to make sacrifices for the general good. Collective problems such as pollution and climate change demand collective responses. Civilization is a shared project.

The Lonely Everywhere

It is impossible to deny that the dispersed city has altered the ways and speeds at which we cross paths with one another. Dispersed communities can squeeze serendipitous encounters out of our lives by pushing everyday destinations beyond the walker's reach. In that way, Mountain House is a lot like Weston Ranch. If you need anything more substantial than a slushie, you have to get into your car and drive to some other town, which is what everyone does. Randy Strausser might have the gas money, but this hypermobility alters his social landscape. That guy watering his lawn down the street is just a passing blur on Randy's eight-mile drive to the FoodMaxx over in Tracy. He might give a nod to a couple of people in the cavernous grocery store, but chances are, he will never see them again. His net-

---

demonstration? Malls and power centers reserve the right to remove unruly patrons, even in the seemingly public concourses and parking areas between stores. Dispersal itself deflates the frisson that comes with meetings between strangers. As sociologist David Brain argued, by omitting strangers from our lives, sprawl leaches away our capacity for dealing with radically different perspectives.

work is stunted, wrapped around a social core, like the roots of a pot-bound tree.

This withering of social capital is not strictly an exurban phenomenon.* But a closer look at those surveys reveals the insidious, systematic power of dispersal to alter our relationships. It is a neighborhood's place in a city, and the distance its residents travel every day, that make the biggest difference to social landscapes. The more time that people in any given neighborhood spend commuting, the less likely they are to play team sports, hang out with friends, watch a parade, or get involved in social groups. In fact, the effect of long-distance living is so strong that a 2001 study of neighborhoods in Boston and Atlanta found that neighborhood social ties could be predicted simply by counting how many people depend on cars to get around. The more neighbors drove to work, the less likely they were to be friends with one another.

Wait a minute, you might say: these days, most of us have friends all over town. Mobility has liberated us from geography, just as urban freeways enable us to travel sixty miles across a metropolitan region to work. This is only partly true. Distance raises the cost of every friendly encounter. Let's say that you and I want to meet for an ice-cream cone at the end of our workday before heading home for dinner. First we both must chart the geographic area each of us can reach in that time. Then we must see if our territories intersect. Then we need to figure out if the journey to and from a rendezvous point in that zone leaves enough time to make the meeting worthwhile. Each of us has an envelope of possibility on the space-time continuum. The more our envelopes intersect, the easier it is for us to actually see each other in person.

Using this model, the geographer Steven Farber and his colleagues at the University of Utah set out to calculate how easy it is for people living in America's biggest cities to meet in a hypothetical 1.5-hour window after work. They used a supercomputer to crunch the numbers on city size, population, geography, form, and land use to

---

*Surveys show that social trust fares better in some suburbs than it does in central cities. But this is partly a product of self-sorting: given the decades-long association between new suburbs and the good life, and the disinvestment in inner cities, America's newest suburbs were almost invariably populated by prosperous homeowners with kids—just the kind of people who stay put and produce the conditions likely to produce strong local connections.

come up with hundreds of millions of possible space-time meet-up envelopes. The result: a rating of what Farber calls the social interaction potential of each city.

The most powerful drag on Farber's social interaction potential should now come as no surprise. It's decentralization: the more thinly a city spreads out, the less access citizens have to one another. "As we continue to sprawl our cities, we are actually making it harder for social interactions to occur," Farber told me. "If you live in a big city, unless you are living and working in the core, you are paying a huge social cost."

But urban distance does more than just limit face-to-face time. It actually changes the shape and quality of our social networks. This was borne out by a 2009 study of commuters in Switzerland, where many people drive to international centers such as Geneva and Zurich. Not surprisingly, the study found that long commutes created a dispersive effect on people's social network: the longer the commute, the farther apart one's friends tended to live from one another, like a web being stretched in all directions. (To be precise, every extra six miles of commute meant that one's friends lived an extra 1.39 miles away from her, and an extra 1.46 miles apart from *each other.*) The upshot of this stretching: long-distance commuters' friends were less likely to be friends with one another, making it logistically more challenging to get face time with each of them. So while the long-distance commuters may have had lots of friends, they just weren't able to get as much support from them.

How much does social time matter? One more survey: a 2008 study by the Gallup Organization and Healthways found a direct relationship between well-being and leisure time. The more people hung out with family and friends in any particular day, the more happiness and enjoyment they reported, and the less stress and worry. It's no surprise that it's good to hang out with people we like. What is remarkable is just how much socializing we can handle. The happiness curve doesn't level off until it hits six or seven hours of social time a day. And yet, like Randy Strausser, more than three-quarters of American commuters now drive to work alone. By the mid-2000s, after a half century of massive investment in highways and urban road expansion, Americans were actually spending more hours commuting than they got in vacation time.

When Kids Pay for Distance

In 2010, I returned to San Joaquin County to see how the exurbs were recovering. I took a cruise through Stockton's Weston Ranch, which had noticeably changed. Lawns and shrubs were shaggy and underwatered. Fences were faded and broken. I stopped to chat with a group of teenagers in the middle of a sidewalk drinking party. They were sons and daughters of parents who had moved to the exurb from Oakland a decade before, hoping to escape the urban gang culture. After proudly showing me their own gang colors—*Norteño* bloodred, on belts and scarves and hoodies—they did what suburban kids have done for generations: they whined about where they lived. They said they were stuck, trapped, miles from anywhere. It was not a new complaint, but it was especially true in this city without a city. Here they were, on the cusp of adulthood, virtually helpless to access jobs or education or stores, never mind parties or movie theaters or restaurants, for that matter. I told them I was researching cities and happiness. One girl pulled her hoodie back over her dreadlocks and said, "You know what would make me happy? A store—something, anything, right here on the corner."

"Quit dreaming," her friend shouted over her. "What we need is a *car* and a tank of *gas*."

These kids had bigger worries than picking up more beer. Before I left them, they warned me to get out of Weston Ranch before dark, when the guns would come out. The warning struck me as pure bravado, but my scans of headlines in *The Record*, Stockton's local newspaper, have since revealed a parade of shootings and assaults in Weston Ranch—from the kid who took a stray bullet in his head when he peered out his window in 2009, to the rapper who was executed on a bench in nearby Henry Long Park in 2012.

Stockton has developed the worst youth gang problem in California. The city faces issues of poverty and immigration, but poor parent-child bonds and weak social ties were key contributors to gang membership. "If we have parents who take care of their kids, provide love and affection, how much of this gang activity would we be curtailing?" asked Stockton mayor Ed Chavez in frustration back when the county was still pitching itself as a rosy alternative to the inner city.

Geography was not helping. One survey found that, with a quarter of all workers commuting to other counties, others driving between San Joaquin's various hamlets, and kids geographically isolated from community services and relatives, nearly half of fifth and seventh graders had no adult supervision at all during afterschool hours. For all its middle-class aesthetics, Weston Ranch was an especially rich gang-recruitment area, Ralph Womack, head of Stockon's youth gang intervention program, told me. Great Valley Elementary School in Weston Ranch resorted to scheduling parent conferences late at night in a desperate attempt to catch those long-distance parents. When latchkey kids have no parents around to guide them, many end up finding a substitute in gangs, he explained.

Many people move to the suburban fringe and suffer the commute as a sacrifice for their children. Unfortunately, that quiet cul-de-sac is a less ideal place to nurture kids and teens than we once thought. This landscape doesn't simply leave them stranded; teens from the suburbs—even affluent suburbs—have proved to be more prone to social and emotional problems than their urban counterparts.

When she studied teenagers from affluent suburbs in the Northeast, Columbia University psychologist Suniya Luthar found that despite their access to resources, health services, and high-functioning parents, these teens were much more anxious and depressed than teens from inner-city neighborhoods who were faced with all manner of environmental and social ills. The privileged suburban teens smoked more, drank more, and used more hard drugs than inner-city teens, especially when they were feeling down. "The implication," explained Luthar, "is that they are self-medicating."

Unhappy youths in these studies all seemed to have one thing in common: they lacked the peace of mind that comes with strong attachment to parents. Kids who actually get to eat dinner with at least one parent get better grades and have fewer emotional problems. Lots of things keep parents busy these days, but it stands to reason that marathon commutes, long-distance shopping trips, and the stringing together of distant appointments unique to the dispersed city can starve children of those crucial parental hours. This phenomenon is certainly not unique to the exurbs. But these communities undoubtedly design time deficits into their residents' lives.

None of this came as a surprise to Randy Strausser, who admitted that his own family had paid the price for his stretched life. Randy first took up the super-commute life when his own daughter and son, Kim and Scott, were toddlers. When the tech boom hit Silicon Valley, real estate prices went through the roof. Like so many people with kids, Randy hit the new highway over the Diablo Range to Tracy, in San Joaquin County. His children barely saw him during the week. His first marriage failed. When they reached their teens, Kim and Scott moved in with Randy's previous wife. But she was an exurban super-commuter too.

In those years, the teens had to fend for themselves most nights. Kim got used to heating up frozen dinners to serve her little brother for dinner. But she could hardly be expected to parent the kid. Scott slid off the rails. First he got into tagging. Then skipping school. Then shoplifting. His troubles got worse and worse.

"Now," said Randy gravely as we finally hit the turnoff for Mountain House, "he is a guest of the county of Salt Lake City." By which he meant Scott was in jail, and it was time to change the subject.

The End of the Road

Sometimes it takes an entire generation to see the life lost between freeway off-ramps.

Randy's daughter, Kim, told me she was drawn into the long-distance life commute herself not long after graduating from high school. That's when she married her high school boyfriend, Kevin Holbrook, and gave birth to a boy. They moved into a modest ranch house in Tracy, as the passage to adulthood seemed to demand. They had bills to pay, but in the dispersed city, it was not as though they could just work around the corner. Kim got a job as an administrative assistant at the Hewlett Foundation in Menlo Park, fifty miles west.

That's how she found herself crawling out of bed at five each morning, dropping her toddler, Justin, at day care, then hitting the highway for two hours, up over the Diablo Range, down through the Castro Valley, across the shallow south end of San Francisco Bay, up to the 280, through the hills above Redwood City, and down into Menlo Park. When she could, she'd catch a ride with her grandmother, Nancy, who also worked for the foundation. Otherwise, she'd go solo in her Chevy Malibu. Two hours in, two hours home.

She was living the long-distance life, just like her mother and father, her grandmother, and her husband, too. It was exhausting, but she endured it for the sake of her son.

One day the phone rang at Kim's office. It was the day-care center back in Tracy. Her little boy had turned beet red. He was as hot as a kettle, and he was vomiting the contents of his stomach all over the playroom. Kim panicked. Her child was dying, she thought, *and he was fifty miles away.* She sprinted downstairs to her Chevy and hit the highway. Her heart pounded as if it were going to break right through her chest. She had no idea how fast she was traveling, but no speed seemed fast enough.

Hot tears were streaming down her face when she heard the sound of a police siren and pulled over on Eleventh Avenue in Tracy. She didn't have the energy to explain her haste to the officer. She just let him write the ticket and kept her eyes on the road ahead, waiting for him to let her go.

By the time Kim burst through the doors of her son's day-care center, his vomit had been mopped up and his fever had settled. She picked him up, wiped the sweaty hair back on his forehead, held him. The boy was on the mend. But that night Kim told her husband that she could not, would not, live as her parents had lived. They vowed to find a way to unstretch their lives.

Kim Holbrook has not been alone in reconsidering her relationship with the city. In the past decade the tide of dispersal has slacked. Central cities from Manhattan to Vancouver to Mexico City have seen an influx of new residents willing to give proximity another shot. But escaping from the effects of dispersal is not as easy as you might think. The system that stretched Kim's life actually flows through architecture, public spaces, infrastructure budgets, laws, and mobility networks, infecting every part of every metropolis in the United States, Canada, and, increasingly, cities all around the world.

If we are going to escape the effects of dispersal, we need to understand it as a system of building, planning, and thinking. We need to consider how it was born in the first place.

4. How We Got Here

The modern city is probably the most unlovely and artificial site this planet affords. The ultimate solution is to abandon it . . . We shall solve the City Problem by leaving the city.
—Henry Ford, 1922

The city we saw from the Repo Tour bus is not a naturally occurring phenomenon. It is not organic. It is not an accident. It was not fashioned by the desires of citizens operating in a free market. It was shaped by powerful financial incentives, massive public investment, and strict rules defining how land and roads can be developed and used. But these are merely tools, put to work in the service of ideas about urban happiness that were born during an age of acute urban trauma. To understand the dispersed city, it helps to take a quick detour into cities that were so full of factory smoke, ugliness, crime, and deprivation that they seemed to threaten the very societies that created them.

Andrew Mearns, a reformist clergyman, produced this report after a trudge into the slums of industrial revolution London in 1883: "Few who will read these pages have any conception of what these pestilential human rookeries are, where tens of thousands are crowded together amidst horrors which call to mind what we have heard of the middle passage of the slave ship." The poor lived several families to a room in filthy tenements, their broken window holes stuffed with rags to keep out the cold. The air was thick with soot and the water infused with cholera.

The city was a flood of sin and misery, which Mearns warned was strong enough to destroy society itself.

The urban slums of America were not much better. In New York

City, the 1894 Tenement House Commission noted that the city's crowded tenement districts were "centers of disease, poverty, vice, and crime, where it is a marvel, not that some children grow up to be thieves, drunkards and prostitutes, but that so many should ever grow up to be decent and self-respecting." In 1885 a contributor to *The American Magazine* described New York's tenement population as "so ignorant, so vicious, so depraved that they hardly seem to belong to our species," adding cruelly that it was "almost a matter for congratulations that the death rate among the inhabitants of these tenements is something over 57 per cent."

High-minded observers were convinced that the urban landscape was corrupting not just the health but also the minds and the very souls of its inhabitants. How would they be rescued? Was the solution to tinker with the city, abandon it, or kill the monster and replace it with a grand, new vision of urbanity? Their proposals ran the gamut, but two design ideologies from those miserable years went on to shape cities right through the twentieth century, and they have driven architects, reformists, and politicians ever since. They seeped into the culture. This is what gave them power.

The first philosophy might be called the school of separation. Its central belief is that the good life can be achieved only by strictly segregating the various functions of the city so that certain people can avoid the worst of its toxicity.

The other we might call the school of speed. It translates the lofty concept of freedom into a matter of velocity—the idea being that the faster you can get away from the city, the freer you will become.

As I explained in Chapter 2, cities have always been shaped by powerful beliefs about happiness. But no philosophies have transformed cities and the world so fully as these.

Everything in Its Place

First, consider the evolution of the idea of separation, which was a natural response to the horrors of the Industrial Revolution. With crowded cities choking on soot and sewage, it was reasonable to wish to retreat from—or at least isolate—the city's unpleasantness. This was the aspiration behind Ebenezer Howard's plans for garden cities, which promised lungfuls of fresh air and conviviality for Londoners who could afford to retreat to their semirural setting. Frank Lloyd Wright's Broadacre City plan promised nothing less than *spiritual* redemption for the tenement dweller who would lead his family away from the gothic verticality of Manhattan. In Europe, the modernists' response was similarly motivated by a horror of the city, but it was much more optimistic. Inspired by almost supernatural advances in technology and the mass-production techniques employed by such industrial pioneers as automaker Henry Ford, they imagined that cities could be fixed by rebuilding them in the image of highly efficient assembly lines. "We claim, in the name of the steamship, the airplane, and the automobile, the right to health, logic, daring, harmony, perfection," Le Corbusier wrote. "We must refuse to afford even the slightest concession to what is: to the mess we are in now . . . there is no solution to be found there."

I suggested earlier that Le Corbusier's happiness formula was a matter of geometry and efficiency. But his ethos was just as separationist as that of his American counterparts: he believed that most urban problems could be fixed by separating the city into functionally pure districts arranged according to the simple, rational diagrams of the master architect. Le Corbusier's Radiant City plan exhibits this philosophy in all its wondrous simplicity: on this quadrant are the machines for living; on that quadrant, the factory zone; on another, the district for shopping—urban units stacked neatly like packages you might see in an IKEA warehouse.

These days such geometrically pure separatist schemes have lost much of their health-related raison d'être. With the help of emission controls and sewage systems, city centers in most advanced economies are no longer toxic, at least in the physical sense. But the ideology of separation has lived on, and nowhere so vividly as in American suburban dispersal. The most casual glance at any contemporary suburban plan, including those that define the territory of the Repo Tour, will reveal a simple set of land uses numbered, color-coded, and laid across the landscape with a paint-by-numbers artfulness best interpreted from thirty thousand feet.

The typical dispersed sprawl plan seems at first to be a fusion between the escapist's garden city and the modernist's perfectly segregated machine idyll. How did such rigid, centrally planned schemes find life in libertarian America? Well, the path that led from the utopias of a century ago to today's sprawl was not straight. It meandered back and forth between pragmatism, greed, racism, and fear.

Americans do not like to think of themselves as a people who easily accept grand plans imposed from above. But they have been just as willing as Canadians, British, and Europeans to support rules that restrict their property rights. In the 1880s, lawmakers in the California city of Modesto introduced a new law banning laundries and washhouses (which all happened to be run by Chinese) from the city core. Later, retailers in Manhattan demanded that properties be zoned to keep industrial interests from sullying the shopping areas along Fifth Avenue. In 1916 the city did just that. Hundreds of municipalities followed. Zoning was intended to reduce congestion, improve health, and make business more efficient. But most of all, it protected property values. Perhaps this is why we so enthusiastically embraced it.

Not that there wasn't pushback. A local real estate developer took the village of Euclid, Ohio, to court to stop it from using zoning to block his industrial aspirations in 1926. That fight went all the way to the U.S. Supreme Court. The village won, and shortly thereafter, the federal government gave all municipalities the same power. Since then, it has been illegal in most American jurisdictions to deviate from very narrow sets of rules governing how cities should be built or altered. Zoning laws and development codes specify what you can build and what you can do on your land. They specify the dimensions of lots, setbacks, and houses long before any of us gets a chance to move to a new neighborhood. Most powerfully, they strictly separate places for living, working, shopping, and recreation. Functional segregation was built into almost every new suburb after World War II.

The separatist project was quickened by massive subsidies in the form of federal mortgage insurance programs that favored new suburban home projects over renovations or inner-city development. You couldn't get a mortgage for a "used" house in many older neighborhoods even if you wanted to live there. You had to move to something new on the edge.

This project was also fueled by fear: not just fear of the noise, fumes, and dirt of industry, but fear of exposure to other people. It is impossible to decouple America's suburban spread from race and class tension. Racial segregation was de facto federal policy for years. The U.S.

Federal Housing Administration, which appraised neighborhoods, regularly excluded entire black communities from mortgage insurance until the advent of civil rights legislation in the 1960s. The policy gutted inner cities, while "white flight" fueled layer after layer of new suburban dispersal. So-called exclusionary zoning, which on the surface bans only certain kinds of buildings and functions from a neighborhood, served the deeper purpose of excluding people who fall beneath a certain income bracket. The tactic still works today. If you want to keep poor people out of your community, all you really need to do is ban duplexes and apartment buildings—which is exactly what new suburbs were permitted to do. The urban strategist Todd Litman summed up zoning's effect thus: "It seemed that segregation was just the natural working of the free market, the result of the sum of countless individual choices about where to live. But the houses were single— and their residents white—because of the invisible hand of government."

What's amazing is how, despite their love of liberty, Americans have embraced the massive restriction of private property rights that the separated city demands. Once a neighborhood is zoned and built, it gets frozen like a Polaroid from the day everyone moves in. As if the power of municipal zoning wasn't enough, suburban developers in the last few decades have set up homeowner associations that encourage residents to exert even more control over one another. Thus, an allegedly government-hating people have embraced an entirely new layer of government.

The color bar is not as visible now in exurban San Joaquin County, but retreatist reassurance can still be seen in the homeowner association rule books that dictate exactly what you can and cannot do with your property. Repo tourists beware: Stockton's Brookside West Owners' Association has a bylaw requiring owners to keep their lawns groomed to standards set by the association board. It's the same across the country: anyone who tries to add a suite in the basement or convert a garage into a candy store or grow wheat in a front yard learns this quickly enough. Even if you do not live in a homeowner association–controlled community, all it takes is one complaint for city inspectors to descend and remind you that your home really is not your castle.

It's important to point out that the ethos of spatial separation favored large-scale retailers and ambitious suburban property developers

who find it easier and cheaper to impose simple designs on large parcels of virgin land than to adapt to existing urban fabric. These interests
lobbied successfully for decades for tax incentives from governments
hungry for new business, a story I'll return to in Chapter 12.

Suburban zoning and development codes grew so powerful and
so entrenched by the end of the twentieth century that the people

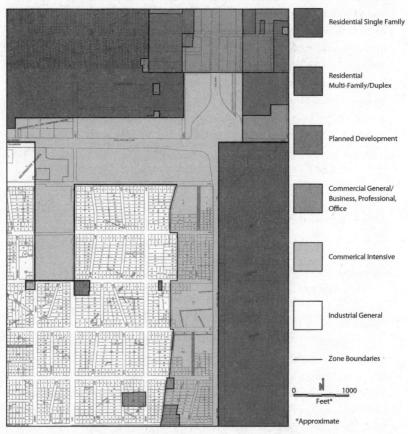

Residential Single Family

Residential
Multi-Family/Duplex

Planned Development

Commercial General/
Business, Professional,
Office

Commerical Intensive

Industrial General

Zone Boundaries

0 — 1000
Feet*

*Approximate

Tampa, Florida: The City as Simple Machine
*The ideology of separation lives on in American suburban plans. This zoning
map of Tampa reveals a strikingly simplistic set of zones that restrict exactly
what can be built—and what can happen—everywhere. Although these
systems are easy for planners to understand, they ban complexity and restrict
freedom.* (Cole Robertson/City of Tampa)

who financed and built most of suburbia had all but forgotten how to make anything but car-dependent sprawl. "We have not had a free market in real estate for eighty years," Ellen Dunham-Jones, Georgia Tech professor of architecture and coauthor of *Retrofitting Suburbia*, told me. "And because it is illegal to build in a different way, it takes an immense amount of time for anyone who wants to do it to get changes in zoning and variance. Time is money for developers, so it rarely happens."

Together, these rules and habits have ensured that the American city is as separated and as static as any Soviet-era housing scheme. They have ensured that first-generation suburbs closer to downtowns do not grow more diverse or dense. They have pushed new development out to the ever-expanding urban fringe and beyond. They are part of the reason that housing supply is so tight in the San Francisco Bay Area that hundreds of thousands of area workers like the Strausser clan are forced to drive two hours north, south, or east. And they have ensured that these new developments will, in turn, resist most efforts to change or adapt them over time.

When Freedom Got a New Name

This reorganization of cities could not have happened without breathtaking subsidies for roads and highways, a decades-long program that itself required a cultural transformation, with roots in a concept that Americans hold especially dear. A century ago, Americans redefined what it meant to be free in cities.

For most of urban history, city streets were for everyone. The road was a market, a playground, a park, and yes, it was a thoroughfare, but there were no traffic lights, painted lanes, or zebra crossings. Before 1903 no city had so much as a traffic code. Anyone could use the street, and everyone did. It was a chaotic environment littered with horse dung and fraught with speeding carriages, but a messy kind of freedom reigned.

Cars and trucks began to push their way into cities a few years after Henry Ford streamlined the mass production process at his automobile assembly line in Highland Park, Michigan. What followed was "a new kind of mass death," says urban historian Peter Norton,

Last Days of the Shared Street
Woodward Avenue, Detroit, circa 1917: When streetcars and private automobiles moved slowly, everyone shared the street. Speed—and a concerted effort by automobile clubs and manufacturers over the next decade—changed the dynamic forever. (Library of Congress, Prints & Photographs Division, Detroit Publishing Company Collection)

who charted the transformation in America's road culture during the 1920s. More than two hundred thousand people were killed in motor accidents in the United States that decade. Most were killed in cities. Most of the dead were pedestrians. Half were children and youths.

In the beginning, private motorcars were feared and despised by the majority of urbanites. Their arrival was seen as an invasion that posed a threat to justice and order. Drivers who accidentally killed pedestrians were mobbed by angry crowds and convicted not of driving infractions, but of manslaughter. At first, all levels of society banded together to protect the shared street. Police, politicians, newspaper editors, and parents all fought to regulate automobile access, ban curbside parking, and, most of all, limit speeds to ten miles per hour.

But drivers joined with automobile dealers and manufacturers to launch a war of ideas that would redefine the urban street.* They wanted the right to go faster. They wanted more space. And they wanted pedestrians, cyclists, and streetcar users to get out of the way. The American Automobile Association called this new movement Motordom.

"They had to change the idea of what a street is for, and that required a mental revolution, which had to take place before any physical changes to the street," Norton told me. "In the space of a few years, auto interests did put together that cultural revolution. It was comprehensive."

Motordom faced an uphill battle. It did not take an engineer to see that the most efficient way to move lots of people in and out of dense, crowded downtowns was by streetcar or bus. In the Chicago Loop, streetcars used 2 percent of the road space but still carried three-quarters of road users. The more cars you added, the slower the going would be for everyone. So Motordom's soldiers waged their psychological war under the cover of two ideals: safety and freedom.

First they had to convince people that the problem with safety lay in controlling pedestrians, not cars. In the 1920s, auto clubs began to compete directly with urban safety councils, campaigning to redirect the blame for accidents from car drivers to pedestrians. Crossing the street freely got a pejorative name—jaywalking—and became a crime.†

Most people came to accept that the street was not such a free place anymore—which was ironic, because freedom was Motordom's rallying cry.

"Americans are a race of independent people, even though they submit at times to a good deal of regulation and officialdom. Their

---

*For example, Charles Hayes, president of the Chicago Motor Club, told friends that the solution was to persuade city people that "the streets are made for vehicles to run upon."

†In 1922, the Packard Motor Car Company built a giant tombstone in Detroit: "Erected to the Memory of Mr. J. Walker: He Stepped from the Curb Without Looking." The next year, the Automobile Club of Southern California paid for police to erect signs prohibiting jaywalking. When M. O. Eldridge, an American Automobile Club executive, was chosen as Washington's traffic director in 1925, he ordered police to arrest and charge anyone caught walking across a street beyond the bounds of a crosswalk. Dozens were rounded up. The court agreed to set the offenders free only if they agreed to join a "Careful Walker's Club."

ancestors came to this country for the sake of freedom and adventure," declared Roy Chapin, president of the Hudson Motor Car Company. "The automobile supplies a feeling of escape from this suppression of the individual. That is why the American public has seized upon motor travel so rapidly and with such intensity."*

The industry and its auto club supporters pressed their agenda in newspapers and city halls. They hired their own engineers to propose designs for city streets that served the needs of motorists first. They stacked the national transportation-safety conferences staged by U.S. commerce secretary Herbert Hoover in the 1920s, creating model traffic regulations that forced pedestrians and transit users into regimented corners of the street such as crosswalks and streetcar boarding areas. When the regulations were published in 1928, they were adopted by hundreds of cities eager to embrace what seemed like a forward-thinking approach to mobility. They set a cultural standard that has influenced local lawmakers for decades.

Futurama

The first American to earn a doctorate in traffic was a bookish young man named Miller McClintock. After his graduation from Harvard in 1924, McClintock called for strict rules that would restrict cars and cities. Efficiency, fairness, and speed limits were the name of the game. But then the Studebaker car company put him at the helm of a new traffic foundation it funded, and McClintock, who had a new wife and child to take care of, had a philosophical change of heart. With Studebaker's quiet backing, he became the national authority on streets and traffic while training America's first generation of traffic experts. His diagnosis for cities came to resemble the aspirations of the auto interests who funded him, and by the time he addressed the Society of Automotive Engineers in 1928, he was sounding a lot like Roy Chapin.

"This country was founded on the principle of freedom," he announced. "Now the automobile has brought something which is an integral part of the American spirit—freedom of movement."

*Chapin eventually joined Herbert Hoover's cabinet as secretary of commerce.

In this new age, freedom had a very particular character. It was not the freedom to move as one pleased. It was the freedom for cars, and cars alone, to move very quickly, unhindered by all the other things that used to happen on streets. The enemy of *freedom*, McClintock declared, was *friction*! The nation needed roads unhindered by the friction of intersections, parked cars, and even roadside trees.

At the 1937 National Planning Conference in Detroit, McClintock unveiled spectacular images of that vision: a futuristic city where pearl-hued skyscrapers poked through a latticework of elevated freeways and cloverleafs unsullied by crosswalks or corner shops or streetcars. The pictures, a collaboration between McClintock and stage designer Norman Bel Geddes, had been paid for by Shell Oil. They would grow into the most persuasive piece of propaganda in the history of city planning, when Bel Geddes expanded the model into Futurama, a vast pavilion for the 1939 World's Fair in New York. Futurama showed people the wondrous world they would inhabit in 1960 if cities embraced the Motordom vision. Visitors were transported in moving chairs over a football field–size diorama where automated superhighways shuttled toy cars between city and country. At the end of the ride, visitors strolled out onto an elevated pedestrian walkway above a perfect street packed with new automobiles. It was a life-size version of the motor age city: the future made real, thanks to the exhibit's sponsor, General Motors.

Although the model was presented as a free-market dreamworld, it bore a striking resemblance to drawings of Le Corbusier's egalitarian Radiant City. Two radically different philosophies had fallen in love with technology to produce a similarly separationist vision. But Futurama was distinguished by its reverence for speed. With its sleek highways propelling citizens from orderly cities to pristine open spaces, it seemed to confirm that the fast city really would set people free, as Frank Lloyd Wright had promised.

More than twenty-four million people waited in line to see the future that year. The exhibit, which was featured in magazines and newspapers, drew an entire nation to the high-speed philosophy of its sponsors and helped cement a massive cultural shift toward the automobile lifestyle.

Meanwhile, a company formed by GM, Firestone Tire and Rubber

Futurama

LEFT: *The future is revealed at the vast General Motors pavilion for the 1939 World's Fair in New York: a city built for cars.* RIGHT: *The Futurama vision has now been built into cities around the world. The fourteen high-speed lanes of Dubai's de facto main street, Sheikh Zayed Road, are impossible for pedestrians to cross for miles at a time.* (*Left:* GM Media Archive; *right:* Charles Montgomery)

Company, Phillips Petroleum, and Standard Oil was busy buying up and dismantling hundreds of private streetcar lines in dozens of cities across the United States. Various conspiracy theories have argued that this was a plan to force people to buy cars by eliminating public transit. This may have been true, but it was hardly necessary. The streetcar had been fatally wounded when the definition of the street changed. It drowned in a sea of cars.

The final assault on the old city arrived via the interstate highway system. In 1956 the Federal-Aid Highway Act funneled billions of tax dollars into the construction of new freeways, including dozens of wide new roads that would push right into the heart of cities. This— along with federal home mortgage subsidies and zoning that effectively prohibited any other kind of development but sprawl—rewarded Americans who abandoned downtowns and punished those who stayed behind, with freeways cutting swaths through inner-city neighborhoods from Baltimore to San Francisco. Anyone who could afford to get out, did.

The System That Reproduces Itself

Cities, like many systems, are prone to a phenomenon known as autopoiesis, which can be compared to a viruslike process of entrenchment, replication, and expansion. The dispersed city lives not only in the durability of buildings, parking lots, and highways, but also in the habits of the professionals who make our cities. Once the system of dispersal was established in early suburbs, it began to repeat itself in plan after plan—not because it was the best response to any particular place, but because of the momentum of autopoiesis. It was simply easier for city builders in communities with modest budgets to repeat what worked before, and their habits gradually hardened into the building and zoning codes that dictated how new places would be built. Thus, a segregated land zoning system created to keep industry from creeping into an Ohio village back in 1926 evolved into a national tool and eventually was distilled into standard, downloadable codes sold by the private online purveyor Municode. Cash-strapped towns can now simply download their property-use laws. Meanwhile, road-design laws developed by Motordom-funded engineers were entrenched in the Federal Highway Administration's *Manual on Uniform Traffic Control Devices*, or *MUTCD*, a traffic bible guiding most urban road projects in the country. Dispersal infected the operating system of city after city, and those cities in turn replicated dispersal's DNA.

The rapid, uniform, and seemingly endless replication of this dispersal system was, for many people and for many years, a marvelous thing. It helped fuel an age of unprecedented wealth. It created sustained demand for the cars, appliances, and furniture that fueled the North American manufacturing economy. It provided millions of jobs in construction and massive profits for land developers. It gave more people than ever before the chance to purchase their own homes on their own land, far from the noise and haste and pollution of downtown.

Had he joined the Repo Tour, Andrew Mearns, the clergyman who trudged into London's slums in 1883, would no doubt note the absence of sewage stench, of desperate crowding, soot, and clambering vermin. He would marvel at the broad lawns, the life-giving sunlight, the peace, plumbing, and privacy afforded each family. And the silence. He would see in the dispersed city a tremendous achievement.

He might not recognize that the pendulum had swung to another extreme. He might have trouble seeing the economic and social devastation caused by the geometries of distance, or the extent to which the system of dispersal had corroded life in other parts of the city. But that system has indeed seeped into every corner of the modern city. It infuses the zoning codes that freeze such first-generation suburban towns as Palo Alto, where Nancy Strausser raised her children, but where none of them or their own children will likely ever be able to afford to live again. It taints central cities, where systems have been reconfigured for speed—not just in neighborhoods lacerated by freeways but also on avenues where traffic signals, asphalt, and sidewalks have been redesigned to favor travelers passing through in private vehicles over the people who live there.

Dispersal has drawn cities into a zero-sum game: as it distilled and privatized some material comforts in detached suburban homes, it off-loaded danger and unpleasantness to the streets of dense cities. It reverberates in the car horns that wake Brooklynites at dawn, and it gets sucked into the lungs of Manhattanites who choose to walk to work.*

It seeps into once-quiet neighborhoods in suburban Los Angeles, where long-distance commuters barrel through residential streets to avoid now-congested freeways, and children have been banned from playing street ball. It exists in the forgotten schools, neglected public spaces, and anemic transit services endured by residents of some unfavored "inner-city" neighborhoods abandoned by governments and prosperous citizens alike more than half a century ago. Meanwhile,

---

*The extent to which central cities were transformed by Motordom has its monument in Manhattan's Park Avenue. Most New Yorkers have no idea that the avenue, now a highway-like thoroughfare with a narrow garden median, got its name in the 1850s because a long section of the avenue actually *was* a park, complete with wide lawns and a six-block brick pedestrian promenade.

dispersal starves the budgets of cities forced to spend sales tax dollars on roads, pipes, sewage, and services for the distant neighborhoods of sprawl, leaving little for the shared amenities that make central-city living attractive. The fact that residents in America's central cities report being even less satisfied and even less socially connected than people in suburbia is not a testament to the superiority of sprawl, but a by-product of received hardships and the pervasive, systemic effects of dispersal.

A new wave of urbanists now pit sprawl against the vertical city, arguing that the physical and cultural density of Manhattan is the model for a sustainable future. But the journey to a happier city cannot simply mean choosing between downtown and the sprawl edge. Most central cities, with these layers of imported traffic, noise, pollution, and road danger, do not currently meet our needs for well-being much better than sprawl. We must redesign both landscapes and the fabric that connects them in ways that answer the needs that led us to retreat in the first place.

To determine what those redesigns might look like, we need to understand how places, crowds, views, architecture, and ways of moving influence the way we feel. We need to identify the unseen systems that influence our health and control our behavior. Most of all, we need to understand the psychology by which all of us comprehend the urban world and make decisions about our place in it.

5. Getting It Wrong

"You see, happiness ain't a thing in itself—it's only a contrast with something that ain't pleasant . . . And mind you,
as soon as the novelty is over and the force of the contrast
dulled, it ain't happiness any longer, and you've got to get
up something fresh."
 —Mark Twain, "Captain Stormfield's Visit to Heaven"

"Nothing in life is quite as important as you think it is while
you are thinking about it."
 —Daniel Kahneman

There is a particularly vexing problem on the road to the happier city,
and it travels with every one of us. The emerging consensus among
psychologists and behavioral economists is that as individuals and as
a species, humans just aren't that well equipped to make decisions
that maximize our happiness. We make predictable mistakes when
deciding where and how to live, and the architects, planners, and
builders who create the landscapes that help shape our decisions are
prone to some of the very same mistakes. I became aware of this at an
especially inconvenient moment.

I was born in Vancouver, the city wedged between sea and forested
mountains on the west coast of Canada, which regularly tops lists of
the world's most livable cities. The setting is gorgeous. Fresh air, mild
climate, and rain forest views attract retirees, investors, and part-
time residents from around the world. All this has made Vancouver a
high-value, high-status destination whose charms are reflected in its
soaring real estate prices.

Like many people born in the 1960s, I could not imagine spending my adult life in some generic apartment. I wanted a house and my own piece of Frank Lloyd Wright's "good ground." I did not base this wish on any particular utilitarian calculation. I was just certain I would be happier once I had achieved it. So in 2006, when the average price of a detached home in Metro Vancouver hit $520,000,* I bought a share of an old friend's house, a two-story fixer-upper on the city's working-class East Side.

The house was perfectly habitable, but it did not resemble the ones pictured in the home and garden magazines that my co-owner, Keri, collected. The place was cut through with awkwardly angled walls and floored with barbershop checkerboard linoleum. The century-old timber frame swayed and lurched in time with any romance conducted on the top floor. It was a little too dark, a little too drafty, and, we decided, a little too cramped. So we signed papers on a second mortgage in order to raise that creaking frame, strip it down to the studs, and transform the place into the home of our dreams. We figured that nine-foot ceilings, reconditioned fir floors, an open-plan kitchen, two living rooms, an extra story, and a couple of extra bathrooms should do it. Like millions of our fellow middle classers, we were sure that the extra square footage would make us happier, despite the quarter-million dollars we had to borrow to get us there. We pictured ourselves sipping wine under blown-glass pendant lights while summer breezes wafted in from the patio.

Construction began the next spring. No sooner had the house been severed from its foundations and propped on story-high columns of railway ties than I was broadsided by the first warning about the psychological trap we had fallen into. This realization arrived by way of Nants Foley, a Realtor in the California town of Hollister. Foley had just written an emotional column that appeared in the Hollister *Pinnacle* warning homebuyers to be wary of the urge to follow their dreams. Foley's own clients invariably wanted to trade up: they all wanted a bigger house on a bigger yard in a more perfect neighborhood, and Foley helped them get it. But after a few sales cycles she noticed that those big homes did not seem to be making her clients happier. "Time and again," she told me when I called her, "I would walk into an absolutely gorgeous home with a beautiful pool that

---

*The average price of a detached home in Vancouver is now more than $1 million.

never got used and a game room that was never actually filled with friends, owned by people who were living really unhappy lives."

People's new homes were so big that they created a whole new layer of housekeeping, and so expensive that they forced their owners to work harder to keep them. One day Foley joined a Realtors' tour of a spacious stucco tract home. The walls were pristine—Foley still remembers the color: Navajo Sand. The carpets were immaculate. But the place felt like a campsite. There was practically no furniture. A lone TV sat on a packing crate, and just about everything else lay on the floor. Clothing, books, and tools, all stacked in neat piles. Mattresses and futons lined the carpets in the bedrooms. It was clear that the house purchase had taken the family right to the edge of its financial wherewithal. They had spent everything they had. There was nothing left for furniture or garden supplies. The yard was a mud pit. The family had joined the ranks of what Foley called "floor people," since floor space was all they had.

How was it that so many people had made decisions that led them into hardship? Foley found her answer in a treatise by the Nobel Prize–winning economist Gary Becker and his colleague Luis Rayo at the University of Chicago. The pair had poured the latest findings in psychology, evolutionary theory, and brain science into an algorithm that describes a trap that the economists believe is endemic to our species. Here it is:

$$H(y_t) = y_t - E\left[y_t \,\middle|\, \varphi_t, \Omega_t\right]_{\varphi_t=1} = w_t - w_{t-1}{}^*$$

Dubbed the evolutionary happiness function, the equation explains the psychological process that both fuels our desire for bigger homes and ensures that we will be dissatisfied shortly after moving in. Dissatisfaction, it suggests, is inevitable. Considering my own rapidly expanding home, I called Rayo in a panic.

He explained that the equation's message is simple:

*A basic translation of evolutionary happiness function: Happiness = your success minus your expectations = your perceived social status. (Courtesy Luis Rayo, from Rayo, Luis, and Gary Becker, "Evolutionary Efficiency and Happiness," *Journal of Political Economy*, 2007: 302–37.)

Humans do not perceive the value of things in absolute terms. We never have. Just as our eyes process the color and luminosity of an object relative to its surroundings, the brain constantly adjusts its idea of what we need in order to be happy. It compares what we have now to what we had yesterday and what we might possibly get next. It compares what we have to what everyone else has. Then it recalibrates the distance to a revised finish line. But that finish line moves even when other conditions stay the same, simply because we get used to things. So happiness, in these economists' particular formulation, is inherently remote. It never stands still.

Framed this way, the happiness function would have served our prehistoric ancestors really well. Hunter-gatherers more oriented to dissatisfaction, those who compulsively looked ahead in order to kill more game or collect more berries than they did yesterday, were more likely to make it through lean times and thus pass on their genes. In this model, happiness is not a condition at all. It is an urge genes employ to get an organism working harder and hoarding more stuff. The human brain has not changed much in the ten thousand years since we began to farm. We have been hardwired for active dissatisfaction.

"We are still slaves to that evolutionary hunting strategy," Rayo insisted. "We are always comparing what we have to something else. But we're not anticipating that no matter what we have, we will *always* be comparing it to something else. In fact, we're not even aware that we are doing this. But there's a difference between what's natural and what's good for us."

Indeed, this trait does not serve the city dweller well, at least not in rich countries. The desire for marble countertops, stainless steel fixtures, and conspicuous purchases clearly doesn't boost the likelihood that we will pass on our genes, and these things cannot, on their own, propel us any closer toward the horizon of shifting satisfaction.

Rayo assured me that it would be a matter of months before I started to compare my own renovated home to a new ideal.

Nants Foley handed in her Realtor's lockbox and turned to farming in 2009.

I, meanwhile, was left with my expanding house and mortgage, and an uncertain place on the spectrum of shifting aspirations.

Wrong Again

Neoclassical economics, which dominated the second half of the twentieth century, is based on the premise that we are all perfectly well equipped to make choices that maximize utility. The discipline's proverbial "economic man" has access to every piece of relevant information, doesn't forget a thing, evaluates his choices soberly, and makes the best possible decision based on his options.

But the more psychologists and economists examine the relationship between decision making and happiness, the more they realize that this is simply not true. We make bad choices all the time. In fact we screw up so systematically that you might as well call behavioral economics the science of getting it wrong. Even when we do get complete information, which is rare, we are prone to a barrage of predictable errors of bias and miscalculation. Our flawed choices have helped shape the modern city—and consequently, the shape of our lives.

Take the simple act of choosing how far to travel to work. Aside from the financial burden, people who endure long drives tend to experience higher blood pressure and more headaches than those with short commutes. They get frustrated more easily and tend to be grumpier when they get to their destination.

Anyone with faith in economic man would think that people would put up with the pain of a long commute only if they enjoyed even greater benefits from cheaper housing or bigger, finer homes or higher-paying jobs. They would weigh the costs and benefits and make sensible decisions. A couple of University of Zurich economists discovered that this simply isn't the case. Bruno Frey and Alois Stutzer compared German commuters' estimation of the time it took them to get to work with their answers to the standard well-being question: "How satisfied are you with your life, all things considered?"

Their finding was seemingly straightforward: the longer the drive, the less happy people were. Before you dismiss this as numbingly obvious, keep in mind that they were testing not for *drive* satisfaction, but for *life* satisfaction. So their discovery was not that commuting hurt. It was that people were choosing commutes that made their entire lives worse. They simply were not balancing the hardship of the long commute with pleasures in other areas of their lives—not through higher income nor through lower costs or greater enjoyment of their homes. They were not behaving like economic man.

This so-called commuting paradox blows a hole in the long-accepted argument that the free choice of millions of commuters can sort out the optimal shape of the city. In fact, Stutzer and Frey found that a person with a one-hour commute has to earn 40 percent more money to be as satisfied with life as someone who walks to the office. On the other hand, for a single person, exchanging a long commute for a short walk to work has the same effect on happiness as finding a new love.* Yet even when people were aware of the harm their commutes did to their well-being, they did not take action to rearrange their lives.

One human characteristic that exacerbates such bad decision making is adaptation: the uneven process by which we get used to things. The satisfaction finish line is actually more like a snake than a line. Some parts of it move away as we approach, and some do not. Some things we adapt to quickly and some things we just never get used to. Daniel Gilbert, Harvard psychologist and author of *Stumbling on Happiness*, explained the commuting paradox to me this way:

"Most good and bad things become less good and bad over time as we adapt to them. However, it is much easier to adapt to things that stay constant than to things that change. So we adapt quickly to the joy of a larger house because the house is exactly the same size every time we come in the front door. But we find it difficult to adapt to commuting by car, because every day is a slightly new form of misery, with different people honking at us, different intersections jammed with accidents, different problems with weather, and so on."

It would help if we could distinguish more broadly between goals that offer lasting rewards and those that do not. Psychologists generally divide the things that inspire people to action into two groups: extrinsic or intrinsic motivators.

As the name suggests, extrinsic motivators generally come with external rewards: things we can buy or win, or things that might

---

*Meanwhile, the misery brought on by a long commute seemed to have a viral effect on the driver's family: the more time a respondent's partner spent commuting, the less happy the respondent tended to be. Call it the delayed road rage effect.

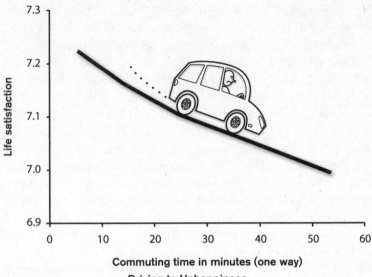

Commuting time in minutes (one way)

Driving to Unhappiness

The longer people choose to commute, the less happy they say they are with their entire life, suggesting that long-distance commuters are systematically failing to maximize utility. (Graphic by Dan Planko, with data from Stutzer, Alois, and Bruno S. Frey, "Stress That Doesn't Pay: The Commuting Paradox," *Scandinavian Journal of Economics,* 2008: 339–66.)

change our status in the world. But while a new granite countertop or an unexpected pay raise makes you happier in the short run, these changes don't do much for long-term happiness. Most of the boost you feel from a leap on the income ladder simply evaporates within a year. The finish line shifts.

Intrinsic motivators, on the other hand, are about the journey rather than the destination. Their rewards come with those activities and states that relate to our deep need to feel connected to other people, to feel competent and effective, and to feel autonomous, or in charge of our actions. They contribute to the resilient kind of happiness that Carol Ryff wrapped up in her map of *eudaimonia*. And they are remarkably durable. Some good things we never get used to: playing sports, creative projects or hobbies, even doing work that requires concentration. When an activity is its own reward, it can actually feel better with every act of consumption. This is especially true in the social world. The more you see your friends, the more intimate and rich those friendships can become.

The problem is, we consistently make decisions that suggest we are not so good at distinguishing between ephemeral and lasting pleasures. We keep getting it wrong.

A Campus Conundrum

This flawed choice calculus is at work in all of us, including some of America's brightest young minds. Consider the anxiety of the Harvard University dormitory resident. Near the end of their first year, freshmen at Harvard get the results of the lottery that determines where they will live for the rest of their undergraduate studies. This is considered a life-changing moment. After all, the lottery determines their home, their neighborhood, and, to some extent, their social life for the following three years.

Harvard's dormitories vary wildly in their architecture, history, and social reputation. The most prestigious, Lowell House, with its grand redbrick facades, is a classic example of the Georgian Revival style. Its blue-capped bell tower is a local landmark, and its alumni include John Updike and Crown Princess Masako of Japan.

Harvard's newest residences, built in the 1970s, lie on the far end of the status and architectural spectrum. The concrete tower of Mather House was described in *The Harvard Crimson*, the student newspaper, as a "riot-proof monstrosity designed by a prison architect," although its bacchanalian soap-foam parties have achieved mythical status. (Noted alumnus: Conan O'Brien.)

News of a bad dormitory assignment is perceived as a psychic and social disaster. Elizabeth Dunn, now a psychologist at the University of British Columbia, endured the housing lottery in 1996, back when results were slipped under dormitory doors before dawn. Dunn recalls that some of her fellows actually performed mock prayers to "the housing gods" to deliver them from being assigned to the wrong house.

"All my friends wanted to be in Lowell House," Dunn told me. "It's so beautiful, it's got that classic dining hall, squash courts in the basement, a wood-paneled library—it's the image of the ideal Harvard life."

When they ripped open their envelopes to discover their collective assignment to Lowell House, Dunn and her friends were overjoyed. They were convinced that the place had the power to make or break their happiness.

But were they right? After a couple of years of watching new freshmen go through the lottery—and studying psychology under Daniel Gilbert—Dunn wasn't so sure. Under his guidance, she set out to find out.

First, she asked a fresh batch of freshmen to predict how happy they would be if assigned to each of Harvard's twelve houses. Then she and a colleague interviewed those students after a year, and then again after two years in their new homes, to see how happy they actually were.

The results would surprise many Harvard freshmen. Students sent to what they were sure would be miserable houses ended up much happier than they had anticipated. And students who landed in the most desirable houses were less happy than they expected to be. Life in Lowell House was fine. But so was life in the reviled Mather House. Overall, Harvard's choice dormitories just didn't make anyone much happier than its spurned dormitories.

Why did the students get their happiness predictions so wrong? Dunn found a pattern that the students share with most of us: they put far too much weight on obvious differences between residences, such as location and architectural features, and far too little on things that were not so glaringly different, such as the sense of community and the quality of relationships they would develop in their dormitory. It wasn't just architecture, history, or interior styling that made people happy. A good campus life was fueled by friendship and the social culture nurtured by longtime house masters and tutors. Mather House's soap-foam parties may have had a more powerful cheering effect than Lowell's stately dining hall.

The curious part was this: most students said that they knew that social life would be more important to their happiness than architecture, yet they still put greater weight on physical features. This is the standard mis-weighing of extrinsic and intrinsic values: we may tell each other that experiences are more important than things, but we constantly make choices as though we didn't believe it.

Lucky for them, the Harvard students were merely predicting their happiness. They weren't actually able to choose their home. In the rest of the city, millions of people get the happiness calculus wrong, time and again, and have to live with the consequences for years.

Distracted by Aesthetics
Students thought they would be happier living in Harvard's Lowell House (left)
than they would be in Mather House (right). *They were wrong.* (*Left*: Jon Chase/
Harvard University; *right*: Kris Snibbe/Harvard University)

Seeing Wrong, Measuring Wrong

Quick: Which would make you happier—living in California or the
U.S. Midwest?

If you chose California, you are like most people—including midwesterners, who told surveyors they were sure that Californians were
happier. Californians agreed. They were all wrong. Californians and
midwesterners report pretty much the same level of life satisfaction.

How is it that most of us get this question wrong? Part of the answer lies in the way we frame decisions and in a cognitive quirk known
as the focusing illusion. We tend to focus on one or two glaring
differences between choices—things we can see or picture, such as
weather—and we ignore or underrate less conspicuous but powerful

details such as crime, commute times, social networks, and pollution. No matter how much more friendly and easy life might be in Ohio, what sticks in our heads is the vivid contrast between that mental image of sunshine and surf and one of dreary winters and roadside slush.

The sad part is that a place's popularity can actually destroy the elements that contribute to happiness. The more we flock to high-status cities for the good life—money, opportunity, novelty—the more crowded, expensive, polluted, and congested those places become. The result? Surveys show that rich, high-status states in the United States are among the least happy in the country. Citizens of Canada's big, high-status cities (such as Toronto and Vancouver, which consistently hover near the top of global quality-of-life lists) say they are much less satisfied with life than people living in small towns and humble backwaters such as Sherbrooke, Quebec, and Brantford, Ontario.* But we keep arriving, and in our collective pursuit we ensure that highly desired places are even less able to make us happy.

We are far less rational in our decisions than we sometimes like to believe. Now neuroscientists are starting to figure out the means by which our brains can turn a supposedly rational decision into a shouting match between logic and emotion.

The Corrupted Decision

David Halpern, an architect and occasional adviser to the British government, once conducted an experiment in which he had a group of volunteers rate the attractiveness of a series of images of human faces and buildings. Some of those volunteers were architecture students. Others were not. The volunteers generally all had the same response to the various human faces, but the longer any one of them had studied architecture, the more his or her taste in buildings diverged from that of the crowd. So while regular people feel delighted

*Surveys in the U.K. show that Londoners are among the least happy people in the entire United Kingdom, despite the city's being the richest region in the U.K.

by the faux-Victorian facades of Disneyland's Main Street U.S.A., most architects can't stand the place. Instead they make pilgrimages to gaze at Ludwig Mies van der Rohe's Seagram Building, a black box in Manhattan whose aesthetic flourish consists of an almost-imperceptible exoskeleton of steel I beams.

Snobbery? Not necessarily. Architects' brains may be physically altered by the act of studying and reading about the philosophy of building. Virginia Tech neurobiologist Ulrich Kirk and his colleagues used fMRI machines to see how the brains of architects and nonexperts would react to pictures of buildings. When a typical architect was asked to rate a building, her medial orbitofrontal cortex (a part of the brain that helps measure how much reward we'll get from decisions) lit up much brighter than the same region in the nonexpert's brain. The architect's hippocampus, a sea horse–shaped instrument that works something like a librarian for all our memories, was also more fully activated.

Not to demean the profession of architecture, but researchers found similar results in the brains of people making that most mundane of choices: Coke or Pepsi. The mere sight of a can emblazoned with the Coke label activated volunteers' hippocampi more than the act of actually sipping the cola, and this caused people to prefer its taste. (The Pepsi label had little effect.) The point here is that exposure to cultural information can change the way our brains function, dredging up images and feelings that alter the way we experience things.* With its complex structures and its billions of neurons, the brain works like a microcosm of human society. Just as the voices and actions of millions of people contribute to societal decisions, groups of neurons collaborate and compete for influence as the brain itself makes decisions.

"In the end, your decision depends on information propagation,"

---

*In another experiment, Kirk observed the culture effect come to life in the brains of all his volunteers. All it took was feeding them a bit of context. He and his colleagues asked volunteers to rate the aesthetics of dozens of pieces of art. Simply telling them that a particular image was from the collection of an art gallery—as opposed to a random image database—caused them to like the image more. Once again, that contextual information lit up different parts of their brains, which biased their preferences.

the neuroscientist Jan Lauwereyns told me. "Certain types of information gain the spotlight, like getting prime-time coverage on television, and this biases our decisions."

Just as architects are biased by their scholarship, we all lug around a heavy bag of cultural messages. The hippocampus and other parts of the brain fight to give these messages a role in each decision, whether we realize it or not.

In the end, our evaluation of what is "good" can be entirely subjective. Our brains are pushed and pulled by the powerful synergy of memory, culture, and images. So our concept of the right house, car, or neighborhood might be as much a result of happy moments from our past or images that flood us in popular media as of any rational analysis of how these elements will influence the moments of our lives.

Given the images that the contemporary city dweller's hippocampus has filed away, this information storm can easily lead to unreasonable expectations. Consider a little girl's first dream home: the dollhouse. When the toy manufacturer Mattel held a contest to create a new home for their iconic Barbie toy in 2011, the winning design was the equivalent of a 4,880-square-foot glass mansion on three acres. Estimated construction cost in real life: $3.5 million. As sure as that house was pink, its dimensions will be transposed onto the aspirations of a generation of girls who grow up playing with it.

I once attended a Christmas party at the house of a single gay man in suburban Seattle. The Christmas tree was huge, and it glistened with lights, but my most striking memory was of his vast living room, his four bedrooms, and his spacious yard. It was clear that except on rare occasions, the house was empty. Nobody slept in three of the four bedrooms. No children played in the yard. The utility of all that square footage lay almost completely in its symbolism. It reminded my host of the convivial home he grew up in. But at the end of the night, his friends drove a dozen-odd miles back to their apartments in Capitol Hill, leaving him alone with his tree.

Of course, today's scorned neighborhoods and designs could be tomorrow's status symbols if the culture was to send us a different set of messages about their worth. This is already happening. For years, television largely depicted American family and social life as suburban, but in the past two decades the hip protagonists of programs such as *Friends* and *Sex and the City* were shown in downtown apartments. Formerly low-status neighborhoods such as Manhattan's East Village have been invaded by the upwardly mobile, and condominium towers designed by starchitects are sprouting between the tenements. New generations are growing up with a different mental library of stories that shape their domestic tastes.

Errors from Above

Unfortunately, when choosing how to live or move, most of us are not as free as we think. Our options are strikingly limited, and they are defined by the planners, engineers, politicians, architects, marketers, and land speculators who imprint their own values on the urban landscape. The city is as much a product of the psychological tics, status urges, and systematic errors in judgment of these powerful strangers as it is one of our own flawed choices or happenstance. Just as each of us makes mistakes when choosing a home or ideal commute time, city shapers have proved themselves to be masters at miscalculating utility on our behalf. Collectively, they make the same predictable cognitive mistakes the rest of us make.

An especially common trap is the tendency to simplify multifaceted problems. The world is wildly complex, and humans have always relied on simplification, metaphor, and story to make sense of it. The pioneering anthropologist Claude Lévi-Strauss discovered this when he lived among preindustrial tribes in Brazil. The forest people organized their knowledge of the world into myths that shared a similar narrative structure: everything was reduced into a system of binary opposites. This structure runs through just about every great myth ever told. There is the idea and its denial, good and evil, friend or enemy. Think about your own life and the way you remember it. Stories tend to get simpler with every telling because they seem to make more sense that way. It is difficult for us to conceive of in-between states, complex arrangements, or overlapping patterns, even though our lives are full of them.

Cities are especially full of contradictions, especially when you consider the complexity inherent in places that mix living, working, shopping, recreation, and other functions. Le Corbusier himself admitted that with all the possibilities and considerations that planners face, "the human mind loses itself and becomes fatigued." Le Corbusier and his acolytes made a religion of extreme simplification. In their "sublime straight lines" and strict functional division, they made cities seem strikingly legible on paper. But cities refuse to behave like simple problems.

Take the most fully realized modernist city. Architect Oscar Niemeyer's* plan for a new capital city for Brazil on a wilderness tabula rasa in the 1950s was meant to embody the country's orderly, healthy, and egalitarian future. Early sketches of Brasilia resembled an airplane or a great bird with its wings outstretched. From above, the plan was exhilarating. Niemeyer segregated functions across the dual axes of his great bird's body. At its head, the Plaza of the Three Powers, a gargantuan square lined with blocks of government ministries and crowned with the national congress complex. Monumental avenues were paved along the bird's spine. Identical residential superblocks were stacked in orderly rows along its wings. The intention was to use simple geometry to free Brasilia of all the chaos of the typical Brazilian city: slums, crime, and traffic jams were banished by the architect's pen. Pedestrians were separated from cars. There was exactly 269 square feet of green space for every resident. The principles of equality ran right through the design: all residents would have similar-sized homes. Everything had its place. On paper, it was a triumph of straightforward and egalitarian central planning.

But when the first generation of residents arrived to live and work in Brasilia, the simple approach showed its weakness. People felt disoriented by the sameness of their residential complexes. They felt lost in their perfectly ordered environment and its vast, empty spaces. They missed their old, cramped market streets, places where disorder and complexity led to serendipitous encounters with sights, scents, and other people. Residents even invented a new word—*brasilite*, or Brasilia-itis—to describe the malaise of living "without the pleasures— the distractions, conversations, flirtations, and little rituals—of

*The original city sketches and master plan, by Lucio Costa, were commissioned and then elaborated by Niemeyer.

Modernist Perfection

Residents of Brasilia's modernist districts invented a new word to reflect their sense of disorientation and alienation in the perfectly ordered, spacious, and green city: brasilite, *or Brasilia-itis.* (© Bruno Daher)

outdoor life in other Brazilian cities." The simple, rational plan extinguished the intrinsic social benefits of messy public space and loaded the city with a psychological burden that was entirely new for its residents. (Eventually the city spilled beyond its plan, and now messy barrios spread like a tangled nest beyond the wings of the great bird.)

Focusing on Danger

The messianic certainty of the high modernists of the last century makes it easy to pick on them. But this tendency toward simplification of inherently complex systems also runs through the decisions of the people who plan the contemporary city, sometimes with disastrous results.

Consider the effort to design safer cities. This noble goal has been stymied by the essential ways in which people—including planners and engineers—assess danger.

The Nobel Prize–winning psychologist Daniel Kahneman argues

that when making decisions about risk, we create simple rules—or heuristics—derived from experience. This makes sense. Get hit by a car or see someone else get hit and you will be more careful the next time you cross the street. The problem is, we generally do not remember the world accurately; nor do we get immediate and compelling access to all our memories; nor do all memories motivate us with the same force.

Think of something that might one day maim or kill you.

Are you picturing a plane crash, a gangster with a knife, or a terrorist with a bomb strapped to his belly? If such shocking images come to mind, then your brain is functioning normally but not accurately. Popular culture is awash with spectacular images and stories of violence and death. These kinds of dangers naturally stick in our heads. We can visualize them and recall them easily. They also carry more emotional wallop—we don't calculate their dangers so much as we *feel* them. Vivid, emotionally charged memories come more easily to mind at moments of decision than mundane ones, and the more easily you can recall or picture a scenario, the more likely you are to think it will happen again. Thus, when making decisions, we tend to pay too much attention to spectacular but rare threats and too little to dangers that creep up on us over time.*

So it's no wonder that societies put tremendous effort into designing alternatives to the horrors of the Industrial Revolution. The dangers were salient. Lung-clogging smog, desperate crowding, dark tenements, poisoned water, and crime born of poverty: the images remain powerful today. But in escaping those horrors, we have built cities infused with new, invisible dangers.

"We've become the victims of our own success," Richard Jackson, professor and chairman of environmental health sciences at the University of California, Los Angeles, told *The New York Times* in 2012. "By living far from where we work, we reduced crowding and improved the quality of our air and water, which drove down rates of infectious disease." All of which are good. But the seemingly safe and

---

*This is one reason why people rate their chance of being murdered much higher than the likelihood that they will die of stomach cancer, even though the latter is four times as likely.

healthy dispersed suburb offers systems of living that can reasonably be considered lethal.

The biggest danger is, by its nature, the least exciting. It is the sickness that comes from doing nothing. Public health experts have even invented a new word—*obesogenic*, or fat-making—to describe low-density neighborhoods like Weston Ranch. This is one of the reasons that, aside from sedentary Saudi Arabians and some South Pacific Islanders, Americans are now the fattest people on the planet. Fully a third of Americans are obese. Nearly one in five American children is overweight. So are more than a quarter of Canadian and 30 percent of British children.* More than three-quarters of obese adults have either diabetes, high blood cholesterol levels, high blood pressure, or coronary artery disease. The Centers for Disease Control warn that lifestyle-related diabetes has reached epidemic proportions. At the same time, living in low-density sprawl puts residents at greater risk of arthritis, chronic lung disease, digestive problems, headaches, and urinary tract infections. Some of these effects come from the toxic air we breathe while we are driving cars or living amid their fumes. But, most critically, they result from living in communities that force people to drive. Just living in a sprawling city has the effect of four years of aging.

Suburbia was once seen as a refuge. Dispersed communities were supposedly protected by sheer distance—and, more recently, gates, guards, and security walls—from people who might rob, steal, or kill. But if the goal is to avoid being hurt or killed by strangers, then the edge neighborhood is a terrible choice. University of Virginia architecture professor William H. Lucy revealed this paradox when he examined the statistics on "death by strangers" in hundreds of U.S. counties. To get a really accurate picture of the danger that strangers pose, Lucy combined the usual figures on homicides by strangers with statistics on traffic fatalities. The conclusion: killer drivers are so common in sprawl that the carnage they create far exceeds the damage done by killers who use other weapons. In fact, someone who walks out her door on the edges of sprawl suburbia is much more likely to die at the hands of a stranger than someone moving

---

*Between 1960 and 2004 the percentage of Americans who were overweight rose from under half to two-thirds of the population.

through most American central cities or inner suburbs. The only difference is that most of suburbia's killers didn't mean it.

Partly because sprawl has forced Americans to drive farther and farther in the course of every day, per capita road death rates in the United States hover around forty thousand per year. That's a third more people than are killed by guns. It's more than ten times the number of people killed in the terrorist attacks of September 11, 2001. Here's an image that sticks: imagine a loaded Boeing 747 crashing every three days, killing everyone aboard. That's how many people die on U.S. highways every year. Globally, traffic injuries are the greatest killer of ten- to twenty-four-year-olds.* A rational actor would be terrified of suburban roads. A rational policy maker would wage war, not on other nations, but on traffic deaths.

The Emotional Engineer

Unfortunately, some of the most favored design responses to road danger have backfired. For decades, road engineers followed standards that strictly separate pedestrians from cars, remove distractions, and widen traffic lanes. Engineering theory long held as gospel the notion that wide, clear roads enhanced safety. The assumption was that cars wouldn't crash so frequently if the things they tended to hit were farther away. In other words, they focused on an expensive but salient and simple solution.

Now the unintended consequences of pursuing seemingly obvious measures have started to pile up. The removal of pedestrians and other distractions from urban roads, a process begun by Motordom during the bloody 1920s, has actually made roads more dangerous. The problem was that the simple fix ignored the complex system of road psychology. By corralling pedestrians with fences, barriers, and dispersed crosswalks, engineers send drivers a message that it is safe

---

*Car accidents are the leading cause of death for people under thirty-five years old. Around the world, more people are killed by cars than by wars—more than four hundred thousand every year. The World Health Organization estimates that beyond the bloodshed, the cost of auto crashes in injuries, medical care, and property damage exceeds $518 billion worldwide.

to put the pedal to the metal. Road studies have found that most of us drive not according to posted speed limits, but according to how safe the road feels. We drive as fast as road designs tell us to drive. The result: drivers kill four times as many pedestrians on spacious suburban residential streets than on the narrow streets of traditional neighborhoods, because those spacious roads make driving faster feel safer. And it is not collisions that kill people, but *collisions at high speed*. A pedestrian hit by a car going 35 miles per hour is ten times as likely to die than if he was hit by a car going 25 miles per hour. Throw in some parked cars or add some trees on the median—just the stuff that was once considered dangerous—and we slow down to less lethal velocities.* Throw in a whole bunch of distractions, including lots of pedestrians, and drivers become so attentive that traffic fatalities plummet (a story I'll return to in Chapter 9).

Another big mistake came with well-meaning efforts to deal with salient dangers such as house fires. Before World War II, the typical residential street in the United States and Canada was only twenty-eight feet wide. If cars were parked on either side, two drivers approaching each other in the middle could barely pass. This was deemed unacceptable, particularly for emergency service vehicle access. If regular cars were in danger of scraping each other on these narrow streets, imagine the spectacular tragedy that might occur if a fire truck failed to get to a burning house. Planners did just that, imagining the smoke, the flames, the children trapped upstairs—just the kind of risk images that hold attention and shape decisions. Consequently, road standards have gotten wider and wider since the 1950s, and pedestrian deaths have grown apace.

Now that many residential neighborhood roads have reached the forty-foot mark, researchers have discovered that this attempt to mitigate spectacular risks has precipitated its own storm of tragedies. Since those newer, wider residential streets encourage faster driving,

---

*For years, engineers recommended clearing such distractions as bushes and trees from road edges. The danger seemed obvious. But Eric Dumbaugh, an assistant professor of transportation at Texas A&M University, found that lines of trees along roads were actually associated with *fewer* crashes because the complexity they added caused people to slow down. Widening shoulders actually increased mid-block crashes.

Designed for Speed
Suburban road designs such as the one shown here lead to more accidents, since drivers tend to go as fast as designs permit. (*Above*: John Michlig; *inset*: Mark Kent)

they are associated with four times as many pedestrian deaths as narrower, older streets.

(In a cruel irony for suburbanites, these fire-truck-friendly roads have not made a whit of difference when it comes to actually putting out fires. Just as many people die in fires in new, wide-street suburbs as were dying in old, narrow-street neighborhoods. Part of the problem is that sprawl's wide streets and big lots take up so much space that cities can't afford to build fire stations close by, so it takes fire trucks longer to reach each blaze.)

The Confusing Thing About Tomorrow Is That It Will Be Different from Today

The cognitive error that may have had more influence than any other on the shape of our cities is known as presentism: we let what we see and feel today bias our views of the past and future. This commonly expresses itself as a tendency to assume that the ways we think and act will not change as time passes.

Imagine being stuck in commuter traffic on one of the three interstate highways that cut through Atlanta, Georgia—one of the world's most dispersed urban regions—back in the 1960s. It might seem perfectly obvious to the commuter you that the pragmatic way to ease the journey would be for the city or state to build more roads. For decades, engineers and politicians have shared this view. Atlanta was encircled by a new beltway—known as the Perimeter—in 1969, and highway expansion programs continued for more than thirty years.

The problem was that new asphalt changed the collective mind of the city. It caused thousands of people to regard the road differently and behave differently. Nondrivers saw open lanes and started driving. Existing drivers altered their routes. Other drivers were inspired to move their homes or work farther away. Meanwhile, property developers took advantage of newly proximate land, offering everyone what seemed like a chance to live or work in the landscape of dispersal.

Given its history of inequity and racial tension, antiurban biases run deep in Atlanta. Historian Kevin Kruse has linked the city's rapid suburbanization to the civil rights movement: when white segregationists lost their battle in cities, they used suburban retreat as a subtle but effective means of insulating themselves from black people. But the impact of the highway explosion was far more dramatic than its origins—it's a pattern that now shapes every resident's experience. The more highway Georgians built, the more thinly people of every color spread their lives across the Georgia hills. Then, like dry streambeds in a storm, those new highway lanes filled up. The region came to exhibit a classic case of what transportation analysts call induced traffic, a phenomenon in which new highway lanes invariably clog up with hundreds of thousands of cars driven by new drivers on their way to new neighborhoods fed by new road capacity, a tendency that creates entirely new traffic jams faster than the time it takes to finish paying off a new car.* The average time it takes for new urban highway capacity to fill up with new demand? Five to six years.

---

*These highways helped scatter 90 percent of Atlanta's growing population out of the urban core.

Now, although it has bloated to twelve lanes in many sections, Atlanta's Perimeter still grinds to a standstill during peak hours.* The driver who once prayed for congestion-easing highway lanes and got them is still stuck in traffic. Through the windshield view of present-ism, he may have forgotten the futility of his old wish for more road space, and now he might well demand that engineers build a few more lanes to solve the problem.

Thinking About Crisis

The errors in individual and collective judgment described above are frustrating and sobering, but they are also trivial—at least when compared with the dangers posed by cognitive blocks that prevent us from recognizing the connection between the way we live in cities and the massive risks now facing our world and our species.

If you don't give a damn about the environment or your descen-dants, then feel free to skip to the next chapter. Just remember that the urban innovations I will later propose in the name of happiness may also save the world.

Here are some things we know:

The earth's atmosphere is warming at an unprecedented pace, mainly as a result of human activity causing greenhouse gas emis-sions. On this point there is agreement from every peer-reviewed journal on the subject, and from the national scientific academies of Canada, China, Brazil, India, Russia, Germany, France, Italy, Japan, Australia, Mexico, the United Kingdom, the United States, and doz-ens of other countries,[†] as well as the United Nations Intergovern-

---

*The travel time in Atlanta grew faster in the 1990s than in any other American city. The average person's time spent in Atlanta traffic rose from six hours a year to thirty-four hours between 1990 and 2000 alone.

[†]A survey of just a few of the national scientific institutions that support the IPCC's findings on climate change: Academia Brasileira de Ciências, the Royal Society of Canada, the Chinese Academy of Sciences, Académie des Sciences, Deutsche Aka-demie der Naturforscher Leopoldina, the Indian National Science Academy, Accademia dei Lincei, the Science Council of Japan, the Russian Academy of Sci-ences, the Royal Society of the United Kingdom, and the National Academy of

mental Panel on Climate Change (IPCC), which synthesizes the work of the biggest group of scientists ever to focus on a single issue. Which is to say that to the very best of human knowledge, we are blowing so much methane, ozone, nitrous oxide, and carbon dioxide into the air that we are throwing the delicate system governing climate and weather out of whack. This we know: climate change is likely to cause more heat waves, droughts, intense storms, cyclones, and tornadoes; the inundation of lowland cities; the spread of infectious diseases; crop failures; and famine that may collectively kill hundreds of millions of people and impoverish many more, not to mention the disappearance of 15 to 37 percent of species by 2050. We know the change has already begun. We know that the longer it takes us to change our ways, the more the earth's surface will warm and the more extreme the effects of climate change will be. We know all these things with enough certainty to keep scientists and global geopolitical strategists awake at night. Certainly the knowledge has alarmed the insurance industry, whose payouts from weather-related natural disasters quadrupled between 1980 and 2009.

At the same time, we know with great certainty that we are consuming plants, animals, soil, minerals, water, and energy at a faster rate than the planet can replenish them. We are using so much of the earth's raw material that we are dooming future generations to poverty and hardship. It would take nine planets to supply all we needed if everyone ate, built, traveled, and threw stuff away as Americans do. It's like maxing out all our credit cards without ever depositing more money in the bank.

This is not a theoretical problem, especially considering that the resource we are running out of most quickly happens to be the one cities currently depend on the most: oil. The majority of forecasters, including those who advise energy companies and military strategists in Western nations, agree that the days of cheap oil are over. Most agree that we will hit peak production of conventional oil sometime

Sciences (from "Joint science academies' statement: Global response to climate change," Washington, DC: The National Academies, 2005), as well as the American Meteorological Society, the American Geophysical Union, the American Association for the Advancement of Science, and the governments of all G8 nations.

in the next twenty years. Oil prices will go through the roof well before then, as Western nations compete with such emerging economies as Brazil, China, and India for fuel. Chinese automakers expect their compatriots to be buying forty million cars a year by 2020—more than three times the American market. The U.S. Joint Forces Command predicts massive energy shortfalls.

Another thing we know: the twin crises of climate change and resource scarcity are going to hit cities especially hard. Sprawling cities experience nearly twice as many extreme heat waves as compact centers, in part because of the vast extent of their paved surfaces. All that hot air causes more smog, which exacerbates problems such as asthma. More heat waves, like the ones that killed more than seven hundred people in Chicago in 1995 or seventy thousand people across Europe in 2003, are on their way. Urbanites, especially the old and the young, are going to suffer from more heat stress and respiratory illness.

We know that some cities will have to absorb millions of climate refugees. Services will become increasingly expensive. Our public and private transportation systems are almost entirely dependent on fossil fuels. Cities won't be able to afford to fund buses to ultra-low-density neighborhoods. These problems will not be confined to slum cities in Africa. People living in sprawl as it is currently configured in North America will be in for a harrowing ride. Distance will no longer be an abstraction. Everyday destinations will be even more expensive and time-consuming to reach, and if they are too dependent on long-distance customers, they may simply disappear.

All these things we know and sometimes acknowledge, yet we build and live in urban systems that actually heighten the threats. With about half the world's population, cities are responsible for three-quarters of energy consumption and 80 percent of greenhouse gas emissions, and the dispersed city is the most wasteful of them all. Detached suburban homes gobble up local farmland and are harder to heat and cool than apartments and town houses. By pushing apart buildings and land uses, sprawl makes it almost impossible to benefit from efficient local energy or transit systems. Even the suburban lawn is a threat: gasoline-powered lawn mowers emit eleven times as much air pollution as new cars. On average, suburbanites pump out about twice the greenhouse gas emissions of people living in dense city centers.

Any clear-eyed analysis confirms that this city and the way we inhabit it pose a direct threat to the well-being of the planet and, arguably, the future of our species. And any rational assessment of well-being should account for risks faced by our children and their descendants. The logical response to these converging crises would be to alter our individual and collective behavior in order to stave off disaster. It demands using less energy and raw materials. It means moving more efficiently and moving shorter distances. It means living closer together and sharing more spaces, walls, and vehicles. It means collecting experiences rather than objects.

Yet in the face of clear threats, most national governments, most cities, and most people have failed to take meaningful action to change their ways. National governments have been unable to agree on a plan that will reduce greenhouse gas emissions enough to avoid a long, grinding climate disaster. Cities have continued to sprawl. People like you and me may recycle our waste and purchase more efficient cars, but few of us have taken anything close to the footprint-reducing action required by the scale of the crisis. We are held back in part by the autopoieisis of urban systems that have their own momentum and staying power. But we are also held back by our own imperfect minds.

It would be hard to design a crisis better suited to provoke inaction than climate change, say psychologists. Many people are simply ignorant of the problem. For some, the science simply conflicts too starkly with our worldview to accept: if you believe that only God or Mother Nature can change the climate, then no amount of evidence is going to convince you otherwise.* But for those who are aware of the science, the dangers are simply not salient enough

---

*The cognitive linguist George Lakoff has described how our understanding of the world assumes a physical form in our brains in the form of neural circuitry he calls frames. These frames can be configured by experiences, long-held moral views, and even advertising, if we hear a message often enough. They define what *feels* true for us, and we use them to understand any new information that comes our way. "If the facts don't fit the frames, the frames stay and the facts are ignored," writes Lakoff. So when someone utters the phrase "climate change," if the information contradicts

to trigger action. They feel so remote, so far in the future, that we discount them. Like a chalkboard covered with mathematical equations, climate science does not scream at us in the night or sting like a bee or actually burn many of us, at least not yet. And while visceral natural disasters such as hurricanes Katrina or Sandy are increasingly linked to the greenhouse effect, the causal chain is, for most of us, as hard to distinguish as water vapor in the sky. Meanwhile, there has been a concerted effort by oil companies, lobbyists, and free-market think tanks to convince us that (a) the crisis is not real, and (b) action to tackle it will destroy our prosperity and lead to years of hardship and misery.

Not even a world-class guilt trip will move us. "People don't respond to campaigns based on guilt and fear. They have a hard time linking their actions to costs far in the future. And they resent governments that fine or punish their behavior, even when they know it is unsustainable," explained Alex Boston, who advises cities on climate and energy policy for the engineering firm Golder.

The result: a perfect calm of inaction. How can we change course when faced with such psychological barriers to action?

The solution lies in appealing to pure self-interest.

The sustainable city has got to promise more happiness than the status quo. It has got to be healthier, higher in status, more fun, and more resilient than the dispersed city. It has got to lure us closer together rather than pushing us apart. It has got to reward people for making efficient choices when they move around. It has got to be a city of hedonic satisfaction, of distilled joys that do not cost the world. The city shapes our decisions. It always has. So, just as the dispersed city limits our choices and pushes us to stretch our lives, the world-saving city must embody lessons from behavioral economics to ensure that the good choice and the happy choice can be the same.

This city is already being born—or rather, pieces of it exist in fragments and threads in cities around the world. It is appearing in downtowns where residents are sick of accepting discomforts offloaded from those who choose long-distance living. It finds life

---

the listener's long-held views, his brain is more likely to access skeptical thoughts and emotions than those that spur action.

in acts of neighborhood rebellion. Sometimes it's an accident. Occasionally it comes in broad strokes made by powerful people in moments of civic audacity. It rarely emerges from earnest concerns about climate change or biodiversity or distant tragedy. Yet that nascent city proves that in the pursuit of happiness, we might build the city that will save the world. That is the story I will tell in the rest of this book.

6. How to Be Closer

This is the true nature of home—it is the place of peace:
the shelter, not only from all injury, but from all terror,
doubt and division . . .

—John Ruskin, *Sesame and Lilies*

The challenge seems at first straightforward: If we are to escape the effects of dispersal, then dense places have got to meet our psychological needs better than sprawl. They have to be places that delight, nurture, and nourish us in return for choosing them. But this is not a simple brief, because we are not simple creatures. We are torn between competing needs. None are more contradictory than the push-pull between proximity and isolation. In some ways our needs are at war with each other.

We need the nourishing, helping warmth of other people, but we also need the healing touch of nature. We need to connect, but we also need to retreat. We benefit from the conveniences of proximity, but these conveniences can come with the price of overstimulation and crowding. We will not solve the conundrum of sustainable city living unless we understand these contradictory forces and resolve the tension between them. How much space, privacy, and distance from other people do we need? How much nature do we need? Are there designs that combine the benefits of dispersal with the dividends of proximity?

The evidence suggests that to get closer to one another, we need a little more distance from one another, and a little more nature—but not too much, and not the sort of nature we might think we need.

To explain, I will first talk about nature.

Then I will talk about the problem of neighbors.

Closer, Part I: The Nature Dividend

In 2011, I was invited by the Solomon R. Guggenheim Museum to join a team examining comfort in New York City. The museum commissioned Atelier Bow-Wow, a Japanese architectural firm, to design a temporary shelter in an empty lot in the East Village, then invited a team of collaborators from around the world to use it as a base for our experiments. The museum's curators hoped that the BMW Guggenheim Lab would be an engine for creating new solutions for city life. They had money to spend and interns to assist. I planned on using their resources to collect data on the effect that city spaces had on people's emotions and behavior. It was a fantastic opportunity: there are few better places to explore extreme urbanity than Manhattan.

The lab's neighborhood, which straddled the boundary between the East Village and the Lower East Side, is a mashup of tenement-style walk-ups and newer mid-rise condo towers bisected by furious traffic arteries and crowded, cracked sidewalks. For a newcomer it is an exhilarating place, a distillation of all of New York City's grit, noise, haste, surprise, and possibility. On my first walk there from my apartment on East Thirteenth Street—a fifteen-minute stroll—I passed every shop I could imagine needing that month. A hardware store, a bank, grocery stores large and small, tattoo shops, manicurists, dry cleaners, artisanal ice creameries, bars, and restaurants by the dozen. Every few blocks there were stairs leading down to the subway. This was a different universe from the empty collector boulevards I had driven on in San Joaquin County. You could live your life here, working, shopping, eating, socializing, and falling in love, all on foot. It was dense, convenient, connected, and endlessly stimulating.

I found the landscape thrilling at first. But I wanted to break down its elements, to understand how different sidewalks and buildings and open spaces in the dense city affected people. So I called in Colin Ellard, a psychologist at the University of Waterloo who had done groundbreaking work on the neuroscience of moving through cities. Colin equipped dozens of volunteers with devices to measure their emotional state as they moved through the neighborhood. He hacked a set of BlackBerry phones so that they would survey people for their levels of affect (happiness in the moment) and arousal (or excitement). We also strapped some volunteers with wrist cuffs that recorded the relative electrical conductance of their skin as they moved. Since skin conductance is directly related to perspiration, it provides an excellent objective measure of emotional arousal.

Why these measures? The affect test was an obvious choice: most people can agree that happiness is preferable to misery. The arousal test added nuance to the data: It can be good or bad to feel excited, depending on the situation. It feels great to be both calm and happy or excited and happy. But sustained arousal can be hard on your immune system, and a combination of high arousal and low affect—in other words, feeling both excited and miserable—is obviously worst of all. It's the state most people call being stressed out.

Every few days, groups of fresh volunteers walked the neighborhood with our tour guides, offering up their psychophysiological data in return. We found that as the urban terrain varied, so did people's emotions. People reported the biggest spike in happiness, and an easing of arousal, just moments after entering the gated M'Finda Kalunga seniors' garden in Sara Roosevelt Park. That was even before the gardeners introduced them to the resident chicken.

This did not surprise us. The garden was almost junglelike in its variety of leafy plants, shrubs, and mature trees, and the last few decades have produced powerful evidence that simply being in, touching, or viewing nature makes people feel good. Hospital patients with views of nature need less pain medication and get better faster than those with views of, say, brick walls. Even simulating a view of nature can help. Heart surgery patients exposed to pictures of trees, water, and forests are less anxious and report less severe pain than those who have to gaze at abstract art all day. Dental patients get less stressed out on days when nature murals are hung on the waiting-room wall. Students do better on tests when nature is within visual range. The natural view is now being prescribed for some of the most stressful built environments. When architects installed a mural depicting a meadowy scene in the booking area of the Sonoma County Jail in Santa Rosa, California, the guards had an easier time remembering things.

All this reinforces the concept that Edward O. Wilson dubbed biophilia, which holds that humans are hardwired to find particular scenes of nature calming and restorative. One theory to explain nature's benefit considers the ways in which we notice the world around us. This theory, developed by biologists Stephen and Rachel Kaplan, posits that we pay attention in two completely different ways: voluntarily and involuntarily. Voluntary attention, the kind we engage when we are consciously solving problems or negotiating city streets, requires plenty of focus and energy, and can tire us out. Indeed, after spending time on a crowded city street, most of us find it harder to focus and harder to hold things in memory. The problem is that much of the built world is so crammed with stimuli, it forces us to constantly decide what to pay attention to—the oncoming bus, the opening door, the flashing stoplight—and what to ignore—say, a billboard advertising liposuction. Conversely, involuntary attention, the kind we give to nature, is effortless, like a daydream or a song washing through your brain. You might not even realize you are paying attention and yet you may be restored and transformed by the act.

The Social Life of Trees

I am not exaggerating when I use that word *transformed*.

In the mid-1990s environmental psychologists Frances Ming Kuo and William Sullivan took a stroll around the Ida B. Wells project, a low-rise social housing complex in Chicago. They were struck by what seemed to be a vivid contrast between the complex's many courtyards. Some were bare tundras of concrete. Others had been planted with grass and trees. The barren courtyards were always empty of people, but the green courtyards, even though they were fairly unkempt and ragged, always seemed to be buzzing with activity, from women sitting around shelling peas to children playing in the corners. "They seemed to be alive, like living rooms," Kuo recalled. "We thought, *geez*, this might be kind of important."

Kuo and Sullivan enlisted residents of nearby projects to watch and record the comings and goings of people at Ida B. Wells. Sure enough, no matter the time of day, those green courtyards hosted some kind of social life, while the barren courtyards were consistently dead. But Kuo also found a stark psychological difference between tenants with green views and those who could see only concrete. "People with the bare views told us they were psychologically fatigued, and more likely to be rude, to fly off the handle, more likely to slap someone in anger. They just had a harder time coping," Kuo said. They even yelled at their children more.

When the researchers began examining police records, they found a mountain of hard data that linked lack of greenness of courtyards to local crime rates. Buildings that looked out on trees and grass experienced about half the violent crime level of buildings that looked out on barren courtyards. The less green the environment, the higher the rate of assault, battery, robbery, and murder. This is especially remarkable given the fact that criminologists have pointed out that bushes and trees provide convenient cover for illicit activity.

Nature deprivation, concluded Kuo, was not merely unhealthy, it was dangerous, partly because it left people feeling more raw and aggressive, and partly because most residents simply abandoned barren spaces, removing the watchful eyes that help keep them safe.

Kuo's discoveries helped establish a clear link between exposure to nature, well-being, and behavior—and a powerful social upshot. People who lived next to green spaces knew more of their neighbors. They reported that their neighbors were more supportive and friendly. They had more people over for get-togethers. They had stronger feelings of belonging.

This was partly a result of the social time people spent in their green courtyards. But there may have been a deeper alchemy at work,

Nice and Green

Access to green space transformed the emotional and social lives of residents of social housing in Chicago. People who lived around the leafier courtyard on the left were happier, friendlier, and less prone to violence than those who lived around the barren courtyard on the right, even though both areas were poorly maintained. (W. C. Sullivan)

one identified more recently by psychologists at the University of Rochester when they had volunteers sit through slide shows depicting scenes of varying biophilic content. After their virtual immersion, volunteers who had viewed nature scenes had strongly different attitudes toward other people than people who viewed images of urban skylines. The nature viewers were much more likely to say they valued deep relationships with other people than the city viewers, who came out more focused on extrinsic goals, such as getting rich. The real test came when the volunteers were handed $5 and invited to either share it with other students or keep it. Amazingly, the more nature students had been exposed to, the more generous they were. These results are now being mirrored outside the laboratory. A study of Los Angeles revealed that people who live in areas with more parks are more helpful and trusting than people who don't, regardless of their income or race. Nature is not merely good for us. It brings out the good *in* us.

The Savanna Trap

At first these findings do not seem to bode well at all for the dense city, especially considering the tricky navigation provided by our own landscape preferences.

In 1993 the Russian artists Vitaly Komar and Alexander Melamid hired a professional polling firm to determine what people living in various countries in Africa, Asia, Europe, and the Americas liked to look at. Using the poll results as a reference, they laid brushes to canvas to create images that were statistically most likely to please the populace of each country. The intent was obviously ironic (the painting *America's Most Wanted* features a perambulating George Washington), but the images revealed a pattern. They all depict similar scenes: open fields with a few trees and shrubs in the near distance, perhaps some wildlife, and, beyond that, bodies of still, clear water. The statistically average Kenyan, Portuguese, Chinese, and American had strikingly common tastes.

The artists thus demonstrated what hundreds of studies into human landscape preference over the last few decades have shown. Most people really like savanna-like views, typically characterized by moderate to high openness; low, grassy ground vegetation; and trees that are either scattered or gathered in small groups. Our preferences are collectively precise: when given a choice, people say they would rather look at trees with short trunks, layered branching systems, and broad canopies.

These happen, of course, to be the sorts of trees and landscapes that nurtured our hunter-gatherer ancestors for thousands of years, including during the era that saw the human brain expand faster than any brain had in the course of animal history. Evolutionary theorists argue that we are genetically inclined to like such landscapes because liking them helped our Paleolithic ancestors survive. Jay Appleton, the English geographer, argued that most of us still unconsciously evaluate terrain for threats and opportunities, leading us to feel better or worse according to the resource quality of our location. We like open views, but we also like to feel safe—values that Appleton called "prospect" and "refuge."

Modern students of landscape architecture have all been inculcated with prospect-refuge theory. Indeed, since the dawn of the profession, its practitioners have been trying to replicate that ideal, sometimes without even knowing it. Humphry Repton, a landscape architect who designed the gardens of dozens of England's famous estates in the eighteenth century, perfected the technique. Repton's manipulations appear in the drawings he made for his landed clientele, in which he would move trees from forest edges into open space, add herds of grazing animals, and create watering hole–like lakes to mimic savanna-like vistas. His contemporaries even built ditches, or *haw-haws*, to keep animals in without interrupting the naturalistic scenes with fencing.

These views have been reproduced complete with shade trees, broad meadows, and lakes in the heart of some megacities, from London's Hyde Park to Mexico City's Bosque de Chapultepec to Frederick Law Olmsted's New York masterpieces, Central and Prospect parks.

In many ways, our landscape preferences support the lingering nineteenth-century idea that the city itself is a toxic and unnatural environment, and that dispersal is the natural response to biological truths. Indeed, the Repo Home Tour through the neighborhoods at the urban edge in San Joaquin County felt like a safari through a vast biophilic compromise. From the raised deck of Interstate 5, you could catch glimpses of the broad parks, golf courses, or artificial lakes that

Evolution of the Ideal Landscape

Psychologists believe that savanna-like views have an inherently calming effect on us, perhaps because they depict landscapes similar to those in which the human brain developed. When architects installed this mural in the booking area of a California jail, the guards experienced lower heart rates and had an easier time remembering things. (istockphoto.com)

The eighteenth-century landscape architect Humphry Repton rendered the ideal landscapes he would then create on British estates. (Repton, Humphry, *Observations on the Theory and Practice of Landscape Gardening,* London: printed by T. Bensley for J. Taylor, 1803)

Modern suburban real estate developers create an atomized savanna for everyone. (Todd Bennett / © 2013 Journal Communications Inc.)

define the suburban savanna. Even the highway berms were treated with naturalistic lawns and shrubbery. The view from every front door of every foreclosed home featured an edited version of the Paleolithic landscape: a broad front lawn, low shrubs gathered along building edges, and at least one low-trunked shade tree.

If the lawn view was universally good for us, the aesthetic dividends of dispersal from central cities would be beyond dispute. But it's not certain that the pseudo-savanna is actually the best view for the human brain.

It turns out that the happiness paradox—that gulf between what we choose and what is good for us—even extends to landscapes.

"I see a big distinction between landscapes that are preferred and those that are beneficial," biologist Richard Fuller explained to me. Fuller and his colleagues surveyed users of parks around Sheffield, England. Visitors said they felt much more healthy, connected, and "grounded" after spending time in parks with many different kinds of trees and birds than in parks that distilled nature down to lawns and a few trees. The "messier" and more diverse the landscape, the better.

This inquiry into the aesthetic value of biological complexity has just begun, but such work suggests that sterile lawns and token trees might be hollow calories for the nature-craving brain. They are better than nothing, but they are not good enough. It would certainly make sense for diverse, complex ecosystems and views to pack a bigger psychological punch than, say, a manicured patch of grass, because they are more likely to draw us into the levels of involuntary attention that are so soothing.

How do we achieve biological complexity in cities? Well, we can either let our green spaces go truly wild or plant and nurture complexity in them. This is hard work. In my travels I have found that the farther I drive into exurbia, the fewer truly complex and rich front yard gardens I see. People burdened with long commutes and huge yards simply have less time for gardening. On the other hand, the high modernists failed the biophilic complexity test at high densities, too. The huge lawns that serve as "green space" between the social housing tower blocks of the last century are deserts compared with what they could be.

So where is the balance between the isolation of the suburban savanna and the unnerving barrens of hyperdensity?

"People read my work and conclude that sprawl is the way to go. They think, lawns, low density, houses far apart," said Kuo. "But that is not at all the case! When you look at the body of research on effects of nature, it can actually work at every scale." What is crucial for healthy living, she insists, is not quantity, but regular exposure, daily doses of nature. So the trick is in finding ways to infuse nature, and nature complexity, into denser places. One experiment worth looking at is my own hometown.

View-Based Urbanism

Vancouver, Canada, has spent the past thirty years drawing people into density in a way that radically reversed a half century of suburban retreat. The experiment began in the early 1970s when citizens rejected a plan to wrap downtown in ribbons of freeway. That made Vancouver the only major city in North America without a single highway running through its core. Since then, the city has steadfastly refused to create any more road space for cars.* On top of that, Vancouver is hemmed in by ocean, steep mountains, and an agricultural land reserve that restricts suburban growth. These conditions, together with a steady flow of immigration, fueled a downtown building boom that gained momentum even during the decades when other North American cities were hollowing out.

Vancouver's urban core, a 20-block-long peninsula bound on two sides by the sea and capped by the magnificent rain forest of Stanley Park, has been rapidly transformed. More than one hundred and fifty residential towers have shot up here since the late 1980s, joining a hundred-odd that sprouted in the 1960s and 1970s. The population nearly doubled between 1991 and 2005. As Americans raced toward suburban horizons, Vancouverites were rushing back downtown, waiting overnight in presale lineups, paying millions of dollars for tower condominiums even before their foundations were poured.

Here is the remarkable paradox: the more crowded Vancouver gets,

---

*In fact, Vancouver's engineers are actively slowing cars down. They install dozens of new pedestrian signals, crosswalks, and traffic lights every year.

the more people want to live there and the higher the city has risen on international surveys ranking the world's best places to live. It now usually sits at or near the top of quality-of-life lists published by Mercer, *Forbes* magazine, and the Economist Intelligence Unit. Prices have doubled on many condominium units in the past fifteen years, and they remained buoyant right through the global economic crisis. To top it off, Vancouver has the lowest per capita carbon footprint of any major city on the continent—a dividend achieved in part by people living closer together, reducing the energy used in transportation and home heating.*

Part of what made Vancouver's vertical experiment both unique and desirable was the way it accommodated residents' biophilic needs. The city's new downtown was shaped to a large extent by the local obsession with views. Despite its dark winters, almost nobody in the city wants to face south, where the sun occasionally appears through the rain clouds. Vancouverites instinctively turn their gaze north and west: to mountains, rain forest, and ocean—in other words, to nature's rugged complexity. Any construction that threatens to block views to the North Shore mountains is met with outrage. City planners have responded with bylaws that shape the skyline, creating a series of "view corridors" through the downtown that allow for unimpeded mountain views from various vantage points to the south. Planners have actually forced some builders to alter the orientation of their towers to protect those sight lines.

This tension between the condo dweller's wish for a panoramic nature view from her window and the public's right to a glimpse of the mountains has helped establish a standard local architecture, just

*Another paradox of density: even though it now takes longer than it ever has to drive across town, Vancouver residents are enjoying easier commutes. Average round-trip commute times in other Canadian cities grew by up to fourteen minutes between 1992 and 2005, but the Vancouver average stayed the same. The city wasn't defying the laws of physics: the numbers were yanked down by all the people who migrated closer to work in the vertical city. Two-thirds of all trips in Vancouver's downtown are now made on foot, by bike, or via public transit. The inhabitants started selling their cars, reversing a continental trend long before the great recession. In 2005, the average family in Vancouver owned 1.25 cars, compared with 1.7 in suburban Surrey. (Even after the economic meltdown, the average American family owned 1.9 vehicles.)

as concerns about building massing and shade determined the form of generations of Manhattan's skyscrapers. New York's 1916 Zoning Resolution forced developers to reduce the mass of their buildings as they got higher, resulting in the stepped form of the iconic Manhattan tower and preserving at least some natural light down on the street. Vancouver's vertical design adaptation borrowed not from New York, but from Hong Kong, the source of so many of its new residents in the 1980s. In land-scarce Hong Kong, builders in that era were accommodating an exploding population by a method you might call extreme stacking. Several levels of shops and services would typically be combined in bulky podium blocks, and then five, six, or

Hong Kongism/Vancouverism

The super-dense, mixed-use podium-and-tower model common in land-scarce Hong Kong (left) was adapted for Vancouver tastes by scaling down street-side podiums and spacing out residential towers (right). Where it succeeds, the Vancouverism model offers both vibrant street life and views for everyone. (*Left*: Charles Bowman; *right*: Charles Montgomery)

more residential towers would stand on top. In some of these complexes, you may be thirty floors up but still have your view of the surrounding hills completely blocked. The model needed adjustment in view-conscious Vancouver. City planners pushed the podiums down to three or four stories. They squeezed the footprint for the towers above and spaced them a minimum of 80 feet apart, so what eventually grew into the skyline were tall, thin shards of glass with plenty of air between them. The result is a place where almost every tower dweller enjoys a visual connection with nature while everyone down on the street gets at least a glimpse. The podiums are lined with town houses or commercial spaces, so that the streets remain lively, safe, and packed with the shops and services that make life as convenient as it is in New York.

The form is so popular—and so profitable for developers—it has spawned a noun: *Vancouverism*. Its shapes have been copied from San Diego and Dallas to Dubai, but the city's followers never quite seem to capture Vancouver's magic. This may be because they lack the city's cinematic natural backdrop. It may also be because few cities push the benefits of density back to the public realm as aggressively as Vancouver does.

Unlike their counterparts in many other cities, Vancouver's municipal planners enjoy broad discretionary power when considering new development. They use that power to squeeze massive community benefits from developers in exchange for the right to build higher. Want to stack a few more stories of condos on your tower? Sure, but only if you repay the city with a public park, a plaza, a day-care center, or land for affordable social housing. In this way, Vancouver manages to claw back as much as 80 percent of the new property value created by upzoning. There is no density without a lifestyle dividend for the community. The result is that as the city gets denser, its residents enjoy more public green space. In Vancouver's downtown neighborhoods you are never more than a few minutes' walk to a park or the spectacular seawall that wraps the entire peninsula.

Small Doses

There is no denying the benefits of an expansive nature view or a big green space. But merely adding up a city's sum total of park space tells us little about each resident's nature diet. I surveyed dozens of New Yorkers at the BMW Guggenheim Lab in Lower Manhattan and found that none of them had been to Central Park during the previous week. They may have been glad the park was there, but they did not benefit from it, because they did not actually see or touch it. This is not to condemn the spectacular park or blame Manhattanites for not trying harder to get to the Sheep Meadow. But it does suggest a problem of scale and access. One big park won't do.

"We can't just build Central Park and say, 'Well, we're done,' " Kuo insisted. "Nature has to be part of your life. It has to be part of your daily habitat and routine." In order for New Yorkers to soak up the benefits of nature, it has to be integrated right into the urban fabric.

Our informal experiments at the lab offered some instructive good news for people who can't live on the edge of grand urban parks: even tiny splashes of nature created a psychological ripple effect.

The unhappiest stop on our emotional tour was the bare brick facade of a social housing project. Just a dozen-odd steps away was a restaurant whose facade was constructed of the same cheap bricks as the social housing. The only difference was that someone had painted the restaurant wall an earthy brown and installed two planters whose rambunctious vines grew high overhead. Our volunteers reported feeling nearly a point higher on a four-point happiness scale here than outside the barren facade down the street—which is to say, they experienced a huge spike in good feelings. Although it would be hard to rule out other factors, from the tone of conversations overheard at each location, to the aroma of pizza that occasionally escaped through the restaurant's doors, feedback from our participants suggested that the green intervention made a big difference.

We were even more surprised by what happened to the people we led out onto the median of Allen Street, a loud and congested arterial road nearby. The median was buffered by a low fence and a bike lane on either side, but it was otherwise stranded in a sea of cars. Taxis honked. Engines roared. Several homeless men had taken refuge there, presumably because nobody else had claimed it. That island sat amid much of the stimulus that drives many people nuts, yet our volunteers recorded feeling both very aroused and very happy there.

Curious about this, I wandered through that space at the end of a particularly hectic day. The location afforded a panoramic view north across the intersection with Houston Street, past a jumble of walls and facades, up First Avenue toward Midtown. It was a great place to observe the city—which may be why out-of-towners reported being much happier than New Yorkers out there on the median. But as I let the site wash over me, its nature dividend was obvious. The entire promenade was lined with mature maples. Even when you were not paying conscious attention to them, their leaves rustled and cast dancing shadows across the path. I sat there, not so much watching those trees as feeling them, and I was calmed and grateful.

Green Interventions

The explosion of research into the benefits of nature suggests that green space in cities shouldn't be considered an optional luxury. As Kuo insists, it is a crucial part of a healthy human habitat. Daily exposure is essential. If you don't see it or touch it, then nature can't do you much good. Proximity matters. But every little bit of nature helps.

This means we need to build nature into the urban system, and into our lives, at all scales. Yes, cities need big, immersive destination parks. But they also need medium-sized parks and community gardens within walking distance of every home. They also need pocket parks and green strips and potted plants and living, green walls. As Gil Peñalosa once put it: cities need green in sizes S, M, L, and XL. Otherwise the human ecosystem is incomplete.

When cities and citizens alter their priorities, the biophilic directive is achievable even where real estate is at a premium. The modern example was set in 2005 by Lee Myung-bak, a daring mayor of Seoul, Korea, who demolished five miles of elevated downtown freeway to restore daylight to the ancient waterway that ran beneath it. Liberated from the concrete shadows, the Cheonggyecheon River now flows through a thousand-acre ribbon of meadows, reeds, landscaped nooks, and mini-marshes. The summer this area opened, seven million people came to stroll, lie on the grass, or dangle their feet in the stream's shallow pools. Birds, fish, and insects not seen in years appeared, too. "Before, you only heard the traffic, but now you can hear the water," a retired driver enthused the next year. With new bus services, cars that once clogged the freeway disappeared and the city found a new biophilic soul. Soon after, the freeway-demolishing mayor was elected president of his country.

Underperforming or unused transportation infrastructures are fine terrain for biophilic retrofits. The High Line, the decommissioned elevated rail line converted into a nineteen-block linear park on Manhattan's West Side, is most famous for the bird's-eye glimpses it offers into offices, private living rooms, and down to the street from viewing platforms that turn evening traffic into rivers of light. But much closer are hundreds of species of flora, from chokecherries and willows to creeping raspberries and autumn moor grass, much of which had already begun to colonize the abandoned platform before its conversion. The High Line's natural caress draws visitors into a playful intimacy. On one warm day I joined a group of strangers who had removed their shoes and splashed in a toe-deep pond amid the wispy moor grass.

Since this park opened, urbanists in every city have clamored for their own High Line, but every city is unique, and so are the opportunities. The City of Los Angeles, for example, is working to turn thirty-two miles of the desolate, concrete-lined Los Angeles River into an "emerald necklace" of parks and paths.

Cities have more room for nature than we might think. The architecture firm partly responsible for the High Line, Diller Scofidio + Renfro, demonstrated this again a few dozen blocks north, in their renovation of Lincoln Center for the Performing Arts, where they created a green hillside by adding a new restaurant building to the Lincoln campus. A sloping, off-kilter roof (hyperbolic paraboloid is the technical name for the form) planted with green grass rears up from the plaza, inviting passersby to collapse on its vertical meadow. Zoom in on Google Earth, and you'll see students from the nearby Juilliard School splayed messily across the lawn.

New research takes the proximity argument further. Extreme intimacy—not just looking at nature, but actually touching or working with plants and dirt—is good for us in ways we never imagined. Biologists have found that the bacteria found naturally in soil boosts seratonin and reduces anxiety in lab mice, and they suspect that it has the same effect when breathed in or ingested by humans. This alchemic discovery is fascinating, but we already know that the act of gardening heightens the biophilic benefits of nature, in part because gardening demands more focus than simply observing nature.

But gardening is also a social act, especially in dense cities. In the summer of 2012, I met up with a group of elderly women on a lawn in the heart of Berolina, a massive Soviet housing cooperative in the former East Berlin. Berolina had all the alienating geometries of high modernism: long housing blocks (one of which stretched an astonishing 437 yards) stood guard over broad green spaces that saw little use. Some of the buildings had been retrofitted with balconies in the 1990s, and the common space between them was adorned with token landscaping. But those lawns retained an empty sterility. Nobody used them.

Many of the women gathered on the lawn that morning had lived at Berolina for more than forty years. That day, for the first time, they laid claim to the common space between the towers. Corrine Rose, a psychologist and BMW Guggenheim Lab team member, had convinced them to work with agronomists at Berlin's Humboldt University to build a small community garden. By the time I got there, the women had pulled on Day-Glo garden gloves and were pouring bags of black soil into raised planters.

"Come on, get to work!" one ruddy ex-Communist with wild white hair barked at me with a smile. We planted basil, thyme, bay leaf, peppers, and lettuce. Everyone got a bit dirty, and everyone had a grand time. The ruddy woman, with Corrine as her translator, told me that several beds had been reserved for them to plant with children from the local elementary school. In September, they would all dig together. Her joy was palpable. The garden was not merely a biophilic intervention. It was a social machine.

This was something we missed when designing our experiment in New York City: we suspected that just looking at urban nature would cheer people up. We should have been testing the effects of actually working with it. But the evidence is out there: people who do "green" volunteer work stay healthier and happier over time than people who do other kinds of volunteer work.* Every time a slice of urban land is transformed into a community garden, the salubrious effects flow

---

*One study in Alameda, California, found that retirees who do "environmental" work were half as likely as non-volunteers to show depressive symptoms after

through the brains and bodies of the people who work it and those who just pass by.

Meanwhile all these green insertions double as environmental system interventions. Plants and water work as urban air conditioners. (During Korea's sweltering summers, temperatures along Seoul's reborn Cheonggyecheon River are now about 6.5 degrees Fahrenheit lower than in surrounding neighborhoods.) Vegetation cleans the air of toxic particulates. It makes oxygen. It captures and stores carbon. City efforts to manage storm water by creating bio-swales (or semi-wild curbside water catchment zones) can also create micro-wildernesses that shrink the city's ecological footprint while easing the urban mind.

So we know that nature in cities makes us happier and healthier. We know it makes us friendlier and kinder. We know it helps us build essential bonds with other people and the places in which we live. If we infuse cities with natural diversity, complexity, and, most of all, opportunities to feel, touch, and work with nature, we can win the biophilic challenge. Quite simply, biological density must be the prerequisite for architectural density.

Closer, Part II: The Social Machine

There is no denying the thrill and sense of possibility that comes with life amid the human densities of Manhattan, with its generous and seething sidewalks. On one short walk to work I witnessed a dog walker tangled in the leashes of his charges, a Guadalajaran man cutting flowers for sale, a pair of shrieking gossips in hot pants, a shawarma vendor carving from a spit of lamb while pinching his cell phone between shoulder and chin, and a procession of uniformed children snaking along hand in hand. There were ancient ladies marching with groceries. I felt the naive enthusiasm of everyone new to New York: I wanted to know everyone. I asked for, and got, help. I caught strangers' eyes, collecting nods, conspiratorial smiles, and brush-offs. The city was so alive, so full of electric potential. In his

---

twenty years, while people who did other forms of volunteering only had their risk lowered by 10 percent.

nineteenth-century masterpiece "Crossing Brooklyn Ferry," Walt Whitman described the sense of communion he experienced in his accidental brushes with thousands of strangers on these streets of Manhattan:

> . . . What gods can exceed these that clasp me by the hand, and
> with voices I love call me promptly and loudly by my nighest
> name as I approach;
> . . . What is more subtle than this which ties me to the woman or
> man that looks in my face,
> Which fuses me into you now, and pours my meaning into you?

For Whitman, it was as though in all that shared seeing, jostling, and touching, the crowded city was somehow creating a common soul. You can still feel it today if you walk its streets long enough.

But anyone living in hyperdensity will tell you that it is not possible to live only amid the crowd. I learned that quickly in my East Village apartment.

The place was on the second floor of an old tenement on East Thirteenth Street. The kitchen, living room, bathroom, and bedroom were arranged in a space the size and dimensions of two on-street parking places. The view consisted of a brick wall punctuated by grimy windows fixed with air conditioners and rusting fire escapes. The first time I opened the window, I drew in a lungful of air scented with what might have been mold and rancid cooking oil. Below me was a dark "yard" strewn with broken furniture and building material. The only green in sight was a forlorn potted palm sitting on a dusty patio beneath me. I leaned out to find the sky. There it was, six stories above, a stingy band of pale blue.

After a day of continuous stimulation in Manhattan, one craves solitude. But the tenement was stingy in this respect. The city found its way inside from my very first night. Shortly after turning out the light, I heard laughter on the street. Then singing. Then, as the hours wore on, the singing devolved into sustained, college-grade hollering, then quarreling, and, finally, the choking gurgle of what could only have been full-force vomiting—right beneath my window. I must have slept, because at 4:00 a.m. I was awoken by the sound of smashing glass and a roaring truck engine. Garbage pickup. At

5:00 a.m. the car horns began. Not tooting cheerily, but blasting in long sets of frustration and ire.

At 6:00 a.m. I gave up and rolled up the blinds. Peering out into the canyon I saw a facelike shape in the dust-caked window across from me. It took a second to realize that it was in fact a human face, and it was staring at me. I pulled back and snapped the blind shut.

The place began to wear me down. It wasn't so much the lack of view or light, or the filth in the canyon below. It was the feeling that I was never quite alone there. I would walk in and feel a simultaneous mix of claustrophobia and loneliness. It got worse when my family arrived for a visit, and every movement, sound, or scent in the cramped space had to be choreographed in order to avoid confrontation.

It struck me that the apartment was exactly the kind of place that first drove the exodus to suburbia. Of course my discomfort was trivial compared with the intense squalor and domestic crowding suffered in these places a century before (or, for that matter, still experienced in tenements from Kowloon to Kolkata). But the place drained the energy I needed to tackle Manhattan and shortened my patience for the crowds outside. I came to feel as hostile toward my neighbors as Randy Strausser was to his in Mountain House. I gained a new sympathy for people who flee to the edge of the city or live in motor homes parked in the Nevada desert, or for the *hikikomori*, the more than seven hundred thousand Japanese who have retreated entirely from society, remaining inside their homes. I felt like one of the rats that researchers forced into overcrowded cages back in the 1970s. Those rats forgot how to build nests. They forgot how to socialize. They eventually started eating their offspring.

This is the other great challenge posed by density: its central tensions are as much social as they are aesthetic.

In the 1940s Abraham Maslow famously drew a pyramid of needs to represent the hierarchy of human motivation. At the base of the pyramid were the basic physiological needs—hunger, thirst, and sexual desire. According to Maslow, once you are satisfied on that level, you move to the next. So once you are well fed, you start worrying about safety. And you don't move on up to the things Carol Ryff talks about in her expansive definition of *eudaimonia*—love, esteem, and self-actualization—until you feel safe. In the modern city, it is not weather or predators that threaten us. For most people it is not hunger, either. It is other people who fill the air with noise; pollute the air we breathe; threaten to punch us, shoot us, steal from us, crowd us, interrupt us during dinner, or just plain make us uncomfortable. Although we are rarely at risk of being robbed or assaulted, exposure to too many people can literally be maddening.

For decades, psychologists believed that dense cities were socially toxic specifically because of their crowding. They found correlations between high population density and such psychosomatic illness as sleeplessness, depression, irritability, and nervousness. Indeed, people who inhabit residential towers, even those with views, report being more fearful, more depressed, and more prone to suicide than people living on the ground.

Being around too many strangers involves a stressful mix of social uncertainty and lack of control. The psychologist Stanley Milgram, who grew up in the Bronx, observed that people in small towns were much more helpful to strangers than were people in the big city. He attributed the difference to overload—the sheer crowdedness of cities creates so much stimulus that residents have to shut out the noise and objects and people around them in order to cope. City life, Milgram felt, demands a kind of aloofness and distance, so that crowding, while pushing us together physically, actually pushes us apart socially.

The evidence supports Milgram's case. People who live in residential towers, for example, consistently tell psychologists that they feel lonely and crowded by other people *at the very same time*. Other studies reveal that people who feel crowded are less likely to seek or respond to support from neighbors. They withdraw as a coping strategy but are thus denied the benefits of social support. And if enough people withdraw often enough, as Milgram pointed out, noninvolvement with other people becomes a social norm: it's simply inappropriate to bug your neighbors.

The Crowd, Moderated

This is not the outright condemnation of urban density that it might seem. Crowding is a problem of perception, and it is a problem of design that can be addressed, at least in part, by understanding the subtle physics of sociability.

First of all, it is critical to understand that human density and crowding are not the same thing. The first is a physical state. The second is psychological and subjective. An example from that most common locus of crowding, the public elevator: Everyone knows how awkward and occasionally claustrophobic a long elevator ride can be. But psychologists have found that merely altering your position inside an elevator full of people changes your perception and your emotional state. Stand right in front of the control panel, where you can select which floor to stop on, and you are likely to feel that the elevator is not only less crowded but bigger. All that really changes here is your sense of control.

We tolerate other people more when we know we can escape them. People who live in areas with crowded streets report feeling much better when they have rooms of their own to which they can retreat. There's a correlation between societal happiness and the number of rooms per person: it's not so much square footage that matters, but the ability to moderate contact with other people. But even people who live in crowded homes tend to feel okay if they can easily escape to a quiet public place.*

We expend a great deal of effort insulating ourselves from strangers, whether it's retreating to the edge of suburbia or adding more security features to our urban apartments. But this habit can deprive us of some of the most important interactions in life: those that happen in the blurry zone among people who are not quite strangers, but not quite friends.

The sociologist Peggy Thoits interviewed hundreds of men and women about the many social roles they played in life, from their positions as spouses, parents, and workers to lighter, more voluntary roles such as working as a school crossing guard. She discovered that the lighter relationships we have in volunteer groups, with neighbors, or even with people we see regularly on the street can boost feelings of self-esteem, mastery, and physical health, all contributors to that

---

*What you look at from your window influences your perception of crowding, too. Even in the suburbs, having windows that face open space rather than other people's windows makes people more likely to feel as though they have enough room, regardless of the square footage they occupy. Your view is not merely a conduit to nature. It is a social device.

ideal state that Carol Ryff called "challenged thriving." The uncomfortable truth is, our spouses and children and coworkers can wear us out. Life's lighter, breezier relationships soothe and reassure us, specifically because of their lightness.*

This leaves us with a conundrum. As Randy Strausser learned back in Mountain House, the detached house in distant dispersal is a blunt instrument: it is a powerful tool for retreating with your nuclear family and perhaps your direct neighbors, but a terrible base from which to nurture other intensities of relationships. Your social life must be scheduled and formal. Serendipity disappears in the time eaten up by the commute and in that space between car windshields and garage doors. On the other hand, life in places that feel too crowded to control can leave us so overstimulated and exhausted that we retreat into solitude. Either way, we miss out on the wider range of relationships that can make life richer and easier.

This is especially worrying as family size shrinks and more of us live alone than ever before. The archetypal 1950s nuclear family, with mother and father raising two-point-something children, is no longer the norm. The average household size in the United States has shrunk to 2.6 people (2.5 in Canada and 2.4 in the United Kingdom). More people now live alone, commute alone, and eat alone than ever before. In fact, the most common household in the United States now consists of someone living *all alone*,† which happens to be the state most associated with unhappiness and poor mental health.

What we need are places that help us moderate our interactions with strangers without having to retreat entirely.

Testing Proximity

The good news is that the crucial blend of control and conviviality can be designed into residential architectures. A hint of this first

*Thoits found that women's "obligatory" roles as spouses, parents, or employees tended to demand lots of time and energy and were more likely to translate into what she called "role strain." That wasn't the case with light, voluntary roles in life, which were unambiguously associated with well-being. The more social roles people have in life, the stronger they become in both mind and body.

†The number of people living alone in America rose from 17 percent in 1970 to 27 percent in 2007 (compared with 22.5 percent married couples with children), and the average household size declined from 3.1 people in 1970 to 2.6.

emerged in a stunning 1973 study in which psychologist Andrew Baum compared the behavior of residents of two starkly different college dormitories at Stony Brook University in Long Island, New York. In one residence, thirty-four students lived in double bedrooms along a single long corridor—a bit like a hotel, except that they shared one large bathroom and a lounge area at the end of the hallway. The other building housed just as many students, but the floors were broken up into suites, with two or three bedrooms each, sharing a lounge and a small bathroom. All the students were randomly assigned, but their reaction to their environment was far from random.

The students who lived in the corridor block felt crowded and stressed out. They complained about unwanted social interactions. The problem was that the long-corridor design made it almost impossible for them to choose whom they bumped into and how often. There was no in-between space. You were either in your room or out in the public zone of the hallway.

The design didn't merely make the students irritated. It changed the way they treated one another. The corridor residents did not become friends. The suite residents did. The corridor residents were less helpful to one another. They actually avoided one another, and they grew more antisocial as the year progressed.

Amazingly, the students carried their behavior with them to other parts of their lives. At one point the students were called to an office and asked to wait for an appointment along with one of their neighbors. Unlike the corridor residents, the suite residents chatted and made eye contact with each other. They reassured each other. They sat closer together.*

How does this tension between conviviality and sense of control translate into built form for those of us who do not live in university dormitories?

*"Normally we presume that the subjective experience of isolation (loneliness) must be at one end of a continuum at the other end of which is excessive social interaction. We can now see that this presumption is misleading. When a person is in a situation where he or she is unable to regulate who, when or where they will meet others, he or she is likely to experience both isolation and over-stimulation," summed up David Halpern. "In the absence of semi-private spaces which allow for informal interaction without commitment, each social interaction becomes an all or nothing experience."

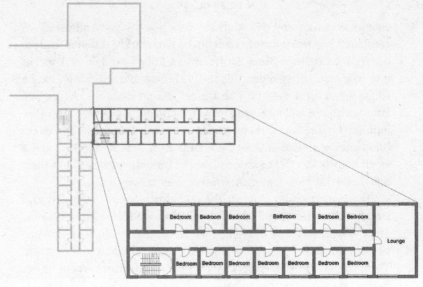

Corridor Residence

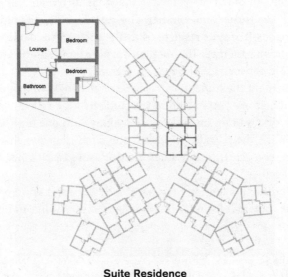

Suite Residence
Friendlier by Design

Students who lived in suite residences where they could control social interactions (bottom) *experienced less stress and built more friendships than students who lived along long corridors* (top). (Valins, S., and A. Baum, "Residential Group Size, Social Interaction, and Crowding," *Environment and Behavior*, 1973: 421; redesign by David Halpern and Building Futures)

The high modernist past offers a lesson. The most spectacular and symbolic failure was Minoru Yamasaki's thirty-three-block Pruitt-Igoe housing complex, built in 1950s St. Louis. The project was an attempt to revive a poverty-stricken inner-city neighborhood by replacing ramshackle row houses and tenements with rows of pristine, identical apartment blocks in a sea of lawn. Yamasaki's architectural drawings featured mothers and children frolicking in common galleries and in parklike spaces that separated the buildings. But the complex grew infamous for squalor, vandalism, drug use, and fear. Nobody used the generous lawns between the buildings. Nobody felt safe.

The architect Oscar Newman toured Pruitt-Igoe at the height of its dysfunction, and he found landscapes of social health that directly corresponded to design: "Landings shared by only two families were well maintained, whereas corridors shared by 20 families, and lobbies, elevators, and stairs shared by 150 families were a disaster—they evoked no feelings of identity or control." In the shared decks of those towers and the vast featureless grounds between the buildings, Newman observed a dysfunction he famously termed indefensible space: where nobody felt ownership over common space, garbage piled up, vandalism took hold, and the landscape was left to drug dealers. After two decades, two-thirds of its flats were abandoned. Although it is true that the community was beleaguered with the problems of poverty and shabby management, design mattered: the Pruitt-Igoe meltdown stood in wild contrast to a row-house project across the street, where people of similar background managed to take care of their environment right through Pruitt-Igoe's worst years. The St. Louis Housing Authority began dynamiting Pruitt-Igoe in 1972.

It must be said that reports of unhappy tower living tend to be skewed by the particular interests of social science researchers. After comparing hundreds of human density studies, David Halpern noted that most of them focused on social housing or slums from the most crowded urban areas in the world, places that tended to be inhabited by desperately poor people with fewer resources. In other words, they were surveying people whose difficult life circumstances would naturally make them less happy. We are now learning that the effect of density is nuanced. For one thing, wealthier people do better in apartment towers than poor people. Not only do they have the money to pay for concierges, maintenance, gardening, decoration, and child care, but, having chosen their residences, they tend to attach greater status to them. Home feels better when it carries a different message about who you are. (A building's status can be altered without any physical change at all. When they were sold on the open market, once-despised social housing blocks in central London became objects of desire for middle-class buyers who fetishized their retro modernism.)

But design influences our social life even in high-status landscapes where conditions are not so dire, and the evidence supports the old dictum that good fences make good neighbors, so much as they allow us to control our interactions. Consider the experience of Rob McDowell, a diplomat who bought a condominium on the twenty-ninth floor of the 501, a hip, design-heavy tower in Vancouver's Yaletown district. Rob was single and had no kids, so five hundred square feet seemed quite enough, especially given the panoramic view from his floor-to-ceiling windows. He could see the ocean. He could see islands in the distance. He could look over the other towers to the forested slopes of the North Shore Mountains. When the fog rolled in, he floated above it. The place wrapped biophilic views, status, and privacy in a neat package.

"I invited all my friends up there to see the view," he told me later. "I was so happy."

But that changed as the months went past.

Whenever McDowell left his apartment, he would follow a hallway he shared with twenty people to an elevator he shared with nearly three hundred people. When the elevator door opened, he could never be sure whom he would see inside, but they were almost never his own neighbors. Standing a foot or two apart, well within the zone of personal space and unable to control the duration of the encounter, McDowell and his neighbors would studiously avoid eye contact, gazing up instead at the LED floor display.* Like Baum's dorm resi-

*The feeling is familiar in the area. People who answered post-occupancy surveys in False Creek North, a Vancouverist neighborhood just across the street from the 501, complained that their fellow condo dwellers were socially skittish. "People don't want to get too close," one resident told a post-occupancy surveyor. "I think they're frightened that if they get too close and then realize that they don't like the person, they're in an impossible situation."

dents, McDowell felt increasingly claustrophobic. His view was no salve for solitude. "You go up the elevator, into your apartment, the door closes, and there you are, stuck alone with your beautiful view," he said. "I began to resent it."

McDowell's Vancouverist tower, so successful in delivering views of nature and a sense of status, was falling short as a social tool. This became clear when his life suddenly changed course.

The city had forced the 501's developer to build a row of town houses along the podium base of McDowell's tower. The town houses were a bit cramped, but their main doors all faced a garden and a volleyball court on the building's third-story rooftop. McDowell noticed that the town house residents regularly played volleyball in the garden. He and his tower-living neighbors had every right to join in, but they never did. It was as though, by their proximity, the town house residents owned that space.

After some friends moved into the town houses, McDowell gave up his view and bought a unit next to them. Within weeks his social landscape was transformed. He got to know *all* his new neighbors. He joined in the weekend cocktail and volleyball sessions in the shared garden. He felt as if he had come home.

McDowell's new neighbors were not inherently more likable or friendly than his tower neighbors. So what had drawn them together? In some ways, their behavior was predicted by decades of sociology similar to Baum's campus studies. The front doors of the town houses all led to semiprivate porches overlooking the podium garden. They provided regular opportunities for brief, easy contact. These porches were a soft zone, where you could hang out or retreat as you wished. (What would happen if a tower dweller decided to just "hang out" in the hallway in the adjoining tower? Not only would he be bored and uncomfortable, but eventually someone would call the police.) Without realizing it, McDowell and his neighbors were testing out a law of social geometry identified by Danish urbanist Jan Gehl. In studying the way people in Denmark and Canada behave in their front yards, Gehl found that residents chat the most with passersby when yards are shallow enough to allow for conversation, but deep enough to allow for retreat. The perfect yard for conviviality? Exactly 10.6 feet deep.

Then there was the issue of social scale. Rather than bumping into any one of three hundred or so strangers each day in the tower elevator,

McDowell experienced repeated contact with fewer than two dozen neighbors, making the social world of the garden more manageable, somewhat like a *fareej*, a domestic enclosure common in the Arab world that is big enough for several extended families. McDowell could remember the names of everyone who passed his door.

These new friendships are not trivial. Nine years on, McDowell babysits his neighbors' kids and keeps spare keys for their doors. His fellow town house dwellers dominate the building's management board. They vacation together. Where the tower pushes people apart, the town house courtyard draws them closer. He considers half of his twenty-two town house neighbors to be close friends.

"How many of them would you say you love?" I asked him the afternoon he showed me around. It was an intrusive question. He blushed, but counted on his fingers. "Love, like they were my family? Six." This is a stunning figure, given the shrinkage that most people report in their social networks these past twenty years. "And we love our home. All of us."

The Magic Triangle

These sentiments—loving your home and loving your neighbors—are related. John Helliwell's most recent studies of national surveys show that the tight web connecting trust and life satisfaction also extends to the misty realm of our sense of belonging. They exist in a perfect triangle:

People who say they feel that they "belong" to their community are happier than those who do not.

And people who trust their neighbors feel a greater sense of that belonging.

And that sense of belonging is influenced by social contact.

And casual encounters (such as, say, the kind that might happen around a volleyball court on a Friday night) are *just as important* to belonging and trust as contact with family and close friends.

It is hard to say which condition is lifting the others—Helliwell admits that his statistical analysis demonstrates correlation rather than causation—but what is strikingly apparent is that trust, feelings of belonging, social time, and happiness are like balloons tied together in a bouquet. They rise and fall together. This suggests that it has been a terrible mistake to design cities around the nuclear family at the expense of other ties. But it also suggests that even the high-status, deeply desired, uniquely biophilic brand of verticalism embodied by Vancouverism and McDowell's high-rise apartment is not a panacea. Helliwell produced a report in which people living in the city's vertical core rated their happiness significantly lower than people living in most other parts of the city. (The Vancouverists are far from miserable: downtown dwellers rated their life satisfaction between 7 and 7.5 on a scale of 1 to 10—about as happy as most Americans—but less dense neighborhoods scored more than a point higher.)

Vancouver just can't escape the persistent link between domestic design and conviviality. People living in Vancouver's downtown peninsula simply don't trust their neighbors as much as people living in neighborhoods where more people live on the ground.* The Vancouver Foundation, the city's largest philanthropic organization, surveyed people about their social connections. People living in towers consistently reported feeling more lonely and less connected than people living in detached homes. They were only half as likely to have done a favor for a neighbor in the previous year. They were much more likely to report having trouble making friends.

Many people love tower living, and many are skilled enough to build a social world in the tower city. They use the tools of the city—the coffee shop, the community center, the social or sports club, the neighborhood garden. They turn uncomfortable intimacies into opportunities. (John Helliwell insists on chatting with strangers in elevators, for example.) Increasingly, they use online tools and mobile applications to find each other. But for those of us who just bumble along, letting our social lives happen to us, the power of scale and design to open or close the doors of sociability is undeniable. The geometries of conviviality are not simple. We cannot be forced together. The richest social environments are those in which we feel free to edge closer together or move apart as we wish. They scale not abruptly but gradually, from private realm to semiprivate to public;

*Part of the problem is that Vancouver's vertical neighborhoods tend to be home to its most transient residents: foreign students, young people, and renters who do not stay long enough to forge deep ties. Tens of thousands of foreign English-language students rent apartments in the downtown's West End, staying for mere months at a time. In 2012, nearly half the people in Vancouver's towers had lived there less than five years.

from bedroom to parlor to porch to neighborhood to city, something most tower designers have yet to achieve.

The Sweet Spot Is Somewhere in Between

If you search hard enough for places that balance our competing needs for privacy, nature, conviviality, and convenience, you end up with a hybrid, somewhere between the vertical and horizontal city.

Just as McDowell and his neighbors found a rich, connected home life three stories above the surface of the earth, cities all over the world offer up surprisingly happy geometries, both by design and by accident. In Copenhagen, architect Bjarke Ingels has attempted to fuse suburban and urban attributes in one building. Ingels's Mountain Dwellings stack eighty apartments with generous patios over eleven stories of sloping roof atop a neighborhood parking lot. Everyone gets a private "backyard" and a coveted south-facing view in a country bereft of mountains, in a district just dense enough to support decent transit.

But the happy geometry need not be so high in concept or cost. It can be found wherever scale and systems intersect with a critical density of human life. It can be found throughout the developing world, where zoning laws have not tamed the bric-a-brac mix of neighborhood housing and commerce. It can be found in Tuscan hill towns, English rail suburbs, South Pacific island villages, and the pueblos swallowed by Mexico City.

One almost-ideal urban geometry was perfected in many North American cities more than a century ago. It was invented not by utopian planners or sociologists, but by cunning men motivated by the constraints of technology and an old-fashioned wish to make as much money as they could.

After the first electrical streetcar was introduced in Richmond, Virginia, in 1887, rail lines rapidly spread across hundreds of cities, luring commuters to new streetcar suburbs from Boston to Toronto to Los Angeles. Almost no one owned a car before World War I, so land developers wishing to attract homebuyers first had to build the rail lines, then offer homes within an easy walking distance from them. Buyers also demanded shops and services and schools, and sometimes parks, all within walking range. If you didn't offer the full package, you would have a hard time selling land. Thus, during the golden age of streetcar suburbia, property development and streetcar development went hand in hand.

"There was a perfect, organic relationship between the purveyors of transit and the purveyors of real estate for business, all of whom wanted to provide enough customers for both business and transit," explains Patrick Condon, an urbanist at the University of British Columbia who has studied the dynamic.

The key to making a profit, said Condon, was to get that math right. The developers assumed (quite correctly, we now know) that most people are happy to walk five minutes, or about a quarter of a mile, from home to shops and streetcars. But in order to provide that critical mass of paying trolley riders and property buyers, they needed to keep residential lots relatively small. The typical street frontage for a single-family house in Vancouver's streetcar neighborhoods was just thirty-three feet, delivering at least eight homes per acre (which makes neighborhoods from two to eight times as dense as many modern suburbs*). Schools were small, too, with classrooms stacked two or three stories high to make room for playgrounds.

As it turned out, the geometry of profit also created a near-perfect scale for happy living. Market streets were lively and bustling, while the residential streets behind them were quiet and leafy. Most people got their own house and yard. There were porches rather than front garages, so people could keep their eyes on the street. Kids had the freedom to walk to school. Without modern suburbia's massive yards, wide roads, and strict segregation of uses, almost everything you needed was a five-minute walk or a brief streetcar ride away. In the streetcar city, greed helped produce density's sweet spot.

Streetcar City 2.0

Most streetcar neighborhoods fell into decline after the 1950s. They suffered multiple wounds. Many lost their streetcars when the systems were bought up by motor interests and replaced with buses. Their ease and charm was eroded by the mass adoption of automobiles, which clogged the main streets and slowed both streetcars and

---

*The human density now required to support transit frequencies of ten minutes or less is estimated at around twelve people per acre. But the average suburban lot over the past two decades in places such as Maryland averages from .5 to 1.2 acres.

buses. Freeways ripped through their vulnerable fabric. Many were abandoned by governments and wealthier citizens in the flight toward increasingly distant suburbs. Tax dollars fled. Schools and services declined. As household sizes shrank and retailers followed the flight to the urban edge, the metrics of scale, system, and human density lost their alchemic balance. But the geometry of the streetcar city has survived, and actually been improved upon, in places like Toronto, Seattle, Portland, and Vancouver.

I discovered the streetcar neighborhood almost completely by accident. My leap into the property market, buying a share of my friend Keri's house in 2006, was driven by the most superficial aspirations. I wanted more rooms, a bigger kitchen, my own piece of ground. I was bugged that the house sat on a tiny lot—twenty-five feet by one hundred, less than a quarter of the size of the lots typically sold in the suburbs in the last three decades. The backyard was the size of a squash court. If you reached out the windows to the north or south, you could scrape the paint on the neighbor's clapboard. At first I felt that the

The Streetcar Suburb

Long after its streetcars were replaced by trolley buses, this district in East Vancouver balances density and land-use mix in a way that responds to human need for privacy, conviviality, convenience, and nature. The market street (bottom right) is not elegant, but it offers commercial destinations, transit, and apartment living. Houses on nearby treelined streets (top right) offer single-family residences and apartments, all within walking distance of schools, transit, and the market street. (Scott Keck; Charles Montgomery/Google Maps)

whole setup was a bit on the stingy side. I didn't realize that these dimensions actually helped my house and my neighborhood achieve the delicate balance between privacy, conviviality, and biophilia. What mattered most was that house's place in the system around it: the density of people per acre, the length of each block, the distance to the nearest market street, and the mixing of all kinds of different activities.

Here is that terrain:

In front of the house there is a yard, a little over thirteen feet deep. All the twelve yards on this street are small enough to make gardening a relatively minor task, and so every stroll leads past a parade of flowers and shrubs and fruit trees. Four minutes' walk away, there is a grassy park where old men play boccie every afternoon and holler at each other in Italian. Five minutes away, down the hill, there is Commercial Drive, a market street of remarkable plenitude. Two minutes up or down that street are a post office, a hardware store, an Italian grocery store, two Chinese veggie markets, a bakery, a fish shop, a parade of coffee shops, two used-furniture stores, some low-rise apartments, a few bars, a gym, a high school, and a community center that holds a library, a pool, and a hockey rink. The Drive feels loose and uncrowded, yet as abundant as a market street in Manhattan. The streetcars are long gone, but buses run both ways along the Drive every six minutes. You can be downtown in fifteen minutes.

Why, when so many streetcar neighborhoods across the continent have fallen ill, had this one stayed so healthy? As it turned out, it was nurtured by many of the same forces that fueled Vancouver's vertical downtown: absence of freeways, geographic constraints, and, especially, local policies that encouraged more human density. While the world was gaping at the rise of Vancouver's vertical downtown, these relaxed streetcar neighborhoods absorbed even more new residents. Between 1991 and 2006 the city's population (not including the outer suburbs) grew by more than a hundred thousand. Most of that growth happened not downtown, but in neighborhoods like my own.

How was this possible? First of all, Vancouver encourages mixed-use development along the old streetcar grid. Single-story structures are constantly being replaced by three- and four-story apartments above restaurants, banks, and shops. Meanwhile, on the leafy residential streets behind those arterials, single-family lots like mine have been quietly transformed.

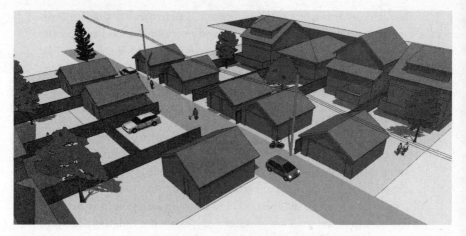

Laneway Revolution

In Vancouver and other cities, new zoning rules allow homeowners to replace their laneway garages (top) with small residences (bottom), one of many ways to add gentle density to existing neighborhoods. (This rendering shows home models designed and built by Lanefab.) (Lanefab.com)

Many detached houses have been divided into apartments. Most basements have been retrofitted with full kitchens, bathrooms, and partial windows to create suites, a practice that has recently been legalized. In 2009 the city also legalized the construction of so-called laneway houses in the backyards behind most detached houses in the city. Think about it: owners of more than seventy thousand properties can now build cottages where their alley garages now stand. Averaging about five hundred square feet, the new cottages aren't much bigger than small apartments, but they give homeowners a chance to house relatives or renters at a comfortable distance. This means that the vast majority of formerly single-family lots in the city can now legally include at least three households—a main residence, a basement suite, and a laneway cottage. Together these rules are enabling one of the biggest urban infill projects on the continent. They are proof that there is plenty of room for more people in almost any of North America's old streetcar neighborhoods.

Diverse Density and Dense Diversity

This neighborhood upcycling provides a stunning range in housing choice, which means room for people of different incomes, mobility, ages, tastes, and tolerance for proximity. On my own street, a family of four lives alone in a three-story million-dollar house, right next to a house split for two couples, next to a house owned by Cynthia, a single woman nearing retirement who chopped her place up into three apartments so she could pay her mortgage and live well without making a bundle. Some people like their apartments. Some people like town houses. Some people will not be content without space between themselves and the nearest neighbor. We all find a place here.

Of course, this model contradicts nearly a century of urban practice in which people with money did their best to avoid people without money and succeeded with the help of city planners. But those of us who live in detached homes owe a debt of gratitude to all those people who either cannot afford a house or simply prefer apartments or sharing space. They help keep the cash registers flowing on Commercial Drive. They are the reason that the First Ravioli Store survives. Their patronage helps heat the public swimming pool and keeps buses coming so frequently that there is no point in checking the schedule. They offer eyes to keep the streets safe. They make life easier for everyone.* Accepting new people at new proximities

---

*Even downtown, Vancouver has convinced people of vastly different status to live close together. New developments are required to devote 20 percent of their land to affordable housing, a practice known as inclusionary zoning. In False Creek North, residents of upscale towers told surveyors that subsidized housing was the "best

certainly saved me from a disaster straight out of Luis Rayo's evolutionary happiness algorithm:

After our renovation, my pal Keri and I strained to carry the burden of a killer mortgage and property taxes, much like the victims of the mortgage crisis in San Joaquin County. But we learned from our neighbors. Rather than move to a cheaper house on the urban fringe, we took a chance and invited our romantic partners to move in with us and pay rent. They agreed. That turned out to be pretty good for our relationships, but it still didn't cover our costs. So we took on two extra tenants in our remaining bedrooms.

I never imagined I would roll into midlife in such a populous domestic assemblage, but this arrangement actually made life easier. Like many houses these days, ours had enough space to allow the six of us to gather or retreat from one another as we wished. We took turns cooking—just one night a week each. I saved on food and on transportation. After a few months of living there, I found I was walking everywhere because *everywhere* was suddenly so close. I rarely needed a car. The geometry of the neighborhood rewrote the pattern of my movements, the pace of my days, and the rhythm of my social world.

Vancouver's experiments in proximity have become so popular that they have helped create a new problem: house and apartment prices have begun to soar well beyond the reach of most people who work in the city. In 2012 Vancouver won the dubious honor of becoming the most expensive city for housing in North America. This means many people who work in the city either can't afford to live there, or have to work so hard they have little time for the social experiences that make life sweet.

To ease the pressure, the city is now scrambling to find ways to add affordable density. As I write this chapter, the Vancouver City Council is in the process of giving one property developer the go-ahead to build three towers of market condominiums above two floors of light industrial space—but only if the developer gives seventy of the apartments back to the city to rent out as affordable housing. The project will mix rich, poor, and work space in a way not seen here in generations.

---

thing to happen" to their area because it drew families to the neighborhood, giving it a greater sense of community.

A System of Voluntary Association

Design alone cannot solve the affordability crisis. Governments simply must invest more in social housing. This is not merely a design question, but a political one. Who will have the right to live in the Vancouver—or any great city—of the future? I will return to this question of equity in Chapter 10.

For now it is important to acknowledge that there are a thousand ways to retrofit proximity and complexity into cities, and they don't all necessarily come from planners and politicians. We might emulate the Danes and build apartments around huge common courtyards. We might learn from the Emiratis of Abu Dhabi, whose traditional neighborhood system, the *fareej*, links courtyard homes with narrow alleys and intimate public spaces in ways that accommodate extended family networks. But in all my travels I have never found a design intervention that strikes a more responsive balance between privacy and conviviality than the one neighbors built for themselves in a typical suburban neighborhood an hour's drive north of Stockton, California.

It started in 1986, when Kevin Wolf and Linda Cloud, a pair of young environmental activists, bought neighboring homes on N Street on what was then the edge of the university town of Davis. At some point they tore down the fence between those homes, and their roommates started sharing meals in the bigger house. As more community-minded people bought or rented the adjoining properties, more fences came down, and more people dropped in for dinner. The residents of the village that came to be known as N Street Cohousing won designation as a planned development from the Davis City Council, enabling them to add larger second units to their homes. In 2005 Wolf and Cloud financed a bigger common house, which became a miniature community center, with laundry facilities and a dining room that could handle dozens of people.

By the time I arrived on a Friday night in 2010, there were more than fifty people living on the two-acre site (at more than five times the typical sprawl density, it still didn't feel crowded). I ducked through a narrow passage between a couple of ranch-style homes to find that the core of the block had been transformed into a lush open green. There were no backyard fences left inside the block. There was an orchard of apple and orange trees, a chicken coop, gardens, and lawns scattered with children's toys.

I told Wolf the place felt a little bit like a commune.

"But it's not!" he corrected me. "None of this land is communal. All the lots are still privately owned. We live in our own homes and have our own yards. It's just that we choose to share those yards and some of our resources."

The setup is remarkably simple. Members of N Street Cohousing pay $25 per month to use the common house, which Wolf and Cloud still own. Some take turns cooking meals for dozens of neighbors in the big kitchen. Some prefer to cook and eat alone at home. Some mix it up. Some have chipped in for a Jacuzzi, which they share with neighbors for a small fee. Others wouldn't dream of hot-tubbing with the gang. People do what they want with their yards, but they agree to maintain common paths through them.

It's a uniquely market-responsive kind of sharing, which allows each person to adjust to a level of engagement or retreat that feels right at any particular moment. People drift together when it suits them and apart when it doesn't. The model pays biophilic dividends: by sharing their block, everyone in effect enjoys a gigantic green backyard. It pays logistical dividends too: parents feel comfortable sending their kids out to play in the super-yard, knowing that dozens of eyes will be watching them from the homes that surround it.

Amid all this voluntary intimacy, remarkable things happen. After I shared dinner with Wolf and a dozen friends, a neighbor arrived with a small child he introduced as Wolf and Cloud's daughter. The child was about five years old, and full of spark. After Wolf put her to bed, he explained that the kid didn't actually begin life as his daughter: she had been adopted as a nine-month-old by another community member, a single woman who later died of cancer. The change in the child's family life was organic. As her mother's health declined, the child spent time with key neighbors, sleeping over at Kevin and Linda's house more and more often. The bonds of intimacy and care were so tight that when her mother finally died, the child had already transitioned into a new loving household (and she was formally adopted). The village had become her extended family and wrapped itself around her like a cocoon.

There is no one perfect neighborhood for everyone. We all have our own tolerance for crowding or quietude, our own thirst for novelty or privacy or music or gardening, and our own complex associations with places, scents, and memories. But the systems in which we live undeniably influence our emotional lives. The lesson of the street-car suburb or N Street is not that cities need to be organized in grids, or that they need streetcars, or that we must all tear down our fences or look a century back for a geometry that works. It is that we can find various geometries to save ourselves and the planet. They do not all involve stacking our lives into the sky, but they are almost all tighter than what the proponents of dispersal have been selling us.

7. Convivialities

The street wears us out. It is altogether disgusting. Why,
then, does it still exist?
                                            —Le Corbusier

Our culture is in need of an art of exposure; this art will not
make us one another's victims, rather more balanced adults,
capable of coping with and learning from complexity.
                                            —Richard Sennett

The architect and the psychologist were trained to disagree. It was 1962, a thrilling time of expansion for European cities. Having recently graduated from the School of Architecture at Denmark's Royal Academy of Fine Arts, Jan Gehl and his colleagues were invited to build entire new city districts using the methods of high modernism. They obsessed about form and efficiency, about tap water, light, and lawns. But Gehl's wife, Ingrid, was an environmental psychologist, and she was deeply skeptical about the design tribe's single-minded mission. She pointed out that architects rarely considered their neighborhoods' relationships with the creatures who inhabited them. Sure, they added human shapes to their renderings—stick children playing on vast lawns and cartoon mothers gathering to chat beneath blank concrete walls—but they did not actually study how people responded to buildings after they were constructed. It was no wonder that after those new towers were completed, the frolicking children and gossiping mothers often failed to appear where they were supposed to.

It took a radical change of scene for the architect to come around to the psychologist's way of thinking. After the couple was awarded a grant to study the medieval towns of Italy, they spent six months among the postcard cathedrals, museums, and palaces. But they paid little attention to such architectural attractions. Rather, they were drawn in by the human activity they saw between buildings in cities and towns that had not yet been reorganized by rational planners or invaded by cars. It was nothing like anything they had experienced back in Copenhagen. They began documenting that life: people wandering along the edges of Venice's canals, the bustle of Perugia's crooked alleyways, Siena's Piazza del Campo and its many happy loiterers. Compared with the sterile sidewalks of home, where nobody paused to so much as have a coffee, public space in Italy's medieval cities seethed with life.

Take the Piazza del Campo, that glorious gathering place at the heart of Siena. The Campo, as it is known, gradually radiates uphill from Siena's Palazzo Pubblico, terminating in a wide semicircular promenade that is lined with dignified five-story villas. With its tremendous sight lines, the Campo functions as a stage across which the entire city parades. There are no cars.

The couple perched on the edges of the Campo and stayed for days. They jotted down the comings and goings of people every half hour, just as biologists might record the movement of ungulates around a watering hole. The mornings were quiet. As the sun climbed, people began to pour into the plaza through the stone arches and dark alleyways that punctured its edges. They stopped to drink and chat. They gathered in the cafés and restaurants whose tables spilled from the piazza's northern fringe. They leaned against the chest-high travertine bollards that stood at regular intervals along the edge of the promenade (which had absolutely no purpose other than to be leaned on). When the dew disappeared, tourists sat cross-legged on the sloping brick surface of the piazza, watching the shadow of the skyscraping Torre del Mangia creep across the amphitheater. After sunset, well-dressed Sienese families came to stroll and chat by the marble Fonte Gaia.

The Campo drew people together. It slowed them down. It held them in its palm.

Gehl was captivated by that human Serengeti. Were Italians really

Designed for Conviviality

With its amphitheater-like shape, its café-lined edges, and its loiter-friendly bollards, Siena's Piazza del Campo is perfectly configured to attract and hold people. (Ethan Kent/Project for Public Spaces)

inclined, by some genetic or ancient cultural impulse, to hang out together in public more than Danes? Perhaps.* But even if urban spaces like the Campo were a reflection of local culture and climate, Gehl suspected that their gracious geometries actually shaped people's behavior by inviting them to come together and to linger.

There was no more ideal place to test the theory than back home in Copenhagen, where the city was embarking on what was then a radical experiment.

After the Second World War, the capital of Denmark had embraced dispersal as fervently as any American city. Everyone bought a car, and suburbs spilled out from the city's medieval heart. Copenhagen did its best to accommodate the flood of private vehicles into the city. Public squares and the off-kilter spaces between buildings, long the shared terrain for all kinds of users, were converted into parking lots. But as the narrow streets of the core were filled with metal, noise, and exhaust fumes, Copenhagen began to seize up. The police simply could not keep traffic moving, and it was impossible to widen the roads in the core without ripping down architectural treasures. When planners proposed running a highway down the middle of the stately lakes on the eastern fringe of the downtown, it was clear that Copenhagen had reached a crossroads. It could either totally redesign its core for cars, as so many other cities had been doing, or it could start pushing back.

In 1962, around the time that New York's freeway king, Robert Moses, was trying to push an expressway through the heart of Lower Manhattan, Copenhagen's City Council took a step in the opposite direction. Nudged by anti-auto protests, they banned cars from the spine of the downtown, a string of market streets collectively known as the Strøget. It was an experiment.

Newspapers predicted disaster. Business owners were terrified. How could a street function without cars? What on earth would

---

*The Campo's location, shape, and design did reflect the evolution of Siena. It began life as a meadow at the intersection of various trade routes and was used as a market hundreds of years before the nine families who dominated the city in the twelfth century paved it with brick and inlaid it with nine rays of travertine to symbolize their rule. Ever since, it has served as the stage for the Sienese clans' cooperation and rivalries—exhibited most famously by the Palio, the annual spectacle in which horses from each clan race one another around the edges of the piazza.

serious, practical Danes do with all that empty space between buildings? Pundits warned that the historical district would be deserted.

"People said, 'We're Danes, not Italians, and we are not going to sit around in outdoor cafés drinking cappuccinos in the middle of freezing winter!'" Gehl told me when I met him in his Copenhagen office half a century later. People believed the city and its civic culture could work only one way. It was the same thing that the engineers would keep insisting in other cities for decades.

But Copenhagen did change, utterly. And nobody is more intimate with its transformations than Gehl. Almost immediately upon his return from Italy, he parked himself on the newly pedestrianized Strøget.

"I sat down every Tuesday and Saturday, in the sun and the rain and the slush, to see what was going on in the winter and summer, day and night, workday and weekend. I watched what children were doing, what old people were doing, and just who was coming there anyway," he told me. "The idea was to study the cycle of the day, the cycle of the week, and the cycle of the year, to see how the rhythm of the city changed. I was trying to make visible to everyone how people react to city forms, so we can start talking about the interaction between form and life."

He spent a year on the Strøget, which changed before his eyes. People poured into the space that had been vacated by cars. They came in the summer, but they also came in the darkest days of winter. Businesses thrived.

What brought the people out? Gehl watched, scribbled down every movement to find out. When the city added a new bench, Gehl counted the people who came and lingered. The benches told a story. A bench facing the passing crowds got ten times as much use as a bench that faced a flower bed. He also noticed that more people gathered on the edges of construction sites than in front of department store display windows. But as soon as the construction crews went home, the audience dispersed. "They were much more interested in watching people doing things than watching flowers or fashion," he noted. His conclusion seems obvious, and yet it was revolutionary at the time: "What is most attractive, what attracts people to stop and linger and look, will invariably be other people. Activity in human life is the greatest attraction in cities."

Making People Visible

In effect, Gehl was doing for human traffic what traffic engineers had once done only for cars. His studies made pedestrians visible to planners for the first time. He figured out, for example, that each square meter of street could handle about fourteen walkers per minute.* Any more than that, and people would start bunching into marching packs to cope with the congestion. The same principles governed all kinds of travel.

"We found that if you make more road space, you get more cars. If you make more bike lanes, you get more bikes. If you make more space for people, you get more people and of course then you get public life."

When Gehl was named a professor at the School of Architecture at the Royal Danish Academy of Fine Arts, the city of Copenhagen came to rely on his work. It used his numbers to justify an incremental but inexorable transformation of the core. Every year, the city reclaimed more streets and poured a little more of the city's road budget into making other streets friendlier and more inviting to people outside of cars.

With the Strøget full up, the city pedestrianized Fiolstræde, a narrow street that sliced north through Copenhagen's university quarter. Then the serpentine Købmagergade. Gradually, a latticework of pedestrian streets and plazas spread through the city's core. As they were linked to the rest of the city with a carefully planned network of bicycle paths, even more people spilled through them. Many of those people came not because of previous plans for shopping or business, but simply because there were so many other people to see. *Things were happening, so more things happened.*

Over the years, Gehl and Lars Gemzøe, a colleague at the School of Architecture, documented every shift in the way people behaved on Copenhagen's streets. They didn't merely measure foot traffic. They also counted people sitting in outdoor cafés, watching street performers, or just sitting on benches or on the rims of fountains. They

---

*The first summer after the Strøget was pedestrianized, 145 people were passing through some eleven-yard-wide sections every minute. The street was handling many more times the traffic than it could handle when cars had ruled, but at this pedestrian volume, the Strøget was pretty much full again.

counted people doing absolutely nothing. (So they can say with authority, for example, that between 1968 and 1995 the number of people to be found just hanging out on the streets of Copenhagen more than tripled.)

In 1968, parked cars were cleared out of Gråbrødretorv, or Grey Monk's Square, a small plaza dominated by a large shade tree near the Strøget. That summer, the owners of a café on the square set up a few tables outside their door. People sat down at those tables and ordered beer and meatballs, and they let the northern sunlight fall on their faces. It seemed a quirky anomaly. But those tables were the drops that led to a torrent. Now the city center is crammed with outdoor cafés, close to nine thousand seats by Gehl's last count. Danish winters are as miserable as they come—the winds from the North Sea deliver wave after wave of rain, sleet, and snowstorms, and the weak sun disappears well before the end of the workday—but now you can see Copenhageners out on their plazas in the dead of winter, wrapped in woolen blankets, sipping little cups of espresso. Gehl collects pictures of them, proof that by redesigning city space, you can actually transform the culture.

A few years after Gehl began his studies, the American journalist and organizational analyst William H. Whyte started counting people on the streets and plazas of New York using time-lapse film footage and painstaking notation. Whyte's studies of behavior on sidewalks and plazas in New York, Melbourne, and Tokyo showed that people almost always chose to sit near one another, even when they had the option of being alone. Strangely, they even tended to stop and gather where pedestrian traffic was thickest. Whyte and his team of note takers and camera-wielding assistants repeatedly found people chatting amid the current of doorways and on busy corners rather than moving aside, as though they actually liked to be jostled a bit.

When you think about it, none of this crowd affinity should be a surprise. Almost all of us will choose a seat in a restaurant with a view of others. People will show up for the most mundane small-town parades. We like to look at each other. We enjoy hovering in the zone somewhere between strangers and intimates. We want the opportunity to watch and be watched, even if we have no intention of ever actually making contact with one another.

This hunger for time among strangers is so widespread that it

Streets for People
Copenhagen's Strøget before and after pedestrianization (Jan Gehl and Lars Gemzøe / Gehl Architects Urban Quality Consultants)

seems to contradict the urge to retreat that helped create the dispersed city in the first place.

The Stranger Deficit

Places like the Strøget carry an increasingly urgent message about the role of public life in cities. For thousands of years, city life naturally led people toward casual contact with people outside of our circle of intimates. In the absence of refrigeration, television, drive-thru, and the Internet, our forebears had no choice but to come together every day to trade, to talk, to learn, and to socialize on the street. This was the purpose of the city.

But modern cities and affluent economies have created a particular kind of social deficit. We can meet almost all our needs without gathering in public. Technology and prosperity have largely privatized the realms of exchange in malls, living rooms, backyards, and on the screens of computers and smartphones. We can enjoy the cinema without leaving bed. We can build new friendships without regard for geography. We tweet our gossip or argue on Facebook walls. We peruse and interview prospective love interests online. We have gotten so good at privatizing our comforts, our leisure time, and our communication that urban life gets scoured of time with people who are not already colleagues, family, or close friends. Tellingly, the word *community* is increasingly used to refer to groups of people who use the same media or who happen to like a certain product, regardless of whether its members have actually met.

As more and more of us live alone, these conveniences have helped produce a historically unique way of living, in which home is not so much a gathering place as a vortex of isolation.

So far, technology only partially makes up for this solitude. Television, that great window to the world, has been an unequivocal disaster for happiness. The more TV you watch, the fewer friendships you are likely to have, the less trusting you become, and the less happy you are likely to be.* The Internet has been a mixed blessing. If you use your computer, iPad, or mobile device much like TV, it has the same negative effect on you as TV. If you use your devices to interact with people, they can help support your close relationships—one study found that after the introduction of an online discussion list in several Boston communities, neighbors actually started sitting out on their porches and inviting each other to dinner more. But our electronic tools are not good enough on their own. A growing stack of studies provide evidence that online relationships are simply not as rich, honest, or supportive as the ones we have in person. (One example: People are more likely to lie to each other when texting than when standing beside each other. But you already knew *that*, didn't you?) The primacy of face-to-face interactions is nothing new. We have spent thousands of years basing our interactions on all our senses: we use not just our eyes and ears, but our noses to receive

*When TV service was introduced to otherwise healthy communities in Canada in the 1980s, it had an almost immediate corrosive effect on civic participation. Watching TV correlates with higher material aspirations, more anxiety, lower financial satisfaction, lower trust in others, and less frequent social activity.

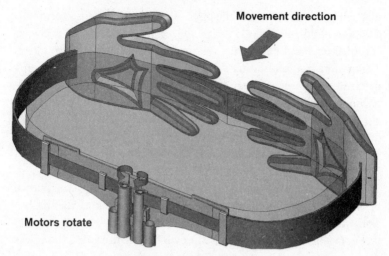

Movement direction

Motors rotate

HaptiHug Telecuddle Interface
This vest concept, part of Keio University Tachi Lab's iFeel IM! system for feeling enhancement, translates the emotions of a distant communicator into a physical hug. The goal, according to creators, is to create "an emotionally immersive experience" in 4-D. Can we ever fully replicate the sensation of actually meeting in person? (Courtesy of Dzmitry Tsetserukou, EIIRIS, Toyohashi University of Technology)

subtle signals about who people are, what they like, and what they want. There is simply no substitute for *actually being there.**

In an age obsessed with virtual space, the quest for conviviality

---

*This concern with touch has led inventors at the Berlin University of the Arts to create mobile phone prototypes that simulate interpersonal sensations. One phone imitates hand-holding by transmitting a sender's squeeze to a tension band around a receiver's hand. Another re-creates a sender's on-phone kiss by pushing a wet sponge against a membrane on the receiver's phone casing. The creepy discomfort experienced even by the inventors of these devices suggests that there are limits to the intimacy-producing potential of technology.

On the other hand, programmers are responding to this reality with applications designed to move online encounters off-line. Some use the GPS in our mobile devices to connect us with nearby strangers—a technique pioneered by the location-based gay online dating app, Grindr. Other apps, such as HeyNeighbor, enable people to ask people in their area for favors or offer help. Some push the limits of altruism: CLOO, for instance, enables you to register your private bathroom so strangers in need can "rent" it in an emergency.

ultimately brings us back to the physical realm. The question remains: Can we build—or rebuild—city spaces in ways that enable easy connnections and more trust among both familiars and strangers? The answer is a resounding yes. The spaces we occupy can not only determine how we feel. They can change the way we regard other people and how we treat one another.

A Science of Conviviality

The great sociologist Erving Goffman suggested that life is a series of performances in which we are all continually managing the impression we give other people. If this is so, then public spaces function like a stage in the same way that our own homes and living rooms do. Architecture, landscaping, the dimensions of the stage, and the other actors around us all offer cues about how we should perform and how we should treat one another.

A man might urinate in a graffiti-covered alleyway, but he would not dream of doing so in the manicured mews outside an old folks' home. He would be more likely to offer a kindness in an environment where he felt he was among family or friends, or being watched, than in some greasy back alley. In Goffman's world, these are conscious, calculated responses to the stage setting. But recently we have learned that some of our social responses occur even without conscious consideration. Like other animals, we have evolved to assess risks and rewards in the landscapes around us unconsciously.

The evolutionary biologists D. S. Wilson and Daniel O'Brien showed a group of nonresidents pictures of various streetscapes from Binghamton, New York. Some of those streets featured broken pavement, unkempt lawns, and dilapidated homes. Others featured crisp sidewalks and well-kept yards and homes. Then the volunteers were invited to play a game developed by experimental economists in which they were told that they would be trading money with someone from the neighborhood they had viewed. You probably already know how they behaved: the volunteers were much more trusting and generous when they believed they were facing off with someone from the tidier, well-kept neighborhood. You might consider this a logical response to clues about each neighborhood's social culture—tidiness conveys that people respect social norms, for example. But even the quality of the pavement—which bore no real relationship at all to the trustworthiness of a street's residents—influenced them.

In fact, we regularly respond to our environment in ways that seem to bear little relation to conscious thought or logic.

For example, while most of us agree that it would be foolish to let the temperature of our hands dictate how we should deal with strangers, lab experiments show that when people happen to be holding a hot drink rather than a cold one, they are more likely to trust strangers. Another found that people are much more helpful and generous when they step off a rising escalator than when they step off a descending escalator—in fact, ascending in any fashion seems to trigger nicer behavior.*

Psychologists stretch themselves trying to explain these correlations. One theory suggests that we experience environmental conditions as metaphors: thus we would translate physical warmth as social warmth, and we would feel an elevated sense of ethics or generosity by gaining elevation. Another line of inquiry known as terror management theory posits that we are all motivated by a constant underlying fear of death. By this way of thinking, those cracked sidewalks in Binghamton would trigger unconscious fears that would cause us to retreat from the people who lived there. Whatever the mechanism, what is certain is that the environment feeds us subtle clues that prime us to respond differently to the social landscape—even if those clues are wholly untethered from any rational analysis of our surroundings.

Neuroscientists have found that environmental cues trigger immediate responses in the human brain even before we are aware of them. As you move into a space, the hippocampus, the brain's memory librarian, is put to work immediately. It compares what you are seeing at any moment to your earlier memories in order to create a

---

*Observing shoppers at a mall, University of North Carolina researchers found that twice as many people stepping off a rising escalator donated to a Salvation Army fund-raiser than did people stepping off a descending escalator. They also found that people who had just watched film clips of views from an airplane window were much more cooperative in computer games than people who had watched clips showing scenes from a car window. The same relationship between altitude and altruism appeared in several experiments. The researchers suggest that being high up, or the mere act of ascending, reminds us of lofty ways of thinking and behaving.

mental map of the area, but it also sends messages to the brain's fear and reward centers. Its neighbor, the hypothalamus, pumps out a hormonal response to those signals even before most of us have decided if a place is safe or dangerous. Places that seem too sterile or too confusing can trigger the release of adrenaline and cortisol, the hormones associated with fear and anxiety. Places that seem familiar, navigable, and that trigger good memories, are more likely to activate hits of feel-good serotonin, as well as the hormone that rewards and promotes feelings of interpersonal trust: oxytocin.

"The human brain is adaptive, and constantly tuning itself to the environment it is in," the neuroeconomist Paul Zak told me the day I met him in Anaheim, California. Zak is the researcher who discovered the key role that oxytocin plays in mediating human relationships. Unlike some more solitary mammals, Zak explained, humans have a huge concentration of oxytocin receptors in the oldest parts of our brain, which can kick into gear even before we have started talking to people.

This should be a concern for city makers because, as much as we are drawn to other people, neither culture nor biological mechanisms ensure that we will always treat strangers well. For example, Dutch researchers found that oxytocin, which should reward us for engaging in cooperative or altruistic behavior, has what might be called a xenophobic bias. After puffing a synthetic version of oxytocin, Dutch students were offered the standard moral dilemma question: Would you throw someone in front of a train if doing so would save five other lives? Exposure to the oxytocin made the students less likely to toss someone with a traditional Dutch name in front of the train, but *more likely* to sacrifice someone whose name sounded Muslim. Such anti-cosmopolitan tribalism can seem depressing until you consider the miracle of trust and cooperation that great cities, and especially great public places, can foster. Design can prime us toward trust and empathy, so that we regard more people as worthy of care and consideration.

To demonstrate this idea, Zak took me for a walk down Southern California's most convivial street, which, in a sad commentary on the state of American public space, sits beyond the fare gate at the entrance to Disneyland.

We crossed under the berm that surrounds the theme park, traversed the faux town square with its veranda-fronted city hall, then paused midway down Main Street U.S.A., that simulacrum of ultra-happy urbanity. The place was full of people of all ages and races, pushing strollers, walking hand in hand, window-shopping, and taking photos among the arcades and eateries.

We inserted some incivility into that crowd. At Zak's urging, I leaned my shoulder toward passing bodies, first brushing passersby, then making full contact. It was just the kind of behavior that would get you slugged on other streets, but time and again I got a smile, a steadying hand, or an apology. I tried dropping my wallet several times and got it back every time with an enthusiasm that bordered on the ceremonial. Then we upped the ante. We accosted random strangers and asked them for hugs. This was a bizarre request from two grown men, but the Main Streeters, men and women, responded with open arms and little hesitation. The place displayed a pro-social demeanor that was almost as cartoonish as the setting.

There are many reasons for the cheeriness on Disney's Main Street U.S.A., not least of which is the fact that people go there intending to be happy. But Zak encouraged me not to ignore the powerful priming effects of the landscape around us. No storefront on this Main Street is more than three stories high, but those unused top floors play a visual trick. They have been shrunk to five-eighths size, giving the buildings the comfortable, unthreatening aura of toys. Meanwhile, from the striped awnings and gilded window lettering to the faux plaster detailing on each facade, every detail on the artificial street is intended to draw you deeper into a state of nostalgic ease.*

The scene enthralled the pioneering neuroimmunologist Esther

---

*Disney and his designers all came from the film industry, and they designed their Main Street to work like a scene in a movie, with props so compelling that every visitor feels as though she has become a part of the scene. They wanted visitors specifically to forget the dehumanizing sprawl that was even then creeping out from Los Angeles. "In the cities we're threatened . . . We don't talk to people, we don't believe everything we hear, we don't look people in the eye . . . We don't trust people. We find ourselves alone. If we keep pulling these blinds down and cutting ourselves off, we die a little bit," explained John Hench, Disney's top lieutenant and leader of the group Disney dubbed his Imagineers back in 1978. "Walt wanted to reassure people . . . There's some nostalgia involved, of course, but nostalgia for what? There was never a main street like this one. But it reminds you of some things about yourself that you've forgotten about."

Sternberg on her first visit. Sternberg, who examines the connection between environment, health, and the human brain, concluded that Main Street U.S.A.'s designers had an uncanny understanding of the neuroscience of place. "They did it brilliantly. They figured out in the 1950s and '60s, long before we understood neuroscience, exactly how to use design to get people from a place of anxiety and fear to a place of hope and happiness," she told me.

The key to the place effect lies in the way that the brain links memory and emotion. On the one hand, Main Street U.S.A.'s evocative landmarks—quaint train station, city hall, distant Sleeping Beauty castle—instantly orient you to the landscape, reducing the anxiety you are hardwired to feel when you are unsure of your location in a complex environment. At the same time, those elements serve as emotional triggers. The hippocampus responds not just to visual signals, but to all our senses, including smell. So whether it is a candy-striped awning or the scent of cooking fudge wafting out over the sidewalk, Disney's references trigger memories that produce feelings of safety and calm—though these memories are just as likely to have been drawn from an invented past as from our own experiences. (The effect is so powerful that developers of care facilities for dementia patients have replicated Main Street U.S.A. in common spaces whose landmarks and street activity are intended to comfort residents with reminders of a small-town past.)

Designing Antisociality

Disney's street may be a simulacrum, an imitation of someone's idea of a real place, but the calming and pro-social effect it has on people is undeniable. This is not to suggest that every public space should attempt Disney's historical trickery, but we should acknowledge that every urban landscape is a collection of memory- and emotion-activating symbols. Every plaza, park, or architectural facade sends messages about who we are and what the street is for.

The effect of aesthetics on emotions has been documented extensively. We know, for example, that the frequent sight of garbage, graffiti, and disrepair produces alienation and depression, especially among the elderly. We know from research on biophilia that infusions of nature don't merely calm the mind, they alter our attitudes, making us more trusting and generous toward other people.

We also know that sharp architectural angles light up the brain's fear centers much like the sight of a knife or a thorn, releasing stress hormones that make us less likely to pause and engage with places and people. (This effect can be witnessed on the street outside Daniel Libeskind's Crystal, an addition to the Royal Ontario Museum in Toronto, where giant prisms of steel, aluminum, and glass slice threateningly toward the sidewalk, managing the amazing feat of emptying people from a once-busy stretch of Bloor Street.)

But the urban landscape does not need to adopt a spectacularly threatening stance to drive people away. Antisocial spaces are as common in the city as blank walls. In fact, blank walls are part of the problem.

Jan Gehl's studies of street edges provide evidence. Gehl and others have found that if a street features uniform facades with hardly any doors, variety, or functions, people move past as quickly as possible. But if a street features varied facades, lots of openings, and a high density of functions per block, people walk more slowly. They pause more often. People are actually more likely to stop and make cell phone calls in front of lively facades than in front of dead ones.

During our experiments at the BMW Guggenheim Lab in New York City, we found that such long, dead facades do not just speed people up physically; they bring them down emotionally. On East Houston Street in Lower Manhattan, the small-lot urban fabric between Orchard and Ludlow was replaced in 2006 by a Whole Foods grocery store that presents a nearly unbroken swath of smoked glass for much of an entire city block. Volunteers who joined our psychological tours of the neighborhood reported feeling markedly less happy on the sidewalk outside this facade than almost anywhere else on their tour. They felt much better once they got to a grittier but lively stretch of shops and restaurants just a block east on Houston.

This points to an emerging disaster in street psychology. As suburban retailers begin to colonize central cities, block after block of bric-a-brac and mom-and-pop-scale buildings and shops are being replaced by blank, cold spaces that effectively bleach street edges of conviviality. It is an unneccessary act of theft, and its consequences

Emotional Landscapes

East Houston Street, New York City: People reported feeling significantly happier along the messy but active street front at top than they did along the blank but tidy facade at bottom. (*Top*: Charles Montgomery; *above*: Alexandra Bolinder-Gibsand)

go beyond aesthetics, or even the massive reduction in the variety of goods and services that results when one giant retailer takes over a block. The big-boxing of a city block harms the physical health of people living nearby, especially the elderly. Seniors who live among long stretches of dead frontage have actually been found to age more quickly than those who live on blocks with plenty of doors, windows, porch stoops, and destinations. Because supersize architecture and blank stretches of sidewalk push their daily destinations beyond walking distance, they get weaker and slower, they socialize less outside the home, and they volunteer less.*

Fortunately, some cities have begun to enact laws to stop developers from killing the sociability of their streets. The Australian city of Melbourne adopted rules banning long, blank facades and forcing new shops and restaurants to have doors or display windows covering at least 80 percent of their frontage. Danish cities have gone further. In the 1980s most large cities in the country actually restricted banks from opening new branches on their main shopping streets. It is not that Danes hate banks; it is that passive bank facades bleed life from the sidewalk, and too many of them can kill a street. It is that the citizenry's right to a healthy, life-giving public realm has trumped anyone's right to kill it—a notion presumably ignored on those Manhattan blocks where four banks compete across corners.

New York City began playing catch-up in 2012, adopting new zoning that limited the ground-floor width of new stores on major avenues on the Upper West Side. On busy Amsterdam and Columbus avenues, buildings on lots wider than fifty feet will have to feature at least two nonresidential businesses, and transparent facades. Banks on Broadway will be restricted to just twenty-five feet of frontage. The move was partly an attempt to stop big national retailers and banks from gobbling up the mom-and-pop stores that give the neighborhood its character. "Stores are the soul of the neighborhood," Gale Brewer, a neighborhood councilwoman, told *The New York Times.* "Small pharmacies, shoe stores, they mean everything to us." By saving small business, the measure would also save human-scale blocks.

Vancouver has proved that dense cities can meet commercial real estate needs while keeping their architecture friendly. Even big-box retailers have had to change up their morphology to get a toehold in the city. Thus, a Costco and its parking lot were buried beneath slim condo towers and rows of street-level town houses on one end of Vancouver's downtown peninsula. And near City Hall, a Home Depot

---

*Studies of seniors living in Montreal found that elderly people who lived on blocks that had front porches and stoops actually had stronger legs and hands than those living on more barren blocks. Meanwhile, those who could actually walk to shops and services were more likely to volunteer, visit other people, and stay active.

and a Winners have been stacked like a hamburger patty *on top* of a row of street-front businesses and *beneath* a leafy garnish of garden apartments. The big boxes get their own entrances on the corner, while the rest of the block facade is shared by a Starbucks, a grocer, and several other shops. The result: the urge for low prices does not kill the street. People actually walk, bike, or take the subway to the big box and sit out front at the Starbucks, sipping their lattes in the rain.

Reoccupation

Some designers work specifically to drive people away. For a time, there was perhaps no greater density of antisocial public spaces on earth than Midtown Manhattan. In 1961 the city enacted a well-meaning ordinance granting developers the right to build higher towers in exchange for building public plazas on their property. What happened in the following decades showed just how dangerous it can be to leave the design of public life to private hands.

Most of these private-public spaces—commonly known as bonus plazas—were deeply misanthropic. General Motors got seven extra stories for building a plaza in front of its monolithic tower on Fifth Avenue in 1968, but the architect sank the plaza deep below the street and capped its ledges with railings that, as William Whyte noted, were perfect for catching you right in the small of the back should you try to sit. This was no anomaly. By 2000, more than half of the bonus plazas in Midtown and the Financial District either did not attract people or actively repelled them. This was exactly their intent. Richard Roth, whose firm, Emery Roth and Sons, designed a quarter of the bonus plaza buildings in midtown and downtown, told sociologist Gregory Smithsimon that his clients explicitly instructed him to build plazas that encouraged people to move through them quickly and not stop. "They kept putting less and less in. The client kept saying, 'No, I want it as minimal as possible,'" Roth recalled. It was acceptable to have people pause and gape at the architecture. It was not acceptable for them to get too comfortable.

Sometimes the designers used gates and fences to achieve the desired antisocial effect, but painful seating, odd edges, and sunken areas that were dark, cold, hard to reach, and scary were just as effective.

Sometimes they left the plaza space entirely blank, creating empty deserts in what were otherwise crowded, space-starved districts. Citizens had traded the air above their cities to property developers for much-needed public space on the ground, only to see developers use design to steal it back.

But the movement to invite people back to city spaces that began in Copenhagen has spread to cities around the world. In New York City, William Whyte's followers have used his theories on sociability to repair the sickliest of places. Whyte's onetime research assistant Fred Kent founded the nonprofit Project for Public Spaces to carry out the social observer's vision. Early on, Project for Public Spaces was asked by the owners of Rockefeller Center to suggest how spikes might be configured to keep people from sitting under or touching the yew trees on their plaza. The plaza management had always seen people as a problem. They did not want the hassle of dealing with vagrants or litterbugs. Kent politely suggested that rather than fortifying their trees, they add benches for people to sit on. The owners took a chance and retrofitted the plazas to accommodate, rather than repel, people. It was the beginning of a gradual transformation that has seen Rockefeller Center become one of the most visited sites in the entire city. Here, and everywhere they intervene, Whyte's disciples employ a method he called triangulation, in which external stimuli are arranged in ways that nudge people close enough together to begin talking. In its simplest form, triangulation might mean positioning a public telephone booth, a garbage can, and a bench beside one another, or simply giving a busker permission to perform near a set of stairs—anything to slow people down in proximity.

Once you become aware of the method, it's possible to see triangulation at work in most of the world's best-loved public places. It works in the Piazza del Campo, where cafés, museums, bollards, and that sloping brick amphitheater create multiple reasons for arrival. The Place des Vosges, the oldest planned square in Paris, was itself conceived as a living room for the city when it was laid out more than four hundred years ago. Today, lawns, sandboxes, and fountains compete for attention with the lure of the shops and cafés that line the arcades at the square's edge.

Triangulation found new life in higher-stakes design when another of Whyte's disciples, Amanda Burden, was hired as New York

City's director of planning. Under Burden's tenure, the repopulation of the city's bonus plazas began in earnest. The once-desolate General Motors Building plaza, for example, has been reinvigorated with a blend of public comforts and commercial panache. Movable chairs and tables sit beneath half a dozen honey locust trees overlooking a shallow pool, creating an inviting lunchtime destination. But the plaza's most memorable feature is the house-size glass cube that sits at its heart. Reminiscent of I. M. Pei's Pyramid in the courtyard of the Louvre, the cube is actually an entrance to a subterranean Apple Store. The space vibrates with life at various speeds and intimacies. On a late September afternoon I observed a young girl poking at her reflection in the pool, a suited businessman crumpled in a power snooze, a dozen couples lunching together, and dozens more simply eyeing the rest of us. It was people that made the space most interesting and worthwhile, but it took design to draw us together and slow us down just enough to transform that landscape of marble, concrete, water, and glass into a social environment.

It can be tempting to see public conviviality as some kind of high science, dependent entirely on master planners and site programmers. But sometimes it is simply a matter of setting street life free around the city's natural systems. For example, I once lived in Copilco, a messy collage of brick and rebar at the south end of Mexico City. My favorite place in this neighborhood was also its ugliest: a small plaza clinging to the edge of Eje Diez Sur, an eight-lane avenue where boxy minibuses known as *peseros* spewed blue smoke and lurched like bulls along the curb. Power transmission lines sagged overhead. Billboards advertising deodorant and mobile phones incised the skyline. For all this dreariness, something special happened on that plaza. The alchemy was twofold: First, a marble staircase at its west edge led down to a subterranean metro station. Every hour, hundreds of people flowed in and out, making connections with the *peseros* on Eje Diez or walking to the nearby National Autonomous University. Second, the plaza's edges were lined with food stalls that intercepted the human flow. Vendors offered fresh-squeezed papaya and orange juice or the unofficial civic dish, *tacos al pastor*, from their corrugated steel shacks. At sunset the ugly skyline disappeared above lines of strung bulbs. Cumbia thunk-thunked through the night air. We travelers would gather in tight circles, plastic plates in hand, squeezing lime onto our tacos in the red-orange light of the *pastor* grill. The rough edge of Eje Diez became a living room, a nexus of conviviality on our journeys.

There is a message for all city makers here. It is that with the right triangulation, even the ugliest of places can be infused with the warmth that turns strangers into familiars by giving us enough reason to slow down. In this case, the subway station provided fuel for the fire of conviviality, but the flame depended on something actually happening in that space. *Something happened because something was allowed to happen,* a rare condition in cities dominated by automobiles or overregulation. But the food cart is starting to become a favorite of urban planners in rich cities. From Portland and Boston to Calgary, planners use mobile vendors as a means of tactical urbanism, infusing enough life to long-dead blocks to draw people and, eventually, brick-and-mortar businesses.

Velocities

For all its rough glory, there is a starker lesson rubbing up against that Copilco plaza. Getting there from the north requires a death-defying sprint through a stampede of *peseros* and even faster-moving taxis and private cars on Eje Diez, one of a network of highway-like arteries laid down across Mexico City in the 1970s. The road edge is hostile. The noise from engines and horns is unnerving. Venture beyond the parked *peseros*, and the danger feels totally enveloping. It changes your mood and your method, hardening you even as you approach it.

Cities that care about livability have got to start paying attention to the psychological effect that traffic has on the experience of public space.

Human bones have evolved to withstand impact with hard surfaces up to a speed of about twenty miles per hour, which is faster than a reasonably fit person can run.* So it is natural to get anxious when confronted with hard objects moving faster than that. Add a bunch of fast-moving objects to a space and make those objects big

---

*In his 2009 World Championship hundred-meter sprint, Usain Bolt's average ground speed was 23.35 miles per hour.

enough to pose a salient danger, and we get even more uncomfortable. Make those objects unpredictable and noisy, and you have created a perfect storm of stimulus to preoccupy anyone who might enter that space without the benefit of his own protective shell. Yet this is the condition we have designed into most modern city streets.

No amount of triangulation can account for the corrupting influence that high-velocity transport has on the psychology of public space. In a classic 1971 study of several parallel streets in San Francisco, Donald Appleyard found a direct relationship between traffic and social life. On a street with only light traffic (two thousand cars per day), children played on the sidewalks and street, people socialized on their front steps, and everyone reported having a tight web of contacts with neighbors on both sides of the street. On a nearly identical street with eight thousand cars passing per day, there was a dramatic drop in social activity and friendships. Another similar street with sixteen thousand passing cars saw almost nothing happening in the public realm, and social ties were few and far between. The only significant difference between these streets was the amount of car traffic pouring through them. But when asked to describe their neighborhood, people on the high-traffic street actually had a harder time remembering what the street edges looked like. In contrast to low-traffic street residents, they described their street as a lonely place to live. Automobiles had the power to turn a neighborhood street into a non-place.

This is partly a result of the danger and uncertainty that auto traffic infuses into a streetscape. But traffic's social corrosion also stems from the noise it produces. We are less likely to talk to one another when it is noisy. We end conversations sooner. We are more likely to disagree, to become agitated, and to fight with the people we are talking to. We are much less likely to help strangers.* We become less patient, less generous, less helpful, and less social, no matter how detailed and inviting the street edge might be.

We are influenced by noise even when we don't know it. Even the sound of light car traffic at night is enough to flood your system with

*In fact, field experiments have shown that in noisy environments, people are systematically less likely to help a stranger pick up a dropped stack of books or to give someone change for a phone call.

Light Traffic Street
- *2,000 vehicles/day*
- *3.0 friends/person on block*
- *6.3 acquaintances*

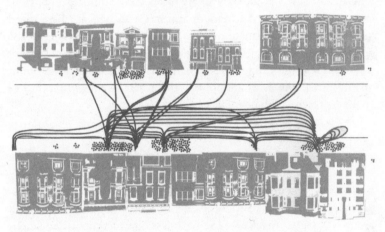

⁂ Where people gather ——————— Where people have friends

Heavy Traffic Street
- *16,000 vehicles/day*
- *.9 friends/person on block*
- *3.1 acquaintances*

How Traffic Alters the Social Life of Streets
In his famous 1972 study, Donald Appleyard showed how traffic influenced patterns of friendship on parallel streets in San Francisco. The more traffic there was, the fewer local friends and acquaintances residents had. (All images based on Appleyard, Donald, and M. Lintell, "The Environmental Quality of Streets: The Residents' Viewpoint," *Journal of the American Planning Association*, 1972: 84–101; redesign by Robin Smith / Streetfilms)

stress hormones. Most city dwellers are conditioned to hear car horns and emergency vehicle sirens as signs of danger, even if we know that these sounds are intended for other people's ears. And when we are stressed, we retreat from each other and the world.

This is perhaps the most insidious way that the system of dispersal has punished those who live closer together. Most of the noise, air pollution, danger, and perceived crowding in modern cities occurs because we have configured urban spaces to facilitate high-speed travel in private automobiles. We have traded conviviality for the convenience of those who wish to experience streets as briefly as possible. This is deeply unfair to people who live in central cities, for whom streets function as the soft social space between their destinations.

You cannot separate the social life of urban spaces from the velocity of the activities happening there. Public life begins when we slow down. This is why reducing velocity has become municipal policy in cities across the United Kingdom and in Copenhagen, where speed limits have been reduced to nine miles per hour on some streets. The city's traffic director, Niels Torslov, told me that his department considers it a rounding success when most of the people they count on any particular street are not moving at all. It's a sign that they've created a place worth being in.

The Social Life of Parking

Even the way we organize car parking can have a social effect. Transportation planner and Brookings Institution fellow Lawrence Frank found that people in cities are actually less likely to know their neighbors if the shops in their area have parking lots in front of them. The dynamic at play is obvious: those parking lots shift the balance of shoppers from local people toward people just passing through. You can't blame a business for wanting to extend its reach. But when an entire city is designed around easy parking, then everyone shops farther from home, and the chances of bumping into people you might actually see again dwindles.

Ample, easy parking is the hallmark of the dispersed city. It is also a killer of street life. A cruise through Los Angeles illustrates the dynamic. The city's downtown has been said to contain more parking spaces per acre than any other place on earth, and its streets are some of the most desolate. Back in the late 1990s, civic boosters hoped that the Disney Concert Hall, a stainless steel–clad icon by starchitect Frank Gehry, would pump some life into L.A.'s Bunker Hill district. The city raised $110 million in bonds to build space for more than two thousand cars—six levels of parking right beneath the hall. Aside from creating a huge burden for the building's tenant, the Los Angeles Philharmonic (which is contractually bound to put on an astounding 128 concerts each winter season in order to pay the debt service on the garage), the structure has utterly failed to revive area streets. This is because people who drive to the Disney Hall never actually leave the building, noted Donald Shoup, a professor of urban planning at the University of California, Los Angeles, and the world's foremost expert on the effects of parking.

"The full experience of an iconic Los Angeles building begins and ends in its parking garage, not in the city itself," Shoup and his graduate student Michael Manville wrote in a damning analysis. The typical concertgoer now parks underground, rides a series of cascading escalators up into the Disney Hall foyer, and leaves the same way. The result? The surrounding streets remain empty, largely bereft of cafés, bars, and shops, as well as the people who might stop in them. It's a lonely place.

As much as we all love the convenience of proximal parking, the garage effect kills life on residential neighborhood streets, too. If all the people in your neighborhood have room for their cars inside their homes or under their apartments, you are much less likely to see them on the sidewalk. You realize how much this matters only when you see a fully realized alternative. I found one in the heart of Germany's Black Forest.

Vauban, an experimental green neighborhood of about five thousand people, is built on a former military base, a 10-minute streetcar ride from the medieval heart of Freiburg. A checkerboard of apartments, town houses, and small parks are arranged amid a grid of roads and pathways, all gathered along a central avenue flanked by broad lawns, pathways, and a streetcar track.

At the crack of dawn on a September morning I joined a five-year-old boy named Leonard and his mother on his first bike ride to school. We wobbled along a quiet street to the main drag, where rush hour was in full swing—rush hour consisting almost entirely of people walking to school, to streetcar stops, and to two futuristic-looking garages on the edge of the village. The place was bubbling with just the kind of life that architects like to drop into their renderings.

That scene was the product of a velocity intervention. You can drive through most of Vauban if you want, but it is much faster and significantly less annoying to walk: on residential streets, the speed limit for cars is a languid five miles per hour. But the city's real innovation is in the way it alters the geography of parking. Long-term on-street parking is forbidden. Meanwhile, Vauban's residential ownership structure turns the economics of residential parking up-side down. In most cities, the cost of parking is rolled into the sale price of your home. But if you move to Vauban, you have two options. If you own a car, you are contractually obligated to purchase a park-ing spot in one of the two garages at the edge of town. (That can be a shock. Leonard's parents bought their parking spot for 20,000 euros.) But if you don't own a car—and you are willing to sign an intimidat-ing "car-free" pledge—you do not have to fork out for a parking spot. Instead, you buy a share of a leafy lot on the edge of town for about 3,700 euros. (This is an investment: if the car-free culture prevails, you will share that park with everyone. If Vauban requires more parking, you stand to make a sizable return.)

This rationalization of car costs means that no matter how Vau-banites get to work, they tend to walk or cycle when they are close to home. That's why the streets are full of people. That's why they are safe for five-year-old commuters.

What Vauban proves is that life can be infused into a community just by adjusting the speed of streets, and the distance between park-ing facilities and people's front doors. The farther away the parking, the livelier the street. It may seem outrageous to parking-obsessed North Americans, but Vauban's parking burden has helped make it one of the most popular suburbs of Freiburg. Leonard sure liked it. When we arrived at his school, the five-year-old turned to me and bellowed something in German. He beamed as his mother, Petra Marqua, translated, "Tomorrow I get to ride to school all by myself."

Those slow streets, filled with so many familiar faces, made the ride so safe that Petra acquiesced.

When Roads Stop Being Roads

Most cities do not have the luxury of planning from scratch. The prime real estate in the densest parts of town has all been accounted for, so cities that want more space for people are left to trade airspace with developers in exchange for bonus plazas, or to invest heavily in acquiring new land. But these are not the only options, especially given the tremendous resource that we, as citizens, already control. All the real estate now used to facilitate the movement and storage of private automobiles is public, and it can be used any way we decide. Cities that are serious about the happiness of their citizens have already begun to confront their relationship with velocity. They are making what once seemed to be radical decisions about what—and whom—streets are for.

This latest wave of experiments in public space can be traced back to Bogotá, and the moment when a quirky idea found its champion in an accidental city bureaucrat. Guillermo Peñalosa began his public life in a supporting role. He campaigned twice on behalf of his older brother, Enrique, who lost his first two mayoral bids in 1991 and 1994. Both brothers saw design as a way to heal a society mired in inequity and civil war, but the younger Peñalosa was particularly obsessed with parks. After youthful wanderings in New York City's Central Park, he found a philosophical role model in the park's co-architect, Frederick Law Olmsted.

"In New York at that time, everyone hated everyone: the blacks and whites and Jews, the locals and the immigrants, they all hated each other," Peñalosa said of the years in the mid-nineteenth century during which Central Park was born. "Olmsted believed that a good public space would help all these people break down the barriers by sharing space and getting to know each other."* He envisioned the same thing for Bogotá.

When his brother lost the 1994 election, Guillermo Peñalosa called the mayor-elect, Antanas Mockus, to convince him to at least

---

*Olmsted did impose his philosophy of social equity on the park. The Mall, the forty-foot promenade carved into the landscape from Sixty-sixth to Seventy-second streets and lined with shade trees, was built specifically to encourage all kinds of people to stroll together in a landscape of formal gregariousness.

try some of his ideas. Guillermo is a softer character than his older brother: less an evangelist and more of a negotiator, a persuader. To his surprise, Mockus hired him as his commissioner of parks, sports, and recreation and gave him free rein. Peñalosa was able to create two hundred new parks by using derelict land the city already owned. But this was only a small dent in the city's public space deficit, and it was just too expensive to buy more land. Peñalosa saw an opportunity in a quirky program known as the Ciclovía, which had, for more than a decade, seen eight miles of busy roads barricaded and opened to cyclists, walkers, and joggers every Sunday. It wasn't so much a car-free day as an ephemeral stretching of parkland. Even in a city where class lines were rigid and violence and fear were rampant, the program drew people from all of Bogotá's social classes together in spaces that had been off-limits to everyone for decades. It embodied Olmsted's philosophies, Peñalosa realized. "I thought that the Ciclovía could be Bogotá's own Central Park!"

If the Ciclovía was going to succeed in nudging the rich and the poor together across the city, it needed a lot more room. Guillermo supersized it, eventually claiming an interconnected network of sixty-odd miles of the city's major roads. It may have been the cheapest public space project ever. There was almost no capital investment at all, beyond the purchase of inexpensive traffic barriers. All it really required was political will.

In an age of car-oriented planning, this pavement grab was still a radical move, but eventually more than a million cyclists, skaters, and strollers began coming out to enjoy the space each week. It was more popular than the pope's visit.

The Ciclovía method has now been taken up across Colombia and exported around the world, from Melbourne to Miami, temporarily transforming streets that nobody could have imagined walking along. The idea had its greatest test on three sunny Saturdays in the summer of 2008, when New York City's Department of Transportation erected barriers so that people on foot, bikes, and Rollerblades could claim several major thoroughfares, including Park Avenue. Thousands of people filled the so-called Summer Streets. They gathered for yoga, street-side samba, and tai chi classes. Many just walked, apparently stunned to see their own feet touching the pavement in the middle of the avenue. Residents along Park Avenue strolled out and plunked

Ciclovía

Every Sunday, hundreds of thousands of people come out to walk, ride, and dance on the street during Bogotá's Ciclovía. The initiative has turned miles of pavement into temporary extensions of the city's park system. (Gil Peñalosa / 8-80 Cities)

down lawn chairs on the grass median, as though it were the park it hadn't been for a hundred years.

Here was New York, with all its awesome vertical geometries, its thrills and social possibilities, now suddenly with space to stretch and breathe. Without the internal combustion roar you could yell at a friend a block away and he would turn and smile. It was, by almost all accounts, a marvelous experience.

It was also an exercise in immersive social marketing. Each Ciclovía or Summer Streets or car-free day offers proof that the city and its roads are fluid and malleable—they can change anytime people really want them to. After a Ciclovía, cities invariably begin to consider large-scale changes in the way that they organize public space and mobility. Participants begin to ask what streets are for, and they invariably seize upon the answer that Copenhageners found decades ago: streets are for whatever we decide they are for, and central cities need not accept the discomforts thrust on them by dispersal.

8. Mobilicities I
How Moving Feels, and Why It Does Not Feel Better

The heavens themselves run continually round, the sun riseth and sets, the moon increaseth and decreaseth, stars and planets keep their constant motions, the air is still tossed by the winds, the waters ebb and flow, to their conservation no doubt, to teach us that we should ever be in action.

—Robert Burton, *The Anatomy of Melancholy*

When we talk about cities, we usually end up talking about how various places look and perhaps how it feels to be there in those places. But to stop there misses half the story, because the way we experience most parts of cities is at velocity: we glide past on the way to somewhere else. City life is as much about moving *through* landscapes as it is about being *in* them.

This is a critical point; not only does the city shape the way we move, but our movements shape the city in return. Jan Gehl rightly pointed out that designing a road for one mode of movement—say, travel in private automobiles—causes the road to fill up with people using that mode, in this case, driving cars. But the relationship goes both ways. The more we choose to drive, the more the urban system gets reconfigured to accommodate drivers, in an endless feedback loop of journeys and changing landscapes.

So we can't fully understand the effect that the city has on happiness without considering how it feels to move through it and how that feeling guides our behavior. But the psychology of mobility is a house of mirrors where what we want, what we do, and what makes us feel good are rarely the same choice.

I have met and interviewed dozens of commuters in cities around the world, people whose journeys are spectacularly varied in texture and difficulty. None of them embodies the complex psychology of the urban traveler as thoroughly as Robert Judge, a forty-eight-year-old husband and father who once wrote to a Canadian radio program explaining how much he enjoyed going grocery shopping on his bicycle. Judge's confession would have been unremarkable if he did not happen to live in Saskatoon, Saskatchewan, where the average temperature in January hovers around 1 degree Fahrenheit. The city stays frozen and snowy for almost half the year. It is the last place you would imagine anyone wanting to depend on a bicycle.

I called Judge up to inquire about his sanity. He told me that he and his wife had decided to go car-free a couple of years back. He liked a challenge. He began by bolting a utility tub to a bike trailer so he could haul as much as a hundred pounds of groceries. He bought studded tires. He acquired expedition ski clothes, including a puff jacket with an arctic collar to protect his lips and windpipe from the chill. Then Judge hit the road.

"Biking in winter is kind of like walking on hot coals: people say you can't do it. They say it's impossible! But then you just go and do it," he told me. "First you feel the cold in your mouth and nose. It's twenty-five below and the wind is blowing. Your eyes fill up with tears for the first few blocks, but then they clear up, and you just keep going."

Judge was especially proud of his trips to Superstore, a big-box grocery outlet about three and a half miles from his house in an inner suburb. He could make it there in about twenty minutes. With his studded tires, he could outmaneuver most cars on the icy road, but people would give him funny looks when they saw him pulling up at the edge of the big-box parking lot. Some people asked if he was homeless. Others offered him a ride. But Judge didn't want their help. He even grew to appreciate the snowdrifts that blew across his route. He would steer his bicycle through fresh drifts just so people would see the tracks and know that the lone cyclist had been there and prevailed.

Judge's pleasure in an experience that seems slower, more difficult, and considerably more uncomfortable than the alternative might seem bizarre. He explained it by way of a story: Sometimes, he said, he would pick up his three-year-old son from day care and put him on the backseat of his tandem bike and they would pedal home along the South Saskatchewan River. The snow would muffle the noise of the city. Dusk would paint the sky in colors so exquisite that Judge could not begin to find names for them. The snow would reflect those hues. It would glow like the sky, and Judge would breathe in the cold air and hear his son breathing behind him, and he would feel as though together they had become part of winter itself.

Few people share Judge's tolerance for discomfort, hard work, and inconvenience, but most of us are more like him than we might imagine. Our urban journeys can meet all kinds of psychological needs. "For many, the commute really is a kind of heroic quest," Patricia Mokhtarian, a University of California, Davis, transportation engineer, said after I told her Judge's story. She said many car commuters feel the same way. "Remember the *Odyssey*, where the heroes launch their ships and head off to face adventures and traumas before making their return? Well, the commute can be this heroic going out into the world, conquering the traffic, surviving, and coming home to the warm reception of family."

People may complain about commuting, but after surveying hundreds of commuters in California, Mokhtarian discovered that the average person actually prefers to be forced to travel for part of every day. "We hear many people say, 'Darn, my commute is not long enough!'" Of course, few people pine for a super-commute. The trip time most people *wish* they had is about sixteen minutes, one way.* Still, Mokhtarian and other travel researchers insist that long or short, every commute is a ritual that can alter our very sense of who we are and what is our place in the world.

---

*Like the people in her studies, Mokhtarian likes the ritual transition between home and work. In fact, rather than living near her office in the cozy hamlet of Davis, she chose to live in the nearby town of Woodland, a conscious choice that forced her to drive to work each day. Commute time? Sixteen minutes, door-to-door.

Driving Sideways

If you were to judge the hedonic utility of various modes of travel by how many people choose them each day, there would be absolutely no substitute for driving an automobile—at least not in North America. Nearly nine in ten American commuters drive to work every day. Three-quarters of Canadians and two-thirds of Brits do the same.

Drivers experience plenty of emotional dividends. When the road is clear, driving your own car embodies the psychological state known as mastery: drivers report feeling much more in charge of their lives than transit users or even their own passengers. Many commuters admitted to Mokhtarian that much of the pleasure of driving came simply from being seen in their fine cars. An upmarket vehicle is loaded with symbolic value that offers a powerful, if temporary, boost in status. The biochemical response is especially strong in young men. Researchers in Montreal found that when male college students spent a mere hour driving an expensive sports car—a $150,000 Porsche—they experienced a heady blast of testosterone, while driving an older, high-mileage Toyota Camry left them slightly drained. "The endocrinological response was substantial, irrespective of whether they had an audience or not," explained study coauthor Gad Saad, associate professor of marketing at Concordia University. In other words, the experience of driving a hot car triggered a hormonal response even when there were no hot babes to impress. No wonder four in ten Americans actually claim to *love* their cars.

Despite these romantic feelings, half of commuters living in big cities and suburbs claim to dislike the heroic journey they must make every day—an unhappy group made up mostly of drivers. Part of the problem is that cars fail to deliver the experience of freedom and speed that we all know they are capable of bestowing in a world of open roads. The urban system neutralizes their power. Luxury and sports cars might still offer their drivers a status bump, but the car's muscles cease to matter when it is surrounded by other cars.

Driving in traffic is harrowing for both brain and body. The blood of people who drive in cities is a high-test stew of stress hormones. The worse the traffic, the more your system is flooded with adrenaline and cortisol, the fight-or-flight juices that, in the short term, get your heart pumping faster, dilate your air passages, and help sharpen your alertness, but in the long term can make you ill. It can take as much as an hour to recover the ability to concentrate after a long urban commute. Researchers for Hewlett-Packard convinced volunteers in England to wear electrode caps during their commutes and found that whether they were driving or taking the train, peak-hour travelers suffered worse stress than fighter pilots or riot police facing mobs of angry protesters.*

If you have ever flown a spaceship through an asteroid belt or driven the Santa Ana Freeway from Anaheim to Los Angeles on a Friday evening, you will understand and have benefited from the heightened focus and alertness offered by the full-on adrenal rush. It can be thrilling in the short term, but if you bathe in these hormones for too long, they can be toxic. Your immune system will be compromised, your blood vessels and bones will weaken, and your brain cells will begin to die off from the stress. Chronic road rage can actually alter the shape of the amygdalae, the brain's almond-shaped fear centers, and kill cells in the hippocampus.

This is part of the reason why urban bus drivers get sick more often, miss work more frequently, and die younger than people in other occupations. One stress-medicine specialist, Dr. John Larson, reported that many of his heart attack patients had one thing in common: shortly before their hearts gave out, they had been enraged while driving. No wonder people start to report steady drops in life satisfaction the more their commute time exceeds Mokhtarian's utopian sixteen minutes, even if they don't attribute their misery to their commute.†

---

*Commuters' hearts raced at 145 beats per minute, well over double the normal rate. They experienced a surge in cortisol. And, in what was apparently a coping strategy, their brains underwent a bizarre temporary transformation that psychologist David Lewis dubbed "commuter amnesia." Their brains simply shut out stimulus from the outer world, and they forgot about most of the trip as soon as it was over.
†When Gallup and Healthways polled Americans, they found that the longer people's commute, the more likely they were to report chronic pain, high cholesterol, and general unhappiness. (People with commutes over ninety minutes have it the worst. They are the most likely to be anxious, tired, and fat. And they are much less likely than people with short journeys to say they enjoy life.)

Cars once promised us unparalleled freedom and convenience, but despite fantastic investments in roads and highways, and the almost complete configuration of North American cities to favor automobile travel, commute times have been getting steadily longer. Americans, for example, clocked in relatively the same average daily commute times for years—about forty minutes round-trip, not including time spent on other errands—since as far back as 1800. But the average American now spends more than fifty minutes commuting. Return commute times have shot past sixty-eight minutes in the New York megalopolis, seventy-four minutes in London, and a whopping eighty minutes in Toronto. Dozens of studies have now confirmed beyond doubt what Atlantans know from experience: the obvious solution to congestion—building more roads—simply produces more traffic, creating a hedonic treadmill of construction and frustration.

Happy Feet

One group of commuters reports enjoying themselves more than everyone else. Their route to happy mobility is simple. These are people who travel on their own steam like Robert Judge. They walk. They run. They ride bicycles.

Despite the obvious effort involved, self-propelled commuters report feeling that their trips are *easier* than the trips of people who sit still for most of the journey. They are the likeliest to say their trip was fun. Children overwhelmingly say they prefer finding their own way to school rather than being chauffeured. These are the sentiments of people in American and Canadian cities, which tend to be designed in ways that make walking and cycling unpleasant and dangerous. In the Netherlands, where road designers create safe spaces for bikes, cyclists report feeling more joy, less fear, less anger, less sadness than both drivers and transit users. Even in New York City, where the streets are loud, congested, aggressive, and dangerous, cyclists report enjoying their journeys more than anyone else.

Why would traveling more slowly and using more effort offer more satisfaction than driving? Part of the answer exists in basic human physiology. We were born to move—not merely to be transported,

Happy Travels

Percentage of commuters reporting
these emotions in the Netherlands:

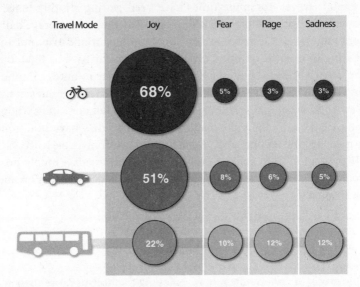

In the Netherlands, where road space is provided for everyone, cyclists are by far the happiest people on the road. Public transit users report being the most miserable, as they do in most other places. (Scott Keck; from Harms, L., P. Jorritsma, and N. Kalfs, *Beleving en beeldvorming van mobiliteit,* The Hague: Kennisinstituut voor Mobiliteitsbeleid, 2007)

but to use our bodies to propel us across the landscape. Our genetic forebears have been walking for four million years.*

How much did we once walk every day? Loren Cordain, a profes-

---

*To put our history of mobility into perspective, try to picture time since the day the first hominid stood tall as a walk across New York's Central Park, all fifty-one blocks from Harlem to Midtown Manhattan. We'd be hunter-gatherers from end to end for thousands of steps, right until the moment we could spot the doorman of the Plaza Hotel on Fifty-ninth Street. The age of farming would almost add up to the sprint across Fifty-ninth. We'd enter the age of cities on the sidewalk right in front of the hotel. The years during which we've let automobiles do the work for us would take up less than the depth of one red carpet–clad step at the hotel's front door.

sor of health and exercise science at Colorado State University, tried to find out by comparing the daily energy expenditure of the average sedentary office worker to modern hunter-gatherers such as the !Kung of southern Africa. In some parts, !Kung women still spend their days collecting nuts, berries, and roots while the men hunt lizards, wildebeests, and whatever else they can track down in the desert. The women tend to walk about six miles per day and the men as much as nine, often burdened by heavy loads. The average American office worker gets barely a fifth of that exercise.

This is a troubling state of affairs, given that immobility is to the human body what rust is to the classic car. Stop moving long enough, and your muscles will atrophy. Bones will weaken. Blood will clot. You will find it harder to concentrate and solve problems. Immobility is not merely a state closer to death: it hastens it. Just spending too much time sitting shortens your life span.

We have evolved to get smarter and cheerier when we exercise, provided we can do it someplace where we aren't burning, freezing, terrified, or in other mortal danger. Robert Thayer, a professor of psychology at California State University, fitted dozens of students with pedometers, then sent them back to their regular lives. Over the course of twenty days, the volunteers answered survey questions about their moods, attitudes, diet, and happiness. The average student walked 9,217 steps a day—much more than the typical American, though much less than a !Kung tribesman.* But within that volunteer group, people who walked more tended to feel more energetic and upbeat. They had higher self-esteem. They were happier. They even felt that their food was better for them.

"We're talking about a wider phenomenon here than just walk more, feel more energy. We're talking about walk more, be happier, have higher self-esteem, be more into your diet and also the nutritiousness of your diet," Thayer said. The psychologist has devoted his life to the study of human moods. In test after test he proved that the most powerful way to fix a dark mood is simply to take a brisk walk. "Walking works like a drug, and it starts working even after a few steps."

As the philosopher Søren Kierkegaard put it, there is no thought

---

*The average walking step is 2.5 feet. So the average student walked around 4.5 miles each day, much more than the typical American.

so burdensome that you cannot walk away from it. We can literally walk ourselves into a state of well-being.

The same is true of cycling, although a bicycle has the added benefit of giving even a lazy rider the ability to travel three or four times faster than someone walking, while using less than a quarter of the energy. A bicycle can expand the self-propelled travelers' geographical reach by an astounding nine or sixteen times. Quite simply, a human on a bicycle is the most efficient traveler among all machines and animals.

Even those who endure the most severe bicycle trips seem to take pleasure in them. They feel capable. They feel free. They feel and are healthier. The average convert to bike commuting loses thirteen pounds in the first year. They may not all attain Robert Judge's level of transcendence, but cyclists report feeling connected to the world around them in a way that is simply not possible in the sealed environment of an automobile or a bus or a subway car. Their journeys are both sensual and kinesthetic.

All this points to two problems in urban mobility. First, people are not maximizing happiness on their commutes, especially in North American cities. Second, and perhaps more urgent, most of us are overwhelmingly choosing the most polluting, expensive, and place-destroying way of moving. As I discussed in the previous chapter, cars, whether they are caught in congestion or moving fast and free, can rip apart the social fabric of neighborhoods. They are by far the biggest source of smog in most cities. They produce more greenhouse gas emissions per passenger mile than almost any other way of traveling, including flying by jet airliner. It seems preposterous that we would choose a way of moving that simultaneously fails to maximize pleasure while maximizing harm. But once again, we are not all as free to choose as we might hope.

Behavior by Design

Of every one hundred American commuters, five take public transit, three walk, and only one rides a bicycle to work or school. If walking and cycling are so pleasurable, why don't more people choose to cycle or walk to work? Why do most people fail to walk even the ten thousand daily steps needed to stay healthy? Why do we avoid public transit?

I was naive enough to ask that question of a fellow diner I met in the food court of the bunkerlike Peachtree Center in downtown Atlanta. Her name was Lucy. She had driven her car in that morning from Clayton County (a freeway journey of about fifteen miles), pulled into a parking deck, followed a skyway a few dozen paces to an elevator and then a few more to her desk. Trip time: about half an hour. Total footsteps: maybe three hundred. She flashed me a broad smile.

"Honey, we don't *walk* in Atlanta," Lucy told me. "We *all* drive here. I can't say why. I guess we're just lazy."

Lazy? The theory doesn't stand up. Lucy's own commute was proof. She could not have made it to work any other way. Suburban Clayton County parked its entire bus fleet in 2010.* In the midst of a cash crunch, the county just couldn't afford to run buses through the sparsely populated dispersed city.

No, the answer to the mobility conundrum lies in the intersection between psychology and design. We are pushed and pulled according to the systems in which we find ourselves, and certain geometries ensure that none of us are as free as we might think.

Few places design travel behavior as powerfully as Atlanta. The average working adult in Atlanta's suburbs now drives forty-four miles a day.† Ninety-four percent of Atlantans commute by car. They spend more on gas than anyone else in the country. In Chapter 5, I explained how the centrifugal force of Atlanta's extensive freeway network enabled its population to spread far across the Georgia countryside—and then left them vulnerable to world-class road congestion. But in a study of more than eight thousand households, investigators from the Georgia Institute of Technology led by Lawrence Frank discovered that people's environments were shaping their travel behavior and their bodies. They could actually predict how fat people were by where they lived in the city.

Frank found that a white male living in Midtown, a lively district near Atlanta's downtown, was likely to weigh ten pounds less than

---

*The bus service in Clayton County carried two million riders in 2009 before it was shut down.

†That's seventy-two minutes a day behind the wheel, just getting to work and back.

his identical twin living out in a place like, say, Mableton, in the cul-de-sac archipelago that surrounds Atlanta, simply because the Mid-towner would be twice as likely to get enough exercise every day.

Here's how their neighborhoods engineer their travel behavior:

Midtown was laid out long before the dispersalists got their hands on the city. It exhibits the convenient geometry of the streetcar neighborhood even though its streetcars disappeared in 1949. Housing, offices, and retail space are all sprinkled relatively close together on a latticelike street grid. A quart of milk or a bar or a downtown-bound bus are never more than a few blocks away. It is easy for people to walk to shops, services, or MARTA, the city's limited rapid transit system, so that's what they do.

But in suburbs like Mableton, residential lots are huge, roads are wide and meandering, and stores are typically concentrated in faraway shopping plazas surrounded by parking lots. Six out of every ten Atlantans told Frank's team that they couldn't walk to nearby shops and services or to a public bus stop. They just didn't have the mix. Road geometry was partly to blame. Frank and others have found that that iconic suburban innovation—the cul-de-sac—has become part of a backfiring behavioral system.

When designers try to maximize the number of cul-de-sacs in an area, they create a dendritic—or treelike—system of roads that feeds all their traffic into a few main branches. The system makes just about every destination farther away because it eliminates the most direct routes between them. Connectivity counts: more intersections mean more walking, and more disconnected cul-de-sacs mean more driving.*

The long-distance story is not unique to Atlanta. In 1940 the average person in Seattle lived less than half a mile from a store. By 1990 the distance had grown to more than three-quarters of a mile, and it has grown since. In 2012, after Facebook and architect Frank Gehry unveiled designs for a new 10-acre base across the Bayfront Expressway from Facebook's old base in Silicon Valley, Gehry explained that his plan strove for "a kind of ephemeral connectivity"

---

*People who live in neighborhoods with latticework-like streets actually drive 26 percent fewer miles than people in the cul-de-sac forest.

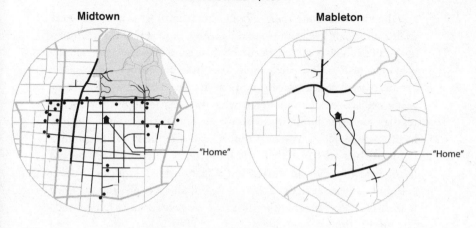

Midtown   Mableton

"Home"   "Home"

——— 1/2 mile (10 minute walk) range from "home"

•   "essential" neighborhood uses

First We Shape Our Streets, Then They Shape Us

A white male living in Midtown (left), near Atlanta's downtown, is likely to weigh ten pounds less than his identical twin living near Mableton (right), a sprawling suburb. This is partly owing to road geometry and land-use mix: a ten-minute walk from a home amid the traditional grid in Midtown will get you to grocery stores, churches, schools, bus stops, restaurants, cafés, a dry cleaner, a bank, and the glorious lawns of Piedmont Park. But the spread-out and homogeneous system of Mableton pushes destinations beyond walking range, which means residents are likely to drive whether they like driving or not. (Each bullet represents a school, church, grocery store, dry cleaner, bank, day-care center, police station, transit stop, or hospital. If restaurants, cafés, bars, and other services were included, the Mableton map would not change, but the Midtown map would be sprayed with dozens more bullets.)

(Erick Villagomez, Metis Design Build)

through its single-level, open-concept floor design. But no magical configuration of the office-park geometry could make up for the fact that half of Facebook's workers actually lived thirty miles away in dense, walkable, networked San Francisco. Facebook would just have to keep busing them in.

Our responses to distance are quite predictable. Most of us will walk to a corner store rather than climb in and out of the car if it's less than a five-minute walk—about a quarter mile—away. We won't walk more than five minutes to a bus stop, but we will walk ten to a light-rail or subway station, partly because most of us perceive rail service to be faster, more predictable, and more comfortable. This is the geometry perfected by streetcar city developers a century ago. It's now being rediscovered by planners who find that simply introducing regular high-quality light-rail service can alter the habits—and the health—of people nearby. Less than a year after the LYNX commuter light-rail line was installed in Charlotte, North Carolina, people living near the line had started walking an extra 1.2 miles *every day* because the system changed their daily calculus. People who switched to the LYNX for their commute lost an average of six and a half pounds during that time.

Kids move by a similar calculus. Frank found that if there is a park or some kind of store within a half mile of their home, school-age youth are more than twice as likely to walk. If destinations are farther, they wait for a parental chauffeur. Think of the implications: a community with one central mega–sports complex with several baseball diamonds and soccer fields can actually be bad for children's health if it replaces small parks scattered every few blocks. In the finer-grained community, instead of begging Mom for a ride to a league game, a teenager might find it easier to organize her own game at the local park.* Nearly two-thirds of parents say there is no place for their children to play within walking distance of home. This is part of the reason that American children now actually gain weight during the supposedly leisure-filled summer break.

"The way we organize most cities actually encourages individuals

---

*The amalgamation and supersizing of schools has been a disaster for children's freedom and health. If school is more than three-quarters of a mile away, children just don't walk there. The journey passes the convenience threshold, and parents frequently deem it too dangerous to let kids go it alone. Less than 13 percent of children walked to school in 2004, compared with half in 1969. Many fears cause parents to limit their children's free time in cities, but the real and present danger to suburban children is posed not by muggers and child-nappers, but by cars. Thanks to generations of safety-engineered and accidentally fast roads, kids walking to school in suburbia face more than fifteen times the risk of being in an accident than car passengers. In a hideous irony, the people who run over school-bound children are often the parents of other children.

to make choices that make everyone's life harder," Frank told me. "The system fails because it promises rewards for irrational behavior."

Put simply, most people do not walk in American cities because cities have designed destinations out of reach. But they have also corroded the experience of walking. Road engineers have not even bothered to build sidewalks in many Atlanta suburbs. Try a Google search for directions near, say, Somerset Road in Mableton, and the map engine will offer a warning you would not expect in a first world city: "Use caution—This route may be missing sidewalks or pedestrian paths."

Aesthetics matter. We walk farther when streets feel safe and interesting. People who live in central New York or London typically walk between a third to a half mile to go shopping. That's a four- to ten-minute stroll. Even in Montreal, with its freezing winters and sweat-soaked summers, people reported walking about a third of a mile (six to eight minutes) between shops, bags in tow. The numbers are almost as high for people arriving at enclosed shopping malls, which mimic the downtown experience, at least once you're in the building. But dump us in a vast parking lot surrounded by big-box outlets, and our inclination to walk evaporates. Even when people are equipped with shopping carts, they won't endure so much as the three-minute stroll between retailers. Researchers observed that a third of the shoppers at one Canadian power center actually parked their cars three or more times during one visit. They just hated trudging across the asphalt desert. It felt ugly, uncomfortable, and unsafe.*

You might speculate that these studies merely demonstrate the

*A survey of shoppers at the forty-eight-acre Kenaston Power Centre in Winnipeg, Canada, found that they behaved like an entirely different species from people in the urban core. Almost none of them were willing to make even the three-minute walk between Walmart and its big-box neighbors. They jumped back into their cars and began the search for a closer parking spot whenever they moved from store to store. A third of Kenaston's visitors actually parked their cars three or more times during one visit.

Why wouldn't they walk, as people do downtown? Shoppers complained that the journey between retail islands meant trudging along the gravel berms of arterial roads, circumnavigating drainage ditches, crossing vast plains of pavement, or all three. The landscape is visible on Google Street View: from the roof of the Google truck the terrain between the Kenaston Power Centre's Safeway and Walmart is as empty and never-ending as the Arctic tundra.

Do Not Walk

Walk

Shoppers in power center environments like this one near Washington, DC (top) don't make even the two-minute walk between stores, while people shopping in traditional market environments like this one in Toronto (bottom) typically walk six to eight minutes to destinations. (Top: Brett VA/ Flickr; *above*: Charles Montgomery)

city's power to sort people by their preferences: maybe Manhattanites walk because they are walkers, while Atlanta's big-lot suburbanites and Canada's power center pilgrims drive because they prefer the air-conditioned comfort and storage capacity of the family minivan. In other words, just because urban designs correlate with travel behavior, it doesn't mean they cause it.

This view is partly true. People do self-sort in cities. In Atlanta, for example, Frank found that people who said they preferred to live in car-dependent neighborhoods tended to drive pretty much everywhere, no matter where they lived. Not surprisingly, people who both liked and lived in lively, walkable places drove less and walked more. But the suburbs were full of people who, like those teenagers I met back in Weston Ranch, wished they could walk places but couldn't. Nearly a third of people living in Atlanta's car-dependent sprawl wished they lived in a walkable neighborhood, but they were mostly out of luck because Atlanta had gone nearly half a century without building such places.

When Atlanta builds differently, people do change their movements. Proof sits on the edge of a tangled freeway interchange three miles north of the city center, where the 138-acre site of a former steel mill has been redeveloped into a dense mix of offices, apartments, retail stores, small parks, and theaters. Despite the fact that much of Atlantic Station, as it is known, sits atop a three-level parking garage, people who have moved there since 2005 have shaved a third of the miles off their driving. Instead, they walk, because some of their destinations have suddenly fallen within the range of a pleasant sidewalk stroll.

Only the Brave

If distance alone determined how we move, then the calculus should be different for cyclists. Seventy percent of American car trips are shorter than two miles, which translates to about an easy 10-minute bike ride. Even a casual rider travels between twelve and twenty miles per hour, which means that she can cross more than five miles during the twenty-five minutes it takes the average American to get to work.* Yet the travel mode rated the most fun, efficient, and joyful has been avoided by all but a tiny fraction of North American travelers, even in dense, connected communities.

For most people, the prospect is unthinkable. Urban cycling is just too scary, and cycle enthusiasts are partly to blame. Beginning in the 1970s, transportation planners and cycle advocates in the United States worked to convert everyone who used a bike into what has become known as a "vehicular cyclist": someone who navigated the streets of the city as though she were driving a car. According to this philosophy, the properly trained vehicular cyclist should play the role

---

*In 2006 the city of St. Petersburg, Florida, installed bike-riding lanes on two streets. The average speed of the bicycle riders even in this often uncomfortably hot city was between eleven and twelve miles per hour, before and after the bike lanes were installed, which works out to about .2 miles per minute.

of hero rather than victim. She should never jump to the sidewalk or cower near the gutter. She should instead claim a whole lane between the cars and demand respect! The philosophy was like a religion, especially among bicycle advocates who saw it as a matter of asserting their right to the street. It found its way into the bible of American traffic planning: the Federal Highway Administration's *Manual on Uniform Traffic Control Devices*, or *MUTCD*. Following the vehicular cyclist mantra—and with the support of hard-core bicycle advocates— road builders avoided creating safe, separate paths for bicycles, in part so cyclists would not be treated as second-class travelers.

The problem is that the vehicular cyclist is almost as rare a creature as economic man. Most people are simply too scared to ride bicycles in traffic. This fear is entirely logical. Nearly half of people struck by cars moving at thirty miles per hour die, and the mortality rate just keeps going up with velocity.

Some say the bicycle helmet is a solution to this reasonable fear. They are dead wrong. As a safety device, the helmet may actually backfire. Ian Walker, an English traffic psychologist, put his body on the line to make this discovery. Walker fitted his bicycle with an ultrasonic distance sensor, then pedaled around the English cities of Salisbury and Bristol to see how close motorists would come when overtaking him. He found that drivers were twice as likely to come dangerously close when he was wearing a helmet. In fact, Walker was struck by a bus and, later, a truck, during the course of the experiment. He was wearing a helmet both times.* It takes a rare hero, someone like Robert Judge, to see hostile conditions as a call to adventure rather than a warning to stay safely behind the wheel of a car.

---

*The problem, Walker speculates, might be semiotic. When drivers see a cyclist wearing a helmet, they read it as a sign that the rider is more experienced and predictable, so they give themselves narrower margins of error when passing. Walker's work suggests that just by wearing a helmet, cyclists make collisions *more* likely. What's remarkable is how drivers tend to adjust their behavior according to less-than-logical assumptions. For example, when Walker wore a wig of long hair, suggesting that he was female, drivers gave him much more room. Walker offers fascinating graphs on his home page: www.drianwalker.com/overtaking/overtaking probrief.pdf.

The Worst Journey in the World

In the last few years, pundits and lawmakers across North America have fretted about what seemed to be an epidemic of dangerous behavior on roads and highways: namely, the habit of texting while driving. A flurry of anti-gadget-play laws resulted, but not before *Wired* columnist Clive Thompson noted, "When we worry about driving and texting, we assume that the most important thing the person is doing is piloting the car. But what if the most important thing they're doing is texting?"

Indeed, the act of driving one's own vehicle has become a serious impediment to our ability to text, tweet, post Facebook updates, watch mobile TV, or get work done. Marketing analysts suggest that this conflict is one of the reasons that young people just aren't as interested in driving or even getting their licenses as they used to be. Almost half of eighteen- to twenty-four-year-olds say they would choose Internet access over owning their own car. And the number of young people applying for driver's licenses is plummeting. But the second we hop on a bus or a train—at least in a favorable wireless environment—the problem disappears. This is one of many compelling reasons to use public transit. It's usually cheaper than driving, and it erases the hassle and worry of car storage. Transit riders travel free from the stress of navigating through traffic. From this narrow perspective, public transit should be a natural and popular choice.

In most cities, it is not. Surveys in the United States and Canada reveal that transit riders are the most miserable commuters of all. American transit users—the bulk of whom rely on buses—are the most likely to feel that their trips take too long and the most likely to be depressed by their journeys. It's not that the experience of public transportation is inherently miserable. It's just that decades of underinvestment mean that the typical transit journey is crowded, slow, uncertain, or uncomfortable. When you starve a system of resources and consistently place it behind other mobility priorities, the experience of using it is bound to disappoint.

Transit riders aren't much happier in train-dependent Britain, where one in five British trains are late. But at least British train commuters can expect a relatively speedy journey. In the United States and Canada, most transit users take double or more the time drivers need to get to work. Bus riders have it the worst. They are generally forced to endure the congestion caused by car drivers, but unlike drivers, they have almost no control over their fate. They experience the stress of uncertainty with every minute of waiting by the side of the road and with every transfer, not to mention the discomfort that comes with unmediated social proximity. There is nothing quite like the beer breath, scowl, or touch of a total stranger to get you thinking about purchasing a car. In cities where transit is meant only as a service for the poor, riding the typical urban bus can be hell on your self-esteem. General Motors actually ran newspaper ads in Canada characterizing bus passengers as "freaks and weirdos" who smelled bad. But transit systems actually go out of their way to ensure the drabness of their infrastructure. The inside of most North American buses and subway cars tends to have all the charm of prison toilets. Planner Jeffrey Tumlin, author of *Sustainable Transportation Planning*, told me that administrators typically choose the most utilitarian-looking materials for bus interiors and stations—even when attractive finishes are no more expensive—simply to avoid the *appearance* of having wasted money. The result are systems that repel wealthier commuters and depress those who have little choice.

Later I will lead you to cities that have inverted the public transit status equation. But my point here is that we all live in systems that shape our travel behavior. And most of us live in systems that give us almost no choice in how to live or get around. Americans have it worst. Even though a majority of Americans now tell pollsters that they would like to live in walkable communities where shops, restaurants, and local businesses are within an easy stroll and jobs are a short commute away, these places are in massive undersupply. Most people live so far beyond the five-minute walk to a frequent bus stop or the ten-minute walk to a rail station that public transit lies beyond imagination.

If you woke up this morning and decided to try a completely different method of getting to work, could you do it? Could you walk there? Ride a bicycle? Or catch a bus or a train that would get you there in the time it took to read the paper? Could you mix and match your modes? Now take it further. Does getting to a grocery store or a doctor's office or a restaurant without a car seem like a pretty big chore? Can your children walk or cycle to school safely on their own? If you think these are unreasonable questions, then chances are, real choice has been designed out of your city. You may still benefit from the tremendous utility of your automobile, but the system is impoverishing you and your family and friends in ways you may never have imagined. How do we build systems that truly make us free in cities? Sometimes it takes a radical shift in the urban imagination to point the way.

9. Mobilicities II
Freedom

Automobiles are in no way responsible for our traffic
problems. The entire responsibility lies in the faulty roads,
which are behind the times.
—Norman Bel Geddes, 1940

Possession is becoming progressively burdensome and
wasteful and therefore obsolete.
—Buckminster Fuller, 1969

In 1969 a consortium of European industrial interests charged a young
American economist with figuring out how people would move
through cities in the future. There was a lot of money to be made by
whoever could divine the single technology most likely to capture the
market in the coming decades. It was the era of James Bond gadgets
and *Apollo 11*. Everyone was sure that some fabulous new machine
would emerge to change everything. Eric Britton dove into the task.
He gave his clients a thorough accounting of even the most fantastical possibilities. He keeps the faded report on a shelf in his apartment, a few blocks from the Luxembourg Gardens in Paris's Sixth
Arrondissement.

In hundreds of tables, Britton soberly cataloged and assessed the
capacity, the energy consumption, and the maximum range of freight
monorails, mini-monorails, carveyor belts, hydrofoils, multiple-speed
moving platforms, and telecanapes, trains that slowed for boarding
without coming to a complete stop. He estimated the congestion that
might be caused by passenger bunching on high-speed walkways and
the energy required for magnetic suspension. He rated technologies

that seemed fantastical at the time, only to reemerge decades later, such as hybrid cars and hydrogen fuel cells.

Britton was swept up in the excitement of the possibilities, but as he shared his dossier of futurist ideas with the people who were actually trying to solve the problems of cities in both the rich and developing world, he was forced to wipe the stardust from his eyes.

"I realized that none of these technologies was going to solve the problems of cities, not in Europe, not in the U.S.A., nor anywhere else in the world," Britton told me as I perused the now-faded report in his Paris apartment. "The future was not going to be defined by some kind of deus ex machina solution to all of our problems, but rather by step-by-step innovations and improvements applied to the tools we already had to work with."

Britton's clients were surprised. In the age of the Jetsons, it was unfashionable to suggest that after a couple of generations, people would still be getting around pretty much the same way they had since the dawn of the internal combustion engine, using trains, buses, cars, bicycles, motorcycles, and, as always, their feet. But history has proved him right. After the decades-long experiment with automobiles, governments simply do not have the money to completely transform urban infrastructure to suit any one radically new technology. Moreover, Britton came to realize that the question of mobility was not merely a matter of technology or economics, but one of culture and psychology, and of the vast variation in our preferences.

To depend on just one technology for urban mobility would be to deny human nature itself. Each of us has a unique set of abilities, weaknesses, and desires. Each of us is compelled and thrilled by a unique set of sensations. Every trip demands a unique solution. Britton likes to begin his journeys around Paris with a stroll down the glorious formal parterre of the nearby Luxembourg Gardens, where he can feel the bone-colored gravel crunching under his brown Rockports and cast his gaze on the patch of grass where he secretly buried his late mother's ashes. His neighbor prefers just to hop in a car and go. Another prefers to dash straight to the Métro. Another carries an iron bicycle down to the street, but walks it for a block before mounting it. Each journey, each aspiration, distinct. This, says Britton, illustrates the essential condition of society and of cities. We are all much more unique in our preferences than planners acknowledge.

"You may think that French people are very different from Americans. But if you look at statistics of their choices and preferences, you see that French people are more different from each other than they are from Americans."

The word for this condition is heteroscedasticity. It suggests that the bigger the size of any group, the harder it is to predict the variation in its characteristics or to find one solution to a problem involving huge numbers of independent variables and actors. "What heteroscedasticity tells us is that everything in cities is going to be a little bit complicated, a bit chaotic," said Britton. "So the first thing you have to do is say, 'Okay, I gotta be able to deal with chaos. There is no single answer to any problem in the city. The solution comes from a multiplicity of answers.'"*

Cities should strive to embrace complexity, not just in transportation systems but in human experience, says Britton. He advises cities and corporations to abandon *old mobility*, a system rigidly organized entirely around one way of moving, and embrace *new mobility*, a future in which we would all be free to move in the greatest variety of ways.

"We all know old mobility," Britton said. "It's you sitting in your car, stuck in traffic. It's you driving around for hours, searching for a parking spot. Old mobility is you devoting a fifth of your income to your car and a good chunk of your tax dollars to road improvements, even as the system performs worse every year. Old mobility is also the fifty-five-year-old maid with a bad leg, waiting in the rain for a bus that she can't be certain will come. It's your kids not being able to walk or bike to school. New mobility, on the other hand, is freedom distilled."

---

*It helps to compare cities and their transportation systems to forests. Rich, diverse ecosystems are always healthier and more resilient than monocultures. Just as a mixed forest can better survive a beetle infestation than a tree farm consisting of one variety of pine, a city that enables endless combinations of mobility will be much more resilient than a city that organizes itself around just one way of moving. It will adjust more easily to shifts in economics, human taste, and energy supply. It will fill in the blanks that master planners cannot see within the tangle of the complex urban system. It will make the most of technologies that can solve the problems particular to cities: tight spaces, congested streets, and, most of all, people with wildly varying preferences.

Britton is one of those people whose ideas seem too theoretical, too pie-in-the-sky to matter, until suddenly they change the world. In 1994, for example, frustrated with planners' myopic view of mobility, he proposed a modest experiment in which cities would simply abandon cars for a single day each year. It would be a way to break old patterns of thinking about streets. "A collective learning experience," is how Britton framed the proposal. He's the one who convinced Enrique Peñalosa to pull off the first big-city car-free day in Bogotá in 2000. Now more than a thousand cities have followed suit. As with the Ciclovía, each city that tries the experiment learns that streets can serve many more purposes than once imagined. People adjust. They find other ways to move. They surprise themselves.

But merely banning cars, Britton admits, is just as simplistic as depending on them entirely. His theory of freedom is better embodied in a proposal he made to the French Ministry of Environment in the early 1970s. At the time, moving by transit in Paris was a bureaucratic nightmare: you had to purchase as many as five different tickets simply to get across town. So few people took buses that Paris was considering abandoning the service. Britton suggested giving everyone in Paris a magic card that would automatically allow them passage on the Métro, trains, and buses. Just as proponents of Motordom once worked to reduce the friction of city roads that slowed cars down in the 1920s, Britton reasoned that by reducing friction and hassle, public transit would become a little more like driving.

Within a couple of years, Paris introduced the Carte d'Orange, a combination subway pass and identity card that gave its holder unlimited access to all of the city's public transportation for a flat monthly rate. The system did not make rides much faster or cheaper, but it chipped away at the anxiety and effort associated with each transit trip. No more fumbling for change or waiting in line for surly ticket agents. Within a year, bus ridership jumped by 40 percent. Gradually the card underwent a series of dynamic upgrades, evolving by 2008 into the Navigo pass, a chip-embedded ID card. With a wave of your Navigo card over an electronic reader, you can ride any Métro, bus, airport shuttle, regional train, express train, or tram in the city.

"The system transforms the city by transforming our choices, and ultimately transforming each of us, the same way a disabled person's life is transformed when they can wheel their chair onto a bus," said Britton. Indeed, the Navigo pass has become a passport to the city, and a powerful distillation of the idea that everybody should be free to move across it. The unemployed get free access to all of Navigo's shared modes. "If you are poor, you can travel right across the city; you can go way the hell out to the suburbs to look for a job. It's all based on a philosophy of how to live—Freedom! Mobility for all!— and it has become part of our daily life now. That card is shaping the culture."*

Feeling Free in Transit

A small club of economists and psychologists devote themselves entirely to the study of how transit makes us feel and behave. They have found that the difficulty we associate with commuting on public transit can have as much to do with mental effort as physical effort. The less you have to think about your trip and the more in control you feel, the easier the journey. This explains part of the magic of the Paris Navigo card, but also its limitations. Although the smart card helps erase mental effort when jumping between modes of travel, it can only go so far in improving the experience of moving by transit, which depends on a matrix of predictability, comfort, and the perception of passing time.

In central Paris, riders need not worry about traffic delays. The Métro and commuter rail systems are woven tightly under the surface of the city, while shared transit has been gradually recolonizing road space. New trams run along grass medians planted down the

---

*Mobility smart cards have proliferated around the world. The smartest of all is Hong Kong's Octopus, a contactless electronic payment card launched in 1997 to collect fares for the city's mass transit system. The Octopus gets you on virtually every public transport in the city. Load it up with cash, and it also works for parking meters, car parks, supermarkets, and service stations. You can even set it to open the lobby door of your apartment building. Most American cities still occupy the old universe. Seattle, for example, has no less than three transit providers, each requiring its own fare either at the beginning or the end of your trip. The city has to post flowcharts explaining when and how you pay to ride.

middle of arterial roads, and a network of road lanes have been handed over to beautiful city buses, which they share with taxis and bicycles.

But speed alone cannot ease all of transit's psychological burden. When you ride a bus or train, your travel time includes the minutes you spend doing nothing but waiting for your ride. Planners spend a lot of time debating the question of "headway elasticity"—or how frequently buses and trains need to come in order to draw the most passengers. The behavioral economics of headway elasticity are impossibly arcane, but the first principle to remember is that if you show up at a stop without checking transit schedules, you will have to wait, on average, half the interval time between buses before stepping on board. So if your bus comes only every twenty minutes, your half-hour journey to work will probably become a forty-minute journey.

But it will feel much longer than that.

Inaction has a warping effect on time: a minute spent waiting seems to pass much more slowly than a minute spent moving. So most transportation planners agree that a bus needs to show up at least every fifteen minutes on any route for people nearby to use it effortlessly—i.e., without feeling as though they need to plan ahead. Cities such as Paris solve the headway problem partly by virtue of density: on most routes, there are enough riders to support bus and train arrivals every few minutes. (This also helps explain the vicious cycle of crummy transit service out in suburbia. Dispersal makes frequent service just too costly to provide, but infrequent service sends potential riders back to their cars.)

Frequent service alone doesn't erase the anxiety of waiting. Just as time decelerates while we are forced to wait, it slows to a crawl when we don't know exactly how long we have to wait. Anyone who has ever stood at a bus stop in the rain or on a train platform, peering into the distance for headlights that refuse to appear, knows that the anxiety produced by delayed service has a very long tail. If your ride is delayed today, you cannot be sure if it will be on time tomorrow. You will carry a little more stress into every trip.

But simply getting more information about the journey can speed the clock back up again. Take the express bus station on Boulevard du Montparnasse, just a couple of blocks from Britton's apartment. There's a covered seating area, but also a prominent screen at the entrance, showing exactly when the next two express buses will arrive.

This subtle change in infrastructure is a powerful psychological intervention. Just having access to real-time arrival data causes riders to feel calmer and more in control. After arrival countdown clocks were mounted in the London Underground, people told surveyors that the wait time felt shorter by a quarter. The clocks also make people feel safer traveling at night, partly by giving them more confidence in the system.

When New York City's Metropolitan Transit Authority installed LED boards displaying train arrival times on some train platforms, the effect was fascinating. People at light board–equipped stations were less likely to lean precariously out over the track, peering down the tunnel. Everyone could make a logical decision whether to wait or head up to the street to walk or catch a cab—becoming, in effect, slightly more like the rational, informed actors that economists tell us we are.

Jarrett Walker, a public transit consultant and author of *Human Transit: How Clearer Thinking About Public Transit Can Enrich Our Communities and Our Lives*, points out that an experiential gulf often separates the people who plan transit services from the people who use them. Take a typical transit map like Seattle's, which until recently featured a latticework of basic lines showing every bus route in the city. Although that map was factually correct, Walker argued that it was functionally wrong at various times, since only a fraction of bus routes offered frequent service. A map-inspired traveler could end up waiting an hour or more for a bus—enough to convince anyone that public transit is a hell best avoided. Luckily, Seattle took Walker's advice and cleared the cognitive fog with new maps that highlight the *real* frequent routes.

But now that the air around us seethes with data, no traveler need be left in the dark. Portland, Oregon, has proved it. In 2005 the city's transit authority, TriMet, opened up access to the digital information produced by its buses, trams, and trains. Since then, independent developers have produced dozens of smartphone applications offering real-time transit data, arrival times, and maps. For those without a smartphone, a service called Transit Board allows any business with Internet access and a cheap monitor to stream bus or tram arrival times for the stop outside its window, so travelers can duck inside for a microbrew instead of waiting in the drizzle. It's cheap, it's good for business, and it takes the anxious edge off the shared ride. Of course, these innovations tend to take place in cities where policy makers actually ride public transit. When transit is seen as a handout to the poor, politicians tend not to invest beyond the most basic levels of service. (People in jurisdictions like Clayton County, Georgia, where transit was cut *entirely* in the great recession, know this too well.)

Freedom from Owning Things

Forty years after Britton's futurist investigations, cities are indeed finding the technology to reshape the future of mobility. As it turns out, that technology has nothing to do with fantastical new devices for moving and everything to do with new ways of thinking, sharing information, and adjusting the way we use the machines we have been using for years. Through open data, smart cards, wireless communications, and geographic positioning systems, familiar machines are being reenergized and woven together into complex systems that are more powerful than the sum of their parts.

To demonstrate how radically urban systems can build freedom in motion, Britton led me down from his office out onto Rue Joseph Bara. From here we could walk two blocks east to a commuter express train station or a couple of more minutes west to the Vavin Métro station, or we could saunter down to the rapid bus station on Montparnasse. Instead we wandered north, up immaculate sidewalks and through the iron gates of the Luxembourg Gardens. We followed the wide promenade beneath the shade trees toward the cream facade of the Luxembourg Palace. Chrysanthemums exploded from great stone urns, catching the early-fall light. Model sailboats drifted across the great octagonal pond. If we happened to be short on time, we could maximize our time in the park to the second, Britton said, because we were never more than a three-minute walk from a personal metro device. It was hard to understand what he meant until we had skirted the palace, crossed the Rue de Vaugirard, and paused by a row of sturdy-looking bicycles. Then, with a theatrical flourish, Britton swept his wallet above a metallic post. I heard a click. He pulled one of a dozen bicycles free from its berth.

"Et voilà! Freedom!" Britton said again, grinning from ear to ear. A sensor in the post recognized Britton's Navigo card and unlocked a sturdy bicycle. Now it would track his time with that bicycle and note the location of the post where he would lock it again.

That bicycle is the most revolutionary item on the new mobility menu. It is a system whose name—Vélib', a fusion of *vélo* and *liberté*— encapsulates its remarkable philosophy and utility. "Yes, a personal metro system that we can take in any direction we want. This changes everything!" said Britton.

Hundreds of cities, including Lyon, Montreal, Melbourne, Boston, Washington, New York, and Chicago, have now launched modest shared-bike programs. But no system in the Western world matches the ambition of Paris.* The Vélib' is everywhere, all the time. More than 20,000 of these bicycles are situated at 1,250 stations around the central city. In most places, you are never more than a quarter of a mile from a station. Unclick a Vélib' from its hitching post and it's yours for half an hour, virtually free.†

With just three gears, and the industrial heft and curvy, solid gray aesthetics of Bauhaus sewing machines, the bikes are certainly not fit for the Tour de France. But since they were introduced, in 2007, they have utterly changed the face of mobility in central Paris.

Each bicycle in the Vélib' fleet gets used between three and nine times every day. That's as many as two hundred thousand trips a day. The flood of bicycles in the streets has risen even higher as newbies try the Vélib', realize the ease of city cycling, and buy their own bicycles.

The Vélib' is more than a tool for convenience; it embodies a political philosophy that many Americans will find radical. It was created to help Parisians simultaneously save the world and become more free *by owning less stuff.*

Denis Baupin, a Paris Green Party leader, spearheaded the Vélib' plan as the city's transportation chief. "If everyone on the planet lived

---

*The Hangzhou bicycle company plans to offer a mind-boggling 175,000 bikes for share across that Chinese city by 2020.

†Subscriptions to the system cost one euro per day, five euros per week, or twenty-nine euros per year. After the first (free) half hour, the system begins to charge an incrementally higher rate for each additional half hour, in order to keep bicycles in circulation.

Personal Metro Systems

With stations (left) never more than a five-minute walk away, the Vélib' bicycle share has become a personal metro system for Parisians. On streets with no bicycle lanes (right), this is still a freedom reserved for the brave. (Charles Montgomery)

like Parisians did," he told me, "we would need three planets to supply all the required energy, materials, and garbage space." Following the chilling math of the environmental footprint theory, the Parisian footprint was a third the size of that left by Americans, but Baupin insisted that Parisians had a duty to shrink their ecological footprint by two-thirds. Baupin, who wore a white linen jacket and had the cheery face of a cherub, didn't see this as a depressing message at all.

"Do we say to Parisians, we must agree to be three times less happy than now in the future? Of course this is impossible! We have to explain that when we restrict our consumption, our waste, and so on, we can be even more happy than today."

For Baupin, the shared bicycle is the ultimate postconsumer machine. It offers a new kind of liberty for anyone willing to share space and equipment. "What is really special about the Vélib' is that you don't own it. Like a park, the bicycle is for everybody to share," he told me. "We don't take shopping carts home after using them at the supermarket. We don't cart around our own elevators or restaurants or airplanes. Why should we be forced by urban design to own cars and bicycles?" he asked.

For most people living in capitalist societies, the "right not to own things" sounds a bit like "deprivation" in disguise. The idea can be especially challenging for Americans, who have been advised by heroes, pundits, and presidents that they will risk democracy itself if they stop shopping.

I told Baupin that where I come from, not owning things generally means you are poor. And when you are poor, you are not free. You are stranded. No, no, he said. In the new Paris, the opposite was true. There was simply no room for everyone to drive. There wasn't enough room for everyone to park. For residents of central Paris, ownership was a tremendous burden. If you owned a car, not only did you have to pay for it, but you had to take care of it and repair it and spend hours on end searching for parking. Ownership could be equally arduous for bike owners, who had to lug their vehicles to their apartments in Paris's six-story walk-ups or risk having them stolen.

The Vélib' was a way to break free of those chains. You didn't have to worry about storing the bike at home or parking it at your destination. You didn't have to fix it. If you got a flat or if it rained, you just clicked it back into a station and hopped on the Métro. You kept moving.*

---

*Ironically, Baupin's postconsumer bike system was built and paid for and is now run by JCDecaux, the biggest advertising company in France. In a complex deal, the city gets all the rental fees while JCDecaux gets revenue from the ad space it sells on more than sixteen hundred on-street billboards throughout the city. So while riders experience the joys of nonownership, their public space is plastered with messages tweaking their status impulses, reminding them that they would be happier if they bought more stuff. This was a compromise between Baupin's Greens and the French Socialist Party, who made up the city's coalition government at the time.

Extreme Sharing

What is true of many purchases—that we don't want the thing so much as we want what it can do for us—is especially true for transportation. Whether it is a train or a bus or a bicycle or a car, any vehicle's utility begins when it starts to move. Most private cars spend the vast majority of their life span sitting, doing nothing but costing their owners money in insurance, lease payments, parking, and depreciation. Not only do automobile owners need to earn substantially more just to be able to afford to drive, but we increasingly work in order to drive to and pay for fitness facilities to get the exercise that should be a side effect of the daily journey.*

In Paris, and around the world, new systems of sharing are setting commuters free.

In 2011 Paris launched Autolib', an electric car-share system that works much like the Vélib', with a fleet of rentable vehicles scattered at recharge stations around the city and accessible using the Navigo card. In more typical car-share systems, such as Zipcar, whose fleet of nine thousand vehicles is spread among cities in the United States, Canada, and the United Kingdom, you book a car by phone or online,

---

*Any honest assessment of travel time has to include the hours you spend working to pay for your vehicle, as well as the time spent on your journey—a concept known as effective speed.

Most drivers tend to wildly underestimate the time they must spend earning money to pay for their trips. (In England, for example, the Royal Automobile Club has found that vehicle expenses are more than double what drivers believed they were.) You must work to purchase gas and oil, of course, but you must also work to pay costs hidden in loan financing, parking fees, repairs, tolls, accessories, maintenance, and depreciation. This stuff adds up. Throw all those work and driving hours together, and you arrive at your effective speed—how many miles you are really traveling for every hour of effort. Let's break it down:

The average American office worker drives twenty-seven miles a day and spends about an hour on the road. According to the American Automobile Association, that drive costs her about $18.36. (In 2013 the AAA estimated that it cost about $9,122 to travel fifteen thousand miles, a rough estimate of the average person's mileage.) Let's say she nets $20 an hour as an office manager. She needs to work an extra forty-five minutes just to pay for her drive, which means, in the end, she takes almost two hours of combined work and travel time to cross those twenty-seven miles. Effective travel speed: just over fifteen miles per hour. Suddenly the average car commute doesn't look so fast.

pick it up from its designated parking spot, and return it when done. But even Autolib' and Zipcar feel clumsy compared with the versatility of what we might call smart sharing. For example, Daimler, the German car company, has scattered hundreds of Smart cars around dozens of cities, including, in 2011, Vancouver. Daimler's CAR2GO concept is deliciously simple. Like Zipcar, you find a car using the Internet or an iPhone or Android application. Like Zipcar, you unlock it with the swipe of a magnetic card over a reader on the windshield. But then you can drive that car wherever you want to go within the service area for as long as you like, and when you arrive at your destination, you *just leave it there.* The system tracks cars with GPS, so you don't need to return it for the next user to find it. No planning required. The thirty-five cents per minute charge covers taxes, insurance, mileage, and even fuel.

The CAR2GO system accommodates the unpredictability and spontaneity of daily life. It has taken Daimler one step toward Britton's new mobility: the cars leave the factory ready for sharing. And it has added one more layer of freedom to my own city. With two car-share outfits, a CAR2GO system, a tight bus network, and three rapid transit lines, people in Vancouver are selling their cars or leaving them at home. (In 2005, the average family in Vancouver owned 1.25 cars, compared with 1.7 in suburban Surrey.) The city is now looking at proposals to repurpose downtown parking garages. The top floor of one has been converted into a produce garden. "The bottom line on all these changes is more choice, less cost for those who can forgo car ownership, less car traffic, more exercise, safer streets, and liberated garages," boasted former Vancouver city councilor Peter Ladner.

Car sharing has now found a particularly American form. Just as Baupin fought the notion that everyone should have to own his own vehicle, a San Francisco start-up called Getaround has enabled those who do own to get more bang out of their vehicles by renting them to complete strangers. In 2010 Getaround began providing car owners in the San Francisco area with small Wi-Fi and GPS-enabled units. Owners choose when and where they want to offer their vehicles, and renters find them and book them via an iPhone app. One peer-to-peer user reported that she left her car in San Francisco while she went hiking in Peru—and earned $350 per week in rentals while she was away.* Meanwhile, even ride sharing has gotten smarter. A smart-phone application called Avego enables drivers and prospective passengers to link up through their phones. At the end of each journey an automated accounting system pays the driver out of the passenger's account.

In some ways, these peer-to-peer systems work like oxytocin, the trust hormone: they offer an inducement and immediate reward for behaving cooperatively with other people. The cooperative impulse manifests in subtle ways: Vélib' users in Paris have adopted the custom of twisting bike seats sideways when they return a damaged bike to a station so subsequent users won't choose them and be disappointed. As these systems grow and eventually guide millions of strangers into mutually beneficial transactions, it will be interesting to observe more changes in user culture and in trust among strangers.

Freedom and Physiology

Car-share devotees may not need to worry about parking and repairs, but they still contribute to—and get stuck in—traffic congestion. This is the great advantage of the bicycle in dense cities, where, moving at between nine and twelve miles per hour, cyclists achieve the same average speeds as drivers (and even shorter trip times, if you take into account time spent parking), in part because they take up so little room.

Britton insisted that without actually riding a bike, it was impossible to understand how the shared bicycle was transforming Paris. He checked the tires on a second bike. Fine. He adjusted the seat. Good. I poked my credit card into the kiosk, pulled my bicycle from its dock, and we rolled out into the Paris traffic, sans helmet, like everyone else. I followed Britton down a narrow side street, we hit Boulevard du Port-Royal, and all hell broke loose. Taxis bounced past like cartoon

---

*Through a deal with Warren Buffett's Berkshire Hathaway, users get the same insurance coverage as owners. The states of California and Oregon have both changed their laws to ensure that car owners cannot be held liable for the accidents of their borrowers.

go-karts. Delivery trucks and motorbikes jostled frenetically. Bus engines screamed as they sucked at the warm air. At first I was disoriented and scared. I had been warned about the pathological aggression of Parisian drivers, and the streets were still full of them.

But Britton and I were not the only ones on two wheels. There were dozens of other Vélib' users around us. There were so many of us out there that drivers had to pay attention. They had to make room. In *The Death and Life of Great American Cities*, Jane Jacobs described the ballet that takes place on crowded sidewalks as people make eye contact and find their way around one another. I felt a similar if supercharged dynamic coming to life in Paris's traffic lanes. With cars and bikes and buses mixed together, none of us could be sure what we would find on the road ahead of us. We all had to be awake to the rhythm of asymmetrical flow. In the contained fury of the narrow streets we were forced to choreograph our movements, but with so many other bicycles flooding the streets, cycling in Paris was actually becoming safer. As more people took to bicycles in Vélib's first year, the number of bike accidents rose, but the number of accidents per capita fell. This phenomenon seems to occur wherever cities see a spike in cycling: the more people bike, the safer the streets get for cyclists, partly because drivers adopt more cautious habits when they expect cyclists on the road. There is safety in numbers.*

I left Britton with a high five and peeled onto Rue Monge, heading toward the Seine.

Between lights and lane changes, through windshields and helmet visors I caught split-second glances of turned heads, nods, angled shoulders—all clues to drivers' intentions. I found my place in the stampede, waving a hand, pointing, moving into open ground, claiming space as I wound my way downhill, across the Seine. I kept riding as the sun fell and the slate roof tiles turned pink. I barreled toward Bastille and the monument to the Revolution of 1830. There, atop the great copper column, the gold figure of Auguste Dumont's Spirit of Freedom was leaping into flight, holding his broken chains to the sky. The last rays of the sun exploded from his wings. The round-

*Even in New York City, where cyclists have the reputation similar to that of Paris drivers, the number of cyclists is growing much faster than the number of cyclist-involved accidents.

about beneath the monument was a spinning whorl of headlights. I joined them, pedaling hard to keep up with the circling taxis and tour buses and motorbikes.

It was absolutely thrilling. I felt free, like Robert Judge the winter rider. But the elements that made this ride thrilling also happened to render it a travel mode unavailable to most other people. You have to be strong and agile to ride a bicycle in city traffic. You need excellent balance and vision. (Children and seniors, for example, have worse peripheral vision than fit adults, and more trouble judging the speed of approaching objects.) Most of all, you must possess a high toler-ance for risk. Even the blood of adventurous riders gets flooded with beta-endorphins—the euphoria-inducing chemical that has been found in bungee jumpers and roller-coaster riders—not to mention a stew of cortisol and adrenaline, the stress hormones that are so useful in moments of fight and flight, but toxic if experienced over the long term.

The biologist Robert Sapolsky once said that the way to under-stand the difference between good and bad stress is to remember that a roller-coaster ride lasts for three minutes rather than three days. A superlong roller coaster would not only be a lot less fun but poison-ous. I personally like roller coasters, and I loved the challenge of rid-ing in the Paris traffic. But what is thrilling to me—a slightly reckless, forty-something male—would be terrifying for my mother or my brother or a child.

So if we really care about freedom for everyone, we need to design for everyone—not just the brave. This means we have got to confront the shared-space movement, which has gradually found favor since the sharing concept known as the *woonerf* emerged on residential streets in the Dutch city of Delft in the 1970s. In the *woonerf*, walkers, cyclists, and cars are all invited to mingle in the same space, as though they are sharing a living room. Street signs and marked curbs are replaced with flowerpots and cobblestones and even trees, encourag-ing users to pay more attention. It's a bit like the vehicular cyclist paradigm, except that in a *woonerf*, everyone is expected to share the road.*

Woonerven zones depend on two critical rules: First, auto drivers don't have equal rights; they are guests, legally bound to give the right-of-way to bicycles and

Before his death in 2008, Hans Monderman, a Dutch traffic engineer, achieved cult status among road wonks for exporting the shared-space concept from Dutch back streets onto busy intersections. Monderman removed road markings and signs to force all travelers to think and communicate more with one another. He insisted that such shared spaces were more safe *because they felt less safe*. As in *woonerven*, pedestrians and cyclists who entered Monderman's shared spaces were confronted with an uncertainty they could solve only by heightening their awareness of other travelers, establishing eye contact, and returning to the social rules that governed movement in busy places before cars took over. When the journalist Tom Vanderbilt joined him in the town of Drachten, Monderman actually closed his eyes and walked *backward* into a busy four-way crossing to prove his point. Drivers avoided him because they were already looking for surprises. When he heard that residents of the area did not feel safe crossing his shared-space intersections, Monderman was pleased. "I think that's wonderful," he told Vanderbilt. "Otherwise I would have changed it immediately."

Accidents and injuries plummeted around Monderman's intersections, but he wasn't recording anyone's stress levels. And there is a vast difference between safe travel and travel that feels safe. Not everyone is as brave or agile as the hero cyclist or the backward-walking traffic expert. If you really want to give people the freedom to move as they wish, you must go beyond accident statistics to consider how people actually feel about moving.

Traffic planners learned this in Portland, Oregon, a city that has spent two decades trying to coax people onto bikes. The city painted bike lanes along busy roads before the turn of the century. But by the mid-2000s the lanes remained mostly empty most of the time. Roger Geller, the city's bicycle coordinator, looked at surveys of the city's commuters and realized that they were building infrastructure for a rare species. Only about 5 percent of Portlanders were strong and fearless enough to negotiate most busy streets by bicycle. Another 7 percent of the population were enthused and confident enough to

---

pedestrians. Second, nobody in a *woonerf* moves much faster than the speed of perceived safety, which amounts to a brisk walking pace.

try the on-street bike lanes. Nobody else had the moxie to ride amid all that fast-moving metal. About a third of the population fell into what Geller called the "no way, no how" group: people who would never be into cycling.

"That made me just really depressed," said Geller, but then he realized that close to 60 percent of the population fell into a group he called the "enthused but concerned." These were people who were interested in cycling but worried about the difficulty, the discomfort, and the danger. They would cycle only if the experience was as safe and comfortable as riding in a car or a bus. So Geller and his colleagues set out to create a network of "low-stress" bikeways that either physically separated cyclists from cars or slowed cars down past the speed of fear on shared routes. It worked. Commuting by bike more than doubled in Portland between 2000 and 2008. But their investment, and the behavior change they engineered, were almost insignificant compared with the European cities where Portland found its inspiration.

A City of Reassurance

What happens when you build mobility systems entirely around safety? I found out the morning I arrived in Houten, a design experiment set amid the soggy pastures of the Dutch lowlands.

I stepped off the train, eyes blurry with an Amsterdam-size hangover, and found a bustling downtown without a car in sight—just throngs of white-haired senior citizens wheeling past on bicycles, their baskets loaded with shopping. I was greeted at Houten's city hall by the mild-mannered traffic director, Herbert Tiemens, who insisted that we go for a ride. He led me down Houten's main road, which was not actually a road but a winding path through what looked like a golf course or a soft-edged set from *Teletubbies*: all lawns and ponds and manicured shrubs. Not a car in sight. We rolled past an elementary school and kindergarten just as the lunch bell rang. Children, some of whom seemed barely out of diapers, poured out, hopped on little pink and blue bicycles, and raced past us, homeward. It was like Vauban, only softer, safer, calmer.

"We are quite proud of this," Tiemens boasted. "In most of the Netherlands, children don't bike alone to school until they are eight or nine years old. Here they start as young as six."

"Their parents must be terrified," I said.

"There's nothing to fear. The little ones do not need to cross a single road on their way home."

Once upon a time, Houten was a tiny village clustered around a fourteenth-century church. But in 1979 the Dutch government declared that Houten needed to do its part in absorbing the country's exploding population. The hamlet of five thousand needed to grow by ten times in twenty-five years—an expansion similar to what many American suburbs would experience. Faced with such an overwhelming change, the local council adopted a plan that turned the traditional notion of the city inside out.

The new Houten was designed with two separate transportation networks. The backbone of the community is a network of linear parks and paths for cyclists and pedestrians, all of which converge on that compact town center and train station (and, incidentally, a plaza laid out with the same dimensions as Siena's Piazza del Campo). Every important building in the city sits along that car-free spine. If you walk or cycle, everything is easy. Everything feels close. Everything feels safe.

The second network, built mostly for cars, does everything it can to stay out of the way. A ring road circles around the edge of town, with access roads twisting inward like broken spokes. You can reach the front door of just about every home in town by car, but if you want to drive there from the train station, you need to wend your way out to the ring road, head all the way around the edge of the city, and drive back in again.

Where bicycles and cars do share roads, signs and red asphalt make it clear that cyclists have priority. It is common to see cars inching along behind gaggles of seniors on two wheels.

The result of this reversing of the transportation order? If you count trips to the train station, two-thirds of the trips made within Houten are done by bike or on foot. The town has just half the traffic accident rate of similar-sized towns in the Netherlands and a tiny fraction of the rate found in most American towns. Between 2001 and 2005 Houten saw only one person killed in traffic—a 73-year-old

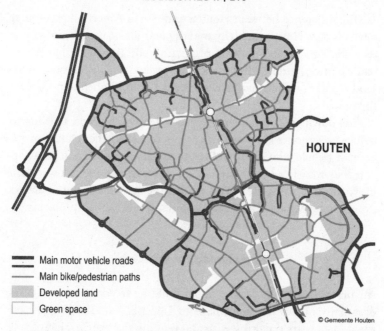

A Town Built for Children

The Dutch suburb of Houten is crisscrossed with paths for cyclists and pedestrians, while roads for cars lead only out to the town's ring road. (Gemeente Houten / José van Gool)

woman on her bike, crushed by an impatient garbage-truck driver. If it was a comparably sized American town, that number would have been twenty times as high.

By the end of the day in safe town, I could barely keep my eyes open. Houten was as sedating as a glass of warm milk at bedtime. This was, of course, the point. The town was *supposed* to be dull: it was the kind of place where young couples moved to have kids, just as North Americans move to quiet cul-de-sacs on the edge of suburbia. Old folks moved in, too. The market streets were packed with them, gliding back and forth on bicycles loaded with groceries and grandchildren. The place is so popular with buyers young and old, it is currently being doubled in size, its ring road looping around a second town center and train station.

The difference between Houten and North American commuter towns is that Houten actually makes good on its promise of safety, security, and good health. If protecting children from harm was really a priority in wealthy economies, we could have built ten thousand Houtens rather than ten thousand Weston Ranches in the past thirty years.

The downside? The reversed road scheme did almost nothing to reduce greenhouse gas emissions compared with other Dutch towns, because people who *did* drive had to take longer routes to go wherever they were headed (though emissions were still much lower than in North American cities). This reflects the externalities cities always experience when they adopt one grand solution to their problems.

Redesigning for Freedom

Anyone who is really serious about building freedom in their cities eventually makes the pilgrimage to Copenhagen. The Danes have spent forty years tinkering with and refining the systems that people use to get around their capital, transforming experiences that are miserable and dangerous in London or Los Angeles into something truly pleasurable. Their success is a product of two ideas: One is that the city itself is a laboratory that invites and rewards experimentation. The other is that planners must concern themselves with not just the physics but also the psychology of mobility.

I joined Copenhagen rush hour on a September morning with Lasse Lindholm, a fresh-faced employee of the city's traffic department. The sun was just burning through the autumn haze as we made our way across the Queen Louise's Bridge, a stately granite span over the shallow, moatlike lake that marks the western edge of the city's downtown. Vapor rose from the lake, swans drifted and preened, and the bridge seethed with a rush-hour scene like none I have ever witnessed. With each light change, cyclists rolled toward us in the hundreds. They did not look the way cyclists are supposed to look. They did not wear helmets or reflective gear. Some of the men wore pinstriped suits and shiny leather shoes. The women dressed in skirts and power suits, high heels and flowing scarves. Nobody was breaking a sweat. These were not Robert Judge adventurists. This was no race. They were calm and sexy and fit.

Lindholm rolled off a list of statistics that bear repeating: About three in ten commuters arriving in Copenhagen would use a car to get to work or school that morning. The same number would use a bus or train as their main mode. But more people would travel by bicycle than by any other mode: 37 percent. If you didn't count the suburbs, the percentage of cyclists in Copenhagen hit 55 percent. And eight of every ten of those cyclists would keep riding right through the dark and sleet-strewn Scandinavian winter. It was stunning, when you think about it: a complex, thriving metropolitan region had managed not just to accommodate heteroscedasticity but to nurture the means of travel that most cities have all but extinguished.

Copenhageners aren't choosing to cycle because of any deep-seated altruism or commitment to the environment, said Lindholm. Nor are they genetically predisposed to cycle any more than Americans are. They are motivated by self-interest. "They just want to get themselves from A to B, and now it happens to be easier and quicker to do it on a bike."

The mayor, Frank Jensen, biked to work that morning. So did several ministers of the national government. So did just about anyone who considered himself part of the city's culture of urban hipness. The height of cutting-edge style in Copenhagen is not a sports car, but the three-wheeled front-end cargo bike dubbed "the Copenhagen SUV." A quarter of families in the city with two children own one of the boxy contraptions.

This behavior is a product of design. People make different choices when they are truly free to choose. Although cycling was hugely popular in Denmark a century ago, Danes gave it up en masse during the first few decades of the auto age.* But persistent congestion and the energy crisis of the 1970s combined to produce a public backlash against auto-centric road design. Tens of thousands of people joined demonstrations calling for bike space. After the pedestrianization of the Strøget, Copenhageners saw that streets were malleable. They could be experimented with. The city had painted cycle lanes onto

*By the 1960s, only one in five Copenhageners cycled to work.

Experience Management
To accommodate surging bicycle traffic, engineers have doubled the width of cycle lanes on Copenhagen's Queen Louise's Bridge. In other areas, planners hope that double-wide lanes will promote conversation between commuting cyclists. (Charles Montgomery)

streets for years, but in the early 1980s traffic director Jens Kramer Mikkelsen began constructing bike lanes physically separated from auto space by low curbs. It changed the psychology of riding. Suddenly cyclists could travel free from fear. This was infrastructure not just for heroes but for children and seniors and people who wished to ride in safety and comfort—in other words, for everyone. It had a *Field of Dreams* effect. Just as highway building in Atlanta produced new drivers, Copenhagen's safe bike routes produced new cyclists. As the separated lane network grew, cyclists filled them, and as they did, they demanded more space. The effect has been supercharged in the past decade. As part of its plan to go carbon neutral by 2025, Copenhagen set itself the goal of knocking Amsterdam off its throne as the world's most bike-friendly city.

"This means that we must be concerned not just about safety," traffic director Niels Tørslov told me. "We care about how safe cycling *feels*."

The city tied together a network of more than two hundred miles of separate bike paths. It installed bike-only traffic lights at congested intersections, giving cyclists a four-second advantage over cars, so they can jump ahead before drivers begin making the right-hand turns that kill cyclists in other cities. Where traffic lights were once synchronized for the convenience of motorists, Copenhagen rejigged the system based on the speed of a brisk bike ride. Now a rush-hour cyclist moving just over twelve miles per hour can surf a wave of green lights through the city without putting a foot down. A cushy network of "green" cycle routes crisscross the city through a necklace of parks, far from the noise and exhaust dust of cars. And the suburbs have not been forgotten. Crews are now constructing a network of wide, separated "bike superhighways" connecting the suburbs to downtown. Oh, and when that Scandinavian snow falls, Copenhagen's bike lanes get cleared before the rest of the roads.

Copenhagen now has a unique dilemma. When the traffic department surveyed cyclists, it found that they are no longer merely fearful of cars, they are scared of one another. The tracks are getting too crowded. The city has had to revisit the conundrum faced by cities a century ago, when cars first arrived: Who has the right to the finite shared resource of city streets?

Tørslov's answer is written right here on Nørrebrogade, the road that crosses Queen Louise's Bridge. Before 2008, Nørrebrogade was clogged beyond capacity with bicycles, buses, cars, and trucks. More than 17,000 cars, 30,000 cyclists, and 26,000 bus passengers rolled down its shop-lined blocks every day. The cars took the most room by far, but cyclists were crowding each other off their path, into traffic, and onto already narrow sidewalks. Buses were waiting behind convoys of commuting motorists. Something had to give.

The solution was to conduct a temporary experiment: redesign the street to be more fair, which meant favoring travelers who use less space. Tørslov's designers created bus-only lanes and diverted commuting cars to other, wider arteries. They used the extra space to double up bike lanes and build wider sidewalks. The effect was almost immediate. By the time I rode across the Queen Louise's Bridge in 2009, commuter car traffic had fallen by half. Bus passengers reported shorter trips. Seven thousand new cyclists had joined the daily parade, which had spilled across two full lanes on each side of the bridge. And the restaurants and shops on Nørrebrogade had spilled out onto the generous sidewalks. It was just the beginning of an ambitious plan to transform the entire arterial skeleton of the city by gradually doing for other arteries what had been started on Nørrebrogade, Tørslov told me. The city's new metric: "conversation cycling infrastructure," or routes that are wide enough so that two people can bike side by side and chat, making the commute just a little more like a social visit.

All of which raises a curious parallel: just as North American cities created more automobile traffic through decades of road building, Copenhagen has induced demand for other ways of moving, especially cycling, by making streets more complete. Are cities that pursue new means of mobility heading for congestion 2.0?

Well, as Anthony Downs pointed out, congestion is an entirely natural feature of any vibrant city. So we should differentiate between types of congestion. It is not moving vehicles per se that nourish the city, but people and goods. Traffic that delivers the highest volume of people and goods for every square foot of infrastructure is clearly best for the city—and arguably best for travelers themselves.

It is a fact of geometry and physics that roads left to the open market—in other words, dominated by private cars—have a hard time supplying cities with their lifeblood. The problem is that cars are space hogs. Even the smallest of private cars takes up about 150 square feet of road space when standing still. That's thirty times the space used by a person standing, and 7.5 times the space used by a person on a bicycle or on a bus. The numbers diverge exponentially as we start moving. Someone driving alone in a car moving at thirty miles per hour takes up twenty times as much space as someone riding on a bus at the same speed. To put this into perspective: if you took all the passengers off a full city bus and put them on bikes, you would take

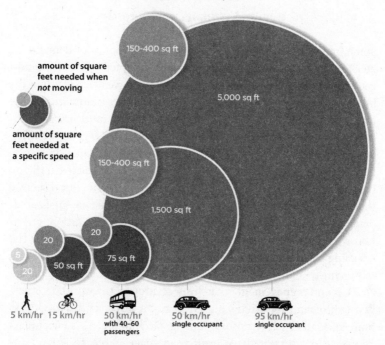

Comparing Travel Space Needs per Person

How fair and efficient are our streets? A car moving at typical city speed uses seventy-five times as much space as someone walking. (Infographic by Matthew Blackett/Spacing.ca, with data from Victoria Transport Policy Institute)

up about a block of bike lane. But if you put them in their own cars, you wouldn't have any street left at all.

This is why any plan to provide real freedom in the city demands more than shared bicycles and cars, or even more buses. Given open competition for road space, some people will choose to drive just enough to gum up the roads for themselves as well as everyone else. They slow down delivery trucks. They ensnare buses, stealing time and certainty from transit riders. They squeeze bicycles and endanger pedestrians. Cities intent on building more variety, freedom, sharing, and sustainability in mobility have no choice but to confront the privilege of private cars.

Demand, Supply, and Surprise

Some brave cities have tinkered with the economics of demand. In 2003 the London mayor Ken Livingstone adopted the world's most geographically extensive congestion charge on vehicles entering the heart of the city on weekdays.* The system uses automatic license plate recognition cameras to identify and charge most private vehicles entering the city core, with exemptions for emergency vehicles, taxis, and residents. The fee started at a hefty £5 but has since been bumped to £10. After three years, the charge had reduced traffic in the core by a quarter and was pulling in £122 million a year. It showed that travel behavior really is elastic: when people start paying the true cost of driving (which, in London's case, includes pollution, greenhouse gas emissions, and the burden imposed on other users by drivers using a disproportionate share of road space), they find other ways of moving.

Demand management is catching on around the world. In Stockholm, the charge for driving into the core climbs as you approach rush hour and falls back to nothing during slack hours. This encourages people to delay their drive until road space is not so scarce. The alternative—public transit—is financed in part by those road and congestion charges. After a brief experiment, in 2006 the citizens of Stockholm voted to make the system permanent because it made their lives easier. Meanwhile, the southern Chinese powerhouse of Guangzhou has introduced an auction and lottery system for license plates that is expected to halve the number of new cars on the road. This represented a real sacrifice, considering the fact that Guangzhou is one of China's main auto manufacturing hubs, but its problems of pollution and congestion were too great to ignore any longer.

These methods raise an ethical question. Should a public resource like city streets be reserved primarily for people who can afford to pay a premium for it? London's answer has been to use revenues from the charge to improve local bus service. But such demand management schemes do little to shift the balance of safety and access to city streets. To do that, you have to physically redistribute the supply of

---

*The zone was briefly extended west to include Kensington and Chelsea, but public opposition led the extension to be canceled in 2010.

this most public resource. This is the lesson of Paris and Copenhagen, and it has finally begun to take hold elsewhere.

Nowhere has the transformational power of redistribution been expressed more vividly than in the heart of New York City. When she was hired in 2007, the city's charismatic new transportation commissioner, Janette Sadik-Khan, mused that she was now the city's largest real estate developer. It was true. The Department of Transportation controlled six thousand miles of streets, more than a quarter of New York City's land base.

For as long as anyone could remember, the city's transportation commissioners had focused on moving cars as fast as possible. That narrow approach was now out the window. Sadik-Khan insisted that she was going to put that real estate—some of the most valuable in the world—to its highest and best use, which did not necessarily mean moving cars.

She began with a reappraisal of the value of city streets, inviting Jan Gehl to study the movement of people in New York using the methods he had developed in Copenhagen. Gehl and his team found that despite the city's preoccupation with vehicle traffic, walkers were much worse off than drivers. Congestion was far more acute on New York sidewalks than out in traffic lanes. They were clogged enough to generate collisions and conflict around bus stops and street furniture, to push people into the path of cars, and to discourage many from walking entirely.* Tellingly, only one in ten pedestrians they counted were children or seniors, even though they made up nearly a third of the population.

This unfair state of affairs had its epicenter at Times Square, where pedestrians outnumbered cars by more than four to one yet were crammed into about a tenth of the space that cars got. More than

---

*Rude behavior on crowded sidewalks is so hard on mental health that Leon James, a University of Hawaii traffic psychologist, created a Pedestrian Aggressiveness Syndrome Scale to measure pedestrian rage. If you regularly fight your way down crowded Midtown Manhattan sidewalks, chances are you have experienced some of James's syndrome traits, which range from "thinking denigrating thoughts" about other walkers, to displaying a mean face, to aggressive passing and bumping maneuvers. Each aggressive thought or action heaps new stress on the walker and the people around her—which means that New Yorkers are in trouble because their sidewalks got 13 percent more crowded between 2007 and 2011 alone.

350,000 pedestrians passed through Times Square every day, from office workers emerging from two of the city's busiest subway entrances to befuddled tourists dragging roller suitcases from curb to curb to curb. If you wanted to get run over, Times Square was one of the best places in the city for it.

Ironically, reserving almost all of Times Square for automobiles did not necessarily benefit drivers. The problem lay in the odd geometry created by Broadway's diagonal jig across the Manhattan grid. Broadway and Seventh Avenue crisscross between Forty-third and Forty-seventh streets, creating a four-block bow tie of conflict. The complex crossings were causing brutally long red-light delays. Vehicle speeds had slowed to four miles per hour.

The square epitomized the futility of trying to solve mobility issues by simply devoting more road space to traffic. A solution had evaded planners for decades. Sadik-Khan addressed it by employing the Copenhagen method: conduct a temporary experiment to see what spatial redistribution might accomplish. On Memorial Day weekend in 2009, Sadik-Khan joined city street crews as they rolled traffic barrels into place like so many orange beer kegs, blocking the flow of cars along five blocks of Broadway in and around Times Square.

"I will never forget it," she told me later. "Have you ever seen *Star Trek*? The way people materialize in the ship's transporter? It was like that. People just appeared! They just poured out into the space we created."

Sadik-Khan's ambitious redistribution of New York City's street real estate—which included painted bike lanes as well as cycle routes separated from traffic by planters and parked cars, bus-only lanes, and public plazas—precipitated some angry backlash. (I will address the psychology of these power struggles in the following chapter.) But there is no denying that by providing for more complexity and different means of moving through Midtown, the streets became simultaneously more efficient, more fair, more healthy, and even more fun. The benefits extended to drivers. A year after the change, the Department of Transportation observed that traffic was actually moving faster on most streets near Broadway. Accidents were down. Injuries to drivers, passengers, and pedestrians plummeted.

The experiment also produced the remarkable dividend that comes when places slow down: more public life.

Before   *After*

Doing It in the Road

Immediately after the barricades went up, people claimed the once-forbidden road space in Times Square. (New York City Department of Transportation)

Before the change, there were two ways of experiencing Times Square. You either sat in a car and cursed the traffic and pedestrians in your way, or you shuffled along an overburdened sidewalk with one hand on your wallet. Times Square lived large in the global imagination, but when you got there, it revealed itself as an obstacle rather than a destination. Its sidewalks were so crowded they were a perfect place to experience Milgram's theory of overload: you coped by either ignoring the people around you or doing subtle battle with them. If you were a tourist, once you got the requisite snapshot, you escaped as fast as the crowd would allow. New Yorkers who could avoid it did so completely.

But after the barriers went up, the place started to breathe. I visited Times Square periodically over the next two years and did not fully grasp its new generosity until I arrived with my eighty-four-year-old mother on a blustery September afternoon in 2011, the year after the mayor had declared the changes permanent. The walk through Midtown's jostling crowds had not been easy. My mother white-knuckled her cane, and I held her close. But as we crossed Forty-seventh Street, the aggressive crowds suddenly eased. She let go of my hand. I paused on the glowing red staircase that does double duty as a roof for the TKTS theater-ticket booth and seating for the public theater of Times Square. Before I knew it, she had stepped down over the curb onto the surface of Broadway. She moved slowly and deter-minedly south among the groves of chairs that the Times Square Alliance had scattered on the asphalt. She paused near the bronze statue of George M. Cohan, made a tripod with her cane, and turned her gaze upward. Her face was lit with the flash and sparkle of the bill-board light show. Waves of people moved around her, but they gave her wide berth. There was room to spare. This was her own Robert Judge moment. She was free in the city, at least for a couple of blocks.

10. Who Is the City For?

> The right to the city cannot be conceived of as a simple
> visiting right or as a return to traditional cities. It can only
> be formulated as a transformed and renewed right to
> urban life.
>
> —Henri Lefebvre, 1968

It would be wonderful if the shapes of our cities maximized utility for everyone. It would be wonderful if city builders were guided purely by an enlightened calculus of utility. But this is not how the world works. Urban spaces and systems do not merely reflect altruistic attempts to solve the complex problem of people living close together, and they are more than an embodiment of the creative tension between competing ideas. They are shaped by struggles between competing groups of people. They apportion the benefits of urban life. They express who has power and who does not. In so doing, they shape the mind and the soul of the city.

Sometimes a self-evident truth does not become salient until you see it written in bold text across the most extreme landscape. This is what I learned in Colombia.

Jaime, my host in Bogotá, was a cautious man from the middle class. His timidity had calcified on the afternoon when a gang of paramilitaries fired a rocket at the office tower where he worked as a television editor. The projectile missed its mark, but Jaime's trust in his fellow citizens never quite recovered. He ordered me not to walk the streets of Bogotá alone. He warned me never to wander at night. Most of all, he forbade me from visiting the ragged slums on the southern fringes of the city, where civil war refugees settled on the plains between the meandering Bogotá and Tunjuelo rivers.

Well-to-do Bogotans imagined that the slums were a nightmare collage of rape, muggings, and murder. But these new neighborhoods were the landscape on which a radical new urban philosophy had been inscribed onto the city over the previous decade. So I snuck out of the apartment early one morning while Jaime was still snoring in his room, crept past the night guard, and walked down through pools of jaundiced lamplight to Avenida Caracas.

I pushed through a turnstile and stepped inside a sleek pavillion of polished aluminum and glass. Polite messages ran silently across an LED screen like quotes on the NASDAQ stock ticker. Four sets of glass doors slid open in unison. I stepped through into an immaculate carriage and took a seat. With a growl, the vehicle eased forward, gaining speed until it was whooshing down the smooth guideway.

It reminded me of the Copenhagen subway—superfast, superclean, superefficient—only instead of rumbling blindly beneath the earth, we could watch the purple glow of dawn over the silhouette of the Andes. And this was no train or high-tech people mover. It was a bus. A bus—just the low-status ride that North Americans love to hate. But the TransMilenio, as Enrique Peñalosa dubbed this bus system, had turned the transit experience upside down. Based on a rapid bus model pioneered in Curitiba, Brazil, the TransMilenio had appropriated the best space on the city's great *avenidas*, leaving car drivers, taxis, and minibuses to fight for the scraps. This is exactly what American streetcar companies had begged for during the car invasion of the 1920s, and which most cities have not seen for decades: a system that aggressively favors those who share space, discourages those who try to grab more than their share, and saves taxpayers from having to fork out for expensive subway lines or new freeways. For a small fraction of the construction cost, the system moves more people per hour than many urban rail-transit systems. Transit fanatics come from around the world to take this ride.

With its lipstick-red coat and gleaming stations, the Trans-Milenio felt downright sexy. That's right: the best way to get to one of the poorest neighborhoods in the hemisphere is to take the sexy bus. We covered about ten miles in twenty minutes. Just as the sun was cresting the Andes, we rolled into a grand airportlike complex at the end of the line. More glass curtains and polished marble. Streams of scruffy commuters pedaled along bike paths into a spacious bicycle-

The Sexy Bus

Bogotá's TransMilenio bus system claimed the best road space in the city from private automobiles and used high-quality finishes in its stations. The intent was not just to cut travel times but also to boost the status of public transit riders. (Courtesy of the City of Bogotá)

storage hall guarded by armed valets. This was Portal de Las Américas, a transit hub appointed with the flair of a bullet-train station.

I jumped in a pedicab and asked the kid at the handlebars to take me to the heart of the barrio misnamed El Paraíso—Paradise.

"Yes, sir," he said in Spanish. "But you must hide your camera." Then he jerked the rusty tricycle around and headed against the current of work-bound cyclists, his breath leaving a contrail in the cold morning air. El Paraíso resembled any other South American aspirational slum: prickly stands of rusted rebar poked from half-built cinder-block walls, monuments to the mansions people imagined completing in their future. Feral dogs chased plastic bags along dirt streets.

But partway along what turned out to be a roundabout journey, the cinder-block walls parted to reveal a monumental white edifice standing in a grassy park. "El Tintal," the kid said as we wheeled past. With its great round windows and tilted skylights, the building looked like a space portal. In fact, it had spent most of its life as a garbage-processing plant before being retrofitted into a library by Daniel Bermúdez, one of the country's most respected architects. The ramp once used by dump trucks was now a grand elevated entrance-way. "Who on earth would come all this way, and to this neighbor-hood, to peruse the stacks?" I wondered aloud, rather stupidly.

"My mother," said the kid. "And me."

The boulevard we found slicing through the middle of Paradise was just as surprising. Usually, the first thing that poor cities do to improve dirt roads is to lay a strip of asphalt down the middle so cars can barrel through. This was different. A wide runway of concrete and tile ran down the middle, but it had been raised knee-high to pre-vent cars from gaining access. The result: a grand promenade reserved exclusively for pedestrians and cyclists. Now and then a car would rumble through the moonscape of potholes and rubble along the edge of the road.

Having arrived by way of Houston, to me the road felt as upside down as the bus system.

If you saw a road like this in Northern Europe or, say, Portland, you'd assume it was the product of some civic committee's carbon reduction plan: a tool for nudging people out of their cars for the good of polar ice caps and future generations. This was not the case in Bogotá. The entire system—the upside-down road, the ultramod-ern bus station, the monumental library, the bike lanes, and the TransMilenio itself—had only one purpose. They were a *happiness* intervention.

Embedded within this landscape are lessons for wealthy cities in an era when budgets will be tight and resources scarce, and when every design decision will inevitably produce clear sets of winners and losers. We can learn from Bogotá because of the way its political leaders chose to act during a few short years, in a time of psychic crisis.

The Worst City in the World

When I began this story, I told you about Bogotá's legendary decline. Colombia spent the last decades of the twentieth century mired in a civil war that left citizens caught between leftist guerrillas, govern-

In developing-world cities with limited resources, roads are first improved by paving them for the few who drive cars, while the majority who do not drive must negotiate the mud and rubble on the shoulder . . .

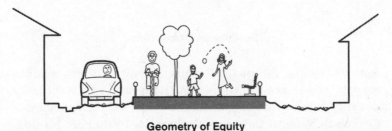

Geometry of Equity

. . . But on Bogotá's Alameda El Porvenir, the paved promenade is reserved for pedestrians and cyclists, while cars are relegated to the edge. (Dan Planko)

ment soldiers, and paramilitary forces. The chaos had crept across jungles and plantations until it infected the capital. How bad was it? Eighty thousand refugees poured into the shanties on the city's edges every year, pushing the population to close to eight million. Those lucky enough to find jobs took hours getting there, stewing under the Andean sun inside a battered fleet of private minibuses whose rainbow colors did not make up for their stunning griminess or inefficiency. There was no public transit system worth taking, and the roads were choked with congestion. The air was a toxic soup. The city ate people's time and chewed on their good nature. People were afraid of one another. In 1995 alone, there were 3,363 murders (a rate of 60 dead for every 100,000 people, or 10 murders a day) and 1,387 traffic deaths. The psychological landscape was depressing: three-quarters of Bogotanos thought that life was just going to get worse. Pundits dismissed the city as terminally ungovernable.

The incivility and violence even seeped into the mayoral campaigns.

During a televised debate between candidates Antanas Mockus and Enrique Peñalosa, a raucous student audience stormed the stage, and Mockus was caught on film brawling with the interlopers.

Peñalosa and Mockus offered Bogotans two radically different visions for urban salvation. In many ways, they represent opposite answers to a critical question: Do you save a broken city by fixing its hardware, its public space and infrastructure, or do you save it by fixing its software—the attitudes and behavior of its citizens? When Mockus won the mayor's seat in 1995, Bogotans got a powerful and sometimes bizarre taste of the latter approach.

The City as Classroom

Antanas Mockus, the son of Lithuanian immigrants, was regarded as slightly odd, even by his admirers. He sported a bowl cut and a chinstrap beard and lived with his mother. He had been president of Colombia's National University until the day he dropped his trousers and mooned an auditorium of unruly students. The move, which he called an act of "symbolic violence," cost Mockus his job, but it afforded him a sudden celebrity status that helped propel him to the mayor's seat. When he won the election, Mockus claimed all of Bogotá as his classroom. "I was elected to build a culture of citizenship," he told me later. "What is citizenship? The notion that along with human rights, we all have duties. And the first priority is to establish respect for human life as the main right and duty of citizens."

Bogotá had never seen a teacher like this. Mockus sent more than four hundred mimes out onto the streets to make fun of rude drivers and pedestrians. He handed out stacks of red cards so that, like soccer referees, people could call out antisocial behavior rather than punching or shooting each other. He invited people to turn in their guns on voluntary disarmament days, and fifteen hundred firearms were ceremonially melted down to make baby spoons. (Only one in one hundred of the city's guns were retrieved, but surveys found the exercise had the effect of making many people *feel* safer and less agressive.)

Mockus actually took to dashing about the city in cape and tights as "Super Citizen" to illustrate his new code of civility, but his out-landish social marketing campaigns were supported by action. He brought in tough new rules against patronage appointments at city hall. He fired all the city's transit police, owing to the department's well-known bribability. It was Mockus who hired Guillermo Peñalosa, his opponent's brother, as his parks czar and empowered him to expand both the parks system and the hugely popular Ciclovía Sunday street-closure program. Upon demonstrating his commitment to clean government, Mockus actually invited citizens to pay 10 percent more property tax to help the city deliver more services. Remarkably, more than sixty thousand households volunteered. Unorthodox as his methods were, Mockus did build a new culture of respect. Those methods may have even prepared citizens for their next mayor, who would test their very ideas of who and what the city was for.

The Urban Equity Doctrine

When Mockus quit his post to run for president in 1997, the murder, crime, and accident rates had begun to fall, but Bogotá's physical and functional problems—congestion; pollution; and a critical lack of schools, safe streets, and public space—were still acute. The city had begun to change its mind, but it was being held back by its body.

Enrique Peñalosa, who finally won the mayor's seat on his third try, insisted that there was an inherent connection between urban form and culture. It was not enough, he felt, to teach people a new citizenship of respect. The city itself had to manifest that philosophy in its forms, systems, and services.

"Only a city that respects human beings can expect citizens to respect the city in return," he said in his inauguration speech. He promised that he would use his term to build that respect into the city, using concrete, steel, leaf, and lawn.

At the start of this book I credited Enrique Peñalosa with a big and simple idea: that urban design should be used to make people happier. Peñalosa is indeed a student of the happiness economists, but his program for Bogotá was grounded in a specific interpretation of well-being that, by its nature, threatens to make many urbanites uncomfortable. It asks: Who should share in the public wealth of the city? Who should have access to parks and beautiful places? Who should have the privilege of easy mobility? The questions are as much political as philosophical. Indeed, they were formed in a place and time where every big idea was political, though most were more likely to lead to revolution than urban innovation.

The Peñalosa brothers were born in the 1950s and raised in upper-middle-class privilege in Bogotá's leafy north end, but they were made acutely aware of their country's grinding inequities by their father, also named Enrique, who administered Colombia's Agrarian Reform Institute. He periodically loaded Enrique junior and his brother Guillermo into a Jeep and carried them into the countryside, where, in a medieval anachronism, millions of peasants still worked the land for Colombia's elite landowners. Enrique senior performed the work of a government-sanctioned Robin Hood, taking land from the rich and redistributing it to the ragged poor who worked it. The journeys imprinted on the boys a sense of familial mission. Since they happened to attend school with the children of the landowning elite, young Enrique and Guillermo found themselves defending their father in playground fistfights. Enrique went on to study economics, and although he wrote a book he unambiguously titled *Capitalism: The Best Option*, he continued to see city life through the lens of equity.

It could barely be otherwise. The city was just as unfair as the Colombian countryside. The biggest green space in the city was a private country club. Well-to-do residents, including Peñalosa's own neighbors, fenced off their neighborhood parks to keep out the riffraff. Merely walking was a challenge because Bogotá's sidewalks had disappeared under parked cars, and hawkers had completely taken over downtown plazas. The most visible injustice lay in the way that Bogotá apportioned the right to get around. Only one in five Bogotan families owned a car, but the city was increasingly using the highway-fed North American metropolis as its role model, building more road space and leaving drivers, cyclists, and bus riders to duke it out on the open road.

Before Peñalosa's election, Bogotá had been getting technical and planning advice from the Japanese International Cooperation Agency (JICA). This was not unusual. Poor cities often accept help from such international aid agencies. Nor was it surprising that in its new development plan for the city, JICA had prescribed a vast network of elevated freeways to ease Bogotá's congestion. The private car and progress were symbolically intertwined. The plan infuriated the new mayor—not just because JICA's $5 billion plan was so transparently tailored to benefit Japan's auto industry, but because Bogotá's elite were so keen on it as well.

"We think it's totally normal in developing-country cities that we spend billions of dollars building elevated highways while people don't have schools, they don't have sewers, they don't have parks. And we think this is progress, and we show this with great pride, these elevated highways!" he complained later.

But Bogotá would not build those elevated highways. Peñalosa began his term by scuttling the plan. He also jacked up gas taxes by 40 percent and sold the city's shares in a regional telephone company and a hydro power utility. He poured the revenues into an aggressive agenda that put public space, transportation, and architecture to the task of improving the urban experience for everyone. His administration bought up undeveloped land on the edge of the city to prevent speculation and ensure that new neighborhoods would get affordable housing with services, parks, and greenways. He built dozens of new schools and hundreds of nurseries for toddlers. He supercharged the expansion of the parks system begun by his brother and Mockus, creating a stunning network of six hundred parks, from neighborhood nooks to Simón Bolívar, a central park more vast than Central Park. He planted a hundred thousand trees. He built three monumental new libraries in the poorer parts of town, including the one I had seen on my ride toward El Paraíso.

All this was in service of a philosophy of radical fairness.

"One of the requirements for happiness is equality," Peñalosa told me as we rode down a side street during the election campaign in 2007. He talked so fast I had to strap a microphone to my handlebars so I could catch his words. "Maybe not equality of income, but equality of quality of life and, more than that, an environment where people don't feel inferior, where people don't feel excluded."

Peñalosa pulled his bike to the curb and slapped one of the thousands of bollards that he had planted along city sidewalks. These bollards were the most symbolic salvo in his so-called war on cars. Before his term, these sidewalks would have been blocked by illegally parked cars. Not anymore. The posts stood like sentries, and indeed, the sidewalk was open and thrumming with people.

"These bollards show that pedestrians are as important as people with cars. We are creating equality; we are creating respect for human dignity. We're telling people, 'You are important—not because you're rich, but because you are human.' If people are treated as special, as sacred, they behave that way. This creates a different kind of society. So every detail in a city must reflect that human beings are sacred. Each detail!"

Later he pointed out two workmen in overalls, pedaling along one of his bicycle roads on Bogotá's wealthy north end. "See those guys?" he said, nodding. "My bikeway gives them a new sense of pride."

The connection was not obvious. How on earth could a bicycle path make someone proud?

"Because it gives them self-respect! Look: before, cyclists were just the poorest of the poor, and they were seen as a nuisance. So the biggest value of the bikeway is symbolic. It shows that a citizen on a thirty-dollar bicycle is equally important as one in a thirty-thousand-dollar BMW.

"It is the same with the bus system. We are not trying to be architecturally cute with these measures, and this is not just an exercise in environmentalism or transport. Social justice, that's what we are constructing!"

The TransMilenio system's director told me later that Peñalosa had insisted on choosing the lipstick-red paint color and even the name for the rapid bus system. Both were supposed to imbue the bus with a hip, modern cachet, so that riders would feel that taking public transit was a high-status experience, even if they had no other choice. Peñalosa also insisted that new libraries such as El Tintal be spectacular architectural icons designed by the country's most respected architects, "in homage to every child, every citizen who would enter there."

Fairness, Felt

There is an assumption in Peñalosa's declarative flood that demands examination. It is that helping people *feel* more equal is a worthy policy goal—as though feeling equal can matter as much as actually *be-*

ing equal. In fact, achieving the former generally demands the latter, as his own interventions acknowledged. But let's not let go just yet of this idea: that status, as a *subjective feeling*, matters.

There's no doubt that we are all compelled by social comparisons. Ask yourself which world you would prefer: one where you drove the only Honda Civic on a highway full of BMWs, or a world where you rode the only tricked-out moped in a city of rusty bikes? Surveys suggest that most people say they would choose the second world— having less is okay, but having less than everyone else feels awful. We can't help but judge our position relative to everyone else.*

Social scientists have known for a long time that poor people are often less healthy than the rich. Some of this health gap can be blamed on lifestyle, long work hours, and lack of access to nutritious food and health care. But not all of it. A decades-long examination of health and mortality in British civil servants—dubbed the Whitehall Studies—found what researchers called "a steep inverse association between social class, as assessed by grade of employment, and mortality from a wide range of diseases." In other words, the more senior you were in the employment hierarchy, the longer you'd live. Messengers, doormen, and other low-ranking employees were more likely to experience heart disease, cancer, lung disease, and depression than higher-status employees. In the United States, poor people in cities with the widest income gaps are less healthy than poor people in more equal cities. Hypertension, high cholesterol, and decreased immunity—all of these come with low status. Changes in social status affects our brain chemistry. Being low in status is like standing in a shower of stress hormones every day. As biologist and neuroscientist Robert Sapolsky puts it, "the disease consequences of feeling poor are often rooted in the psychosocial consequences of being made to feel poor by one's surroundings." If you've got food and a roof over your head, the worst part of poverty may in fact be the *feeling* of being poorer than other people.

Big gaps in socioeconomic status can mean trouble for society in

---

*Status comparisons are an almost inescapable habit. Most people say they would forgo a pay raise if it means that their colleagues will get an even bigger raise. Other surveys find that people tend to be less happy with their jobs the more their spouses earn.

general. In their book, *The Spirit Level: Why Greater Equality Makes Societies Stronger*, British epidemiologists Richard Wilkinson and Kate Pickett demonstrate how gross inequality can lead to higher rates of violent crime, drug use, children born to teenagers, and heart disease. "If you fail to avoid high inequality, you will need more prisons and more police," they warn governments. "You will have to deal with higher rates of mental illness, drug abuse and every other kind of problem."* Some economists argue that status gaps are so harmful that we should treat them like pollution and use the tax system to close them.

All this may be valid, but it would be wrong to reduce the Bogotá program to a strategy for managing people's feelings. By any objective assessment, the happy mayor's efforts to make the poor feel more equal actually made them more equal. Consider Fabien Gonzáles, a lanky young man I met at Portal de las Américas, whose story was typical of the city's poor: he pedaled his bike a mile to the Portal, then rode the TransMilenio fifteen miles to his job as a cashier at the Home Center, a big-box outlet on the wealthy north side of town. His monthly pay: the equivalent of about $240. Gonzáles had no choice but to use his feet, his bike, and the bus to get to work. He did not find the TransMilenio particularly sexy. But it did give him the gift of time.

"Before the TransMilenio I had to leave home two hours before starting work," he told me as he squeezed onto a northbound express. "Now, forty-five minutes, maximum."

This is the essence of Peñalosa's happy city program. It actively redistributes the benefits of city living in order to make it fairer and more tolerable for the biggest number of people. The color of the bus matters, but even more important is the way it speeds riders across the city. (The average TransMilenio rider saves forty minutes a day.) While the upside-down road's relegation of cars to the rubbly edge

---

*This may be part of the reason for the strong connection being found between inequality and the happiness of societies in general. If economic growth makes a country richer but less equal, it can actually corrode general happiness. This is terrible news for the United States, where there has been a steady upward sucking of wealth and power in the past three decades. Thirty years ago, an American CEO would make forty times as much as the lowest-paid person in the company. Now the ratio is more than four hundred to one.

might please a status-conscious cyclist, what really matters is the ability of millions of poor people to move quickly and safely. El Tintal library may well inspire its poor neighbors with its postindustrial grace, but more practically, it gives them access to books, and to a place where they can gather and learn. And while it's possible that the Ciclovía program creates warm and fuzzy feelings between the rich and the poor who gather on becalmed roads, what really matters is that millions of people who have no backyards or cars in which to escape the city can enjoy an ephemeral park and a sense of freedom for a few hours each Sunday.

War and Peace

Peñalosa learned when he was a boy that the redistribution of privilege always meets with resistance. But he was not one for compromise. He ordered the removal of thousands of cluttering commercial billboards, and he tore down the fences residents had erected around neighborhood parks. He went to war not just with cars but with anyone who appropriated public space in Bogotá, even if they were poor—in one case forcing thousands of struggling street vendors to remove stalls that had choked off public plazas. The city's amenities were for everyone. Peñalosa campaigned to turn the city's grand country club into a public park. Even the dead were targeted: while Mockus had the words "Life Is Sacred" painted on the walls of a cemetery in the central city, Peñalosa attempted to remove the graves so that the living could have more park space. (Both the country club and cemetery initiatives failed.)

This aggressive plan created plenty of enemies for him at first. Private bus operators and drivers who were pushed from Trans-Milenio routes were furious. So were the vendors and hawkers who were swept from popular plazas. But none were as vociferous as the business lobby, who were outraged by the bollards that went up along city sidewalks, effectively killing their free parking. They could not imagine customers arriving by foot, bike, or bus.

"He was trying to *Satanize* cars," Guillermo Botero, the president of FENALCO, Colombia's national federation of retailers, told me. "The car is a means of subsistence. It is an indispensable means for people to develop their own lives. If we keep squeezing roads, the city will eventually collapse."

FENALCO and its allies threw the full force of their connections and their bank accounts into a campaign to impeach the mayor. For a while, it looked as though Peñalosa would lose his job.

Equity Wars

The Bogotá backlash was not unique. It is mirrored in cities around the world. No matter how desperate, dysfunctional, or unfair the circumstances, and no matter how rational the initiative, new plans that threaten the urban design status quo face deep and emotional opposition.

In New York City, efforts to redistribute street space—including the creation of 255 miles of painted or separated bike lanes—have met with near-hysterical response from some quarters. In 2011, opponents of a new separated bike lane on the edge of Brooklyn's Prospect Park actually sued the city to have the lanes removed, though the suit was eventually dismissed.* City councilors and columnists alike accused Mayor Michael Bloomberg of launching a culture war, favoring a "faddist minority" of bike-riding elitists over car commuters and anyone not rich enough to live in Manhattan. The argument was a complete reversal of the status narrative in Bogotá, and it was false. Two-thirds of the people who work in New York City commute on transit or by walking. Fewer than half of the city's households even own a car. Only one in a hundred regularly commutes by taxi. The claims of elitism were dripping with irony: in New York and all over America, it is not the rich but the poor who are most likely to travel by bicycle.†

Resistance to urban renovations is driven partly by deeply held beliefs about the relationship between urban form and culture, and

---

*The opponents' various claims—that the lanes are neither safe nor popular—contradict reality. City studies found that cycling doubled in the city between 2006 and 2010, and that when protected bike lanes were installed, crashes causing injury for all road users typically drop by a whopping 40 percent.

†A 2011 study found that the poorest quarter of all Americans make nearly one-third of all bike trips.

what it means to be free in cities. The system of dispersal is entrenched not just in roads and curbs and traffic signals and shopping malls; it has infused our very way of thinking about what streets and cities are for. In 2007, when Mexico City closed several major avenues to car traffic in its own version of the Ciclovía, I witnessed a woman attempting to push a police officer out of her path with the bumper of her Ford Fiesta. "You are violating my human rights!" she hollered out the window to the astonished Sunday strollers and rollers. Later, Mexican radio host Angel Verdugo called on drivers to simply run over cyclists. "They want to be like Europeans," he complained. "They believe they are living in Paris and riding along the Champs-Élysées!"

Some of this backlash stems from stakeholders' fear of losing the right to live and move as they have become accustomed. This is natural. As the benefits of urban systems get reapportioned, some people will be inconvenienced. But opponents of happy city redesigns generally lose the equity debate. Today's urban mobility systems are flat-out unfair, especially in North America. As I detailed earlier, a third of Americans—those too young, too old, too poor, too infirm, or simply not interested—do not drive at all. In an auto-dependent city, that leaves one in every three people at the mercy of scarce public transit or dependent on someone else to chauffeur him around. Children and teenagers are the most obvious victims of this. They are trapped at home and denied the freedom to walk to school or to see friends as they wish.

Nondriving seniors are even worse off: they end up making it to the doctor, to restaurants, to social events, and to religious gatherings only half as often as seniors who can drive. Older African Americans and Latinos are twice as likely to depend on transit as Caucasians and much more likely to be stuck at home.

This unfairness is compounded by the way cities are organized. We have known for decades that poor people and minorities in the United States have less access to parks, green space, and recreation centers, and they even have fewer trees on the streets where they live. This is one reason their children are more likely to suffer the ailments that go with obesity. After decades of sprawl construction, they also have less access to jobs. (A third of low-income African Americans don't even have access to a car.) They also have less access to food.

(More than 2.5 million households in the United States live more than a mile from a supermarket and don't have access to a car. And the less white the neighborhood, the worse access to supermarkets or healthy food tends to be.)

You might suggest that people simply walk to those stores—walking being the most basic of urban liberties—but minorities in the United States are much less likely than white people even to have sidewalks in their neighborhoods. In Los Angeles, where the wealth has been poured into freeways, the city has admitted that 40 percent of its sidewalks are in disrepair.*

It should be no surprise to anyone familiar with this state of geographic inequity that black and Latino Americans are much more likely to die on the road than whites are. This became salient for me when reviewing news stories of pedestrian fatalities around Atlanta. I found a tragic succession of similar narratives, in which poor people, usually black and usually children, were killed simply trying to dash across the highwaylike byways of suburban Atlanta to reach a suburban bus stop. One might dismiss them as foolish until you note that crosswalks on some of these suburban byways are more than a mile apart.

This is not merely an American problem. Poor children in the United Kingdom are twenty-eight times more likely to be killed on roads than wealthy children are. In Britain, which lost a fifth of its local services to big-boxing and car-focused growth between 1995 and 2000, the New Economics Foundation found that people without cars were finding it harder and harder to shop, get medical services, or even get to work. Eight hundred towns lost their banks. One in four young people reported missing a job interview because it was just too hard to get there.

The financing of this inequity is deeply unfair, too. Because they drive more and farther, the richest 10 percent of the population in the U.K. benefit from four times as much public spending on transport as the poorest 10 percent. In the United States, only about half of roadway expenses are financed by user fees such as gas taxes,

---

*Sidewalks in Los Angeles and other California cities are in such bad shape that they are facing civil rights lawsuits from disabled people, who find cracked and broken surfaces, and curbs without ramps, totally impassable.

vehicle registration, or tolls (and most of that money goes to highways, which pedestrians and cyclists tend not to use). The rest comes from property and income taxes paid by everyone. Here is where equity and efficiency collide: because of their light footprint, infrastructure for walkers and cyclists costs only a tiny fraction of auto infrastructure to build and maintain. So cyclists and pedestrian commuters who pay property and income tax actually end up subsidizing their car-driving neighbors.*

The dispersal system also happens to be unfair even to those capable of driving. In *The Option of Urbanism*, the land-use strategist Christopher Leinberger explained how patterns of sprawl development punish poor drivers: Most cities develop "favored quarters" where the (mostly white) rich tend to live and shop. In sprawl, those favored quarters are fed by investment in new highways, malls, and job centers. Priced out of such districts, poor people are forced to drive farther to work, meaning they buy more gas and contribute more in gas taxes, which have traditionally gone toward funding more highway improvements in the favored quarters that exclude them.

Now the poorest fifth of American families pour more than 40 percent of their income into owning and maintaining cars. When working families move far from their jobs in order to find affordable homes, they can end up blowing their savings just getting there—which is exactly the condition that led so many of San Joaquin County's super-commuters to foreclosure.†

Residents of favored districts have long guarded against new density that might bring in poorer people. Their preferences have been woven right into zoning codes, and they have found their way into infrastructure decisions. (In Los Angeles, a subway linking downtown with the ocean in Santa Monica was delayed for nearly two decades partly because residents in affluent Hancock Park and Beverly Hills did not want their community to be directly accessible from poorer East and South L.A.) American cities have actually

*The number crunchers at the Victoria Transport Policy Institute estimate that for every mile that someone in the United States travels in an automobile, on a bike, or on foot, the costs in public infrastructure are 29.3 cents, .9 cents, and .2 cents, respectively.
†In American cities, extra commuting costs incurred after a move of twelve to fifteen miles can eat up all the savings offered by cheaper housing.

been getting more segregated by income class for the past three decades.

To Be Fair

These inequities need to be confronted: in part for the sake of the poor, who have every bit as much right to the public benefits of the city as the wealthy; in part for the soul of the city, which, as the Greeks knew, was above all a *shared* project; and in part for purely pragmatic reasons—in a fairer city, life can be better for everyone.

In the fair city, people who share space on transit enjoy the right-of-way on congested roads.

In the fair city, streets are safe for everyone, especially children. (As Peñalosa points out: your streets are not inclusive until you can imagine an eight-year-old or an eighty-year-old walking safely and independently. This might seem an audacious goal until you actually see the very old and the very young walking and cycling on the streets of Copenhagen or Vauban, and now El Paraíso.)

In the fair city, everyone has access to parks, shops, services, and healthy food.

This access is almost never realized by accident. Public parks, for example, tend to reflect the preferences of the socioeconomic class whose members designed them—typically middle-class professionals with kids. But kid-friendly design is not necessarily friendly to everyone else. I realized this in Copenhagen when planners walked me through the recently renovated Nørrebro Park, an inner-city green space. There was the lawn for lovers' picnics and pickup soccer. There was the children's playground. But off to one side, there was also an unadorned hut surrounded by a high wooden fence. This was the zone designed by and for a demographic that some people call drunken bums.

"We asked everyone in the neighborhood to come to our planning meetings, but we realized that the alcoholics, the guys who just sit around all day and drink in the park, never showed up," planner Henrik Lyng told me as we wandered through the park. "So we just bought a case of beer, came down here, and found them."

The drinkers told Lyng they wanted a place to hang out where they wouldn't be bothered by or bother other park users. They wanted a place to meet. They also wanted a toilet. That's what they got.

I met a few of the regulars in that compound: rough, red-eyed men accompanied by rather fierce dogs. The guys said that the fence ensured that their dogs didn't scare the children in the playground. They picked up the litter and looked out for each other. The compound was their common living room. Nørrebro Park works for everyone because it acknowledges through design that everyone has a right to be there.

But we face a couple of daunting challenges getting to the fair city. First of all, in most places, the happy redesigns I've been talking about—from bike lanes, traffic calming, good transit, and pop-up plazas to bylaws that ensure vibrant commercial streets—appear first in favored districts because their residents have the time, money, and political influence to make them happen. That's one problem. The other is that wherever they are implemented, such livability measures actually drive up land values. This may be good news for property owners and city coffers, but it is a disaster for renters. For example, a new light-rail line through Seattle's Rainier Valley has attracted lots of new investment—but it has also begun to squeeze out people of color. New York City's celebrated High Line Park has caused lightning-fast gentrification: the cost of residential property within a five-minute walk of the park more than doubled during the eight years straddling the park's opening in 2009.

No wonder these measures are viewed with suspicion. In a reversal of the last century's prevailing trend, wealthy people are increasingly colonizing inner cities while poor people and new immigrants are pushed to the suburban fringes. Some of the less wealthy who still manage to occupy a place in the connected city understand the relationship between amenities and affordability. In Berlin, activists sucesfully prevented the BMW Guggenheim Lab from staging three months of free events in the gritty district of Kreuzberg, knowing it would speed up gentrification in the area. In my own neighborhood in East Vancouver, the renovation of a public park in 2010 prompted organized protests by people who were worried that the spruced-up green space would cause nearby rents to rise. The fear is justified: the forces of supply and demand have helped make housing in some of the world's most livable cities—such as Vancouver and Melbourne—the least affordable.*

So any sincere effort to build the fair city must also confront the unfairnesses wrought by markets and geography. Just as Peñalosa infused civic benefits into Bogotá's slums, wealthy cities must provide affordable housing, and different kinds of housing, in even the most favored neighborhoods.

Some cities have been making that slow journey toward equity. In the last century, Americans came to admit that rules that effectively banned poor people or people of color from certain neighborhoods were wrong. Similarly, governments and the courts have acknowledged that land zoning that excludes apartments and affordable housing from neighborhoods also constitutes a form of segregation. In 1973 the wealthy county of Montgomery, Maryland, passed a bylaw stating that 15 percent of dwellings in every new subdivision in every part of the county must be suitable for people of low or moderate income. That way the people who work in the county could actually live there. It worked: thousands of lower-income residents have since found homes in one of the wealthiest parts in the state. The bylaw has been copied in hundreds of other cities.

Lately though, the housing equity challenge has boomeranged. As wealthy people rediscover the convenience and pleasure of central city living, poor people are being pushed out to the urban fringe. Cities that care must take aggressive and creative design interventions to ensure these neighborhoods serve everyone. What might that look like in the age of scarce public funds?

Vancouver again provides inspiration, this time on the site of Woodward's, an abandoned department store that marked the frontier between super-shiny Vancouverism and the grit of Canada's poorest neighborhood. Housing activists, private developers, the City,

*Vancouver and Melbourne, frequent winners on surveys of livability, ranked just behind Hong Kong as the least affordable in Demographia's 2012 International Housing Affordability Survey of cities in Canada, the United States, the United Kingdom, New Zealand, Australia, and Hong Kong. The survey is ideologically driven—its founder, Wendell Cox, is a vocal opponent of smart-growth policies and a paid consultant for various free-market think tanks—but it does make a clear point about the cost of housing. (Detroit was the most affordable among surveyed cities.)

and senior levels of government collaborated on a plan to populate the site with a university, retail stores, and the usual clutch of cafés—all beneath three residential towers.* The model was unprecedented: One of the towers contains subsidized housing for families. Another offers bomb-proof rooms for dirt-poor singles, most of whom arrive with addictions and mental illness. The tallest of the three towers, dubbed the W, offers fancy condominiums at market prices.

The subsidized component of the project depended in part on public dollars, but it also depended on the willingness of hundreds of buyers to pay top dollar for upscale condos situated amid the maelstrom of poverty and open drug use. Bob Rennie, the marketer selling the W, challenged buyers with the slogan "Be Bold or Move to Suburbia." It was an audacious (and, some in the neighborhood charged, unforgivably classist) dare, but it worked. The tower's suites, priced from $350,000 to $1.4 million, sold out within a month.

How could design help people of such disparate means live in such proximity? The project architect, Gregory Henriquez, employed a keen appreciation for status aspirations and anxieties in his solutions. Each tower got its own lobby: a segregation that was requested both by Rennie and by the Portland Hotel Society, the agency that would run the social housing component. (Poorer residents could not afford the lobby upgrades inevitably requested by the wealthy. And their representatives admitted that it might be psychologically hard for the poor to ride the elevator daily with people who were so much richer.) Another nod to privacy and status: Henriquez fitted the windows of the singles housing with hardy sliding blinds. Residents dealing with mental illness and paranoia could shut out the light of the world without taping up their windows with tinfoil and newspaper, thus preserving the views from market condominiums across the courtyard. The Woodward's block's street edges may be disappointingly bare, but inside that block is a grand public atrium through which the entire spectrum of neighbors pass and occasionally mingle, while students take shots at the basketball hoop at its heart. Woodward's has proved so convivial that it has accelerated

---

*The project contains 536 market condos, 125 subsidized apartments for singles, and 75 family nonmarket housing units.

gentrification in the area, but it has done so while locking two hundred affordable homes in place.

It's not enough to nudge the market toward equity. Governments must step in with subsidized social housing, rent controls, initiatives for housing cooperatives, or other policy measures. I don't want to stray beyond the scope of this book—which is about design rather than social policy—but I must acknowledge that such mixing rarely happens if governments don't step in to smooth the way. What's clear is that fairness demands that cities stop concentrating subsidized housing in poor zones so all residents and their children can enjoy equal access to decent schools and services. This mixing is the mark of a civilized, democratic, and ethical society.

The Equity Dividend

The Bogotá experiment may not have made up for all the city's grinding inequities. But it was a spectacular beginning, and to the surprise of many, it proved that the fairer city is not a radical proposition at all.

The campaign to impeach Peñalosa failed, partly because the mayor implemented his program so swiftly. He enjoyed broad executive powers and hired a motivated, partisan team to carry out a vision he had been fine-tuning for years. What it lacked in public process, it made up for in deliveries. As he moved into the second and third years of his three-year term, the equity program began to pay off for everyone, and the mayor's approval rating hit 80 percent.

The changes after three years were stunning: the downtown core was revitalized, school enrollment grew by 30 percent, and running water was provided to hundreds of thousands more homes. By 2001, almost twice as many people were cycling to work in the city, saving the average minimum-wage worker the equivalent of a month and a half's salary that year.

But here is the amazing thing: the happy city program, with its aggressive focus on creating a fairer city, did not only benefit the poor. It made life better for almost everyone.

The TransMilenio moved so many people so efficiently that car drivers crossed the city faster as well: commuting times fell by a fifth.

The streets were calmer. By the end of Peñalosa's term, people were crashing their cars less and killing each other less frequently, too: the accident rate fell by nearly half, and so did the murder rate, even as the country as a whole got more violent. There was a massive improvement in air quality: along all the TransMilenio routes, the noxious fumes and dust clouds cleared, and real estate values along the routes spiked, too.

Bogotans got healthier. Those who lived near the new parks, especially seniors, started walking more. Bogotans over the age of sixty actually reported getting more exercise if they lived in a neighborhood with a TransMilenio station. Just like the LYNX light-rail line in Charlotte, the TransMilenio changed people's behavior, but it did it at a fraction of the cost by giving the formerly lowly bus the highest status on the road.

The city had experienced a massive spike in feelings of optimism. People believed that life was good and getting better, a feeling they had not shared in decades, not even during Mockus's super-citizen years. After Peñalosa's term (sequential terms are illegal in the city), Mockus ran for mayor again. He gained Peñalosa's endorsement—and won the race—in part by promising to continue the ambitious infrastructure plans, which he carried out in his second term. The next mayor, Luis Garzón, continued some of those plans. In their terms, the software and hardware agendas merged, and the city experienced its best times in anyone's memory.

Ricardo Montezuma, an urbanist at the National University of Colombia, told me that Mockus and Peñalosa proved to Bogotans that they could have any city they wished for. Over their terms, Bogotanos' perception of the city utterly changed. "Twelve years ago, eighty percent of us were completely pessimistic about our future. Now it's the opposite. Most of us are optimistic," Montezuma told me in 2007. "Why is this important? Because in a big way a city is really just the sum of what people think about it. The city is a subjective thing."

Montezuma's point is not that form doesn't matter. It is that the city is an idea to which each citizen contributes and from which each citizen should benefit.

Whether you call it a happiness program, a fairness agenda, or a straight-up war on cars, Peñalosa's program was more than ideology written onto the city. It brought the benefits of the city to a much greater number of people. It maximized utility in a way that would have pleased Jeremy Bentham himself. It was deeply rational, in a way that American cities have not been for decades.

Sadly, Bogotá's fortunes have since declined. The TransMilenio system is plagued by desperate crowding as its private operators fail to add more capacity—yet more proof that robust public transit needs sustained public investment. Optimism has withered. Neither Peñalosa nor Mockus has occupied the mayor's chair again. The urbanist momentum has been seized by other Colombian cities, such as Medellín.

But Bogotá's transformative years still offer an enduring lesson for rich cities. By spending resources and designing cities in a way that values everyone's experience, life can get easier and more pleasant for everyone. We can make cities that are more generous and less cruel. We can make cities that help us all get stronger, more resilient, more connected, more active, and more free. We just have to decide who our cities are for. And we have to believe that they can change.

11. Everything Is Connected to Everything Else

The rigid, isolated object . . . is of no use whatsoever. It
must be inserted into the context of living social relations.
—Walter Benjamin, 1934

In 2010 Copenhagen and its neighbor municipalities held an international competition to design a new power plant in Amagerforbrænding, an industrial pocket northeast of the city's old battlements. There was nothing remarkable about the competition. New power plants are being built all the time. They are generally ugly, utilitarian structures that most cities like to keep out of both sight and mind. But the winning proposal set the international design world aflutter. It came from the Bjarke Ingels Group (BIG), the firm whose eponymous principal had verticalized suburbia on the outskirts of Copenhagen with Mountain Dwellings. The mop-topped thirty-seven-year-old had spent his career blending modernist ambitions and aesthetics with an almost fantastical sense of playfulness. Ingels had already convinced Denmark to pluck the iconic Little Mermaid statue from Copenhagen's shoreline so he could set her inside a whorl he designed for the country's pavilion at the 2010 Shanghai World Expo. He had codesigned a swimming pool to sit in the inner harbor so that citizens could do laps in the clean waters. And he had tried to sate Copenhageners' desire to bike absolutely everywhere by creating an apartment building whose figure-eight shape allowed residents to cycle a gentle promenade all the way up to their tenth-floor apartments.

Much of Ingels's previous work had broken down the separation of uses that so often characterizes architecture and urban planning. The power plant would take this theme further. As per the brief, the facility would create heat and electricity by burning the city's garbage. But rather than letting the new waste-to-energy facility stand alone, Ingels proposed wrapping the giant structure in an exoskeleton whose winding roof would serve as an artificial ski slope the size of seven football fields (333,700 square feet). Suddenly the city's industrial district would be transformed into a shining fun zone, and Copenhageners would not have to travel to Sweden to have a mountain adventure.

"The new plant is an example of what we at BIG call 'hedonistic sustainability'—the idea that sustainability is not a burden, but that a sustainable city in fact can improve our quality of life," Ingels boasted at the time.

The building would also perform an educative function. Skiers would ascend to the mountain's 330-foot peak in elevators that would face inward, so they would see exactly what happened to their city's waste. And since even a waste-to-energy plant releases some carbon dioxide into the atmosphere, the plant's smokestack would be fitted with a giant piston that would blow a smoke ring into the sky each time it produced an extra ton of CO_2, providing a whimsical reminder of the product of Copenhageners' consumptive habits.

Early on in this book I posed a conundrum: If guilt and shame and fear do not lead us to action, how can we hope to solve the urgent ecological challenges of our time? Ingels offers a utopian response in the monumental form of his smoke-ring-blowing ski hill: with creative design, the sustainable life can actually be more pleasurable.

Ingels's functional mashups—the working harbor as lap pool, the apartment roof as bicycle promenade, the energy plant as source of both green power and playtime—point toward a deep truth about cities. As much as we have tried to separate the functions of the city into discrete units spread out across the landscape, everything remains inherently connected to everything else. The ways we move, the things we buy, the pleasures we take, the trash we produce, the carbon we blow into the atmosphere, and the economy itself are intertwined and interdependent. If you follow these threads far enough, they lead to a point of intersection where the projects of urban prosperity, sustainability, and happiness really do converge—not in a single object or building, but in the complex weave of energy, mobility, economics, and geometric systems that define city life.

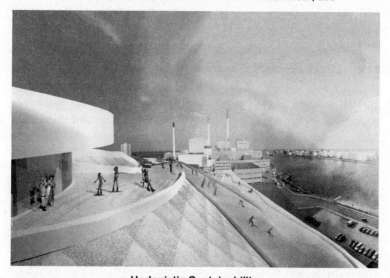

Hedonistic Sustainability
Bjarke Ingels's waste-to-energy-plant concept combines green energy production with a ski hill for mountain-deprived Copenhageners. (BIG & Glessner)

We have all heard the skeptics who warn that serious action to fight climate change and energy scarcity will lead us into decades of hardship and sacrifice. When it comes to cities, they are absolutely wrong. In fact, sustainability and the good life can be by-products of the very same interventions. Alex Boston, the Golder planner who advises dozens of cities on climate and energy, doesn't even ask civic leaders about their greenhouse gas reduction aspirations when they first start talking. "We ask, 'What are your core community priorities?'" says Boston. "People don't talk about climate change. They say they want economic development, livability, mobility, housing affordability, taxes, all stuff that relates to happiness." These are just the concerns that have caused us to delay action on climate change. But Boston insists that by focusing on the relationship between energy, efficiency, and the things that make life better, cities can succeed where scary data, scientists, logic, and conscience have failed. The happy city plan is an energy plan. It is a climate plan. It is a belt-tightening plan for cash-strapped cities. It is also an economic plan, a jobs plan, and a corrective for weak systems. It is a plan for resilience.

The Green Surprise

Consider the by-product of the happy city project in Bogotá. Enrique Peñalosa told me that he did not feel the urgency of the global environmental crisis when he was elected mayor. His urban transformation was not motivated by a concern for spotted owls or melting glaciers or soon-to-be-flooded residents of villages on some distant coral atoll. Still, a funny thing happened near the end of his term. After making Bogotá easier, cleaner, more beautiful, and more fair, the mayor and his city started winning accolades from environmental organizations.

In 2000 Peñalosa and Eric Britton were called to Sweden to accept the Stockholm Challenge Award for the Environment, for pulling 850,000 vehicles off the street during the world's biggest car-free day. Then the TransMilenio bus system was lauded for producing massive reductions in Bogotá's carbon dioxide emissions.* It was the first transport system to be accredited under the UN's Clean Development Mechanism—meaning that Bogotá could actually sell carbon credits to polluters in rich countries. For its public space transformations under Mayors Peñalosa, Antanas Mockus, and their successor, Luis Garzón, the city won the Golden Lion prize from the prestigious Venice Architecture Biennale. For its bicycle routes, its new parks, its Ciclovía, its upside-down roads, and that hugely popular car-free day, Bogotá was held up as a shining example of green urbanism.

Not one of its programs was directed at the crisis of climate change, but the city offered tangible proof of the connection between urban design, experience, and the carbon energy system. It suggested that the green city, the low-carbon city, and the happy city might be exactly the same destination.

Other cities have also realized that boosting quality of life and reducing their environmental footprints are complementary goals and should be part of the same plan. You can experience one without realizing you are accomplishing the other. Take London's congestion charge, which has been touted as a powerful greenhouse-gas-reduction strategy.† But this was not its purpose. The charge was a response to a

---

*By nearly 250,000 tons a year.
†After the charge was introduced in 2003, the city reduced emissions by almost a fifth when most city's emissions were climbing.

host of issues that Londoners felt were much more pressing than future climate change. There was so much traffic that people couldn't get to work. It was killing Londoners' quality of life and costing the city in productivity. People were incredibly frustrated about spending so much time on the road. The charge eased pressure on the roads, allowed the city room to construct more public space through the West End, and made the city more convivial and safe. The climate benefits were a bonus, gradually emphasized as climate change grew in the public consciousness.

In Paris, climate and hedonic benefits are being explicitly rolled out as part of the same program. If you have visited Paris during August over the last decade, you will likely have been drawn to the Left Bank of the Seine, where every summer the city has been burying the Pompidou Expressway under a swath of golden sand dotted with beer gardens, boccie ball courts, and potted palm trees, all the way from the Louvre to the cast iron arches of the Pont de Sully. Paris Plages has seen pavement all through central Paris wrested away from cars and converted into sandboxes, plazas, and dance floors. The beachification is widely understood to be a scheme for easing the misery of people stuck in Paris during its humid summer months, but it is an official part of the plan to shrink the city's environmental footprint and cut its greenhouse gas emissions from vehicles by 60 percent by 2020. It works specifically because it makes driving in the city more difficult. The beaches are now being made permanent. By the time you read this, the Pompidou Expressway will have been narrowed, and a mile-and-a-half car-free zone will have replaced the road space on the Left Bank. Hedonic sustainability will have been built right into the fabric of the city. Drivers must either wait in traffic or shift to the city's networked system of shared transport.

Mexico City has caught the happiness bug, too. The city's last mayor, Marcelo Ebrard (who famously prescribed free Viagra for the city's senior citizens so they might reap the salubrious effects of sexual intercourse more regularly), built a giant ice rink and igloos on the city's central plaza so that poor Mexicans could enjoy a white Christmas without jetting to Whistler as the elite did. He built replicas of Paris Plages and launched a homegrown version of Bogotá's Ciclovía, shutting down miles of downtown roads on Sundays so that citizens could treat their streets like parks. He copied Bogotá's mobility system,

The Freeway Is Not a Freeway
Every summer for the last decade, the Pompidou Expressway in Paris has been converted to Paris Plages. Now pedestrian zones are being made permanent, part of a plan that addresses both climate and livability issues. (Charles Montgomery)

laying down a network of metrolike rapid buses that have even lured the public-transit-phobic business class out of their cars. He called in Gil Peñalosa and Jan Gehl to create a plan to wrestle 186 miles of road space away from drivers and hand it over to cyclists. As part of the city's Plan Verde, the measures not only shrink the city's carbon footprint and make commuting easier (these days in the Mexican capital, just about any cyclist can move faster than cars, which have slowed to an average of about 7.5 miles per hour), but most important, they are intended to give a new sense of security to citizens who have for years been afraid of their streets. Despite the attention given to the country's bloody drug war, more Mexicans die on the roads every year than as a result of narco-violence.* Martha Delgado, the city's environmental secretary until 2012, told me, "A city that lives under the hostility and insecurity of car traffic can change only if its citizens retake ownership of its public spaces."

Quality of life and climate action are complementary goals. It's just easier to get people excited about plans that improve their lives. That's why, when the City of New York explains its remarkable transformation in the way the city uses roads, it boasts about its huge improvements in safety, speed, efficiency, and people's taking coffee on public plazas, leaving its goal of reducing the city's greenhouse gas emissions by 30 percent to a footnote.

Death and Taxes

Still, this focus on quality of life risks obscuring other, increasingly urgent synergies emerging between climate action and happy urban design. For one thing, public health researchers have discovered that designs that lower greenhouse gas emissions also make entire societies healthier. *The Lancet*, the prestigious British medical journal, argued that whether you are in London or Mumbai, interventions to make walking and cycling safe and comfortable are radically more effective at bringing down emissions than the technological fixes being pushed by the transportation industry. This is because every journey we make burns some form of energy—usually some form of fossil fuel— and there is an inverse relationship between the carbon we burn in our machines and the food calories we burn when choosing how to get around.[†][‡]

---

*Mexico experiences an average of twenty-three pedestrian deaths a day. For the drug war to beat that, there would have to be more than 8,395 killings a year.

†When we walk or cycle, we burn food calories and get fit. When we drive, we burn fossil fuels but few calories. Imagine getting from, say, the Mableton Post Office in suburban Atlanta down to the Big Kmart at the Village at Mableton. According to the rough online calculator at Reroute.it, you would burn 159 calories walking the 1.5 miles (burning roughly the energy contained in two chocolate-chip cookies or a bottle of beer), 47 calories biking (burning a mandarin orange), or blow 1.2 pounds of carbon dioxide by driving.

‡Proponents of electric cars have argued that they fall outside this carbon equation.

Even if you don't care about your own health or the health of the environment, the relationship between urban design, health, and climate change planning touches your life and your bank balance. That's because the dispersed city that nudges millions of people toward inactivity—and exposes them to air pollution and traffic crashes—simultaneously creates financial burdens for all of society. We know that obese people have more medical troubles. But they also miss work more frequently owing to illness and disability. They also work fewer years than healthy people. In the United States, this costs society a thundering $142 billion every year.* Meanwhile, pollution from auto-dominated roads causes tens of billions more in health-care costs. And then there are the costs incurred by traffic accidents, which run as much as $180 billion annually. Since the damage is directly related to the distance people drive every day, just reducing the frequency and length of automobile trips can ease the burden on emergency services, productivity, and the health-care system.†

For years, none of these expenses were considered when transportation departments funded new roads and highways; they were the responsibility of other people working in other agency silos. But when you take the wide view, it becomes clear that Bogotá's TransMilenio, New York's bike lanes, and Vancouver's laneway housing project are all exercises in long-term austerity. In fact, just about every measure I've connected to happy urbanism also influences a city's environmental footprint and, just as urgent, its economic and fiscal health. If we understand and act upon this connectedness, we just may steer hundreds of cities off the course of crisis.

Indeed, electric vehicles charged from systems that derive their power from hydro-electric or nuclear power plants produce fewer emissions. But this ignores the emissions created just building any car. Given the energy used to manufacture a new, energy-efficient Toyota Prius, for example, one would actually save more energy and emissions by continuing to drive a mid-'90s Geo Metro.

*This includes health-care costs, lost wages due to illness or disability, and value of future earnings lost by premature death. Direct medical costs alone add up to $61 billion (adjusted to 2008 dollars).

†Society reaps even more indirect emergency service and health-care savings when cities provide attractive transit service, because for every mile traveled, riding a bus is ten times safer than driving a car.

There Is No Such Thing as an Externality

Even before widespread acknowledgment of human-caused climate change, Jane Jacobs warned that the city is a fantastically complex organism that can be thrown into an unhealthy imbalance by attempts to simplify it in form or function. In *Cities and the Wealth of Nations* she warned specifically about the tendency for designers and planners to overscale: the larger an organism or economy, the more unstable it would become in changing times, and the less the likelihood that the system would be able to self-correct. Most city builders paid no attention. They pursued greater integration with global systems, relied more heavily on national and multinational industries and retailers to fuel their economies, and altered their cities' very bone structure to accommodate extreme dispersal. The dispersalists saw order and efficiency in their segregated systems, but in many cases they were merely transferring energy costs from industry to regular citizens and governments.

Americans are learning the hard way that everything is connected to everything else. The modern urban landscape, whose construction fueled both the economic boom and a storm of carbon emissions and other pollution, is also responsible for many of the costs now crippling families and local governments alike, thanks to the indivisible relationship between land use, energy, carbon, and the cost of just about everything.

Consider the geography of the foreclosure crisis. As we've seen, the communities that fell hardest during the subprime implosion, places like exurban San Joaquin County, were classic low-density, segregated-use zones of single detached homes on plenty of acreage. This is because classic sprawl depends on cheap energy, and lots of it, to function. That dependence means that these neighborhoods are also climate killers because huge energy costs for households translate to huge greenhouse gas emissions. The relationship is clear: as emissions go up, operational affordability goes down.*

*According to the Housing and Transportation Affordability Index (http://htaindex .cnt.org), an average household in 2008 in Weston Ranch emitted more than eleven metric tons per year from auto use and spent more than $5,000 on gas (assuming that they did not commute outside of Stockton for work). In comparison, the average

260 | HAPPY CITY

Exurban homeowners have felt this pain for half a decade. But now city governments are being forced to reckon with this long-unaccounted relationship between distance and energy. Not only does sprawl development cost taxpayers more to build, it costs more to maintain, because each home in a typical community of dispersed single-family homes on big lots needs so much more paved street, drainage, water, sewage, and other services than a home in a denser, more walkable place. A neighborhood of detached homes and duplexes on small lots can be serviced for about a quarter of the cost of servicing typical large-lot detached homes. Dispersed communities also need more fire and ambulance stations than dense neighborhoods do. They need more school buses. The waste is astounding: in the 2005–06 school year, more than 25 million American children were bused to their public schools. The country spent $18.9 billion getting them there—that's $750 for each bus-riding student, which could have been spent on actual learning.

Across the United States, broke city governments have found themselves unable to fund police, fire, and ambulance services, let alone school buses or the maintenance of roads, parks, and community centers. Cities stretched so far, so fast, for so long, at such low densities that the country now faces a massive unfunded liability for infrastructure maintenance. The American Society of Civil Engineers (ASCE) has warned that repairing the country's major infrastructure will cost more than $2 trillion.

Many North American cities are just waking up to the fact that they have been engaging in a massive urban Ponzi scheme, with new development creating short-term benefits in development fees and tax revenues but even bigger long-term costs that pile up faster than cities' ability to pay them off. In the boom years, cities kicked the great reckoning down the road. But now the maintenance costs are coming due, the development fee revenues from the boom years have dried up, and giant potholes are appearing in civic budgets. Building more of the same will not help cities get back on track or on budget. Cities have got to find ways to draw strength rather than weakness from the essential interconnectedness of land use, energy systems,

---

household in San Francisco's Mission District emitted about four metric tons per year from auto use and spent about half as much on gas.

Save the Planet and Your Bank Account

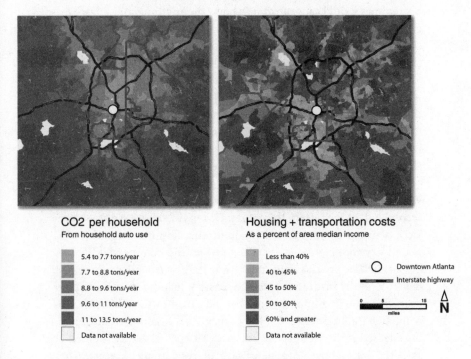

CO2 per household
From household auto use

5.4 to 7.7 tons/year
7.7 to 8.8 tons/year
8.8 to 9.6 tons/year
9.6 to 11 tons/year
11 to 13.5 tons/year
Data not available

Housing + transportation costs
As a percent of area median income

Less than 40%
40 to 45%
45 to 50%
50 to 60%
60% and greater
Data not available

Downtown Atlanta
Interstate highway

0   5   15
miles

Residents of denser, more connected neighborhoods in central Atlanta are not only saving money by paying less in combined housing and transportation costs (right). *They are also fighting climate change by producing less greenhouse gas emissions* (left) *than residents in Atlanta's sprawling suburbs. In both cases, the savings are a result of system design.* (Scott Keck/Cole Robertson and Center for Neighborhood Technology: Housing and Transportation Index)

and their own budgets. This means policy makers—and voters—need to start saying no to what once seemed like obvious paths to prosperity.

Jobs, Money, and Geometry

Most of us agree that development that provides employment and tax revenue is good for cities. Some even argue that the need for jobs outweighs aesthetic, lifestyle, or climate concerns—in fact, this argument comes up any time Walmart proposes a new megastore near a small town. But a clear-eyed look at the spatial economics of land, jobs, and tax regimes should cause anyone to reject the anything-and-anywhere-goes development model. To explain, let me offer the story of an obsessive number cruncher who found his own urban laboratory quite by chance.

Joseph Minicozzi, a young architect raised in upstate New York, was on a cross-country motorcycle ride in 2001 when he got sidetracked in the Appalachian Mountains. He met a beautiful woman in a North Carolina roadside bar and was smitten by both that woman and the languid beauty of the Blue Ridge region. Now they share a bungalow with two dogs in the mountain town of Asheville.

Asheville is, in many ways, a typical midsize American city, which is to say that its downtown was virtually abandoned in the second half of the twentieth century. Dozens of elegant old structures were boarded up or encased in aluminum siding as highways and liberal development policies sucked people and commercial life into dispersal. The process continued until 1991, when Julian Price, the heir to a family insurance and broadcasting fortune, decided to pour everything he had into nursing that old downtown back to life. His company, Public Interest Projects, bought and renovated old buildings, leased street-front space out to small businesses, and rented or sold the lofts above to a new wave of residential pioneers. They coached, coddled, and sometimes bankrolled entrepreneurs who began to enliven the streets. First came a vegetarian restaurant, then a bookstore, a furniture store, and the now-legendary nightclub, the Orange Peel.

When Price died in 2001, the downtown was starting to show signs of life, but his successor, Pat Whelan, and his new recruit, Minicozzi, still had to battle the civic skeptics. Some city officials saw such little value in downtown land that they planned to plunk down a prison right in the middle of a terrain that was perfect for mixed-use redevelopment. The developers realized that if they wanted the city officials to support their vision, they needed to educate them—and that meant offering them hard numbers on the tax and job benefits of revitalizing downtown. The numbers they produced sparked a eureka moment among the city's accountants because they insisted on taking a spatial systems approach, similar to the way farmers look at land they want to put into production. The question was simple:

What is the production yield for every acre of land? On a farm, the answer might be in pounds of tomatoes. In the city, it's about tax revenues and jobs.

To explain, Minicozzi offered me his classic urban accounting smackdown, using two competing properties: On the one side is a downtown building his firm rescued—a six-story steel-framed 1923 classic once owned by JCPenney and converted into shops, offices, and condos. On the other side is a Walmart on the edge of town. The old Penney's building sits on less than a quarter of an acre, while the Walmart and its parking lots occupy thirty-four acres. Adding up the property and sales tax paid on each piece of land, Minicozzi found that the Walmart contributed only $50,800 to the city in retail and property taxes for each acre it used, but the JCPenney building contributed a whopping $330,000 per acre *in property tax alone.* In other words, the city got more than seven times the return for every acre on downtown investments than it did when it broke new ground out on the city limits.

When Minicozzi looked at job density, the difference was even more vivid: the small businesses that occupied the old Penney's building employed fourteen people, which doesn't seem like many until you realize that this is actually seventy-four jobs per acre, compared with the fewer than six jobs per acre created on a sprawling Walmart site. (This is particularly dire given that on top of reducing jobs density in its host cities, Walmart depresses average wages as well.)

Minicozzi has since found the same spatial conditions in cities all over the United States. Even low-rise, mixed-use buildings of two or three stories—the kind you see on an old-style, small-town main street—bring in ten times the revenue per acre as that of an average big-box development. What's stunning is that, thanks to the relationship between energy and distance, large-footprint sprawl development patterns can actually cost cities more to service than they give back in taxes. The result? Growth that produces deficits that simply cannot be overcome with new growth revenue.*

*In Sarasota County, Florida, for example, Minicozzi found that it would take about three times as long for the county to recoup the land and infrastructure costs involved in developing housing in a sprawl pattern as compared with downtown. If

"Cities and counties have essentially been taking tax revenues from downtowns and using them to subsidize development and services in sprawl," Minicozzi told me. "This is like a farmer going out and dumping all his fertilizer on the weeds rather than on the tomatoes."*

Price, Whelan, and Minicozzi helped convince the city of Asheville to fertilize that rich downtown soil. The city changed its zoning policies, allowing flexible uses for downtown buildings. It invested in livelier streetscapes and public events. It stopped forcing developers to build parking garages, which brought down the cost of both housing and business. It built its own user-pay garages, so the cost of parking was borne by the people who used it rather than by everyone else. All of this helped make it worthwhile for developers to risk their investment on restoring old buildings, producing new jobs and tax density for the city.

Retail sales in the resurgent downtown have exploded since 1991. So has the taxable value of downtown properties, which cost a fraction to service than sprawl lands. The reborn downtown has become the greatest supplier of tax revenue and affordable housing in the county—partly because it relieves people of the burden of commuting, and partly because it mixes high-end lofts with modest apartments. All of this, while growing what one local newspaper emotionally described as, "a downtown that—after decades of doubt and neglect—is once again the heart and soul of Asheville."

By paying attention to the relationship between land, distance,

---

all went well, the county's return on investment for sprawl housing would still be barely 4 percent.

*The productive richness of the new Asheville approach becomes even clearer when you consider the geographic path taken by dollars spent at local businesses. Money spent at small and local businesses tends to stay in a community, producing more local jobs, while money spent at big national chains tends to get sucked out of the local economy. Local businesses tend to use local accountants, printers, lawyers, and advertisers, and their owners spend more of their profits in town. National retailers, on the other hand, tend to send such work back to regional or national hubs, and their profits to distant shareholders. Every $100 spent at a local business produces at least a third more local economic benefit and more than a third more local jobs. The arrival of a Walmart in any community has been shown to produce a blast radius of lower wages and higher poverty.

The Unequal Geography of Density

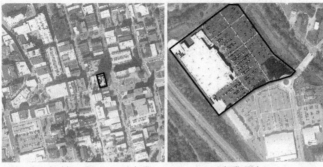

Mixed-use building, downtown Ashville   Ashville Walmart

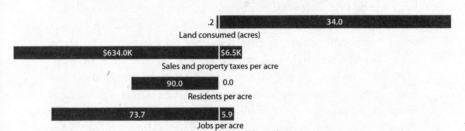

By investing in downtowns rather than dispersal, cities can boost jobs and local tax revenues while spending less on far-flung infrastructure and services. In Asheville, North Carolina, Public Interest Projects found that a six-story mixed-use building produced more than thirteen times the tax revenue and twelve times the jobs per acre of land than the Walmart on the edge of town. (Walmart retail tax based in national average for Walmart stores.) (Scott Keck, with data from Joe Minicozzi / Public Interest Projects)

scale, and cash flow—in other words, by building more connected, complex places—the city regained its soul and its good health.

Growth Within Limits

By now you won't be surprised to hear that what Joe Minicozzi and his friends are doing to improve downtown Asheville also happens to be a strategy for fighting climate change. In Asheville, everything is just as connected to everything else as it is in large cities.

Efforts to create nodes of jobs density, residential density, and tax density also produce nodes of energy efficiency that lower the cost of running the city. "The low carbon community is also about ensuring that you can finance the sewage, the water, and roads to sustain your community on the long-term basis," Alex Boston points out.

An average city can end up collectively spending more than $4,000 per household per year on energy, typically moving vehicles or heating and lighting buildings. Most of that money gets sucked right out of the community and paid to distant energy utilities or oil companies. How do you turn that around? By changing the city's relationship with distance and with energy.

Few cities have done this as dramatically as Portland, Oregon. Back in the 1970s the state of Oregon ordered its cities to create urban growth boundaries in order to protect agricultural land. Then, while other cities kept pouring resources into freeways, Portland began investing in light-rail, streetcars, and bicycle lanes. Between 1990 and 2007, as people in most cities drove farther and farther every day, Portlanders were reversing the trend. Drivers now travel about 20 percent fewer miles every day than citizens of other major cities in the United States, shaving about nine minutes off the average daily commute. Traffic fatalities fell by 80 percent between 1985 and 2008, again bucking the national trend.

Aside from the millions saved in emergency and medical services, the trip shortening has had a salubrious effect on the local economy. Thanks to their shorter commutes, by 2008, people in the Portland region were saving about $1.1 billion every year on gas, or 1.5 percent of all personal income in the region. This means that Portlanders send less money out of the city to car companies and oil barons and spend more at home in their city on food, fun, and microbrewed beer.* The result: Portland has more restaurants per capita than any large city in the country other than Seattle and San Francisco. All this good living allowed Portlanders to spare the world about 1.4 million tons of greenhouse gas per year. It was a gift to

*About 73 percent of the retail price of gas and 86 percent of the retail price of a new car immediately leaves the local economy, according to a report by CEOs for Cities.

their children and to their planet, but what got people really excited was that Portland's climate-friendly systems attracted wealth. An investment of $100 million in slow-moving downtown streetcars actually pulled in $3.5 billion in new office, retail, and hotel development within a couple of blocks of the new lines.

Portland's experience proves that a city can make massive carbon reductions without turning to hyperdensity, argues Boston. "Density alone doesn't lead to carbon reductions, or happiness for that matter. You can live in a forest of apartment towers and still be forced to drive everywhere. But when cities find ways to mix housing and jobs and places to shop, then carbon goals and lifestyle goals start to converge."

Boston has experienced these dividends firsthand. First he helped create a climate action plan for the City of North Vancouver, a mountainside suburb just across a broad saltwater harbor from Vancouver. His metrics were straightforward: if the city was going to reduce its carbon footprint, it needed to give lots more people a chance to do a lot more things closer together. This did not necessarily mean building a mini-Manhattan. It meant weaving more apartments, more town houses, more shops, and more jobs along Lonsdale Avenue, the city's central spine. Indeed, that's what the city was already doing in the name of prosperity. The area had attracted hundreds of new residents—including Boston and his partner, who moved there to start a family two years after he helped hammer out the city's climate action plan. They bought a duplex beneath a huge cedar tree on a quiet street, just a couple of blocks off Lonsdale. They immediately started reaping the benefits of the climate-friendly system.

For one thing, it made them richer: Since 2005, the city's efforts to build more efficient communities had cut per capita energy costs by about 10 percent—saving citizens each about $400 every year. Boston's utilities bill (which covers water, sewage, garbage collection, and recycling) was about three-quarters what it would have been if he had moved to the similarly named but more sprawling District of North Vancouver, which bordered the city.

The changes also made Boston's everyday life easier, healthier, and more convenient. This was apparent when I joined him on his daily commute to downtown Vancouver. The ritual included a twenty-minute walk and a fifteen-minute ride across the harbor on the Sea-Bus, a small passenger ferry. As we walked, he pushed his rosy-cheeked year-and-a-half-old son, Kenson, along in a stroller.

The most remarkable thing about the trip was not the ease of the transition from quiet backstreet to busy Lonsdale. Nor was it the wonderful urban collage Boston noted as we walked—from typical main street businesses to light industrial shops, including a metalworks, an auto body repair garage, and a cabinetmaker—land uses that meant people could live, shop, and work steps from home. What impressed me most was the detour Boston took just before getting on the SeaBus.

We headed past the market at the foot of Lonsdale and past the office block that sat above the bus exchange, and Kenson grew increasingly excited. As we approached a spiffy-looking mid-rise condominium tower, he broke into a wide-mouthed grin. He pointed and cawed as a white-haired gentleman emerged from the lobby. His babysitter for the day was Boston's own father. The climate technician had convinced his aging parents to trade their home in sprawl for a condominium in North Vancouver's low-carbon complexity.

"So you moved for the sake of the climate?" I prompted Boston senior.

"Well, it rains here just as much as it did at our old house," he replied.

"No, Dad, he's talking about climate change. About greenhouse gas emissions," Boston junior interrupted.

Boston senior gave me a wink. He didn't seem to give a damn about the city's carbon credentials, but he loved its sheer handiness. They walked to pretty much everything they needed. The price? More babysitting—a dividend for Alex that would have been much more difficult to collect in the dispersed city.

The Boston family is not alone in appreciating the city's low-carbon payoff. During the years that the City of North Vancouver was making its carbon U-turn, pollsters found that citizens were getting happier and happier with their quality of life.

Body Heat

Sometimes the dividends of proximity and complexity are invisible, intangible among the myriad relationships, geometries, and systems of the city. But sometimes they are clearer than even Bjarke Ingels's architectural metaphors, and they reveal new truths about the interconnectedness of city systems.

In its role as host city for the 2010 Olympic Winter Games, Vancouver built a village for athletes on the southeast shore of False Creek, a former industrial waterway on the edge of its downtown. The Village, as the area is now known, is a showcase of green urbanism, from its rainwater-fed mini-wetland to its LED-lit central plaza. Eventually sixteen thousand people will live in the low-rises and town houses that line its narrow pedestrian-friendly streets. The last time I strolled through—about three years after the Olympics— residents had colonized the new bakery-café, children were clambering over the feet of the giant sculpted fiberglass starlings that rule the plaza, and the seawall hummed with skaters, stroller-pushing joggers, and bike commuters. Outside the new community center, teams of Lycra-clad paddlers stretched and chatted, preparing to launch their dragon boats off a nearby dock into False Creek.

The social energy converging on the Village is impressive. But this energy convergence goes beyond metaphor: all those human bodies are vessels of *thermal* energy. As human density increases at the Village, so does the density of energy its residents cycle through the air and water systems of their buildings, through their machines, and through their own bodies, concentrating a resource that has now been harnessed by a remarkable new power system. This is how the Southeast False Creek Neighbourhood Utility works: Every time residents of the Village do their dishes or take a shower or use the toilet, they flush thermal energy—either in the form of room-temperature water or considerably warmer human waste—down the drain. The wastewater gets piped to a sewage pumping station submerged under a nearby bridge. Inside that station is a small energy plant that uses a process of evaporation and compression to suck the heat from the wastewater. That energy gets transferred to clean water, which is then sent back to provide radiant heat and hot water for everyone in the

Village. This is one reason that residents have cut their household greenhouse gas emissions by three-quarters.

The energy plant emits no odor or toxins, but its exhaust flues have been turned into public art: five stainless steel pipes reach several stories into the sky, like the outstretched fingers of a giant robot hand. The designers Bill Pechet and Stephanie Robb fitted the flues with LED lights, so that when energy output is high, the steam puffing from them is tinted with a hot-pink glow. Once upon a time, smokestacks symbolized all that was toxic and unpleasant about inner cities. Not anymore. These pink fingertips are a reminder that residents are heating their homes, in part, *with their own bodies.*

This model has begun to realize the aspiration contained in Bjarke Ingals's power-producing mountain: a system where energy production, consumption, and human experience are drawn into a hedonic loop. But it suggests that we don't need grand architectural metaphors to solve the challenges posed by human settlements. Real power lies not in singular objects, but in the sinew and systems and invisible relationships that run through everything, from emotions to urban geometry to systems of energy distribution. We have only begun to understand the potential of these overlapping systems, but we do know that when regular people and city builders alike embrace complexity and the inherent connectedness of city life, when we move a little closer, we begin to free ourselves from the enslaving hunger for scarce energy. We can live well and save the world at the very same time.

12. Retrofitting Sprawl

First they built the road, then they built the town
That's why we're still driving round and round
—Arcade Fire, "Wasted Hours"

There is a rash of studies under way designed to uncover the bad consequences of overcrowding. This is all very well as far as it goes, but it only goes in one direction. What about undercrowding? The researchers would be a lot more objective if they paid as much attention to the possible effects on people of relative isolation and lack of propinquity. Maybe some of those rats they study get lonely too.

—William H. Whyte

There is a problem with almost all the urban innovations I have been describing, and a creeping disparity at play in cities that borrow ideas from places like Bogotá, Paris, Vancouver, and Copenhagen. Jeremy Bentham would call this problem a failure to maximize utility. Ethicists would call it a problem of equity. It is both. The problem is that the happy city's matrix of freedom, rich public spaces, leisure time, and safe streets is not much use to people like Randy Strausser and his family, or anyone else who lives far from denser, more connected places. As the wealthy recolonize downtowns and inner suburbs, and as property values rise accordingly, millions of people are simply being excluded. Meanwhile, many of these improvements are next to impossible to pull off in the city of dispersal and segregated functions, whose systems and forms are too inflexible to accommodate them and too stretched to make the civic investments affordable.

This unfairness, and its intractability, gnawed at me until the afternoon I met a die-hard suburbanite named Robin Meyer.

I last saw Meyer in the spring of 2010. She was standing in the middle of the parking lot in front of the neocolonial facade of the U.S. post office in Mableton, insisting that this spot, right here, was the center of town. If you didn't know about her plan, you might have thought Meyer was crazy. She was surveying what looked to me like the middle of nowhere.

Mableton, you may recall, showed up in Lawrence Frank's urban-health studies as one of those towns that is so unwalkable that people get fatter just living there. The unincorporated community fifteen miles west of downtown Atlanta is the kind of place where you could drive for days and never quite feel that you had arrived anywhere. Tendrils of asphalt braid and curl through the semi-urban sprawl northeast of Atlanta's Perimeter beltway, with cul-de-sacs and strip malls and business parks evenly scattered over the rolling terrain. If you circled the dying mall down on Veterans Memorial Highway—cruelly misnamed the Village at Mableton—or doubled back and headed up to the big-box power centers that cling to the East-West Connector, you would find yourself increasingly disoriented, and you would not have found anything you'd call a downtown—certainly not the view from the post office parking lot.

From where we stood, a lawn fell away past a looping access drive and a deep swale. Beyond that, cars and trucks sped along Floyd Road's five wide lanes. Beyond more parking lots and lawn, we could see the clapboard plantation house built in 1843 by the Scottish settler and town founder Robert Mable. South of the old house, across another broad parking lot, was the Mable House Arts Center and beyond that, a new park-and-ride lot where hundreds of spaces sat entirely unoccupied on this, a weekday. The busiest place in sight was the twenty-bay RaceTrac gas station down at the intersection of Floyd and Clay roads.

Every destination in Mableton was an island, isolated by those formidable swaths of asphalt and grass. Everywhere we looked, parking space exceeded building footprints by at least three to one. You'd be crazy to walk from the post office to the library behind the gas station, or the shopping plaza beyond that, or even to the arts center right across Floyd Road. "That would be a death march," Meyer said, referring to both the frying rays of the Georgia summer sun and Floyd Road itself, which has grown over the years into a commuter highway, speeding people between distant mega-schools, power centers, business parks, and dollar stores. But this was it, she said. This was the place that mattered. This is where Mableton would reinvent itself.

Meyer had spent years being perfectly content with the horizontal suburb. She and her husband built a house on a four-acre lot a few miles from the post office back in 1984, and they made the weekday freeway commute into Atlanta for years. But now that she had retired, given up her commute, and gotten involved in the Mableton Improvement Coalition (she was chairman of the board), Meyer was acutely aware that there is no *there* in Mableton. "There's no center—no place for people to gather and have all the sorts of things that communities are *supposed* to have," she said. She didn't want anything radical. Just a village where she could park her car, walk around and do a few errands, and feel as though she were someplace.

Meyer could see the outlines of that place as she squinted out across the collage of asphalt and lawn. The two architects who stood with us could see it too.

"The town square could be right here," offered Galina Tachieva, a partner at the urban planning firm Duany Plater-Zyberk (DPZ). She pulled off her bug-eye sunglasses and swept a hand across the scene. "And there could be a row of shops or live-work studios lining it. And this *disastrous* road needs to be slowed down so that old people and children can actually walk across it. We might add parking along the curbs, or split the road in half, like a zipper."

That was a beginning. But why stop there? they said. Why not build some veranda-fronted two- or three-story buildings in the parking lots of the sickly plazas along Floyd Road? Why not push those buildings right up against the sidewalks like the streets of old towns everyone likes to visit? Why not turn the field just north of the post office—a farm owned by former Georgia governor Roy Barnes— into a village center with housing for seniors? Why not connect nearby roads so folks could actually walk places? It was a tremendous fantasy for a spring afternoon. It was also illegal.

Urgency and Imagination

Once upon a time, urban pioneers stood upon the untamed ground across North America and summoned up enough imagination to proclaim that towns, and maybe even cities, would rise from the wilderness on which they stood. It takes similar resolve to stand on the tarmac outside the Mableton post office—or any other spot on the suburban savannas that surround North American cities—and imagine anything like a town replacing the durable landscape of sprawl. But it is an idea that has grown steadily more urgent, and it is more than an aesthetic concern.

I have already outlined how this landscape can make people sicker, fatter, more frustrated, socially isolated, and broke. I have shown how it makes streets more dangerous. But this urban form also happens to deny a growing majority of people the life they actually want. In 2011 a survey by the National Association of Realtors found that six in ten Americans say they would rather live in a neighborhood that has a mix of houses, stores, and businesses within an easy walk than one that forced them to drive everywhere. But in places like Atlanta, only about 10 percent of homes can access such wonders.

The sprawl city is also facing a slow-moving crisis that is arguably just as dire as the foreclosure meltdown that singed American cities these past years. In 2009 the Atlanta Regional Commission issued a warning: by 2030, one out of every five residents in the Atlanta metro region would be over the age of sixty. And Atlanta's suburbs are currently hell on the elderly. With everything so far away, many seniors can't get anywhere on foot—leaving many in a homebound state that actually hastens the aging process. Those who can't drive have a tough time getting services, and they are starved of the casual social encounters that keep people connected, strong, and healthy. In a sprawl future, millions of Atlantans will be stranded, alone in their homes or warehoused in retirement institutions, a fate even worse than the one currently experienced by kids and poor people in suburbs across the continent.

The commission made a call to action: it was time to figure out how to turn places like Mableton into communities that would work for people of all ages—even those who could not drive. Starting in 2009, they invited community members to meet with experts in health care, mobility, aging, transportation, accessibility, architecture, and planning in a brainstorming session known as a "charrette."

Sprawl Repair

This is where Tachieva and her colleague Scott Ball came in. The two architects specialize in a kind of urban surgery that reverses the damage done by sprawl. Tachieva sees their task as nothing short of reversing a century of dispersal.

"Cities have been blown out of proportion, as though we were designing them for giants. What we were doing, of course, was designing for the scale of cars," she said. "Now we are returning cities to a human scale. We are returning the balance of life to neighborhoods."

Tachieva is driven by more than altruism. There's money in the work she calls sprawl repair. The U.S. population is projected to grow by 120 million by 2050. Where will those people live? Downtowns and first-ring, streetcar-style suburbs will be able to accommodate only a fraction of the new demographic tidal wave. Most jobs have already moved out beyond city limits anyway. The masses, Tachieva says, will still need suburbia.

But these people won't look at all like suburbia's first few waves of migrants. Demographers project that most homebuyers in the next couple of decades will be empty-nest baby boomers or their single adult children. Only about one in ten buyers are likely to have children of their own. Those childless buyers won't be in the market for traditional detached suburban homes. Neither will many new immigrants, who are simply not used to nor enthusiastic about endless auto commutes. Some analysts suggest that the United States already has enough large-lot single-family homes to meet demand right up to 2030.

"The party is over for sprawl," Tachieva said. "The market is changing, and young people and old people are demanding something different. They want lively, sophisticated places where they can walk, and where they can still have freedom beyond the age of eighty."

Tachieva literally wrote the book on the subject. Her how-to guide, the *Sprawl Repair Manual*, offers some wildly ambitious prescriptions: Business parks can be fixed by inserting streets and shops onto their tarmacs. Urban highways can be morphed into main streets by putting them on diets and slowing them down with narrower lanes, streetlights, and crosswalks. Disconnected tangles of cul-de-sac can be made walkable by strategic grafting of new roads and lanes between them. Huge, unaffordable McMansions can be divided into apartments. Gas stations can be humanized by wrapping their parking lots in new street-front businesses.

Parts of the *Sprawl Repair Manual* read like a blueprint for a fantasy urban universe; anything is possible on paper. But some of Tachieva's prescriptions have already come to life in pockets across the continent.

One of the most striking retrofits is growing on the former site of a vast mall surrounded by parking on 104 acres in Lakewood, southwest of Denver. At the turn of the twentieth century, customers of the mall then known as Villa Italia had been sucked away by newer, bigger malls on the urban periphery. Some suggested turning the superblock site into a big-box power center. But what people in Lakewood really wanted was a downtown.

The city worked with a developer to turn the superblock into twenty-three smaller blocks, with streets woven into the network of the surrounding neighborhoods, combining shopping, offices, housing, and public space. Larger buildings and parking structures were "wrapped" with small street-fronting retail spaces, keeping streets active and slow, as Jan Gehl has counseled. The site is anchored not by its national retailers but by a block-size town green and a central plaza where people come and hang out without any need to shop. More than fifteen hundred people now live on the unfinished site in town houses, apartments above stores, lofts, and houses built up against the streets.

The important difference between a meaningful sprawl repair such as the Lakewood Towne Center and main street–imitating faux downtowns appearing across the continent is that the former achieves more than just the aesthetic feat of turning malls inside out. The true repair addresses the systemic problems of sprawl. By mixing shopping, services, and public space with housing, it allows people to escape the

Megablock Redux

Sprawl-repair plans turn parking oceans (top) *into walkable town centers* (above) *with parking stacked behind apartments and streets connected to surrounding neighborhoods.* (Copyright © Duany Plater-Zyberk & Company)

bonds of their seat belts and walk if they wish. It creates a critical mass of demand for transit, and comfortable places to wait for it. It links streets to surrounding networks, making walking easier and extending tendrils of easier living, good health, sociability, and connectivity. It offers truly public space—that is, owned and controlled by the local municipality, not the mall owner or developer. On the plaza at Lakewood you can loiter, stage a piggyback fight, or a demonstration, for that matter, without depending on the goodwill of the private security forces that have come to dominate public-private spaces from Disneyland to Midtown Manhattan. These mall retrofits are not quite the same as a downtown, and not quite as fine-grained and unpredictable as the old streetcar neighborhood, but they do infuse choice and freedom into the homogeneity of sprawl.

The Law of Sprawl

If so many people want to live in or near walkable urban spaces, why have so few been built in the last few decades? Why can't any town just retrofit its troubles away?

One reason stems from contradictions within our own preferences. Although it is true that most of us say we would prefer a walkable community over one that forces us to drive long distances, most of us *also* want to live in a detached home with plenty of privacy and space. In other words, we would like to have our cake and eat it too, the ideal world being one in which we reap the benefits of *other people* choosing to live in apartments and town houses nearby, but not close enough to disturb our sleep.*

This ideal world happens to be pretty much what Robin Meyer wants in Mableton, which is a fine coincidence because it is exactly what sprawl repair can provide her, thanks to the heteroscedasticity of society. More than a third of Americans would actually be willing to live in an attached home or apartment if it also gave them an old-style walkable neighborhood. Millions of people are waiting for those places to be born, and they are increasingly willing to pay a premium to enjoy them. There's evidence of this in the real estate market, which is showing a tectonic shift. In the Washington, DC, area, for example, the highest housing price per square foot in 2000 was in

*According to the National Association of Realtors "2011 Community Preference Survey," eight in ten people still say they would prefer to live in single-family detached houses over other types of housing such as town houses, condominiums, or apartments.

estatelike suburban neighborhoods—25 to 50 percent higher than the price in walkable urban neighborhoods. But by the end of the decade the situation had reversed, with home prices 50 to 70 percent higher per square foot in walkable urban neighborhoods. So demand is not the issue.

The problem is that most of sprawl has already been sold, zoned, and occupied, locking the existing system of land use into place. In order for sprawl repairs to function as complete systems, they need to work at a significant scale. That can mean rezoning and redesigning many acres of land. Sometimes all it takes to put the brakes on redevelopment is one stubborn property owner. Governments do have the power to exercise "eminent domain," or the right to seize private land for its own use or for resale in the interest of the community, but doing so can involve a hell of a court battle, not to mention ethical concerns. This is why most retrofits have grown from dead and dying malls—large parcels of land with single owners.

But the biggest obstacle to the retrofit project has almost nothing to do with demand or landowners' resistance to change. It is that the system that built sprawl—huge state subsidies, financial incentives, and powerful laws—is still in place. In fact, in most jurisdictions in the United States and Canada, the sprawl-repair vision is not merely unfamiliar. It is totally against the law.

Mableton is a perfect example. Most of the things that Robin Meyer imagined—things that would make Mableton more walkable, slower, safer, healthier, and more welcoming for kids and seniors— are forbidden by zoning codes and road standards in Cobb County. You cannot build the kind of apartments above shops that you see in Paris or Copenhagen, or in any of North America's best-loved neighborhoods, because county codes strictly segregate the various functions of the city onto separate parcels of land. Not only do these rules keep housing away from business and jobs, but Cobb County has different zones for residences on two-acre lots, one-acre lots, three-quarter-acre lots, half-acre lots, and so on, right on down to duplexes, condominiums, and rental apartments, and there are strict controls about what can happen on those lots. Everything has its place—far from everything else.

It is also against the law to build anything in Mableton without surrounding it in a sea of parking. The requirement for every professional office to have one parking spot per 250 square feet or for every bowling establishment to provide five spaces per alley might seem reasonable, but the rules also forbid two different businesses from sharing parking, even if one attracts daytime visitors (say, accountants) and the other attracts nighttime visitors (say, bowlers). Such inanely simplistic rules mean there are an estimated eight parking spaces for every car in the United States.

It doesn't stop there. You cannot push a commercial building close to the street. Nor can you squeeze streets down to the friendly dimensions of the old main streets that people love to visit. Nor can you take a state-controlled artery such as Floyd Road and give it dimensions that will slow drivers down when they pass through town; that would violate state highway standards and safety regulations.

Look at your own city. Zoning and building codes have shaped almost everything you see. Code controls the way everything looks and feels. It controls the width of streets and the height of curbs. It controls the distance between your front step and the sidewalk. It organizes the system of the city, and thus the lives led in it. Code is the reason you can or cannot walk from your home to a corner store. It is not market-based, nor is it democratic. Chances are you did not vote on the code that shaped your city. As I wrote earlier, these days most American municipalities take the easy route and simply adopt their code from Municode, the generic online source.

A city's traditional zoning code functions as an organism with very strong intentions about how city life should work. The best neighborhoods in America could not be replicated in Mableton or in most other places on the continent, because all the things that are great about them would break the rules.

Code Wars

The godlike power of code struck Tachieva's mentor, Andrés Duany, shortly after he began his career as an architect in Miami in the 1970s, when he realized that every commission began with a search through a four-inch-thick binder titled *City of Miami Zoning Ordinance 11000.*

"I remember the book—that horrible book always waiting on my desk. I was aghast that there was something that would tell me, the architect, what to do in terms of form. Then I realized that the power that shapes our city is in the code, not in the people. Miami looks the way it does, and Savannah the way it does, Paris the way it does, and New York City the way it does, and San Francisco the way it does, because of codes," Duany told me. What was worse, the codes he worked under were forcing him to create structures that he knew would destroy the human scale and social life of the city. "Code appears to be neutral, but it isn't. However neutral the language is, however neutral the metrics, however fair it seems to be, the outcome it has in mind is sprawl. What we needed to do to make great places was not to fight the code, but *take it over.*"

The code revolution began in the wilderness. Duany and his creative partner and wife, Elizabeth Plater-Zyberk, famously found their opportunity on eighty acres of private property on a desolate stretch of Florida's Gulf Coast, in a county with no zoning regulations whatsoever. The property's owner, Robert Davis, wanted to re-create the aesthetic and the functional appeal of towns built before the age of dispersal. It would be impossible to accomplish that dream by following the rules that had governed almost all suburban development for the better part of a century. They had to invent an entirely new code.

The trio toured such classic old towns as Savannah and Charleston, taking photos and sketching along the way. Then they created a set of basic design rules to approximate the best of what they had seen. Their new code prescribed a compact town of narrow, interconnected streets, alleys, and small parks, populated by traditional-looking houses with deep front porches, wood siding, pitched roofs, and quirky one-room towers—and it encouraged the mix of uses that new towns had been missing for fifty years. Within those standards, Davis let buyers and their architects design whatever they wanted for each lot.

The resulting resort town of Seaside was the most influential piece of urbanism of its era—and among the most controversial. It was an almost dreamlike idyll of pastel-painted cottages, picket fences, and picture-perfect squares. Many critics hated it for Duany's prescriptive aesthetic codes. They dismissed it as a manufactured fantasy of instant urbanism, a criticism heightened by the choice of Seaside for the setting of the 1998 dystopian film *The Truman Show*. But Seaside turned out to be exactly the kind of place people loved. Davis sold lots for as little as $15,000 in 1982, but land values climbed 25 percent almost every year in the next decade. Even after the real estate bust of 2008, town houses several blocks from the ocean were selling for nearly $2 million, and condominiums sitting above shops in the town center—a form that had been considered unsellable for decades—were fetching $800,000. These days, the most common criticism of Seaside is its lack of socioeconomic diversity—a condition created *specifically* by its wild popularity. People will pay a premium to live or even spend a few days in places that feel and function like traditional villages and towns.

The experiment has inspired copycats around the world. But its real value is in the way it demonstrated the power of the zoning code: change the code and you change the city.

In 1993 Duany, Plater-Zyberk, and a group of like-minded architects and planners came together to wage war against the rules and practices that had produced sprawl. They called their movement the Congress for the New Urbanism—the name a cheeky reference and reaction to the CIAM—Congrès Internationaux d'architecture moderne—the fraternity formed by Le Corbusier and other European modernists in 1928. The New Urbanists were determined to undo the modernists' work. They wrote a manifesto calling for compact, mixed-use, mixed-income neighborhoods of walkable street networks, with transit and attractive public spaces, all framed by buildings that responded to the local culture and climate.

The Congress for the New Urbanism has now grown into a powerful movement with thousands of members. Their ideas, which incorporate much of what Jane Jacobs and Christopher Alexander and Jan Gehl first proposed decades ago, have become accepted thinking among new generations of city planners. But for all their influence, the New Urbanists have been responsible for only a tiny fraction of built America, even during the boom years. The places they envision—no matter how loved they are, no matter how well they sell—are still essentially illegal in the vast majority of cities. The result: most New Urbanist communities have been built far from city limits, out along the highways, in swamps and farmers' fields, or on dead mall sites or abandoned industrial lands—which means, of course, that they are unavailable to any family not wealthy enough to also operate a couple of cars—while the urgent work of repairing existing cities and suburbs languishes.

The greatest problem facing anyone who would repair sprawl remains the godlike power of code. Code is to the city what an operating system is to a computer. It is invisible, but it is in charge. So the battle for American cities has moved from architectural drafting tables to the dense, arcane pages of the zoning codebooks. The winners will determine the shape of cities and the fate of suburbia.

There are many fronts in the code war, but the New Urbanists' favorite weapon has become the form-based code, a set of rules that prescribes the shape of spaces and buildings without necessarily dictating what can happen there. Most form-based codes specifically do away with the strict segregation of uses that characterized twentieth-century zoning plans, so that work, play, domesticity, and commerce could begin to intermingle again. To develop his own base code, Duany drew from the ecological sciences, using a transect, or cross section, to show how human activities should occur in a gradual spectrum from wilderness to city center, just as natural ecosystems gradually change from mountainside to seashore. Dubbed Smart-Code, it basically states that the closer you get to an urban core, the denser buildings and uses should become.

The code ends the intrusion of essentially rural forms such as highways into village and town centers, and the plunking down of downtown forms such as apartment buildings in the middle of nowhere. It offers certainty to people like Robin Meyer, who want a village to drive to, but do not want an apartment tower next to their four-acre lots. It also offers developers more certainty about what growth will look like. Someone who builds or buys into a block of spiffy town houses can be assured that the immediate neighborhood will grow with a similar scale rather than being surprised by a glass skyscraper next door, or a mini-mart fronted by a big parking lot. It helps towns avoid what happened down the road from Mableton in Smyrna, where, after having secured building rights on a chunk of land beside the new town green, a developer turned around and built a strip mall–like structure, with its ass to the green and its face to a big parking lot.

Mableton's New Operating System

A code can't be smart if it is imposed from a distance. In the summer of 2010, a year after the Atlanta Regional Commission first spurred them to action, more than a hundred residents, bureaucrats, politicians, architects, designers, and traffic engineers spent a week in the cramped cafeteria of Mableton Elementary School, hashing out a plan to fix the town. It was a sweatbox. There were no windows, and the air conditioner was broken. The ideas came like fire. The architects drew them on poster board as fast as the people could throw them out.

What they came up with looked a lot like what Meyer had envisioned that sunny day in the post office parking lot. They saw Floyd Road tamed—although the county would have to regain control of it from the state of Georgia to do so. They saw the patchwork of parking and lawn and vast, empty spaces along Floyd disappear underneath a pleasant town center. They saw the Racetrac gas station receding behind a curtain of shops. Just north of the post office, Governor Barnes's farm would sprout old-folks housing and services around a public square. Disconnected streets would be connected. The closer you got to the new town square, the tighter the urban fabric would become. The dying mall, the Village at Mableton, would become a real village, with new customers for its shops living above them, around them, and in the gently densified neighborhoods—where people would gain the right to add an extra residence or two to their own properties—within the magic five-minute walk.

Mableton would not be a passing blur in a windshield. It would be a place for slowing down, for staying. Hundreds of people would get to live in or near a core that could offer them an easier, richer, more resilient existence. They would get what people in old downtowns and streetcar suburbs have enjoyed all along. By their very proximity, they would provide the body heat to support businesses, vibrant streets, and a commuter train station on the rail line that now cuts through town without stopping. And people like Meyer, who prefer their cars, would get a town center worth driving to.

By giving some people the choice of living close together and close to the necessities of life, everyone in Mableton would eventually come out ahead. That was the vision.

Mableton today

The Mableton people want

Mableton town center (top) is configured like a rest stop, with destinations dispersed amid seas of lawn and parking astride highwaylike Floyd Road. Residents have set out a vision (above) to turn the town center into a walkable village core with a mix of housing, retail, public buildings, and parks, with car parking tucked behind buildings and Floyd Road tamed into a boulevard. (Copyright © Duany Plater-Zyberk & Company)

But the plan would have died in the elementary school classroom had it not been accompanied by new rules—a new operating system. So, after the people traced out their aspirations, Tachieva and Ball translated them into a new form-based code, a straightforward set of rules to guide the design of new developments in the area around Mableton. Meyer and her allies worked to convince Cobb County's governing board of commissioners to take a chance on the new code. They were more than successful. The following year, that code was adopted for all of Cobb County. Rather than totally replacing the county's old code, it now runs alongside it: property developers can choose which code they wish to have applied to their project applications.

The new Mableton won't be built without investment from property developers. The form-based code contains some honey for them by making the building permit process easier, simpler, and more predictable. At the same time, Cobb County will fast-track projects that choose the new code. It will take years for a new generation of developments to repair Mableton, but at least the system is now stacked to favor the future that people actually want.

Changing the Game

As the people in Mableton realized, the battle to repair sprawl on a large scale means convincing developers that they can make money by building stuff they have avoided for decades.

To this end, Tachieva insists that form-based codes do not go far enough. Even when communities and decision makers agree that the old sprawl patterns are not sustainable, the dispersal system can rumble on like a runaway truck, propelled by the momentum of a century of rules, guidelines, and state-mandated community plans. Every level of government offers incentives for sprawl-style development and penalties for smart growth, sometimes without even knowing it.

The lingering incentives for sprawl are too numerous to name, but here are a few glaring examples:

First there is the "traffic impact exaction," a standard fee that municipalities charge developers who create new density, based on the superficial assumption that density creates more automobile traffic and thus more costs. It backfires horribly because it actually punishes the kinds of mixed-use development that can support transit, and it spreads new development farther and farther across the landscape, creating even more traffic.

Then there is the U.S. government's accelerated depreciation tax deduction, which gives developers a generous tax break for creating new buildings rather than renovating or reusing old ones. It effectively rewards Walmart for abandoning older stores and building in regional power centers far from the communities they first promised to serve.

Another misguided gift to sprawl is the home mortgage interest tax deduction. The United States is one of only a handful of countries in the world that gives individuals a tax break on interest for home mortgages. In practice, the deduction has given the biggest tax break to people who can afford to buy new homes on the suburban fringe rather than those who buy cheaper, modest homes in older neighborhoods. (Personal loans for renovations, for example, don't get the deduction.) By encouraging homeowners to delay paying down big mortgages, it helped cause the foreclosure crisis. And it apparently does little to boost home ownership. In Canada, where there is no such tax break, the rate of home ownership is slightly higher than in the United States. By rewarding sprawl buyers, it passes massive new costs on to municipalities, which then have to build new schools, fire stations, and roads to service horizontal growth.

To top it off, governments have continued the decades-old practice of pouring tax dollars into highways and low-density infrastructure while spending a tiny fraction of that amount on urban rail and other transit service. For example, of the 18.4 cents per gallon the U.S. government took in gas taxes in 2012, only 2.86 cents went to public transit and almost all the rest was poured into highways. (Thus, as fuel costs and the recession drove more people than ever to transit, the Metropolitan Atlanta Rapid Transit Authority, or MARTA, actually consolidated bus routes and cut subway services.) Complicating matters, almost all major developments and road changes have to be approved by state governments, whose own regulations may have their origins back in the early years of dispersed city building.

"Sprawl was incentivized," Tachieva says. "Now we want to get similar incentives for mixed-use and walkable places. We need to level the playing field and give an equal chance for efforts to improve the places we already have."

She and other sprawl-repair activists are taking the lead by writing model sprawl-repair acts as unsolicited gifts for state governments. The acts enable states and municipalities to change infrastructure-funding rules, tax incentives, and permit requirements to make it just as easy to retrofit dead malls into dense, walkable, mixed-use town centers as it is to build big-box deserts. They allow fast-tracked permitting for sprawl repairs and tax incentives for the kinds of places that people actually love. (At the time of writing, the Commercial Center Revitalization Act, inspired by Tachieva's work, was gradually making its way through the South Carolina state legislature.)

If all this sounds like a big fat bonus for property developers, well, it is. But the truth is, as long as we inhabit a capitalist system, the future of suburbia depends on them.

The vast majority of real estate developments in the United States are controlled by a handful of huge Wall Street–controlled real estate investment trusts. Wall Street traders are not interested in the complexity of urban life. They are interested in easily tradable commodities, explains Christopher Leinberger, the land-use strategist. Leinberger has found that in the last couple of decades, real estate has come to be sorted into a limited set of product types, all based on the segregated, drivable model set out by the modernists a lifetime ago. Retail development, for example, will either be a neighborhood center, a lifestyle center, or a big-box-anchored power center, product types that Wall Street financiers can quantify, approve, and exchange without ever actually visiting the building site or so much as talking to anyone from the community about what they actually want.

"Bank loan officers now specialize in just one of these types of real estate; bring them something different and they will generally show you the door," writes Leinberger in *The Option of Urbanism*. Despite the apparent recklessness that led to the 2008 financial crisis, lenders generally recoil from complexity and risk, so their funding formulas have ended up reinforcing simplistic, separatist patterns of development. Mixed-use retrofits demand more care and attention, and a cognitive break for these developers. If you cannot offer them certainty and attractive returns, says Tachieva, then the vast drosscapes and dead malls left behind by sprawl's horizontal charge are unlikely to be repaired for many years.*

The Aesthetic Trap

One other force complicates sprawl repair. It lives in the way each of us perceives the relationship between architecture and the urban system. Every one of us carries an idea of what the ideal town is supposed to look like, but that idea is most often represented by a set of images in our head rather than by deep consideration of the complex systems that make the place function in a particular way. As Elizabeth Dunn discovered in her Harvard dorm studies, most people exaggerate the life-changing power of aesthetics and architectural details. We tend to judge the character and health of a place—and even its residents—by the very material used on building facades.† Most of us are drawn to and comforted by designs that remind us of pleasant times in the past or in our imagination. This is one reason why New Urbanist retrofits are frequently wrapped in neo-traditional packages. It's a form of subversive marketing, as Ellen Dunham-Jones, coauthor of *Retrofitting Suburbia*, explained to me. New Urbanist designers and developers know that what they are selling is entirely unfamiliar for many people—mixed use, mixed income, density, and transit. So they use nostalgic, unthreatening forms to gently build acceptance for what are essentially progressive public

*In Tachieva's opinion, this even means offering tax incentives for builders of multistory parking garages, the argument being that such garages attract needed customers to denser retail nodes in suburbia, making them robust and busy enough to warrant the construction of public transit in the future. Transportation activists argue that good public transit should come first. It's a chicken-and-egg argument that has gone on for years. Whoever is right, we do know that without either ample parking or sexy public transit, retailers simply won't occupy new space.
†Sociologists have found that even the materials used to clad a home's facade can shape visitors' perceptions about the resident's personality. If a house is clad with wooden shingles, for example, people are more likely to think that its owners are artsy, friendly, and of a relatively high social class. Red brick suggests that they are not so artistic, but still friendly and high in social standing. If we see cinder block, we tend to lump the occupants in with the unfriendly, the inartistic, and the low class. Stucco gets the lowest status rating of all.

goals. Form is the spoonful of sugar that helps the good medicine go down. Superficial but effective.

But this focus on aesthetics can blind us to crucial elements of design. This is what seems to have happened just down the road from Mableton, where the town of Smyrna demolished its moribund former core and built a hedonic landscape on the ruins. I wandered Smyrna's new Market Village with the mayor, Max Bacon, in 2010. The main drag, Spring Street, was lined with faux-antebellum mansions, complete with white columns, expansive porches, and brick facades. There was a classical fountain at one end and a gazebo at the other, and beyond that, instead of Sleeping Beauty's Castle, was the Romanesque facade of a new city hall, capped with a miniature tower.

The project's architect, Mike Sizemore, was pleased to hear me compare Spring Street to Disney's Main Street U.S.A. "The style was an attempt to tie Smyrna into a past that people wish they had, a past they aspire to," he said. "The solid, tapered columns and the porches

Reinventing the Familiar

Like Disneyland's Main Street U.S.A., Smyrna's Market Village was designed to remind people of an idealized past. (Courtesy of Sizemore Group Architects)

with their rocking chairs all speak of the elegance and stability of the Old South."

The village, with its quaint restaurants, ice-cream parlor, art shops, and fitness center, was a huge hit when it opened in 2003. The apartments above the shops sold within months of being finished. So did the cottages nearby. Smyrna's council members had risked their political necks, raising property taxes in order to help bankroll the project, but after the village opened, land values within a mile radius went through the roof, inflating the city's tax revenue twentyfold. The city started raking in so much money that the city council cut the tax rate by 30 percent, making it near the lowest in the state. "It sounds like a Bernie Madoff scheme, but it's true!" one councilor gushed.

The success made Mayor Bacon, who spearheaded the scheme, something of a hero in Smyrna. On the day of our walk through the Market Village, passersby kept slapping him on the back and thanking him. Village Sushi, a restaurant on the strip, even named a dish after him: the Max Bacon Sushi Roll.

Yet the aesthetic appeal of the Market Village obscures a deep flaw in the Smyrna redesign. This became apparent when I visited the mayor's ninety-one-year-old mother, Dot, a frail, elegant woman who lived in an old yellow cottage behind the new city hall. Unable to walk very far, Dot had to beg rides from her neighbors to buy food and staples. There was no place to buy groceries in the Market Village, and the nearest supermarket was more than a mile away. Here she was, living steps from her son's new downtown, and Dot was stranded. To support the grocery store Dot Bacon needed, the Market Village would need a heck of a lot more people. (It usually takes eight hundred dwellings to support a small corner store, for example, and Smyrna's new downtown features just a few dozen homes.) There was land to build on near the impressive new community center and library, but Sizemore told me that the people of Smyrna had refused to consider adding buildings that might obscure the view of these impressive edifices from the five-lane Atlanta Road. In a common replaying of the focusing illusion, they chose the salience of form over function. They chose a design that felt like a village but did not actually perform like one.

This is the lesson for all retrofits: the system is ultimately more important than the package it comes in, and the greatest hurdle for sprawl repair may be challenging the way each of us views the city.

Backlash and Reality

This has become painfully clear in the last decade, where efforts to tackle the problems of sprawl in a more systematic way have begun to draw shrill outrage from some conservative urbanists and libertarians, some of whom have found a voice in the Tea Party movement. Tea Party activists have taken to storming otherwise humdrum city and regional planning meetings across the United States whenever they catch wind of plans to introduce rail transit or transit-friendly zoning or regional growth boundaries. In Tampa, Florida, for example, Tea Party activists defeated a tax measure that would fund light-rail and road improvements in Hillsborough County. *Hillsborough County Conservative Examiner* columnist Warren Pledger issued this phantasmagorical warning: by paying for light-rail, "tax payers will be purchasing the cattle cars that sneaky government officials hope to utilize in the forced transportation of proletariat workers traveling between their apartment buildings and the government owned factories seven days a week."

Such imaginative interpretations are actually pretty standard among Tea Party urbanists. In city after city, opponents to New Urbanism and "smart growth" claim that local planners are part of an international conspiracy to force everyone to abandon their cars, give up their private property rights, and live in United Nations–mandated "habitation zones." In the 2010 midterm elections, Colorado Republican gubernatorial candidate Dan Maes accused his Democratic opponent of using a Paris-style bicycle-share program to convert Denver into a "United Nations Community."*

In this debate, the city emerges not merely as a system for living, but as a symbol, an expression of political values. The backlash is grounded in a deep-seated mistrust of government and a fear of losing property rights and freedoms. These anti-planning tendencies are quite natural in a nation that holds its sense of liberty close, but they

---

*As proof of a high-level conspiracy between local planners, national governments, and the United Nations, opponents point to Agenda 21, an action plan adopted after the 1992 U.N. Earth Summit in Rio de Janeiro, when 178 governments resolved to consider the environmental impacts of development. Ironically, the first time most urban planners ever hear of Agenda 21 is when Tea Party activists bring it up at public consultation meetings.

are not based in a clear view of reality. For one thing, they ignore the fact that their tax dollars are already being used to massively subsidize the sprawl model. They also forget that the purely libertarian city simply does not exist. The vast majority of cities in the developed world have been shaped by rules that might already be considered totalitarian for the level of control they exert. Ironically, the dispersed city that Tea Partiers defend so passionately is, itself, a product of centralized control and legislation. That city is grounded at least partly in the ideas of the high modern European socialist Le Corbusier, evangelist of strict controls and segregation of land use, road geometry, and city life.

Tachieva, for her part, wishes she could reassure every one of sprawl repair's libertarian opponents. Even if the sprawl-repair movement is wildly successful, she says, there will be plenty of auto-oriented suburbia around for those who prefer, and can afford, that way of living.

"Anyone who wants to can keep their big house, live wherever they want, go to malls, and commute for four hours if they like," Tachieva says. "We just want the chance to fix a few little spots here and there. We want to create some space so that the hundred million people who are coming to American cities will have some choice about where to live and how to live."

I think that opponents of the retrofit movement also misunderstand the fundamental relationship between urban form and individual freedom. Every urban dweller's freedom to live, move, and experience the city as he chooses is inherently conditioned by what every landowner does with his or her property. If a developer builds an auto-dependent neighborhood for ten thousand people at the far end of my city, that system will soon infringe on my own right to enjoy safe and navigable roads. Its drivers will crowd the public right-of-way road until the point of gridlock, and then they will demand that it be widened. They will suck up my tax dollars with their demands for dispersed water, sewage, and electricity systems. If they forbid their neighbors from building new density on their own land, then new settlers will have to move even farther down the road, propagating the system of dispersal that—through geometry and sheet distance—has forced millions of people into one way of moving and living, regardless of their preferences.

Cities have always expressed a tension between individual property rights and common benefits. But the Tea Party urbanists take a dangerously narrow view of liberty. Surely a city of true freedom would provide maximum choice about where and how to live. Some visionary citizens understand that achieving such freedom means paying not less but *more* taxes, if they result, say, in a wider palette of mobility options. (In 2008, for example, two-thirds of Los Angeles County residents agreed to a new half-cent sales tax that will raise $40 billion for transportation projects over thirty years, including new subway, bus, and light-rail networks, bike lanes, and, yes, freeway improvements. The transit investments are reinventing the city whose name is synonymous with sprawl, pouring new pedestrian life onto boulevards around transit stops and responding to a new generation of Angelinos who prefer iPhones and souped-up bicycles to cars.) Local code retrofits are even more transparently empowering because they provide citizens with the tools first to visualize the life they want beyond their front doors and then to shape the city that will offer that life. The new codes actually give people in growth centers *more* freedom to build up their own land than they had before.

Thankfully, the code warriors are gaining ground. More than three hundred cities in Canada and the United States have now adopted some kind of form-based code (or bylaws, as typically known in Canada) for at least some neighborhoods. In 2010 Miami, Florida, became the first major city to toss out its entire zoning book in favor of a homegrown form-based code.

Mableton found its own local code because citizens like Meyer took hundreds of hours to plan, to draw, to argue, and to dream their town's future. They came to understand that the town is not just a picture, and not just an idea, but a system for living they could shape together. They were not guided by the state or by large developers, but their plan will harness the energy of development when the economy picks up. And when sprawl's most devoted citizens grow old or run out of gas money, Meyer hopes her village will be waiting for them, too.

13. Save Your City, Save Yourself

Cities have the capability of providing something for everybody, only because, and only when, they are created by everybody.

—Jane Jacobs

Sometimes the forces that shape our cities can seem overwhelming. It is easy to feel small in the face of the monumental power of the real estate industry, the tyranny of zoning codes, the inertia of bureaucracies, and the sheer durability of things that have already been built. It is tempting to believe that the job of fixing cities is the untouchable terrain of distant authorities whom the state has deemed responsible. It is a terrible mistake to give in to this temptation.

Who has the right to shape the city? The French philosopher Henri Lefebvre once offered a straightforward answer. This right is not something that can be bequeathed by the state. It is not an accident of ethnicity or nationality or birthplace. It is earned through the act of habitation. If you live out your life in the shared urban landscape, then you have a natural right to participate in shaping its future. Lefebvre invented a new name for his naturally enfranchised city shaper, who was both citizen and denizen of the city: the *citadin*.

Lefebvre was talking about more than design. He was calling for a total restructuring of social, political, and economic relations so that *citadins* could wrest power over their common urban future back from the state. Whether you support his revolution or not, it is impossible to deny the truth in his message: We are all *citadins*. We are all, through the very geography of our lives, natural stewards and owners of the city. Those who acknowledge it claim immense power.

I have learned this from people who have stopped waiting for mayors or planners or engineers to remake their streets and neighborhoods. Some, like the neighbors who tore down their fences on N Street in Davis, just want to build a community that makes more sense for them than the one that planners handed them. Some are driven by a wish to reclaim an almost intangible sense of belonging. Others want safer spaces for their kids. Some are trying to save the planet. Some want more freedom to live and move as they please. They rarely use the language of neuroscience or behavioral economics or even architecture, but they are proving that the happy city revolution can start right at the front door, and that every one of us has the power to alter our city. Some of them find that in changing their cities, they also change themselves.

Freedom Rider

On a spring morning in 2009 a bespectacled twelve-year-old named Adam Kaddo Marino announced to his mother, Janette, that it was National Bike to Work Day.

"School is my work," Adam told his mother. "So I should get to bike to school, right?"

The pair left their home in Saratoga Springs, New York, on their bicycles, and they followed the city's main drag, Broadway, north until it was swallowed by a hardwood forest. They biked on a slick rock trail through the trees. The light of the rising sun streamed through the canopy, which was bursting with new growth. It was a glorious ride, much better than sitting in the back of a diesel school bus. They emerged from the forest near the back of Maple Avenue Middle School and locked Adam's bike up just as the buses were pulling in. Adam felt great.

That was the end of the fun. First the parking attendant warned Adam's mother that she had made a big mistake. Then the vice principal laid into her. Then Principal Stuart Byrne came out to explain that biking and walking to school had been banned by the school district since 1994. Byrne confiscated Adam's bicycle. ("I would be a nervous wreck every day if kids were riding to school," he later told *The Saratogian*, noting the modern-day dangers of traffic and lurking child abusers. "If anything happened, it would weigh on me for the rest of my life.") What had been a ritual for generations of children in Saratoga Springs was now deemed too risky. Adam's bicycle was locked in the school boiler room.

"As time went on, my blood started to boil," Janette Kaddo Marino told me later. "Here we were, trying to encourage freedom, and I was reprimanded by my child's principal! Shouldn't I have the right to take my child to school any way I can?"

It's easy to see why the school district made the rule. Maple Avenue Middle School is a gigantic amalgamated institution plunked down north of town on its namesake avenue, which looks more like a rural highway than an urban boulevard. Although Maple Avenue does have a painted bike lane—part of a nationally designated bike highway—at the time there were no sidewalks, and the road was engineered for speed, right down to the geometry of the school entrance, where the street corners looked more like curves on a racetrack. Saratoga Springs had designed danger right into the school experience.

But this story does not end like so many others in the country of fear. Adam had too much at stake. Born with partial achromatopsia, a congenital vision disorder, Adam knew he might never see well enough to get a driver's license, but he could walk and cycle at slower speeds with ease. The family had moved to Saratoga Springs specifically because they thought it was the kind of place where Adam could be free to ride his bike. That was one thing. Adam was also bugged by the sheer idiocy of the ban on walking and biking.

"I'm a safe rider. I wear a helmet. I use hand signals when I am turning. My mom taught me all that stuff long ago. Why would they have a rule saying I can't bike or walk to school? It just didn't make sense to me," Adam recalled.

His mother warned him that defying the school district would not be easy. He would be in the spotlight. She said he didn't have to take on this fight. "But I said I'm totally game. We had to change the school so kids in the future could decide for themselves how to get there. We couldn't back down."

Adam fought against the architecture of fear. After the school relinquished Adam's bike, he insisted on riding to school whenever he felt like it. His mom rode with him. They would whiz by the long line of vehicles full of chauffeur-parents and kids on Maple Avenue, and Adam would wave when he saw the faces of his fellow students pressed against the window of the school bus or their parents' cars. They kept riding even after the day the following autumn when the police were called to school to give Janette hell. They kept riding, and Janette kept harassing the school district until the story started hitting newspapers, TV news, and finally the *Drudge Report*.

That did the trick. Humiliated, the school district finally backed down and legalized the journey. Now there's a bike rack at the school, and sometimes Adam rides with a posse of seven or eight friends.

The Kaddo Marinos have launched a wider campaign to force Saratoga Springs to start building sidewalks and safer routes near schools. It will be a long fight: even though the district now has a safe-routes-to-schools committee, the last big infrastructure investment at Maple Avenue school was a renovation of the school's vast parking lot to ease car congestion. But by insisting on their right to move as they pleased, the Kaddo Marinos have begun to force their city to reconsider what roads are for.

Anger and Action

Another morning, this one on Clinton Street in Brooklyn, just before Christmas in 2001: for what seemed like the hundredth time, Aaron Naparstek, an interactive media producer, was awoken at the crack of dawn by the honking of car horns. The morning racket had driven him crazy for months. Naparstek knew that drivers weren't honking because they were worried about hitting someone. They were honking because they were backed up at the light at Clinton and Pacific, not moving at all. He could hear their anger in the way they let their horns wail. Not *toot, toot*, but *maaaaaaaaaa! maaaaaaaaaa!* It didn't help that most American car horns are built for highway travel: they are designed to be heard far ahead of fast-moving vehicles.

That sense of aggression seeped into Naparstek's psyche. Some days he would wake up even before the horns started blowing, and he would lie in bed, anticipating that first honk. And when it came, it was like a punch in the chest.

"My chest would tighten, my heart rate would go up. It felt like someone was about to fucking attack me—you know, do violence to me," he told me. "And finally it was like, someone needs to pay for this."

On that winter morning, one impatient driver laid his hand to his horn and did not remove it. The blast continued as Naparstek strode to the window of his third-floor brownstone apartment and identified the offending honker stuck near the intersection in a faded blue sedan. He swore that if the guy was still wailing on the horn in the time it took him to stroll to his refrigerator, grab a carton of eggs, and stroll back to his window, the guy was going to get it.

The honk went on.

The first egg was a direct hit, and deeply satisfying. After three or four more, the driver leaped out of his vehicle, spotted Naparstek, and started screaming. The stoplight cycled. The cars backed up even farther down Clinton. The guy kept yelling, and Naparstek probably yelled back. Among other threats, the driver promised to return that night, break into Naparstek's apartment, and kill him. By the time the guy returned to his car, every driver on the street seemed to be honking, and Naparstek was a trembling mess.

After a few days of wondering when the stranger would show up with a bat, Naparstek realized that he needed to find a more constructive response to the dysfunction of New York traffic and his own anger. He tried a Zen approach. He started writing haiku about honking horns, taping them to lampposts in the neighborhood. They looked like this:

When the light turns green
like a leaf on a spring wind
the horn blows quickly.

It felt good. After a few weeks Naparstek noticed that his public haiku were joined by others. After a few more weeks the haiku writers and readers began meeting to talk about their frustrations. They started attending local community-policing meetings together, where they demanded that the police start ticketing the honkers. Amazingly, the police did just that. But the honking would always return after a day or so.

"Finally," said Naparstek, "I realized I needed to step back, try some empathy, understand that these drivers are in pain down there, and help them solve the problem that was leading them to such rage."

He took to sitting in his window with a pencil and pad of paper in order to document the geography of honking. A predictable dynamic revealed itself. First, traffic would back up on Atlantic Avenue, a feeder road for the Brooklyn Bridge and the Brooklyn Queens Expressway, a block away. If the light at Clinton and Atlantic was green but there was no way out of the intersection, the first driver would rightfully stay put. But lacking a clear sight line to anything but that green light, the drivers behind that first car would lay on their horns.

It was clear that the problem could not be fixed by creating more road space. There was no space left to distribute. It didn't lie in moving cars more quickly through intersections. Physics wouldn't allow it. Naparstek studied traffic engineering reports. He befriended transportation planners. He showed up at community meetings and buttonholed anyone who knew anything about congestion management.

He finally found his answer at the intersection between the economics of impatience and the arcane art of light-signal programming. The city had timed the signals along many blocks of Clinton Street in order to create a "green wave" that drivers could theoretically cruise without stopping, all the way to Atlantic. In practice, that system created a bottleneck of cars at Atlantic that backed up well past Naparstek's intersection at Clinton and Pacific. But he deduced that if the green-light cycles along Clinton could instead be "feathered," or staggered in duration, then drivers would be held back a little bit longer at other intersections and experience less of a bottleneck once they got to Atlantic. Drivers' pain would be rationed and relieved in increments along the route, easing their feeling of entrapment at the end.

Naparstek proposed the idea to the Department of Transportation. He bugged the bureaucrats for months until they finally made that change. It was a little miracle. The honking had died down to an occasional toot on the morning I sat on the brownstone step on the corner of Clinton and Pacific.

By then Naparstek and his fiancée had moved to a quieter street, but he had been convinced that the entire city needed a new approach to streets. He had also been emboldened by the notion that

SAVE YOUR CITY, SAVE YOURSELF | 301

anyone who cared enough could change the way the city worked. He fought to get cars out of nearby Prospect Park and Grand Army Plaza. He joined Transportation Alternatives, a six-thousand-member network of livable street activists. He convinced Mark Gorton (who had made a fortune from his algorithm-based hedge funds and the file-sharing website LimeWire) to help him launch *Streetsblog* and *Streetfilms*, a Web-based campaign calling for safer, fairer, saner, and healthier streets.

These days, when pundits around the world discuss the massive changes that began occurring on the streets of New York City in 2007, they invariably credit the city's mayor, Michael Bloomberg, or his Department of Transportation chief, Janette Sadik-Khan. In truth, credit should also go to citizen activists like Naparstek.

In a campaign they launched in 2005, Naparstek and his activist friends started organizing, letter writing, shouting, blogging, networking, and educating convinced citizens and policy makers throughout the five boroughs to make the case not only that the city needed to change, but that it was capable of changing. It was the activists who raised the money to fly in Jan Gehl for streetscape studies and pep talks with policy makers. It was they who coordinated pedal-powered summits between Enrique Peñalosa, local politicians, and bike-loving celebrities such as David Byrne. It was Naparstek himself whose media campaign vilified the city's old guard transportation commissioner, Iris Weinshall, until she retired, creating an empty desk space that would be filled by a member of the livable streets tribe. (Sadik-Khan had been a board member of the Tri-State Transportation Campaign, a nonprofit dedicated to reducing auto dependency in the region. A slew of her new advisers, planners, and technical staff had roots with Transportation Alternatives, Project for Public Spaces, or one of Naparstek's community groups in Brooklyn.*)

*Jon Orcutt, Sadik-Khan's senior policy adviser, had been executive director of the Tri-State Transportation Campaign and a *Streetsblog* contributor. Assistant commissioner Andy Wiley-Schwartz came from Project for Public Spaces. Deputy commissioner for planning and sustainability Bruce Schaller had consulted for Transportation Alternatives (TA). The group's director of communications, Dani Simons, became the DOT's director of e-media. Ryan Russo, a TA activist in Brooklyn known for his custom orange bike, became the DOT's director of street management and safety. Chris Hrones, a volunteer for Naparstek's Grand Army Plaza

It was the livable streets activists who ran the barricades at Sadik-Khan's Ciclovía-like Summer Streets. And when the bike lane backlash came, it was they who packed school gyms and community board meetings to defend the streets renaissance. Some of them gave time. Some of them gave brainpower. Some of them gave cash. (Gorton contributed more than $2 million to the campaign between 2005 and 2008.) But it was people, lots of people, who changed New York City, not any one mayor, administrator, or superstar.

In 2010 Naparstek spent an hour sitting with me on the stoop of his old brownstone, watching the cars idle at the intersection of Clinton and Pacific. The guy was still up for a fight: the battle over bike lanes on the edge of Prospect Park was just heating up. But he remained calm as a driver started laying on the horn at the intersection. He chuckled and said, "A few years ago I wouldn't have been able to stand this." Maybe it was because he was older. Maybe just knowing that he could do something about the problem gave Naparstek peace of mind (after all, such a sense of empowerment is a key ingredient of that ideal state of challenged thriving). But one thing was clear. His egg-throwing days were over.

Painting the Town

One last story, this one from just above the muddy waters of the Willamette River, in an inner suburb of Portland, Oregon. This one matters most.

If you had driven through Sellwood in the late 1980s, you might have noticed a tall young man with an unruly shock of black hair sullenly mowing the lawn in front of a farm-style house on Southeast Ninth Avenue. That would be Mark Lakeman. He had lived there most of his life, and he was desperately unhappy. His malaise matched that of his neighborhood. With its modest lots and treelined streets, Sellwood approximated the streetcar suburb sweet spot, yet it was the kind of place where you could walk the sidewalks and never meet

---

Coalition, was hired as the DOT's Downtown Brooklyn coordinator. Mike Flynn, who worked with Naparstek's Park Slope Neighbors group, was hired as the DOT's director of capital planning.

anyone. Most people drove when they had to go anywhere. The streets were empty of children and, not coincidentally, full of cars cutting through on their way downtown from distant suburbs. Lakeman couldn't extinguish his feelings of disconnection. Trained as an architect and steeped in the culture of design, he had a hunch that something was broken in the shape of his neighborhood, but he couldn't put a finger on what it was.

When he was twenty-seven, Lakeman quit his corporate architectural job and went searching for the solution to his unhappiness. The quest was personal, but it was also architectural. You might say he was searching for what the architect-philosopher Christopher Alexander once called "the quality without a name," a sense of aliveness in the city, and in himself.

Lakeman took a plane across the Atlantic. He visited the ruins of meeting places built by his Celtic ancestors, circles of stone now sinking into the heather of England's Lake District. He studied the daily rhythm of light and human activity in the piazzas of the Tuscan hill towns, and he was as moved by them as Jan Gehl had been thirty years before. Finally, after three continents and years of searching, he ventured into the lowland rain forests near Mexico's frontier with Guatemala. The region is home to the Lacandon, a people whose ancestors resisted the Spanish conquest and who still live beyond the reach of modern urban planners.

Lakeman found the quality he was looking for in an unpaved village called Naja. It was hardly a romantic scene. The villagers cooked on earthen hearths and built their huts from rough-hewn mahogany. Lakeman was moved by the richness of their lives and the way it was reflected in the form of their settlement. The place was constantly being redesigned for reasons of pragmatism or imagination. The Lacondon would meet at the merging dirt pathways between their homes and gardens, and those intersections would gradually flatten and widen into gathering spaces. When they gathered, they would gather in circles. As conversations merged, circles would merge and grow. Those shapes reflected the intimate political and social dynamic in the village. Everyone participated on this earthen agora. There was no separation between children and adults.

Over months, Lakeman befriended the village leader, Chan K'in Viejo, an ancient man with a deeply crevassed face, two wives, and twenty-one children. In the smoky shadows of the leader's hut Lakeman admitted that it was not until he entered Naja that he was able to extinguish his feelings of disconnection. This was the first time he had seen a community of people actually behaving like a community: gathering, talking, and helping one another every day. It would have been nice to stay, he said. The old man told him to go home and fix his own village.

The Hegemony of the Grid

When he returned to Portland, Lakeman recognized what might have been the heart of his village, buried under asphalt right there at the intersection of Southeast Sherrett Street and Ninth Avenue. "Why didn't people in Sellwood know each other's names or talk to each other or meet each other?" Lakeman recalled later. "Why didn't they behave like villagers? I realized that part of the answer was in design." In that straight, empty street grid he saw a kind of institutionalized, village-killing prison—the opposite of Naja's convivial circles.

Lakeman's reaction to the street grid might seem melodramatic, but history supports his framing. The orthogonal road grid that defined Sellwood—and most North American cities—really is a hand-me-down from empires who used streets as tools of aggression. The Assyrians used the grid design for garrisons and detention camps in conquered regions. So did the Romans. The rectilinear lines of their garrison towns, and eventually their basilicas, ran right over the circular gathering spaces of Lakeman's ancestors in northern England. Thomas Jefferson convinced his fellow Founding Fathers of the American republic to adopt the Roman grid barely four years after their victory against the British Empire. The national Land Ordinance of 1785 set the grid as the approved form for all settlements west of the Ohio River. It was part of the tool kit of colonization and nation building. The grid was the fastest, simplest way to divide land so that it could be commodified. Rectangular units were easy to survey, buy, sell, and tax. They made it easier to provide services. The grid was a spectacular success as an economic tool, but it created some seriously unbalanced cities. The Land Ordinance of 1785 did not have provisions for parks or open space. Its cities comprised private lots and

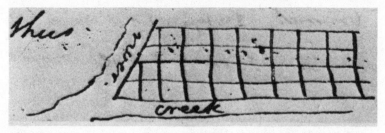

Grid Thinking

Thomas Jefferson's 1790 plan for a capital city on the site of Carrollsburg, District of Columbia, echoed plans for Roman garrison towns. The grid would be repeated in cities across the continent. (From papers of Thomas Jefferson, untitled sketch in the margin of a manuscript note, "Proceedings to be had under the Residence Act," dated November 29, 1790, LC-MS)

public roads, as though the city existed purely for commerce rather than for the people that commerce was thought to enrich. In town after town, planners subdivided, overlooked, or avoided public parks and plazas. Cities that wanted parks actually had to buy the land from private holders.

The result was that in most neighborhoods, the streets themselves became the only shared public space. As they came to be dominated by cars, the public living room—and the village that might have been born within it—disappeared.

The grid has its defenders, especially when compared with the stunning inefficiency of the freeway and cul-de-sac development of sprawl. New Urbanists admire the clarity and connectivity that can make grid neighborhoods so conducive to walking. Traffic engineers point out that a tight grid of arterial roads is less vulnerable to the nightmarish delays that accidents can cause on dendritic systems and freeways.

But the imposition of the grid or any other plan from on high has another, ultimately more profound effect on the people who must inhabit it: it estranges them from the process of shaping their own world.

"None of the people who have ever lived on my street had a say on how it was laid out. None of them ever held a vote and said, 'Let's make this bilaterally symmetrical, and let's make the rules on this side of the street the same as on the other side of the street. Let's make sure the intersections won't be the gathering places that our ancestors made back in the lands that we came from,'" Lakeman told me. "How many of us actually said, 'Hey, let's not have even one public square in the typical American neighborhood,' where in the typical village there were many."

Whether or not you share Lakeman's conception of the evils of the urban grid, he does identify that great irony of the American city: a nation that celebrates freedom and weaves liberty into its national myth rarely gives regular people the chance to shape their own communities. Municipal governments, often with the counsel and assistance of land developers, lay down community plans complete with restrictive zoning long before residents arrive on the scene. Residents have no say about what their streets and parks and gathering places will look like. And once they move in, it is illegal for them to tinker with the shape of the public places they share, or, as I have illustrated, to use their homes for anything beyond the dictates of strict zoning bylaws.

Most people in wealthy cities do not make their own homes or neighborhoods. They simply decorate and inhabit the dwellings they are offered. And we know that the ultimate villageless city—sprawl—has effectively sapped its residents of social and political wherewithal. As I have shown, people who live in sprawl are among the least likely of Americans to volunteer, vote, join political parties, or rise up and raise hell. There are many reasons for this apathy; not least among them might be genuine contentment. But the fact is, it's hard to find the agora in the dispersed city. You can't hold a demonstration in a Walmart parking lot or inside a Starbucks. Scant few neighborhoods in North America feature places that draw people together regularly for anything other than buying stuff.

This is why what happened when Lakeman got back to Sellwood that spring was so revolutionary. He challenged his neighbors to take control of the shape of their community.

First, Lakeman and a few friends built a ramshackle teahouse of salvaged wood and old windows around the base of an old tree on his parents' property on the corner of the intersection of Southeast Sherrett and Southeast Ninth, and they invited the neighbors to come for tea. Sellwood had never seen anything like it. Curious, people from up and down the blocks popped in. As spring grew lush and the cottonwood seeds began to fly in the breeze, a few dozen people would arrive to share Monday-night potluck dinners. By summer, there were hundreds.

The neighbors got to talking about the state of their neighborhood: the commuters who roared through the grid on their way to the Sellwood Bridge, the kids who had been struck by cars while trying to reach a nearby park, and the fact that none of them had ever talked to each other before. To Lakeman's delight, one Monday evening the crowd pushed right out into the middle of the intersection, and the cars stopped, and some of the people started to dance in the warm evening air.

When Portland's Bureau of Buildings ordered the teahouse, an unauthorized structure, torn down, the neighbors looked to the intersection and imagined a village square that was as desirable as it was forbidden.

The way that neighbors remember it now, someone's kid, a girl of thirteen, gathered the other children around a map of the four blocks around the intersection. The kids drew lines on that map with red felt-tip pens, connecting neighbors. There was a chef, and lots of people who liked to eat. There was a social worker, and people who had social problems. There was a musician, and people who liked music. There was an electrician. A plumber. A roofer. A designer. A landscaper. A carpenter. A contractor. Then they added the stay-at-home parents and the kids, too. Eventually the map was so crisscrossed with red it was hard to read. All these people drove out of the neighborhood to eat, to socialize, to work, and to spend. "We realized that we had a full-on village right here," Lakeman said. "All we were missing was a central place to connect." In other words, the neighborhood did not have a human resources problem. It had a design problem.

The neighbors gathered one weekend in September, thirty of them, and they brought paint, and they coated the asphalt in concentric circles radiating from the manhole at its center so that all four corners were linked. From then on, the intersection would be a piazza. They called it Share-It-Square.

Portland's Office of Transportation promptly threatened to fine the neighbors and sandblast the circles off the street. The intersection was a public space. "That means nobody is allowed to use it!" one city staffer infamously declared.

But Lakeman charmed city councilors with his village tales. The mayor pulled rank on the city's engineers. Within a few weeks the square had a conditional permit.

The neighbors built a telephone booth–size library on one corner of the intersection so people could come and trade books. They built a message board and chalk stand on the northeast corner, and a produce-sharing stand on the southeast, and a kiosk on the southwest with a big thermos that they agreed to keep full of hot tea.

Eventually the lines between public and private space began to blur. Just as the neighbors had appropriated the public right-of-way, so they began to open their own lots. One couple built a community sauna in their backyard. Fences between yards came down. People from blocks away came to help themselves to vegetables from the produce stand—and leave other greens in their place. People went out of their way to help one another. One elderly woman left town for a week and returned to find that her neighbors had painted the peeling exterior of her house.

I visited Portland on the spring day when the piazza was getting its annual new coat of paint. There were cans and brushes and kids all over the street, smearing the asphalt with coats of electric pink, turquoise, and leaf green. There was Wayne, a homeless bottle collector, pausing for a smoke and a chat on the cob bench the villagers had built, with Pedro Ferbel, the guy who built a community sauna in his backyard. A young mother put down her paint roller and told me that she had moved nearby for the sake of her daughter, who had met most of her friends around this intersection. Betty Beals, a woman with long gray hair, poured me a cup of tea from the thermos at the covered kiosk and told me how she once felt scared to walk these streets because she just didn't recognize or trust the people she encountered. Not anymore. Other people spoke of spending less money than they used to—they borrowed tools from friends, for example, and were more likely to host neighbors for dinner rather than going out. This was partly a result of the financial crisis that had hit the country so hard, but it would not have happened if the door of conviviality had not been opened.

The place felt like that mythical, possibly imagined past in which

Intersection Repair

Neighbors repaint the "piazza" on their intersection in Sellwood, Portland. The intervention spawned a movement known as City Repair. (Charles Montgomery)

everybody knows your name and cares about how you are. It felt almost cartoonlike, perhaps because the scene is so rare these days anywhere but on TV, yet this scene was real.

So is the psychological effect of intersection repair. We know this thanks to Jan Semenza, a Swedish-Italian epidemiologist who arrived to teach public health at Portland State University a couple of years after Share-It-Square was born. Semenza had his own special interest in getting people together. The story of his introduction to the geography of loneliness is worth remembering.

Semenza had just begun training as an investigator at the Centers for Disease Control in Atlanta in the summer of 1995 when an unprecedented heat wave struck the American Midwest. By July 13 the temperature in Chicago had hit 106 degrees. The heat index—a combination of heat and humidity that measures the temperature a typical person would feel—soared above 120. Roads buckled. Apartments baked. Kids riding buses to summer school programs got so nauseated from heat and dehydration that they had to be hosed down by the fire department. Other people were so desperate to cool down, they forced open thousands of fire hydrants. When crews came to shut the water off, the street bathers threw bricks and stones at them. By July 15 the old and the sick were running out of steam. More than three hundred people died from the heat that day alone.

The CDC sent Semenza to Chicago to figure out who was dying, and why. By the time he flew into O'Hare, seven hundred people had expired from heat-related illness. Semenza and his team of eighty investigators, including his wife, Lisa Weasel, fanned out across the city, interviewing the families and friends of those who died.

On one of their first days out, Semenza, Weasel, and a colleague attempted to learn about a middle-aged man who had died in his residential hotel room. They couldn't locate the man's family or any of his friends, so they approached the manager of the run-down apartment hotel where the man lived. The manager sat in a little booth in the hotel's cramped lobby. The air was thick and heavy. The lobby walls were painted red and the lights dim. Coming in off the street was like entering the maw of a great beast, remembers Semenza.

The manager wouldn't let the investigators climb the stairs. There was no point, he told them. The dead man had left no trace, and his room had already been rented.

"What can you tell us about him?" asked Semenza.

"Nothing. I don't know anything about this guy," replied the manager gruffly.

Did he have family? None that visited. Friends? Nope. The guy had never entertained a single guest.

Semenza remembers the heat pressing down from the ceiling and the manager scowling. Semenza's shirt was soaked in sweat. He tried again. Surely there was some detail, something that could be learned about the deceased.

"No! There's nothing to be known about this man," the manager replied. "He was totally alone. He was no one."

Semenza heard that story of solitude over and over during weeks of harrowing investigation. So many of the dead had lived alone. So many of them lived lives of anonymity. It was the one thing they had in common.

The investigators had expected the heat to claim those with previous medical problems or the bedridden. They expected it to kill people who lived on the hot-plate top floors of buildings, or people with no air-conditioning or access to cool spaces. Indeed, those people were disproportionately represented among the dead. But nobody had fathomed just how deadly it was to be friendless.

"We found, if you're socially isolated, your risk for heat wave mortality goes up sevenfold," Semenza told me later. This was a conservative estimate. The CDC surveys didn't include individuals who had no relationships whatsoever, because Semenza's team was not able to learn a thing about such people. So there were hundreds of invisible dead, forgotten soon after their corpses were hauled off in refrigerated trucks hired by the county's medical examiner. In the end, the heat wave claimed more than seven hundred people. Semenza was haunted by the experience and had been looking for a solution to the epidemic of urban isolation ever since.

It was one reason why Semenza and Weasel were so enthralled with the Sellwood piazza. Seeing a concrete opportunity to battle urban loneliness, they convinced their neighbors in nearby Sunnyside to build their own. Being a compulsive empiricist, Semenza wanted solid data on its effects.

First they called City Repair, the nonprofit that Lakeman and his friends had created after building Share-It-Square. With their help, the Sunnyside neighbors got organized. In 2001, after nine months of potlucks, workshops, and block parties, dozens of neighbors came together to paint a giant sunflower mural across the intersection of Southeast Thirty-third Avenue and Yamhill Street. Later they built a sculpted wall from cob—a mix of earth and straw. They also built an iron-framed gazebo on one corner. When it came time to raise that gazebo's heavy roof frame, one of Semenza's neighbors offered to lift it with his crane.

"No way!" said Semenza. "We're lifting it by hand. All of us, together." After his encounters with isolation and death in Chicago, he would use any excuse to get people together. It took dozens of them, but the neighbors did lift that roof. Then they threw a party to celebrate their success.

All the while, Semenza was studying the effect the intersection repair was having on mental health. He had enlisted a team of his public health students to survey hundreds of neighbors before and after the Sunnyside project, as well as two other repair projects, and they compared them with people in other neighborhoods.

The data was stunning. It suggested that the interventions transformed not just the physical but the psychological landscape. After intersection repairs, fewer people reported experiencing depression than before. They slept better. They claimed that life seemed easier and more fun. They found that their neighbors got friendlier. They rated their own health as better than before—which is no small matter, since how we feel about our health can matter more to psychological well-being than how our doctors feel about our health. In short, people who lived near intersection repairs got happier and healthier even as well-being flatlined in untouched neighborhoods nearby. The repairs also coincided with a drop in burglaries, assaults, and vehicle thefts within a one-block radius—an improvement that simply did not occur in nearby neighborhoods.

New Space, New Life

City Repair demonstrates the truth of the message that Lakeman brought back from the Lacandon village: that the meeting place, the agora, and the village square are not trivial. They are not civic decoration or merely recreational. The life of a community is incomplete without them, just as the life of the individual is weaker and sicker without face-to-face encounters with other people.*

But the color and shape of the neo-piazzas are only half the story. In both Sellwood and Sunnyside, the act of working together to battle city bureaucrats, and then to design and build piazzas, gave neighbors a new sense of their collective power. They learned to rely on one another. It was a little like the effect of a play-off game on a high school basketball team. To use the language of social capital, they bonded. At the same time, each core group was also forced to reach out to the rest of the neighborhood—the skeptical, the suspicious,

---

*Semenza is now so convinced of the City Repair model's power for building social connections that he promotes it as a public health intervention in his work with the European Centre for Disease Prevention and Control. Specifically, he sees it as a way to keep vulnerable people alive during the extreme weather events that climate change is making more common.

the homeless, and the fellow who was just plain pissed off that nobody was going to plant honeysuckle by the sidewalk. They bridged. They did the things that so many city dwellers have forgotten. They changed the city, and then it changed them.

You can see it in Lakeman himself, who, though still not quite satisfied—he wants bends in his streets and a raised piazza and a car-free zone with garages at its edge—is no longer the brooding, alienated loner. The morning after the Sellwood painting party Lakeman and I tromped over from his house to survey the updated piazza. His knees were scuffed and stained, as though he had spent the dawn hours crawling through his garden, which in fact he had. He sipped from a tall glass of water, watching a couple of children pause to hop between the painted lily pads in the intersection. A woman appeared halfway down Ninth. Recognizing Lakeman, she marched up and fixed her eyes on him.

"Lakeman," she said. "You're babysitting my kid next week."

He nodded and smiled.

If you didn't know his story, you would have thought it was the reluctant smile of a man who had been caught, trapped. Ten years before, no neighbor would have dared ask such a thing. They would have been strangers. But Sellwood had changed. No one was anonymous anymore, and village life came with obligations. Lakeman was home.

Epilogue: The Beginning

The right to the city is far more than the individual liberty to access urban resources: it is a right to change ourselves by changing the city.

—David Harvey, 2008

No age in the history of cities has been so wealthy. Never before have our cities used so much land, energy, and resources. Never before has the act of inhabiting a city demanded converting so much primordial muck into atmosphere-warming gas. Never before have so many people enjoyed the luxury of private domesticity and mobility. Despite all we have invested in this dispersed city, it has failed to maximize health and happiness. It is inherently dangerous. It makes us fatter, sicker, and more likely to die young. It makes life more expensive than it has to be. It steals our time. It makes it harder to connect with family, friends, and neighbors. It makes us vulnerable to the economic shocks and rising energy prices inevitable in our future. As a system, it has begun to endanger both the health of the planet and the well-being of our descendants.

Our challenge lives in the way we build, but also in the way we think. It is a design problem, but it is also a psychological problem. It lives in the tensions that exist within each and every one of us—that endless tug-of-war between fear and trust, between status aspirations and the cooperative impulse, between the urge to retreat and the need to engage with other people. As much as they embody a philosophy of living, cities also reflect our cognitive frailties, and the systematic errors every one of us tends to make when deciding what will make us happy in the long run.

We have made mistakes.

316 | HAPPY CITY

We have been seduced by the wrong technologies. We gave up true freedom for the illusory promise of speed. We valued status over relationships. We tried to stamp out complexity instead of harnessing it. We let powerful people organize buildings, work, home, and transportation systems around too simplistic a view of geography and of life itself.

Most of all, we let the urban project be guided by what the sociologist Richard Sennett once called a "great, unreckoned fear of exposure," wherein we translated the uncertainty of city life into retreat instead of curiosity and engagement. We let the fear of being uncomfortable, inconvenienced, or hurt guide us into cities that not only isolate us but rob us of all the ease and pleasure and richness we might enjoy if the city were just a little bit more layered, a little bit more complex, a little bit messier.

It is not too late to rebuild the balance of life in our neighborhoods and cities and, in so doing, to build a more resilient future. The task demands that we listen to the parts of ourselves that are more inclined toward curiosity, trust, and cooperation. It demands that we acknowledge truths that we have long told each other, but which we have forgotten in making our cities: we may have been hardwired for dissatisfaction and for status anxiety, but we are also built to feel good when we trust and cooperate with one another. We all need privacy, but we are uniquely suited to get along in settings where, when the stage is right, we manage to turn complete strangers into people worthy of respect and care. We find our best selves not alone on the savanna or on the highway, but in the group, on a team, in the village. The truth is woven into human history, the architecture of our brains, and the spirals of our DNA. We all carry within us the person that Henri Lefebvre called the *citadin* and Mark Lakeman simply called the *villager*.

The city that responds to those truths, that respects the cooperator, the walker, the villager in each of us also happens to be a healthier place to live. It nurtures our relationships. It insulates us against economic hardships. It offers a thrilling new freedom to choose how to move and how to live. It manifests that ineffable but undeniably good feeling we all get when we know we are most truly alive.

The struggle for the happy city is going to be long and difficult. The broken city lives in the rituals and practices of planners, engineers, and developers. It lives in law and code, and in concrete and asphalt. It lives in our own habits, too. Those of us who care about the living city are going to have to fight for it in the streets, in the halls of government, in the legal and social codes that guide us, and in the ways we move and live and think.

The champions of the happy city have begun to show us the way.

There have been victories at city hall. Visionary mayors, planners, and even traffic engineers have demonstrated that the urban experience can be transformed by changing the city's hardware.

There have been victories in law. In adopting new sets of rules about how to build places, hundreds of cities have abandoned the high modernist code of separation and segregation and have set themselves on a course of slow but certain change.

There have been victories in thousands of neighborhoods where people have challenged the written and unwritten rules of how we move, live, and share space. Whether it's hauling furniture onto the street, staging neighborhood car-free days, tearing down the fences between their yards, turning metered parking stalls into miniature parks, or planting guerrilla gardens under cover of night, urban activists are taking design—and their future—into their own hands. They are proving that stubbornness and imagination can hack the old urban operating system. Victory is not guaranteed, not in every fight, but every time one of us stands up to dispersal, we chip away at its power and get a chance to find new life within ourselves.

Changing Places

It's also true that not all of us have the wherewithal to wrestle our cities into shape. It takes more than guts and imagination. It takes time. If you happen to live in dispersed sprawl, you may well be too busy working, commuting, ferrying kids to appointments in distant destinations, and coping with the demands of the horizontal city to start a revolution. It may be all you can do to pursue your own happiness as best you can in systems that were terribly designed for the challenge. Sadly, relief is unlikely to come to your door in the form of a monorail or a teleport or even a New Urbanist retrofit. There is too much sprawl to repair, and not enough money to do it. No matter how much you complain or rant or pray, the roads that entrap you will not suddenly become free of traffic, at least not without an economic meltdown even more severe than the last one.

This does not mean it is not possible to slip the shackles of dispersal. You can reengineer your relationship with the city simply by changing your place in it. That is what Kim Holbrook did. Remember Kim: the daughter of super-commuters, she spent her teen years playing mom to her younger brother in Tracy, California, while her parents drove back and forth to work in the Bay Area. By her early twenties Kim was out on the highway, driving alone to a job sixty miles away, just like her father and her grandmother. It took an emotional earthquake, a violently ill boy, and a frantic, tearful drive back to her son's day-care center to convince her to break the long-distance habit. The last time I saw her, Kim and her husband, Kevin, had rented a little house in a humble neighborhood right in Sacramento, close to schools, shopping, and Kim's new job as a lease administrator. They were saving $800 a month in gas bills, but more important, they could eat dinner every night with their young son, who was thriving. It's a start.*

This kind of personal retrofit demands that you confront your own habits and relationship with the city. It means redefining your notion about what the good life is supposed to look like. It means pursuing a different kind of happiness. It is, in itself, a course of urban activism that can have a dramatic effect on you and, because everything is connected, your city. To demonstrate, let me leave you with one last story—that of a life transformed.

A decade ago Conrad Schmidt lived unremarkably. The South African expatriate drove his Jeep YJ to work every weekday morning in the suburbs of his adopted city of Vancouver. That took an hour. He spent most of his day in front of a computer, writing software to control the robots that made cars, toys, and cigarettes in American factories. At the end of his workday Schmidt drove home again.

*Kim's father, Randy Strausser, has moved, too. In 2011 he and his wife, Julie, gave up on Mountain House and moved to Discovery Bay Golf and Country Club, another twenty minutes away from his work in the Bay Area. Around that time, he was also involved in a car accident (his fourth in twenty years) on his long commute. The truck was totaled, but Randy was unhurt. He has now upgraded to a bigger, safer truck. He has been making friends on the golf course.

Another hour. Sometimes, when traffic got really bad, he would grip the steering wheel as tightly as Randy Strausser had, and fight the overwhelming urge to scream. That sense of panic, of being trapped, stayed with him even after he parked his car. But drive he did, year after year, for the sake of that job. A layer of fat spread across his stomach and buttocks. Sometimes he would drive to a gym in order to work off the pounds and the frustration. Most days he just had no time for that.

Schmidt survived until, at the age of thirty-four, he realized that his decision to fit his days to the demands of sprawl shaped most everything about him. It dictated how he got around, how much stuff he bought, the shape of his body, even the amount of carbon dioxide he pushed into the atmosphere. Carbon—that was the one that stung him. He had studied the science, and he couldn't stand the thought that he was helping fuel the climate crisis. One day he'd have kids. He felt like he was stealing from them.

Schmidt reengineered his life in stages. First he followed his fancy to a neighborhood with a reputation for street culture, a place where he could walk to buy his milk and newspaper, and enjoy the journey, to boot. He may not have considered the dynamics of population density, average lot size, or zoning regulations when he moved. He did not realize that he was enjoying the benefits of a century-old calculus, or that a long-gone streetcar line had shaped his new neighborhood. He knew only that the place felt good. It felt easy. There were people out on the main street all the time. He got to know some of them.

I know how Schmidt felt, because he had landed in my own accidental neighborhood. Like every truly great community, Commercial Drive functions much like the places people in sprawl pay to visit on their vacations. It is not at all elegant, but because the architecture, the street, and life itself have assumed a human speed, it is a place where you feel good walking, grocery shopping, or just hanging out.

The next step: One day Schmidt left his car at home. He walked to the SkyTrain, the elevated rapid transit line that crossed Commercial Drive a few blocks from his apartment. As the train carried him above the city and then the suburbs, Schmidt gazed down at the stop-and-go traffic. After twenty minutes he stepped off the train and made another life-changing decision. He did not wait for a bus. He took a deep breath and started to run.

Schmidt ran over a bridge and along a river. He ran along the road where he had once gripped his steering wheel in frustration. He ran all the way to work. When he got there, Schmidt could not stop laughing. He felt like a hero. He felt free. He decided to run to work again the next day.

After a few of these trips Schmidt realized that he didn't need his Jeep anymore, so he sold it. Now he had a few hundred extra dollars in his pocket every month. This emboldened him. One workday morning, still feeling his runner's high, Schmidt walked into his boss's office.

"I'd rather not come in on Fridays," he said.

"Fine," replied his boss. "But I will have to cut your salary by twenty percent."

"Fine," said Schmidt.

It really was fine. With no car, Schmidt didn't need the money.

He got stronger every day, and he felt younger. He gave up his trips to the gym—why bother with a treadmill when your commute is your workout? He walked up and down the Drive, and he made friends there. They were a lot like him. Many of them had traded their life in dispersal for more time.

When the economy tanked, Schmidt didn't feel the pain. He didn't have a big house to lose. He had already sold his home and squeezed into a one-bedroom apartment along with a pretty woman he had met in the neighborhood. After their first baby arrived, they moved to a humble bungalow nearby. These places weren't fancy, but his life on the Drive was rich with experiences.

It dawned on Schmidt that the less money he made, the better his life was becoming. He had time to pursue the dreams he had never managed to get around to in his old life. For one thing, he began staging costume parties where hundreds of his neighbors would come and dance. He started a new political party based in part on the economics of his own experience, and he called it, naturally, the Work Less Party.

Conrad Schmidt's new life did not come for free. He earned it by trading away stuff as well as square footage. It was a deliberate journey. But here is the thing: the geometry of our neighborhood set the stage for that new life. The density and mix of buildings and jobs, the scale of streets and parks, the frequency of buses, the speed of roads, and the relationship of the Drive to the rest of the city, especially the nearby downtown, constituted a life-shaping *system*. That system did not just make his days easier, healthier, more connected. It did not just make Schmidt stronger and give him more control over his days. It shrunk his footprint on the city, and on the earth. At the same time, by consciously embracing a local life on the Drive, Schmidt gave right back to it. He gave the neighborhood his money, his time, and, it would not be an exaggeration to add, his love. In so doing, he made it stronger. He became a part of it.

Some people, like me, arrive in the happy city by accident. Some seek it in desperation. Some build it. Some fight for it. Some, like my neighbor Conrad Schmidt, experience a conversion moment. They realize that their place in the city, and the ways in which they move, have tremendous power to shape their own lives, the life of their city, and the future of their world. They realize that the happy city, the low carbon city, and the city that will save us are the same place, and that they have the wherewithal to create it.

This is the truth that shines over the journey toward the happy city. We do not need to wait for someone else to make it. We build it when we choose how and where to live. We build it when we move a little bit closer. We build it when we choose to move a little slower. We build it by choosing to put aside our fear of the city and other people. We build the happy city by pursuing it in our own lives and, in so doing, pushing the city to change with us. We build it by living it.

Notes

1. The Mayor of Happy

3   *Christopher Alexander*: Alexander, Christopher, *The Timeless Way of Building* (New York: Oxford University Press, 1979), 109.

5   *five billion of us will be urban*: United Nations Human Settlements Programme, "State of the World's Cities Report 2006/7," 2006.

5   *most of the world's pollution*: International Bank for Reconstruction and Development/World Bank, "Cities and Climate Change: An Urgent Agenda," Washington, DC, 2010, 15.

5   *civil war and sporadic terrorism*: Martin, Gerard, and Miguel Arévalo Ceballos, *Bogotá: Anatomía de una transformación: políticas de seguridad ciudadana 1995–2003* (Bogotá: Pontificia Universidad Javeriana, 2004).

8   *nobody was killed in traffic*: Stockholm Challenge, www.stockholmchallenge .org/project/data/bogot&-car-free-day-within-world-car-free-day-forum (accessed January 2, 2011).

9   *While the elder proselytized*: Peñalosa has influenced more than a hundred cities. On his advice, cities such as Jakarta, Delhi, and Manila have reclaimed streets from their usurpation by private cars, creating vast linear parks or handing the space to rapid bus systems modeled on Bogotá's own. "Peñalosa's philosophy on public spaces had a great impact on our perception of model cities," Moji Rhodes, an assistant to the mayor in the seething megacity of Lagos, Nigeria, told me after Peñalosa convinced Lagos to start building sidewalks along new roads.

10n *Americans used to get by*: U.S. Census Bureau, "Statistical Abstract of the United States 2009," Washington, DC, 2009; The World Bank, "Motor Vehicles (per 1,000 People)," http://data.worldbank.org/indicator/is.veh.nveh.p3/coun tries (accessed April 28, 2013); U.S. Department of Transportation, Research and Innovative Technology Administration, Bureau of Transportation Statistics, "Table 1-37: U.S. Passenger-Miles," www.rita.dot.gov/bts/sites/rita.dot.gov .bts/files/publications/national_transportation_statistics/2009/html/table_01 _37.html (accessed April 29, 2013); U.S. Census Bureau, "Median and Average Square Feet of Floor Area in New Single-Family Houses Completed by Location," www.census.gov/const/C25Ann/sftotalmedavgsqft.pdf (accessed

April 29, 2013); National Association of Home Builders, "Facts, Figures and Trends for March 2006," 2006; U.S. Environmental Protection Agency, "Municipal Solid Waste in the United States: Facts and Figures for 2010," 2010.

11 *power in China*: Crabtree, Steve, and Tao Wu, "China's Puzzling Flat Line," *Gallup Business Journal*, 2011, http://businessjournal.gallup.com/content/148853/china-puzzling-Flat-line.aspx? (accessed August 31, 2012).

11 *By 2005 clinical depression*: Faris, Stephanie, "Depression Statistics," *Healthline*, March 28, 2012, www.healthline.com/health/depression/statistics (accessed April 29, 2013); Easterbrook, Gregg, "The Real Truth About Money," *Time*, January 9, 2005, www.time.com/time/magazine/article/0,9171,1015883,00.html (accessed December 28, 2010).

11 *Depression scales*: The Minnesota Multiphasic Personality Inventory, a questionnaire used by medical health professionals, is one of the most widely used tests in psychological assessment. The test consists of ten scales: Hypochondriasis, Depression, Hysteria, Psychopathic Deviate, Masculinity/Femininity, Paranoia, Psychasthenia, Schizophrenia, Hypomania, and Social Introversion. See Twenge, Jean M., "Birth Cohort Increases in Psychopathology Among Young Americans, 1938–2007: A Cross-Temporal Meta-analysis of the MMPI," *Clinical Psychology Review*, 2010: 145–54.

11 *One in ten Americans*: Olfson, Mark, and Steven C. Marcus, "National Patterns in Antidepressant Medication Treatment," *Archives of General Psychiatry*, 2009: 848–56.

11 *"correlates of subjective well-being"*: Wilkinson, Will, "In Pursuit of Happiness Research: Is it Reliable? What Does It Imply for Policy?" Policy Analysis, Cato Institute (April 11, 2007).

11 *gap between material and emotional wealth*: Bartolini, Stefano, Ennio Bilancini, and Maurizio Pugno, "Did the Decline in Social Capital Decrease American Happiness? A Relational Explanation of the Happiness Paradox," Department of Economics, University of Siena, Italy, August 2007, www.econ-pol.unisi.it/quaderni/513.pdf (accessed January 1, 2011).

11 *almost all urban growth*: In 1910, only three in ten Americans lived in cities. Now eight in ten do, but five of them actually live in the suburbs. Hobbs, Frank, and Nicole Stoops, "Demographic Trends in the 20th Century," Special Reports, Series CENSR-4, Washington, D.C.: U.S. Census Bureau, 2002.

12 *turning of the tide of urban dispersal*: Frey, William H., "Demographic Reversal: Cities Thrive, Suburbs Sputter," The Brookings Institution, June 29, 2012, www.brookings.edu/research/opinions/2012/06/29-cities-suburbs-frey (accessed April 29, 2013).

2. The City Has Always Been a Happiness Project

17 *Sigmund Freud*: Freud, Sigmund, *Civilization and Its Discontents*, vol. 1, in *The Complete Psychological Works of Sigmund Freud*, ed. J. Strachey (London: Hogarth Press, 1953) 75–76.

17   *Aristotle*: Aristotle, "Rhetoric." *The Internet Classics Archive*, ed. W. Rhys Roberts, Web Atomics, 350 B.C., http://classics.mit.edu//Aristotle/rhetoric.html (accessed December 27, 2010).

17   *"Do not all men desire happiness"*: Modified from *The Dialogues of Plato*, 4th ed., vol. 1, trans. Benjamin Jowett (Oxford: Clarendon Press, 1953), 278e–282d.

19   *for pleasure alone*: Aristotle, *Nicomachean Ethics* trans. W. D. Ross (Adelaide: ebooks@adelaide, 2006), http://classics.mit.edu/Aristotle/nicomachaen.html (accessed December 27, 2010).

19   *behaving virtuously*: Ibid.

19   *deck of a ship*: Kotkin, Joel, *The City: A Global History* (New York: Modern Library, 2005), 21; Kitto, H.D.F., "The Greeks," in *The City Reader*, eds. Richard T. Le Gates and Frederick Stout (London: Routledge, 1996), 32–36.

21n   *The Roman sense*: Kotkin, *The City*, 29.

22   *Medieval churches*: Sennett, Richard, *The Conscience of the Eye: The Design and Social Life of Cities* (New York: W. W. Norton, 1990), 15.

22n   *Happy the man*: Horace, Epode II (Beutus ille), in *Horace: The Complete Odes and Epode*, trans. David West (New York: Oxford University Press, 1997), 4.

23   *felicific calculus*: Bentham, Jeremy, *An Introduction to the Principles of Morals and Legislation* (Oxford, U.K.: Clarendon Press, 1789), Chapter 4.

23n   *Bentham made his own*: Bentham, Jeremy, *The Panopticon Writings*, ed. Miran Bozovic (London: Verso, 1995), 29–95.

24   *Vauxhall Gardens*: Collinson, Peter, *"Forget not mee & my garden . . ."*: *Selected Letters, 1725–1768 of Peter Collinson, F.R.S.*, ed. W. Alan Armstrong (Philadelphia: American Philosophical Society, 2002); Coke, David E. and Alan Borg, *Vauxhall Gardens: A History* (New Haven, CT: Yale University Press), 211.

25   *proposed a City Beautiful*: Boyer, P. S., *Urban Masses and Moral Order in America, 1820–1920* (Cambridge, MA: Harvard University Press, 1978).

26   *Stalin's proclamation: Happy: Cities and Public Happiness in Post-War Europe*, ed. Cor Wagenaar (Rotterdam: NAi Publishers, 2005), 65.

26   *Le Corbusier*: Cohen, Jean-Louis, *Le Corbusier and the Mystique of the USSR: Theories and Projects for Moscow 1928–1936* (Princeton, NJ: Princeton University Press, 1992), 93.

26n   *Robert Pemberton*: Pemberton, Robert, *The Happy Colony* (London: Saunders and Otley, 1854), 80–82, 111; from Reps, John, "Queen Victoria Town," www.library.cornell.edu/Reps/DOCS/pemberto.htm (accessed March 3, 2012).

27   *"Why should not he"*: Wright, Frank Lloyd, *When Democracy Builds* (Chicago: University of Chicago Press, 1945). As quoted in Hall, Peter, *Cities of Tomorrow: An Intellectual History of Urban Planning and Design in the Twentieth Century* (Malden, MA: Blackwell, 1988).

30   *electroencephalogram (EEG) monitor caps*: Davidson, R. J., D. C. Jackson, and N. H. Kalin, "Emotion, Plasticity, Context, and Regulation: Perspectives from Affective Neuroscience," *Psychological Bulletin* 126 (2000): 890–909.

31   *Daniel Kahneman: Well-Being: The Foundations of Hedonic Psychology*, eds.

326 | NOTES

Daniel Kahneman, Ed Diener, and Norbert Schwarz (New York: Russell Sage Foundation, 1999).

31   *women happiest of all*: Kahneman, Daniel, and Alan B. Krueger, "Developments in the Measurement of Subjective Well-Being," *Journal of Economic Perspectives*, 2006: 3–24.

31n *Other studies have shown*: Frank, Robert, *Luxury Fever* (Princeton, NJ: Princeton University Press, 1999).

32   *Disney entertainment machine*: *Designing Disney's Theme Parks: The Architecture of Reassurance*, ed. Karal Ann Marling (New York: Flammarion, 1997).

33   *"experience machine"*: Nozick, Robert, *Anarchy, State, and Utopia* (New York: Basic Books, 1974).

34n *If you were to ask*: Gilbert, Daniel, *Stumbling on Happiness* (Toronto: Vintage Canada, 2007).

35   *People in small towns*: Brereton, Finbarr, Peter J. Clinch, and Susana Ferreira, "Happiness, Geography and the Environment," *Ecological Economics*, 2008: 386–96.

35   *money cannot buy*: Helliwell, John, "How's Life? Combining Individual and National Variables to Explain Well-being," *Economic Modelling*, 2003: 331–60.

35   *London borough of Greenwich*: Interviews with Hilary Guite, director of public health and well-being, National Health Service, Greenwich, U.K.

35n *In a groundbreaking 2009 study*: Oswald, Andrew J., and Stephan Wu, "Objective Confirmation of Subjective Measures of Human Well-Being: Evidence from the U.S.A.," *Science*, 2010: 576–79.

36   *measures of well-being*: Ryff, Carol D., and B. H. Singer, "Know Thyself and Become What You Are: A Eudaimonic Approach to Psychological Well-Being," *Journal of Happiness Studies*, 2006: 13–29.

37   *relationships with other people*: Helliwell, John, "Well-Being, Social Capital and Public Policy: What's New?" *Economic Journal*, 2006: C34–C35.

38   *50 percent raise*: Helliwell, John, and Christopher P. Barrington-Leigh, "How Much Is Social Capital Worth?" working paper, Cambridge, MA: National Bureau of Economic Research, 2010.

38   *get their wallets back*: Helliwell, John, and Shun Wang, "Trust and Well-Being," working paper, Cambridge, MA: National Bureau of Economic Research, 2010.

39   *set up various games*: Zak, Paul, "The Neuroeconomics of Trust," University of Nebraska-Lincoln, Hendricks Symposium—Department of Political Science, 2006.

39   *trust other people*: Zak, P. J., A. A. Stanton, and S. Ahmadi, "Oxytocin Increases Generosity in Humans," *PLOS ONE*, 2007: e1128; Ross, H. E., et al., "Characterization of the Oxytocin System Regulating Affiliative Behavior in Female Prairie Voles," *Neuroscience*, 2009: 892–903.

40   *Animals that live in groups*: Dunn, Elizabeth W., Daniel T. Gilbert, and Timothy D. Wilson, "If Money Doesn't Make You Happy, Then You Probably Aren't Spending It Right," *Journal of Consumer Psychology*, April 2011, 115–25 (www.sciencedirect.com/science/article/pii/S1057740811000209).

40n *Why, Darwin wondered*: Darwin, Charles, *On the Origin of Species by Means of Natural Selection: Or the Preservation of Favoured Races in the Struggle for Life* (New York: Appleton, 1869), 80, 209.

40n *The debate was recently renewed*: Johnson, Eric Michael, "The Good Fight," in *The Primate Diaries* (blog), *Scientific American*, July 9, 2012, http://blogs .scientificamerican.com/primate-diaries/2012/07/09/the-good-fight (accessed August 20, 2012).

41 *fashion a common good*: Sandel, Michael, *Liberalism and the Limits of Justice* (Cambridge, U.K.: Cambridge University Press, 1998), 183.

3. The (Broken) Social Scene

44 *Aristotle*: Aristotle, *Politics* trans. Benjamin Jowett, (Adelaide: eBooks@Adelaide, 2007) (originally published 350 B.C.).

45 *more people had lost their homes*: RealtyTrac staff, "Detroit, Stockton, Las Vegas Post Highest 2007 Metro Foreclosure Rates," *RealtyTrac*, February 13, 2008, www.realtytrac.com/ContentManagement/pressrelease.aspx?ChannelID =9&ItemID=4119&accnt=64847 (accessed January 3, 2011).

46 *U.S. construction in the last three decades*: Dunham-Jones, Ellen, "New Urbanism's Subversive Marketing," in *Worlds Away: New Suburban Landscapes*, ed. Andrew Blauvelt (Minneapolis: Walker Arts Center, 2008).

46 *"edge cities"*: Garreau, Joel, *Edge City: Life on the New Frontier* (New York: Doubleday, 1991).

48 *commuters escaping high home prices*: Roberts, Ronnie, "Southwest Stockton, Calif., Neighborhood Attracts Commuters," *The Record*, accessed from High Beam Research, March 3, 2002, www.highbeam.com/doc/1G1-120566678.html (accessed January 7, 2011).

48 *gas prices doubled*: Cortright, Joe, "Driven to the Brink: How the Gas Price Spike Popped the Housing Bubble and Devalued the Suburbs," white paper, CEOs for Cities, 2008.

48n *At the time*: "Welcome to Stockton: Foreclosure Capital USA," *China Daily*, September 17, 2007, www.chinadaily.com.cn/world/2007-09/17/content_6111808 .htm (accessed January 7, 2011).

49 *spends twice as much*: Center for Transit-Oriented Development and Center for Neighborhood Technology, "The Affordability Index: A New Tool for Measuring the True Affordability of a Housing Choice," Washington, DC: Brookings Institution, 2006; Center for Neighborhood Technology, "Penny Wise Pound Fuelish: New Measures of Housing + Transportation Affordability," Chicago, 2010.

49 *spent more on transportation*: Laitner, John A. "Skip," "The Price-Induced Energy Trap: Exploring the Impacts of Transportation Expenditures on the American Economy," New America Foundation, October 2011, http://newamerica .net/sites/newamerica.net/files/policydocs/102111energy_trap_working_paper .pdf (accessed June 14, 2012).

49n *By 2011, nearly three-quarters*: Depaul, Jennifer, "The Angriest Democrat in Congress Attacks Obama," *The Fiscal Times*, November 30, 2011, www.thefis caltimes.com/articles/2011/11/30/The-Angriest-Democrat-in-Congress-Attacks -Obama.aspx (accessed August 20, 2012).

49n *"metropolitan areas with the weakest"*: Cortright, *Driven to the Brink*.

49n *A 2012 report by the Demand Institute*: Keely, Louise, Bart van Ark, Gad Levanon, and Jeremy Burbank, "The Shifting Nature of U.S. Housing Demand: The U.S. Housing Market Is Growing Again—but Not as We Knew It," Demand Institute, May 2012, www.demandinstitute.org/sites/default/files/blog-uploads /tdihousingdemand.pdf (accessed March 20, 2013).

52n *When the* Toronto Star: Helliwell, John, and Shun Wang, "Trust and Well-Being," working paper, Cambridge, MA: National Bureau of Economic Research, 2010; Ackerman, G., et al., "Crime Rates and Confidence in the Police: America's Changing Attitudes Toward Crime and Police," *Journal of Sociology and Social Welfare*, 2001: 43–54; Truman, Jennifer, "Predictors of Fear of Crime and the Relationship of Crime Rates and Fear of Crime," *University of Central Florida Undergraduate Research Journal*, 2005: 18–27.

53 *the country's declining social capital*: Bartolini, Stefano, Ennio Bilancini, and Maurizio Pugno, "Did the Decline in Social Capital Decrease American Happiness? A Relational Explanation of the Happiness Paradox," Department of Economics, University of Siena, August 2007, www.econ-pol.unisi.it/quaderni /513.pdf (accessed January 1, 2011).

54 *people are losing ties*: Brashears, Matthew E., "Small Networks and High Isolation? A Reexamination of American Discussion Networks," *Social Networks*, October 2011: 331–341.

54 *ate together every night*: Kiefer, Heather, "Empty Seats: Fewer Families Eat Together," *Gallup*, www.gallup.com/poll/10336/empty-seats-fewer-families-eat -together.aspx (accessed March 3, 2012).

54 *social desert*: Halpern, David, *Mental Health and the Built Environment: More Than Bricks and Mortar?* (London: Taylor and Francis, 1995).

54 *psychotic disorders*: Park, Alice, "Why City Life Adds to Your Risk of Psychosis," *Time*, September 7, 2010, http://healthland.time.com/2010/09/07/living-in -cities-can-add-to-risk-of-psychoses/ (accessed September 11, 2010).

55 *parents' stress*: McConnell, D., R. Breitkreuz, and A. Savage, "From Financial Hardship to Child Difficulties: Main and Moderating Effects of Perceived Social Support," *Child: Care, Health and Development*, 2011: 679–91.

55 *sleep better*: Kurina, L. M., K. L. Knutson, L. C. Hawkley, J. T. Cacioppo, D. S. Lauderdale, and C. Ober, "Loneliness Is Associated with Sleep Fragmentation in a Communal Society," *SLEEP* 2011; 34(11):1519–26.

55 *live longer*: Putnam, Robert D., *Bowling Alone* (New York: Simon and Schuster Paperbacks, 2000); Frumkin, Howard, Lawrence Frank, and Richard Jackson, *Urban Sprawl and Public Health: Designing, Planning, and Building Healthy Communities* (Washington, DC: Island Press, 2004); Seeman, T. E., "Social Ties and Health: The Benefits of Social Integration," *Annals of Epidemiology*, 1996:

442–51; Hirdes, J. P., and W. F. Forbes, "The Importance of Social Relationships, Socioeconomic Status, and Health Practices with Respect to Mortality Among Healthy Ontario Males," *Journal of Clinical Epidemiology*, 1992: 175–82; Veenstra, Gerry, "Social Capital and Health (Plus Wealth, Income Inequality and Regional Health Governance)," *Social Science and Medicine*, 2002: 849–68; Berkman, Lisa F., "The Role of Social Relations in Health Promotion," *Psychosomatic Medicine*, 1995: 245–54.

55 *Citizens of sprawl*: Leyden, Kevin M., "Social Capital and the Built Environment: The Importance of Walkable Neighborhoods," *American Journal of Public Health*, 2003: 1546–51; Williamson, Thad, *Sprawl, Justice, and Citizenship: The Civic Costs of the American Way of Life* (New York: Oxford University Press, 2010).

55n *The 2011 study*: "Long-Distance Commuters Get Divorced More Often, Swedish Study Finds," *Science Daily*, May 25, 2011, www.sciencedaily.com/releases /2011/05/110525085920.htm (accessed March 3, 2012).

56 *evidence that the ethnic diversity*: Putnam, Robert, "E Pluribus Unum: Diversity and Community in the Twenty-first Century—The 2006 Johan Skytte Prize Lecture," *Scandinavian Political Studies*, 2007: 137–74.

57 *the more neighbors drove to work*: Freeman, Lance, "The Effects of Sprawl on Neighborhood Social Ties," *Journal of the American Planning Association*, 2001: 69–77.

57 *Using this model*: Farber, Steven, and Xiao Li, "Urban Sprawl and Social Interaction Potential: An Empirical Analysis of Large Metropolitan Regions in the United States," *Journal of Transport Geography*, 2013, http://dx.doi.org/10.1016 /j.jtrangeo.2013.03.002 (accessed April 29, 2013).

57n *Surveys show that social trust*: Williamson, *Sprawl, Justice, and Citizenship*, 94–97.

58 *long-distance commuters' friends*: Viry, G., V. Kaufmann, and E. D. Widmer, "Social Integration Faced with Commuting: More Widespread and Less Dense Support Networks," in *Mobilities and Inequality*, eds. T. Ohnmacht, H. Maksim, and M. M. Bergman (Surrey, U.K.: Ashgate Publishing, 2009), 121–44.

58 *happiness curve doesn't level off*: Harter, James, and Raksha Arora, "Social Time Crucial to Daily Emotional Wellbeing in U.S.," Gallup, June 5, 2008, www .gallup.com/poll/107692/social-time-crucial-daily-emotional-wellbeing.aspx (accessed January 7, 2011).

58 *drive to work alone*: U.S.Census Bureau, "Most of Us Still Drive to Work—Alone," June 13, 2007. www.census.gov/newsroom/releases/archives/american _community_survey_acs/cb07-cn06.html (accessed January 7, 2011).

58 *more hours commuting than*: U.S. Census Bureau, "Americans Spend More Than 100 Hours Commuting to Work Each Year, Census Bureau Reports," March 30, 2005, www.census.gov/newsroom/releases/archives/american_community _survey_acs/cb05-ac02.html (accessed January 7, 2011).

59 *youth gang problem in California*: Phillips, Roger, "SUSD Post to Combat Gangs: New Position for Stockton Unified Funded by Grant," *The Record*,

November 23, 2008, www.recordnet.com/apps/pbcs.dll/article?AID=/20081123/A_NEWS/811230316 (accessed January 7, 2011).

59 *key contributors to gang membership*: Wyrick, Phelan A., and James C. Howell, "Strategic Risk-Based Response to Youth Gangs," *National Criminal Justice Reference Service*, September 2004, www.ncjrs.gov/html/ojjdp/203555/jj3.html (accessed March 3, 2012).

59 *mayor Ed Chavez*: "Failing Health: San Joaquin County in Crisis: High Homicide Rate Points to Mental-health Issues," *The Record*, March 21, 2006, www.recordnet.com/apps/pbcs.dll/article?AID=/20060321/SPECIALREPORTS14/603210301/-1/A_SPECIAL04 (accessed January 7, 2011).

60 *no adult supervision at all*: Children Now, "2010 California County Scorecard of Children's Well-Being," September 29, 2010, www.childrennow.org/index.php/learn/reports_and_research/article/726 (accessed January 7, 2011).

60 *parent conferences*: Johnson, Zachary K., "Stockton Helps Commuting Parents: Schools Work to Keep Commuter Parents in Touch," *The Record*, April 16, 2007.

60 *even affluent suburbs*: Luthar, Suniya S., and Karen D'avanzo, "Contextual Factors in Substance Abuse: A Study of Suburban and Inner-City Adolescents," *Development and Psychopathology*, 1999: 845–67.

4. How We Got Here

63 *Henry Ford*: Henry Ford, *the Modern City: A Pestiferous Growth, in Ford Ideals: Being a Selection from Mr. Ford's Page in the Dearborn Independent, 1922* (Whitefish, MT: Kessinger, 2010), 154–57.

63 *Andrew Mearns*: Mearns, Andrew, *The Bitter Cry of Outcast London: An Inquiry into the Condition of the Abject Poor* (London: James Clarke, 1883).

64 *Tenement House Commission*: Deforest, Robert W., and Lawrence Veiller, *The Tenement House Problem* (New York: Macmillan, 1903), 10.

64 *New York's tenement population*: Hall, Peter, *Cities of Tomorrow: An Intellectual History of Urban Planning and Design in the Twentieth Century* (Malden, MA: Blackwell, 1988), 36–37.

65 *Le Corbusier wrote*: Fishman, Robert, *Urban Utopias of the Twentieth Century: Ebenezer Howard, Frank Lloyd Wright, and Le Corbusier* (New York: Basic Books, 1977), 186.

65 *"We must refuse"*: Scott, James C., *Seeing Like a State: How Certain Schemes to Improve the Human Condition Have Failed* (New Haven, CT: Yale University Press, 1998), 106.

66 *Zoning was intended*: Hall, *Cities of Tomorrow*, 292–93.

67 *excluded entire black communities*: Hall, *Cities of Tomorrow*, 293–94, and Todd Litman, *Where We Want to Be: Home Location Preferences and Their Implications for Smart Growth*, Victoria Transport Policy Institute, 2010.

69 *Cars and trucks began*: Hall, *Cities of Tomorrow*, 275.

70   *killed in motor accidents*: Norton, Peter D., *Fighting Traffic: The Dawn of the Motor Age in the American City* (Cambridge, MA: MIT Press, 2008), 21.
70   *mobbed by angry crowds*: Ibid., 69–77.
71   *three-quarters of road users*: Ibid., 161.
71n *Charles Hayes*: Ibid., 66.
71n *In 1922*: Ibid., 76–77.
72   *"The automobile supplies"*: Chapin, Roy, "The Motor's Part in Transportation." *Annals*, 1924: 1–8.
72   *"This country was founded"*: Norton, *Fighting Traffic*, 168.
72n *Chapin eventually joined*: Ibid., 205.
73   *unhindered by the friction of intersections*: "Transport: Four Frictions," *Time*, August 3, 1936, www.time.com/time/magazine/article/0,9171,770337,00.html (accessed January 9, 2011).
73   *1937 National Planning Conference*: "Present System of City Streets Completely Inadequate to Handle Heavy Traffic, Expert Declares," *Evening Independent*, June 1, 1937: 5.
73   *motor age city*: Leinberger, Christopher, *The Option of Urbanism: Investing in a New America Dream* (Washington, D.C., Island Press), 18.
73   *More than twenty-four million people*: Gelernter, David, *1939, The Lost World of the Fair* (New York: Free Press, 1995), 25.
73   *a company formed by*: Hall, *Cities of Tomorrow*, 291; Bianco, Martha J., "Kennedy, 60 Minutes, and Roger Rabbit: Understanding Conspiracy-Theory Explanations of the Decline of Urban Mass Transit," discussion paper, Portland: Center for Urban Studies, College of Urban and Public Affairs, Portland State University, 1998; United States v. National City Lines, 186 F.2d 562 (United States Court of Appeals for the Seventh Circuit, January 3, 1951).
74   *Federal-Aid Highway Act*: Hall, *Cities of Tomorrow*, 291.
77   *new wave of urbanists*: Such as David Owen, author of *Green Metropolis*.

5. Getting It Wrong

78   *Mark Twain*: Twain, Mark, "Captain Stromfield's Visit to Heaven," in *The Best Short Stories by Mark Twain*, ed. Lawrence Berkove (New York: Modern Library, 2004), 234.
78   *Daniel Kahneman*: Kahneman, Daniel, interview by Gallup Business Journal, "Are You Happy Now?" (February 10, 2005), http://businessjournal.gallup.com /content/14872/happy-now.aspx (accessed March 3, 2012).
79n *The average price*: "Greater Vancouver Housing Market Trends Near Long-term Averages as Spring Market Approaches," Real Estate Board of Greater Vancouver, March 2, 2012, www.rebgv.org/news-statistics/greater-vancouver-housing-market-trends-near-long-term-averages-spring-market (accessed March 8, 2012).
80   *Dubbed the evolutionary happiness function*: Rayo, Luis, and Gary Becker, "Evolutionary Efficiency and Happiness," *Journal of Political Economy*, 2007: 302–37.

82 *people who endure long drives*: Stutzer, Alois, and Bruno S. Frey, "Stress That Doesn't Pay: The Commuting Paradox," *Scandinavian Journal of Economics*, 2008: 339–66.

83 *adaptation*: Frey, Bruno S., *Happiness: A Revolution in Economics* (Cambridge, MA: MIT Press, 2010), 131–33.

83 *extrinsic or intrinsic motivators*: Ibid., 131; Deci, Edward L., and Richard M. Ryan, "The 'What' and 'Why' of Goal Pursuits: Human Needs and the Self-Determination of Behavior," *Psychological Inquiry*, 2000: 227–68.

84 *activity is its own reward*: Frey, *Happiness: A Revolution*, 130.

85 *freshmen at Harvard*: Baker, Meredith C., and Cara K. Fahey, "The Housing Market, 2009: Mather House," *Harvard Crimson*, March 9, 2009, www.thecrim son.com/article/2009/3/15/the-housing-crisis-mather-house (accessed January 9, 2011).

85 *concrete tower of Mather House*: "Dictionary of Harvardisms from A to Z: The Vocabulary You Need to Get Through Your Life at Harvard," *Harvard Crimson*, August 24, 2009, www.thecrimson.com/article/2009/8/24/dictionary-of -harvardisms-2-am-1 (accessed January 9, 2011).

86 *were they right?*: Dunn, Elizabeth W., and Timothy D. Wilson, "Location, Location, Location: The Misprediction of Satisfaction in Housing Lotteries," *Personality and Social Psychology Bulletin*, 2003: 1421–32.

87 *Californians were happier*: Schkade, D., and D. Kahneman, "Does Living in California Make People Happy? A Focusing Illusion in Judgments of Life Satisfaction," *Psychological Science*, 1998: 340–46.

88 *flock to high-status cities*: Oswald, Andrew J., and Stephan Wu, "Objective Confirmation of Subjective Measures of Human Well-Being: Evidence from the U.S.A.," *Science*, 2010: 576–79; Sharpe, Andrew, Ali Ghanghro, Erik Johnson, and Anam Kidwai, *Does Money Matter? Determining the Happiness of Canadians*, Research Report, Ottawa: Centre for the Study of Living Standards, 2010.

88 *conducted an experiment*: Halpern, David, "An Evidence-Based Approach to Building Happiness," in *Building Happiness: Architecture to Make You Smile*, ed. Jane Wernick (London: Black Dog, 2008), 160–161.

88n *Surveys in the U.K.*: Hall, James, "Men in Their Late 40s Living in London Are the Unhappiest in the UK," *The Telegraph*, February 28, 2012, www.telegraph .co.uk/news/newstopics/howaboutthat/9110941/Men-in-their-late-40s-living -in-London-are-the-unhappiest-in-the-UK.html (accessed March 3, 2012); Office for National Statistics, "Analysis of Experimental Subjective Well-Being Data from the Annual Population Survey, April to September 2011," February 28, 2012, www.ons.gov.uk/ons/rel/wellbeing/measuring-subjective-wellbeing -in-the-uk/analysis-of-experimental-subjective-well-being-data-from-the-an nual-population-survey–april—september-2011/report-april-to-september -2011.html (accessed March 3, 2012).

89 *Architects' brains*: Kirk, U., M. Skov, M. S. Christensen, and N. Nygaard, "Brain Correlates of Aesthetic Expertise: A Parametric fMRI Study," *Brain and Cognition*, 2008: 306–15.

89   *Coke or Pepsi*: McClure, S. M., J. Li, D. Tomlin, K. S. Cypert, L. M. Montague, and P. R. Montague, "Neural Correlates of Behavioral Preference for Culturally Familiar Drinks," *Neuron*, 2004: 379–87.

89n *Kirk observed*: Source: Kirk, U., M. Skov, O. Hulme, M. S. Christensen, and S. Zeki, "Modulation of Aesthetic Value by Semantic Context: An fMRI Study," *Neuroimage*, 2009: 1125–32.

90   *Barbie toy*: Rochon, Lisa, "Blueprint for Architect Barbie! Think Pink—and Give Her a Monster Home," *The Globe and Mail*, August 13, 2011.

91   *Claude Lévi-Strauss*: In conversation by telephone before his death in 2004.

92   *"the human mind"*: Le Corbusier, quoted in Scott, James C., *Seeing Like a State: How Certain Schemes to Improve the Human Condition Have Failed* (New Haven, CT: Yale University Press, 1998), 110.

92   *Brasilia-itis*: Holston, James, *The Modernist City: An Anthropological Critique of Brasilia* (Chicago: University of Chicago Press, 1989), 24.

94   *heuristics*: Tversky, A, and D. Kahneman, "Judgment Under Uncertainty: Heuristics and Biases," *Science*, 1974: 1124–31.

94   *Richard Jackson*: Brody, Jane E., "Communities Learn the Good Life Can Be a Killer," *Well: New York Times Health and Science*, January 30, 2012, http://well .blogs.nytimes.com/2012/01/30/communities-learn-the-good-life-can-be-a -killer/ (accessed March 14, 2012).

94n *This is one reason*: Lichtenstein, S., P. Slovic, B. Fischhoff, M. Layman, and B. Combs, "Judged Frequency of Lethal Events," *Journal of Experimental Psychology: Human Learning and Memory*, 1978: 551–78.

95   *considered lethal*: Gardner, G., and E. Assadourian in *State of the World 2004: The Consumer Society*, ed. Linda Starke (New York: W. W. Norton, 2004), 3–21.

95   *obesogenic, or fat-making*: O'Brien, Catherine, "Sustainable Happiness: How Happiness Studies Can Contribute to a More Sustainable Future," *Canadian Psychology*, 2008: 289–95.

95   *fattest people on the planet*: World Health Organization, "Global Database on Body Mass Index," http://apps.who.int/bmi/index.jsp (accessed January 11, 2011).

95   *Fully a third of Americans*: National Institute of Diabetes and Digestive and Kidney Diseases, "Overweight and Obesity Statistics," http://win.niddk.nih .gov/statistics (accessed January 11, 2011).

95   *Nearly one in five*: Centers for Disease Control and Prevention, National Center for Health Statistics. "Prevalence of Obesity Among Children and Adolescents: United States, Trends 1963–1965 Through 2007–2008," www.cdc.gov/nchs /data/hestat/obesity_child_07_08/obesity_child_07_08.htm (accessed January 11, 2011).

95   *more than a quarter of Canadian*: Statistics Canada, "Canada Yearbook Overview 2009—Children and Youth," http://www41.statcan.gc.ca/2009/20000 /cybac20000_000-eng.htm (accessed January 11, 2011).

95   *30 percent of British children*: "Statistics on Obesity, Physical Activity and Diet—England, 2010," Health and Social Care Information Centre, U.K., February 10, 2010, www.hscic.gov.uk/pubs/opad10 (accessed April 29, 2013).

95 *more than three-quarters of obese adults*: Lachapelle, Ugo, "Public Transit Use as a Catalyst for an Active Lifestyle: Mechanisms, Predispositions, and Hindrances," thesis, University of British Columbia, Vancouver, 2010.

95 *Centers for Disease Control*: Gardner, Gary, and Erik Assadourian, "Rethinking the Good Life," in *State of the World 2004*, 164–79.

95 *living in low-density sprawl*: Sturm, R, and D. A. Cohen, "Suburban Sprawl and Physical and Mental Health," *Public Health*, 2004: 488–96.

95 *"death by strangers"*: Lucy, William H., "Mortality Risk Associated with Leaving Home: Recognizing the Relevance of the Built Environment," *American Journal of Public Health*, 2003: 1564–69.

96 *per capita road death rates*: "Safety Tips to Keep Your Family Safe: Accident Statistics from the National Safety Council," *Safety Times*, www.safetytimes.com/statistics.htm (accessed January 11, 2011).

96 *killed by guns*: Violence Policy Center, "About the Violence Policy Center," www.vpc.org/aboutvpc.htm (accessed January 11, 2011).

96 *September 11, 2001*: Centers for Disease Control and Prevention. "Years of Potential Life Lost (YPLL)," Injury Prevention & Control: Data & Statistics (WISQARS), www.cdc.gov/injury/wisqars/years_porential.html (accessed January 11, 2011). Also, the National Center for Injury Prevention and Control estimates that car crashes lop a whopping 5 percent off the average American life span.

96 *an image that sticks*: Nozzi, D., *Road to Ruin: An Introduction to Sprawl and How to Cure It* (Westport, CT: Praeger, 2003).

96n *Car accidents*: Brown, David, "Traffic Deaths a Global Scourge, Health Agency Says," *Washington Post*, April 20, 2007, www.washingtonpost.com/wp-dyn/content/article/2007/04/19/AR2007041902409.html (accessed January 11, 2011).

97 *drivers kill four times as many*: Condon, Patrick M., *Seven Rules for Sustainable Communities: Design Strategies for the Post Carbon World* (Washington, DC: Island Press, 2010), 54.

97 collisions at high speed: Swift, Peter, *Residential Street Typology and Injury Accident Frequency* (Longmont, CO: Swift and Associates, 1998).

97 *the forty-foot mark*: Condon, *Seven Rules*, 42.

98 *build fire stations close by*: Patrick Condon explains these dynamics beautifully in *Seven Rules for Sustainable Communities*, 56–57. He draws on earlier research by Peter Swift from 1998 and a report by Bill Dedman in *The Boston Globe*, January 30, 2005.

99 *Five to six years*: Cervero, Robert, "Road Expansion, Urban Growth, and Induced Travel: A Path Analysis," Department of City and Regional Planning, Institute of Urban and Regional Development, University of California, Berkeley, 2001.

99n *These highways*: Todd Litman, *Generated Traffic and Induced Travel Implications for Transport Planning* (Victoria, BC: Victoria Transport Policy Institute, 2010); interview with Howard Frumkin of the Centers for Disease Control in the Web series *American Makeover*, episode 1, "Sprawlanta," www.americanmakeover.tv/episode1.html (accessed February 2, 2011).

100 *United Nations Intergovernmental Panel on Climate Change*: core writing team, R. K. Pachauri, and A. Reisinger, eds., *Climate Change 2007: Synthesis Report. Contribution of Working Groups I, II and III to the Fourth Assessment Report of the Intergovernmental Panel on Climate Change* (Geneva: Intergovernmental Panel on Climate Change, 2008).

100n *The travel time*: Green, Charles, Health Plenary Address, Congress for New Urbanism 18, Atlanta, May 20, 2010.

101 *This we know*: Thomas, C., et al., "Extinction Risk from Climate Change," *Nature*, 2004: 145–48.

101 *alarmed the insurance industry*: Fogarty, David, "Climate Change Growing Risk for Insurers: Industry," *Planet Ark*, January 20, 2011, http://planetark.org /wen/60947 (accessed January 21, 2011).

101 *It would take nine planets*: WWF, Zoological Society of London, and Global Footprint Network. *Living Planet Report 2008* (Gland, Switzerland: World Wide Fund For Nature, 2008).

102 *in the next twenty years*: Froggatt, Antony, et al., "Sustainable Energy Security: Strategic risks and opportunities for business," white paper, London: Lloyd's, 2010; Industry Task Force on Peak Oil and Energy Scarcity, "2010 Peak Oil Report," 2010; Hess, Werner, "Energy for Tomorrow's World—Trends, Scenarios, Tomorrow's Markets," Allianz/Dresdner Bank AG, Frankfurt/M., Germany, 2005); International Energy Agency, *World Energy Outlook 2008* (Paris: IEA Publications, 2010); Hirsch, Robert L., "Peaking of World Oil Production: Recent Forecasts," National Energy Technology Laboratory, 2007; U.S. Joint Forces Command, "The Joint Operating Environment," Norfolk, VA, 2010.

102 *forty million cars*: Mouawad, Jad, "Rising Demand for Oil Provokes New Energy Crisis," *New York Times*, November 9, 2007, www.nytimes.com/2007/11 /09/business/worldbusiness/09oil.html (accessed January 21, 2011).

102 *massive energy shortfalls*: Macalister, Terry, "US Military Warns Oil Output May Dip Causing Massive Shortages by 2015," *The Guardian*, April 11, 2010, www.guardian.co.uk/business/2010/apr/11/peak-oil-production-supply (accessed January 21, 2011).

102 *extreme heat waves*: Tillett, Tanya, "Temperatures Rising: Sprawling Cities Have the Most Very Hot Days," *Environmental Health Perspectives*, 2010: A444.

102 *More heat waves*: Committee on the Science of Climate Change, *Climate Change Science: An Analysis of Some Key Questions* (Washington, DC: National Academy Press, 2001).

102 *cities are responsible*: Grimm, N. B., et al., "Global Change and the Ecology of Cities," *Science*, 2008: 756–60.

102 *the suburban lawn is a threat*: U.S. Environmental Protection Agency, "Green Landscaping: Greenacres, A Source Book on Natural Landscaping for Public Officials," Landscaping with Native Plants, www.epa.gov/greenacres/toolkit /chap2.html (accessed March 3, 2012).

103 *twice the greenhouse gas emissions*: Hoornweg, Daniel, Lorraine Sugar, and

Claudia Lorena Trejos Gómez, "Cities and Greenhouse Gas Emissions: Moving Forward," *Environment and Urbanization*, 2011.

103 *better suited to provoke inaction:* Gifford, R., "The Dragons of Inaction: Psychological Barriers That Limit Climate Change Mitigation and Adaptation," *American Psychologist*, 66, (2011), 290–302.

103n *The cognitive linguist:* Lakoff, George, "George Lakoff Manifesto," a summary of his thoughts from his book *Don't Think of an Elephant: Know Your Values and Frame the Debate* (White River Junction, VT: Chelsea Green, 2004).

6. How to Be Closer

106 *John Ruskin:* Ruskin, John, *Sesame and Lilies* (New York: Metropolitan Publishing, 1891), 136.

108 *Hospital patients with views of nature:* Ulrich, Roger S., "View Through a Window May Influence Recovery from Surgery," *Science*, 1984: 420–21.

108 *Sonoma County Jail:* Farbstein, Jay, Melissa Farling, and Richard Wener, "Effects of a Simulated Nature View on Cognitive and Psycho-physiological Responses of Correctional Officers in a Jail Intake Area," final report, National Institute of Corrections, 2009.

109 *Stephen and Rachel Kaplan:* Berman, Marc G., John Jonides, and Stephan Kaplan, "The Cognitive Benefits of Interacting with Nature," *Psychological Science*, 2008: 1207–12.

110 *to local crime rates:* Kuo, F. E., and W. C. Sullivan, "Environment and Crime in the Inner City: Does Vegetation Reduce Crime?" *Environment & Behavior*, 2001: 343–67.

110 *lived next to green spaces:* Kuo, F. E., W. C. Sullivan, R. L. Coley, and L. Brunson, "Fertile Ground for Community: Inner-City Neighborhood Common Spaces," *American Journal of Community Psychology*, 1998: 823–51.

110 *deeper alchemy:* Weinstein, N., A. K. Przybylski., and R. M. Ryan, "Can Nature Make Us More Caring? Effects of Immersion in Nature on Intrinsic Aspirations and Generosity," *Personality and Social Psychology Bulletin*, 2009: 1315–29.

111 *live in areas with more parks:* Kuo, Frances, "Parks and Other Green Environments: Essential Components of a Healthy Human Habitat," National Recreation and Park Association, 2010.

111 *Vitaly Komar and Alexander Melamid: Painting by Numbers: Komar and Melamid's Scientific Guide to Art*, ed. JoAnn Wypijewski (New York: Farrar, Straus and Giroux, 1997).

115 *population nearly doubled:* City of Vancouver.

116 *lowest per capita carbon footprint:* City of Vancouver, Sustainability Group, "Climate Protection," 2008, http://vancouver.ca/sustainability/climate_protection .htm (accessed January 29, 2011).

116 *"view corridors":* Berelowitz, Lance, *Dream City: Vancouver and the Global Imagination* (Vancouver: Douglas & McIntyre, 2005).

116n *Another paradox of density*: Turcotte, Martin, "The Time It Takes to Get to Work and Back," General Social Survey on Time Use: Cycle 19, Statistics Canada, 2005; "2005 Annual Report Livable Region Strategic Plan," Regional Development Policy and Planning Department, Greater Vancouver Regional District, Burnaby, 2005; "City of Vancouver Transportation Plan Update: A Decade of Progress," City of Vancouver, 2007; U.S. Department of Transportation Federal Highway Administration, 2009 National Household Travel Survey.

118 Vancouverism: "Vancouverism is characterized by tall, but widely separated, slender towers interspersed with low-rise buildings, public spaces, small parks and pedestrian-friendly streetscapes and facades to minimize the impact of a high density population." From Chamberlain, Lisa, "Trying to Build the Grand Central of the West," *New York Times*, December 28, 2005, www.nytimes.com/2005/12/28/realestate/28transbay.html (accessed January 24, 2011).

120 *Cheonggyecheon River*: Vidal, John, "Heart and Soul of the City," *The Guardian*, November 1, 2006.

121 *High Line*: High Line and Friends of the High Line, "High Line: Planting," www.thehighline.org/design/planting (accessed September 15, 2012).

121 *bacteria found naturally in soil boosts seratonin*: "Can Bacteria Make You Smarter?" *Science Daily*, May 24, 2010, www.sciencedaily.com/releases/2010/05/100524143416.htm (accessed March 3, 2012).

122n *One study in Alameda*: Pillemer, K., T. E. Fuller-Rowell, M. C. Reid, and N. M. Wells, "Environmental Volunteering and Health Outcomes over a Twenty-Year Period," *The Gerontologist*, 2010: 594–602.

124 "*Crossing Brooklyn Ferry*": Whitman, Walt, "Crossing Brooklyn Ferry," in *Leaves of Grass, 1891–92 Edition* (Philadelphia: David McKay, 1892).

125 hikikomori: Hoffman, Michael, "Nonprofits in Japan Help 'Shut-ins' Get Out into the Open," *The Japan Times* online, retrieved October 21, 2011.

125 *hierarchy of human motivation*: Maslow, A. H., "A Theory of Human Motivation," *Psychological Review*, 1943: 370–96.

126 *psychologists believed that*: Thanks to the environmental psychologist Robert Gifford for collected insights, both in conversation and in his article "The Consequences of Living in High-Rise Buildings," *Architectural Science Review*, 2007: 2–17.

126 *overload—the sheer crowdedness*: Milgram, S., "The Experience of Living in Cities," *Science*, 1970: 1461–68.

127 *your sense of control*: Rodin, Judith, Susan K. Solomon, and John Metcalf, "Role of Control in Mediating Perceptions of Density," *Journal of Personality and Social Psychology*, 1978: 988–99.

127 *it's not so much square footage*: Organization for Economic Co-operation and Development, "Compendium of OECD Well-Being Indicators," 2011, www.oecd.org/std/47917288.pdf (accessed August 12, 2013).

127n *What you look at*: Day, Linda L. "Choosing a House: The Relationship Between Dwelling Type, Perception of Privacy and Residential Satisfaction," *Journal of Planning Education and Research*, 2000: 265–75.

128   *2.4 in the United Kingdom*: Macrory, Ian, "Measuring National Well-Being—Households and Families, 2012," Office for National Statistics, U.K., April 26, 2012, www.ons.gov.uk/ons/dcp171766_259965.pdf (accessed April 29, 2013).

128   *poor mental health*: Halpern, David, *Mental Health and the Built Environment: More Than Bricks and Mortar?* (London: Taylor and Francis, 1995).

128n   *Thoits found that*: Blau, Melinda, and Karen Fingerman, *Consequential Strangers: Turning Everyday Encounters into Life-Changing Moments* (New York: W. W. Norton, 2009), 67, 100–101. See also Thoits, Peggy A., "Personal Agency in the Accumulation of Multiple Role-Identities," in *Advances in Identity Theory and Research*, ed. Peter J. Burke, Timothy J. Owens, Richard T. Serpe, and Peggy A. Thoits (New York: Kluwer Academic Publishers, 2003), 179–94.

128n   *The number of people*: U.S. Census Bureau, "America's Families and Living Arrangements: 2007," U.S. Department of Commerce Economics and Statistics Administration, 2009.

129   *college dormitories at Stony Brook*: Valins, S., and A. Baum, "Residential Group Size, Social Interaction, and Crowding," *Environment and Behavior*, 1973: 421.

129n   *subjective experience of isolation*: Halpern, *Mental Health and the Built Environment*, 137–39, 153.

131   *Pruitt-Igoe housing complex*: Newman, Oscar, *Creating Defensible Space*, Center for Urban Policy Research, Rutgers University (U.S. Department of Housing and Urban Development Office of Policy Development and Research, 1996), 10.

131   *Oscar Newman*: Ibid., 11.

131   *Pruitt-Igoe meltdown*: Hall, *Cities of Tomorrow*, 237–40; also see von Hoffman, Alexander, "Why They Built the Pruitt-Igoe Project," Joint Center for Housing Studies, Harvard University, www.soc.iastate.edu/sapp/PruittIgoe.html (accessed January 24, 2011).

132n   *The feeling is familiar*: Wenman, Christine, Nancy Hofer, Jay Lancaster, Dr. Wendy Sarkissian, and Larry Beasley, C.M. "Living in False Creek North: From the Residents' Perspective," School of Community and Regional Planning, University of British Columbia, Vancouver, 2008.

133   *The perfect yard*: Gehl, Jan, *Life Between Buildings* (Skive: Danish Architectural Press, 2006), 38, 67, 191.

134   *feelings of belonging*: Helliwell, John, and Christopher P. Barrington-Leigh, "How Much Is Social Capital Worth?" working paper, Cambridge, MA: National Bureau of Economic Research, 2010.

135n   *Part of the problem is*: Helliwell and Barrington-Leigh, "How Much Is Social Capital Worth?"; "Connections and Engagement: A Survey of Metro Vancouver, June 2012," Vancouver Foundation, 2012; Halpern, *Mental Health and the Built Environment*, 262.

137   *"business and transit"*: Condon, Patrick M., *Seven Rules for Sustainable Communities: Design Strategies for the Post Carbon World* (Washington, DC: Island Press, 2010), 12–22.

137n   *The human density*: Durning, Alan Thein, *The Car and the City: 24 Steps to Safe Streets and Healthy Communities* (Seattle: Northwest Environment

Watch, 1996); Kopits, Elizabeth, Virginia McConnell, and Daniel Miles, "Lot Size, Zoning, and Household Preferences: Impediments to Smart Growth?" discussion paper, Washington, DC, Resources for the Future, 2009.
139 *You can be downtown*: City of Vancouver.
142 *most expensive city for housing*: Economist Intelligence Unit.

7. Convivialities

146 *Le Corbusier*: Le Corbusier in S. Von Moos, *Le Corbusier: Elements of a Synthesis* (Cambridge, MA: MIT Press, 1979), 196.
146 *Richard Sennett*: Sennett, Richard, *The Conscience of the Eye: The Design and Social Life of Cities* (New York: W. W. Norton, 1990), xiv.
150 *a year on the Strøget*: Gehl, Jan, *Life Between Buildings* (Skive: Danish Architectural Press, 2006).
151n *The first summer*: Gehl, Jan, and Lars Gemzøe, *Public Spaces—Public Life, Copenhagen*, 3rd ed. (Copenhagen: Narayana Press, 2004), 12.
152 *streets and plazas of New York*: Whyte, William H., *The Social Life of Small Urban Spaces* (New York: Project for Public Spaces, 2004).
153 *the Internet*: Hampton, Keith N., "Neighborhoods in the Network Society: the e-Neighbors study," *Information, Communication & Society*, 2007:10:5, 714–48.
154n *When TV service*: Frey, Bruno S., Christine Benesch, and Alois Stutzer, "Does Watching TV Make Us Happy?" working paper, Center for Research in Economics, Management and the Arts, University of Zurich, 2005, 15.
155 *no substitute for actually being there*: The first generation of research into Facebook sociology has arrived and has found that among other things, it helps people with low self-esteem make new connections. Shyness may prevent you from winking at someone in a bar, but you might still poke them online. Among university students, Facebook use correlates with *slightly* higher social capital and life satisfaction. But maxing out on Facebook friends does not produce stronger social dividends. For one thing, most people lack the brain capacity to maintain an unlimited number of true friends. Research by the evolutionary anthropologist Robin Dunbar suggests that the maximum number of acquaintances most of us can maintain is 150, but when it comes to good friends, the people we can actually count on, we are limited to between six and twelve. That number doesn't change much whether friends meet online or in person, and so far, online friends do not seem to be measuring up as proxies. When surveyed about their online relationships, most people describe friendships that are not as deep or committed and don't involve the interdependence or understanding of their face-to-face relationships. A study of youths in highly networked Hong Kong found that young people who developed friendships in person shared more subtle codes of communication—they could more easily read between the lines of what each other were saying. They were more likely to know each other's family or friends. They confided more deeply in each other. They felt they knew each other better.

The online social environment can warp our well-being in surprising ways. One new insight is that maxing out on Facebook friends can actually make you unhappy. The phenomenon has its roots in the evolutionary happiness function: that never-ending compulsion to compare ourselves to other people. The problem, explains study author Dilney Goncalves, a professor at IE Business School in Madrid, is that people typically post Facebook updates that contain good news and achievements, creating the false impression of a world of super-successful people. So the more Facebook friends you have, the more time you spend checking their skewed status updates, and the worse you feel about your own life. (The tipping point? Three hundred and fifty-four Facebook friends.)

See Valenzuela, Sebastián, Namsu Park, and Kerk F. Kee, "Is There Social Capital in a Social Network Site?: Facebook Use and College Students' Life Satisfaction, Trust, and Participation," *Journal of Computer-Mediated Communication*, 2009: 875–901; Dunbar, R., *Grooming, Gossip, and the Evolution of Language* (Cambridge, MA: Harvard University Press, 1996); Krotoski, Aleks, "Robin Dunbar: We Can Only Ever Have 150 Friends at Most . . ." *The Guardian*, March 14, 2010, www.guardian.co.uk/technology/2010/mar/14/my-bright -idea-robin-dunbar (accessed January 7, 2011); Darius, K. S., "A Comparison of Offline and Online Friendship Qualities at Different Stages of Relationship Development," *Journal of Social and Personal Relationships*, 2004: 305–20; Pappas, Stephanie, "Facebook with Care: Social Networking Site Can Hurt Self-Esteem," *LiveScience*, February 6, 2012, www.livescience.com/18324-face book-depression-social-comparison.html (accessed March 3, 2012); Mesch, Gustavo S., and Ilan Talmud, "Similarity and the Quality of Online and Offline Social Relationships Among Adolescents in Israel," *Journal of Research on Adolescence*, 2007: 455–65.

155n *This concern with touch*: Li, Shan. "'Emotional' Phones Simulate Hand Holding, Breathing and Kissing," *Los Angeles Times*, September 8, 2011, http:// latimesblogs.latimes.com/technology/2011/09/phone-breathing-kissing.html (accessed April 30, 2013).

156 *pictures of various streetscapes*: O'Brien, Daniel T., and David S. Wilson, "Community Perception: The Ability to Assess the Safety of Unfamiliar Neighborhoods and Respond Adaptively," *Journal of Personality and Social Psychology*, 2011: 606–20.

157 *temperature of our hands*: Kang, Y., L. Williams, M. Clark, J. Gray, and J. Bargh, "Physical Temperature Effects on Trust Behavior: The Role of the Insula," *Social Cognitive and Affective Neuroscience*, 2011: 507–15, Steinmetz, J., and T. Mussweiler, "Breaking the Ice: How Physical Warmth Shapes Social Comparison Consequences," *Journal of Experimental Social Psychology*, 2011: 1025–1028.

157n *Observing shoppers*: Sanna, L. J., E. C. Chang, P. M. Miceli, and K. B. Lundberg, "Rising Up to Higher Virtues: Experiencing Elevated Physical Height

Uplifts Prosocial Actions," *Journal of Experimental Social Psychology*, 2011: 472–76. (Since this paper's publication, some researchers have called into question the validity of the authors' data.)

158 *mental map*: Sternberg, Esther, *Healing Spaces: The Science of Place and Well-Being* (Cambridge, MA: Belknap Press of Harvard University Press, 2009).

158 *anti-cosmopolitan tribalism*: de Dreu, Carsten, "Social Value Orientation Moderates Ingroup Love but Not Outgroup Hate in Competitive Intergroup Conflict," *Group Processes Intergroup Relations*, 2010: 701–13.

159 *Esther Sternberg*: Sternberg's *Healing Spaces* is a thorough and accessible exploration of the science of place and well-being.

159n *Disney and his designers*: Haas, Charlie, "Disneyland Is Good for You," *New York*, December 1978: 13–20.

160 *effect of aesthetics*: Semenza, Jan, "Building Healthy Cities: A Focus on Interventions," in *Handbook of Urban Health: Populations, Methods, and Practice*, eds. Sandro Galea and David Vlahov (New York: Springer, 2005), 459–78.

161 *in front of lively facades*: Gehl, Jan, Lotte Johansen, and Reigstad Solvejg, "Close Encounters with Buildings," *Urban Design International*, 2006: 29–47.

163 *on their main shopping streets*: From *Improving Urban Spaces* (Dansk Byplanlaboratorium), a study of the quality of the main streets in practically all Danish cities of any reasonable size (ninety-one cities). Published by the Danish Town Planning Laboratory.

163 *on the Upper West Side*: New York City Department of City Planning. "Special Enhanced Commercial District Upper West Side Neighborhood Retail Streets—Approved!" *NYC.gov*, June 28, 2012, www.nyc.gov/html/dcp/html/uws/index .shtml (accessed October 11, 2012); Berger, Joseph, "Retail Limits in Plan for the Upper West Side," *New York Times*. February 2, 2012, www.nytimes.com/2012 /02/03/nyregion/zoning-proposal-on-upper-west-side-could-reshape-commerce .html (accessed March 3, 2012).

163n *Studies of seniors*: Brown, S. C., C. A. Mason, T. Perrino, J. L. Lombard, F. Martinez, E. Plater-Zyberk, A.R. Spokane, and J. Szapocznik, "Built Environment and Physical Functioning in Hispanic Elders: The Role of 'Eyes on the Street,'" *Environmental Health Perspectives*, 2008: 1300–1307; Richard, L., L. Gauvin, C. Gosselin, and S. Laforest, "Staying Connected: Neighbourhood Correlates of Social Participation Among Older Adults Living in an Urban Environment in Montreal, Quebec," *Health Promotion International*, 2008: 46–57.

164 *bonus plazas*: Smithsimon, Gregory, "Dispersing the Crowd: Bonus Plazas and the Creation of Public Space," in *The Beach Beneath the Streets: Exclusion, Control, and Play in Public Space* by Benjamin Shepard and Gregory Smithsimon (New York: SUNY Press, 2011).

167n *2009 World Championship hundred-meter sprint*: Hamilton-Baillie, B., "Urban Design: Why Don't We Do It in the Road?" *Journal of Urban Technology*, 2004: 43–62.

168 *influenced by noise*: Jha, Alok, "Noise of Modern Life Blamed for Thousands of Heart Deaths," *The Guardian*, August 22, 2007, www.guardian.co.uk/science /2007/aug/23/sciencenews.uknews (accessed March 3, 2012).

168n *field experiments*: Cohen, S., and S. Spacapan, "The Social Psychology of Noise," in *Noise and Society*, ed. D. M. Jones and A. J. Chapman (Chichester, U.K.: Wiley, 1984): 221–45.

171 *"The full experience"*: Manville, Michael, and Donald Shoup, "People, Parking, and Cities," *Access*, 2004, http://shoup.bol.ucla.edu/People,Parking,Cities.pdf (accessed March 3, 2012).

8. Mobilicities I: How Moving Feels, and Why It Does Not Feel Better

176 *Robert Burton*: Burton, Robert, *The Anatomy of Melancholy*, ed. Jackson Holbrook (London: Rowman and Littlefield, 1975), 71.

179 *Nearly nine in ten American commuters*: U.S. Census Bureau, "2010 American Community Survey Highlights," www.census.gov/newsroom/releases/pdf/acs _2010_highlights.pdf (accessed March 3, 2012).

179 *Three-quarters of Canadians*: Statistics Canada, "Commuting Patterns and Places of Work of Canadians, 2006 Census," 2008, Ottawa.

179 *two-thirds of Brits*: Department for Transport, "National Travel Survey, Table NTS0409, Average Number of Trips by Purpose and Main Mode: Great Britain, 2009," 2010.

179 *drivers report feeling*: Gatersleben, B., and D. Uzzell, "Affective Appraisals of the Daily Commute: Comparing Perceptions of Drivers, Cyclists, Walkers, and Users of Public Transport," *Environment and Behavior*, 2007: 416–31.

179 *in their fine cars*: Ory, David T., and Patricia L. Mokhtarian, "When Is Getting There Half the Fun? Modeling the Liking for Travel," *Transportation Research Part A: Policy and Practice*, 2005: 97–123.

179 *"The endocrinological response"*: Harris, Misty, "Hot Cars Make Men More Manly, Study Shows," *Vancouver Sun Health Blog*, not dated, www.vancouver sun.com/health/cars+make+more+manly+study+shows/1870063/story.html (accessed April 30, 2013).

179 *love their cars*: Langer, Gary, "Poll: Traffic in the United States. A Look Under the Hood of a Nation on Wheels," *ABC News*, February 13, 2005, http://abcnews .go.com/Technology/Traffic/story?id=485098&page=1 (accessed June 24, 2010).

179 *an unhappy group*: Langer, "Traffic in the United States."

179 *stress hormones*: Evans, G., and S. Carrere, "Traffic Congestion, Perceived Control, and Psychophysiological Stress Among Urban Bus Drivers," *Journal of Applied Psychology*, 1991: 658–63.

180 *fight-or-flight juices*: White, S. M., and J. Rotton, "Type of Commute, Behavioral Aftereffects, and Cardiovascular Activity: A Field Experiment," *Environment and Behavior*, 1998: 763–80.

180 *immune system will be compromised*: McEwen, B. S., "Allostasis and Allostatic

Load: Implications for Neuropsychopharmacology," *Neuropsychopharmacology*, 2000: 108–24.

180 *Chronic road rage*: Fenske, Mark, "Road Rage Stressing You Out? Crank the Tunes," *The Globe and Mail*, October 6, 2010, www.theglobeandmail.com/life /health-and-fitness/health/conditions/road-rage-stressing-you-out-crank -the-tunes/article1322066 (accessed January 14, 2011).

180 *urban bus drivers*: Aronsson, G., and A. Rissler, "Psychophysiological Stress Reactions in Female and Male Urban Bus Drivers," *Journal of Occupational Health Psychology*, 1998: 122–29.

180 *heart attack patients*: Larson, John, and Carol Rodriguez, *Road Rage to Road Wise: A Simple Step-by-Step Program to Help You Understand and Curb Road Rage in Yourself and Others* (New York: Tom Doherty Associates, 1999).

180n *Commuters' hearts*: Lewis, David. "Commuting Really Is Bad for Your Health," *Hewlett Packard Newsroom Home*, Hewlett Packard, November 1, 2004, http://h41131.www4.hp.com/uk/en/press/Commuting_Really_is_Bad_for _Your_Health.html (accessed 10 05, 2012).

180n *commutes over ninety minutes*: Crabtree, Steve, "Wellbeing Lower Among Workers with Long Commutes: Back Pain, Fatigue, Worry All Increase with Time Spent Commuting," Gallup, August 13, 2010, www.gallup.com/poll /142142/wellbeing-lower-among-workers-long-commutes.aspx (accessed December 3, 2010).

181 *average daily commute*: Condon, Patrick M., *Seven Rules for Sustainable Communities: Design Strategies for the Post Carbon World* (Washington, DC: Island Press, 2010), 23.

181 *eighty minutes in Toronto*: Toronto Board of Trade, "Toronto as a Global City: Scorecard on Prosperity—2011."

181 *solution to congestion*: Williams-Derry, Clark, "Study: More Roads = More Traffic," *Sightline Daily*, December 14, 2011, http://daily.sightline.org/2011/12/14 /study-more-roads-more-traffic/ (accessed March 3, 2012).

181 *self-propelled commuters*: Gatersleben and Uzzell, "Affective Appraisals of the Daily Commute," 416–31.

181 *Children overwhelmingly say*: O'Brien, Catherine, "Sustainable Happiness: How Happiness Studies Can Contribute to a More Sustainable Future," *Canadian Psychology*, 2008: 289–95.

181 *cyclists report*: Harms, L., P. Jorritsma, and N. Kalfs, *Beleving en beeldvorming van mobiliteit* (The Hague: Kennisinstituut voor Mobiliteitsbeleid, 2007).

182n *To put our history*: My comparison of human history to the walk across the length of Central Park is based on these figures:

Appearance of Australopithecus: 4 million years
Agricultural revolution: 10,000 years ago
Sumerian and Egyptian cities of cut stone: 3,000 years
Length of Central Park: about 2.5 miles
Width of Fifty-ninth Street: much more than 11 yards

Width of New York sidewalk at Fifty-ninth: more than 3 yards
Depth of a stair: much more than 4 inches

See Wright, Ronald, *A Short History of Progress* (Toronto: Anansi Press, 2004), 35–69; Stringer, Chris, and Robin McKie, *African Exodus: The Origins of Modern Humanity* (New York: Henry Holt, 1997); Cordain, Gotshall, and Eaton, "Evolutionary Aspects," 49–60; also drawn from interviews with Ronald Wright.

183 *daily energy expenditure*: Cordain, L., R. W. Gotshall, and S. B. Eaton, "Evolutionary Aspects of Exercise," *World Review of Nutrition and Dietics*, 1997: 49–60.

183 *immobility is to the human body*: Patricia Montemurri, "Excessive Sitting Linked to Premature Death in Women," *USA Today*, August 16, 2011, http://usatoday30 .usatoday.com/news/health/healthcare/health/healthcare/prevention/story /2011/08/Excessive-sitting-linked-to-premature-death-in-women/49996086/1 (accessed April 29, 2013).

183 *when we exercise*: Taylor, Paul, "Boosting Your Brain Power Could Be a Walk in the Park," *The Globe and Mail*, October 14, 2010, http://m.theglobeandmail .com/life/health/health-and-fitness/health/conditions/boosting-your-brain -power-could-be-a-walk-in-the-park/article623387/ (accessed January 14, 2011).

183 *"feel more energy"*: Gloady, Rick, "Walk Your Way to More Energy," *Inside CSULB*, California State University, Long Beach, 2006, www.csulb.edu/misc /inside/archives/vol_58_no_4/1.htm (accessed August 12, 2013).

184 *human on a bicycle*: Illich, Ivan, *Energy and Equity* (New York: Harper & Row, 1974).

184 *convert to bike commuting*: Howard, John, *Mastering Cycling* (Champaign, IL: Human Kinetics, 2010), 22.

184 *more greenhouse gas emissions*: Sightline Institute, "How Low-Carbon Can You Go: The Green Travel Ranking," www.sightline.org/maps/charts/climate -CO2byMode (accessed March 3, 2012).

184 *Of every one hundred*: Per the U.S. Census Bureau, in 2010, 76.6 percent of American workers sixteen years and over drove alone to work. About 5 percent of people carpooled. Just under 3 percent walked to work, and less than 1 percent rode a bicycle.

185 *commute by car*: Paumgarten, Nick, "There and Back Again," *New Yorker*, April 16, 2007, www.newyorker.com/reporting/2007/04/16/070416fa_fact_paumgarten (accessed August 12, 2013).

185n *That's seventy-two minutes a day*: Goldberg, David, Lawrence Frank, Barbara McCann, Jim Chapman, and Sarah Kavage, "New Data for a New Era: A Summary of the SMARTRAQ Findings," Atlanta: SMARTRAQ, 2007.

186 *couldn't walk to nearby shops*: Frank, L., B. Saelens, K. Powell, and J. Chapman, "Stepping Towards Causation: Do Built Environments or Neighborhood and Travel Preferences Explain Physical Activity, Driving, and Obesity?" *Social Science & Medicine*, 2007: 1898–914.

186 *average person in Seattle*: Vanderbilt, Tom, *Traffic: Why We Drive the Way We Do (and What It Says About Us)* (Toronto: Knopf Canada, 2008), 138.

186n *People who live in neighborhoods*: Wieckowski, Ania, "Back to the City," *Harvard Business Review*, May 10, 2010, http://hbr.org/2010/05/back-to-the-city/ar/1 (accessed January 9, 2011).

187 *Facebook's workers*: Russell, James S., "Facebook, Gehry Build Idea Factory for RipStik Geeks," *Bloomberg*, August 24, 2012, www.bloomberg.com/news/2012-08-24/facebook-gehry-build-idea-factory-for-ripstik-geeks.html.

188 *perceive rail service to be*: Schlossberg, Marc, Asha Agrawal, Katja Irvin, and Vanessa Bekkouche, *How Far, by Which Route, and Why? A Spatial Analysis of Pedestrian Preference* (San Jose: Mineta Transportation Institute College of Business, 2007).

188 *LYNX commuter light-rail*: McDonald, John M., Robert J. Stokes, Deborah A. Cohen, Aaron Kofner, and Greg K. Ridgeway, "The Effect of Light Rail Transit on Body Mass Index and Physical Activity," *American Journal of Preventive Medicine*, 2010: 105–12.

188 *summer break*: Playful City USA: *KaBoom!* National Campaign for Play, "Play Matters: A Study of Best Practices to Inform Local Policy and Process in Support of Children's Play," *Kaboom.org*, October 12, 2009, http://kaboom.org/docs/documents/pdf/playmatters/Play_Matters_Case_Summaries.pdf (accessed October 4, 2012).

188n *The amalgamation*: University of Michigan, "Why Don't Kids Walk to School Anymore?" *Science Daily*, March 28, 2008, www.sciencedaily.com/releases/2008/03/080326161643.htm (accessed January 9, 2011); Condon, *Seven Rules*, 4; Ernst, Michelle, and Lilly Shoup, "Dangerous by Design: Solving the Epidemic of Preventable Pedestrian Deaths (and Making Great Neighborhoods)," Transportation for America/Surface Transportation Policy Partnership, 2009.

189 *to go shopping*: Burnfield, J. M., and C. M. Powers, "Normal and Pathologic Gait," in *Orthopaedic Physical Therapy Secrets*, eds. Jeffery D. Placzek and David A. Boyce (Philadelphia: Hanley and Belfus, 2006).

189n *A survey of shoppers*: Lorch, Brian, "Auto-dependent Induced Shopping: Exploring the Relationship Between Power Centre Morphology and Consumer Spatial Behaviour," *Canadian Journal of Urban Research*, 2005: 364–84.

190 *the suburbs were*: Frank, L., et al., "Stepping Towards Causation," 1898–914.

192 *separate paths for bicycles*: Conversation with Greg Raisman, City of Portland planning department, 2009.

192 *mortality rate*: Hamilton-Baillie, B., "Urban Design: Why Don't We Do It in the Road?" *Journal of Urban Technology*, 2004: 43–62.

192n *The problem*: Walker, Ian, "Drivers Overtaking Bicyclists: Objective Data on the Effects of Riding Position, Helmet Use, Vehicle Type and Apparent Gender," *Accident Analysis and Prevention*, 2007: 417–25.

193 *number of young people*: DeGroat, Bernie, "Fewer Young, but More Elderly, Have Driver's License," *The University Record Online*, University of Michigan, December 5, 2011, http://ur.umich.edu/1112/Dec05_11/2933-fewer-young-but (accessed March 3, 2012).

193 *American transit users*: Ory and Mokhtarian, "When Is Getting There Half the Fun?" 97–123.

193 *British trains*: Clark, Andrew, "Want to Feel Less Stress? Become a Fighter Pilot, Not a Commuter," *The Guardian*, November 30, 2004, www.guardian.co .uk/uk/2004/nov/30/research.transport (accessed October 06, 2012).

194 *"freaks and weirdos"*: See http://www.boingboing.net/2003/04/15/gm-apologizes -for-fr.html for correspondence.

9. Mobilicities II: Freedom

196 *Norman Bel Geddes*: Bel Geddes, Norman, *Magic Motorways* (New York: Random House, 1940).

196 *Buckminster Fuller*: Fuller, R. Buckminster, *Operation Manual for Spaceship Earth* (Carbondale: Southern Illinois University Press, 1969).

200 *also its limitations*: Evans, Gary, Richard Wener, and Donald Phillips, "The Morning Rush Hour: Predictability and Commuter Stress," *Environment and Behavior*, 2002: 521–30.

201 *anxiety of waiting*: Evans, John E., "Transit Scheduling and Frequency," in *Traveler Response to Transportation System Changes*," TCRP Report 95 (Washington, DC: Transportation Research Board, National Academy Press, 2004.)

202 *arrival countdown clocks*: Schweiger, C. L. "Customer and Media Reactions to Real-Time Bus Arrival Information Systems," in *Real-Time Bus Arrival Information Systems: A Synthesis of Transit Practice*, TCRP Report 48 (Washington, DC: Transportation Research Board, 2003).

202 *traveling at night*: Dziekan, Katrin, and Karl Kottenhoff, "Dynamic At-Stop Real-Time Information Displays for Public Transport: Effects on Customers," *Transportation Research Part A: Policy and Practice*, 2007: 489–501.

202 *Metropolitan Transit Authority*: Metropolitan Transit Authority, "New Technology Helps Keep Customers Informed," http://new-mta.info/news/new -technology-helps-keep-customers-informed (accessed April 30, 2013).

202 *a service called Transit Board*: TriMet App Center: http://trimet.org/apps; "Transit Board," *Portland Transport*, August 13, 2007, http://portlandtransport .com/archives/2007/08/transit_board_1.html (accessed March 3, 2012).

207n *Any honest assessment*: Tranter, Paul J., "Effective Speeds: Car Costs Are Slowing Us Down," Australian Greenhouse Office, Department of the Environment and Heritage, 2004; U.S. Department of Transportation Federal Highway Administration, "2009 National Household Travel Survey"; American Automobile Association, "Your Driving Costs," Heathrow, FL: annual issues, April 16, 2013; Research and Innovative Technology Administration, Bureau of Transportation Statistics, "Table 3-17: Average Cost of Owning and Operating an Automobile," *National Transportation Statistics*, http://www.rita .dot.gov/bts/sites/rita.dot.gov.bts/files/publications/national_transportation _statistics/html/table_03_17.html (accessed April 29, 2013).

208 *people in Vancouver*: "2005 Annual Report Livable Region Strategic Plan," Regional Development Policy & Planning Department, Greater Vancouver Regional District, Burnaby, 2005.

208 *proposals to repurpose*: Bula, Frances, "Vancouver Tax Hike Drives Home Message That Cars Have No Place Downtown," *The Globe and Mail*, January 2, 2012.

208 *Car sharing has now found*: Andersen, Michael, "Five Secrets from the Future of Car Sharing," *Sightline Daily*, December 14, 2011, http://daily.sightline.org /2011/12/14/five-secrets-from-the-future-of-car-sharing (accessed April 29, 2013); Geron, Tomio, "Getaround Brings Car-Sharing to Oregon with Federal Grant," *Forbes*, December 13, 2011, www.forbes.com/sites/tomiogeron/2011 /12/13/getaround-brings-car-sharing-startup-to-oregon-with-federal-grant (accessed March 3, 2012); "Getaround," *Portland Afoot*, www.portlandafoot .org/w/Getaround#Testimony_from_Getaround_Users_in_Mountain_View .2C_Calif (accessed March 3, 2012).

209 *advantage of the bicycle*: P. Jensen, J. B. Rouquier, N. Ovtracht, and C. Robardet, "Characterizing the Speed and Paths of Shared Bicycles in Lyon," *Transportation Research Part D: Transport and Environment*, 2010: 522–24.

210 *safety in numbers*: Price, Gordon, *Price Tags*, 101, March 11, 2008; Pucher J., R. Buehler, and M. Seinen, "Bicycling Renaissance in North America? An Update and Re-Appraisal of Cycling Trends & Policies," *Transportation Research Part A: Policy and Practice*, 2011; 45(6): 451–75; Nussbaum, Paul, "More Bicyclists Means Fewer Accidents, Phila. Finds," *Philly.com*, *Philadelphia Inquirer* and *Philadelphia Daily News*, September 17, 2012, http://articles.philly.com /2012-09-17/business/33881208_1_bike-sales-bike-lanes-bicycle-coalition.

210n *Even in New York City*: Walsh, Bryan, "New York City's Bicycle Wars," *Time*, July 3, 2012, www.time.com/time/health/article/0,8599,2118668,00.html (accessed February 2, 2013).

211 *worse peripheral vision*: Conversation with Greg Raisman.

211 *high tolerance for risk*: Hennig, J., U. Laschefski, and C. Opper, "Biopsychological Changes After Bungee Jumping: β-Endorphin Immunoreactivity as a Mediator of Euphoria?" *Neuropsychobiology*, 1994: 28–32.

212 *Tom Vanderbilt*: Vanderbilt, Tom, *Traffic: Why We Drive the Way We Do (and What It Says About Us)* (Toronto: Knopf Canada, 2008), 199.

213 *Commuting by bike*: Pucher J., et al., "Bicycling Renaissance in North America?," 459.

216 *pilgrimage to Copenhagen*: City of Copenhagen Technical and Environmental Administration Traffic Department, "Copenhagen, City of Cyclists: Bicycle Account 2008," Copenhagen, 2008.

217 *"the Copenhagen SUV"*: Ibid.

217n *By the 1960s*: "Cycling in the Netherlands," The Hague: Ministry of Transport, Public Works, and Water Management, Directorate-General for Passenger Transport, and Expertise Centre for Cycling Policy, 2009, 13.

220 *cars are space hogs*: "Comparing Per Person Travel Space Needs," infographic courtesy of *Spacing* magazine, data: Victoria Transportation Policy Institute.

222 *reduced traffic in the core*: Transport for London, "Central London Congestion Charging: Impacts Monitoring," Fourth Annual Report," London, 2006.

222 *Chinese powerhouse of Guangzhou*: Bradsher, Keith, "A Chinese City Moves to Limit New Cars," *New York Times*, Global Business, September 4, 2012, www .nytimes.com/2012/09/05/business/global/a-chinese-city-moves-to-limit-new -cars.html (accessed April 29, 2013).

223 *one in ten pedestrians they counted*: New York City Department of Transportation, "World Class Streets: Re-making New York City's Public Realm," consultant report, New York, 2008.

223n *Rude behavior*: James, Leon, "Pedestrian Psychology and Safety: Sidewalk Rage/ Pedestrian Rage," DrDriving.org, www.drdriving.org/pedestrians (accessed March 3, 2012); "Study: NYC Sidewalks Getting More Crowded," CBS New York, August 6, 2011, http://newyork.cbslocal.com/2011/08/06/study-nyc-side walks-getting-more-crowded (accessed March 3, 2012).

224 *Injuries to drivers*: Figures from NYC DOT study, available at the NYCDOT website's about DOT, Broadway section: www.nyc.gov/html/dot/html/about /broadway.shtml (accessed January 22, 2011).

10. Who Is the City For?

227 *Henri Lefebvre*: Henri Lefebvre, "The Right to the City," in Kofman, Eleonore, and Elizabeth Lebas, trans. and ed., *Writings on Cities: Henri Lefebvre* (Oxford, UK: Blackwell, 1996).

228 *But the TransMilenio*: Interview with Angelica Castro Rodríguez, general manager of the public-private alliance that runs the TransMilenio service.

231 *1,387 traffic deaths*: Martin, Gerard, and Miguel Arévalo Ceballos, *Bogotá: Anatomía de una transformación: políticas de seguridad ciudadana 1995–2003* (Bogotá: Pontificia Universidad Javeriana, 2004).

231 *three-quarters of Bogotanos*: Gallup Poll.

237 *low-ranking employees*: University College London Research Department of Epidemiology and Public Health, "Whitehall II Study," July 8, 2010, www .ucl.ac.uk/whitehallII/publications/year/2010 (accessed January 29, 2011).

237 *poor people in cities*: Wilkinson, R., *Mind the Gap: Hierarchies, Health, and Human Evolution* (London: Weidenfeld and Nicolson, 2000).

237 *Changes in social status*: The UCLA neuroscientist Michael McGuire discovered that changes in social status affect serotonin levels in the brains of vervet monkeys as well as college undergraduates. See Frank, Robert, *Luxury Fever* (Princeton, NJ: Princeton University Press, 1999), 141; McGuire, Michael T., M. J. Raleigh, and G. L. Brammer, "Sociopharmacology," *Annual Review of Pharmacology and Toxicology*, 1982: 643–61.

237 *"psychosocial consequences"*: Adler, Nancy, Elissa Epel, Grace Castellazzo, and Jeannette Ickovics, "Relationship of Subjective and Objective Social Status

with Psychological and Physiological Functioning: Preliminary Data in Healthy White Women," *Health Psychology*, 2000: 586–92.

237n *Status comparisons*: Layard, Richard, *Happiness: Lessons from a New Science* (London: Penguin/Allen Lane, 2005), 43–48.

238 *higher rates of mental illness*: Wilkinson, Richard, and Kate Pickett, *The Spirit Level: Why Greater Equality Makes Society Stronger* (London: Bloomsbury, 2009).

238n *This may be part of the reason*: Harris, Gregory, "Liberal or Tory, Minority Gov't Would Hit 'Sweet Spot,' Profs Say," University of Calgary press release, January 18, 2006, www.ucalgary.ca/mp2003/news/jan06/third-way.html (accessed January 12, 2011); Helliwell, John F., *Globalization and Well-Being* (Vancouver: UBC Press, 2002).

240 *Michael Bloomberg*: Cassidy, John, *Rational Irrationality*, "Battle of the Bike Lanes," *The New Yorker*, March 8, 2011, www.newyorker.com/online/blogs/johncassidy/2011/03/battle-of-the-bike-lanes-im-with-mrs-schumer.html (accessed March 3, 2012).

240 *commutes by taxi*: U.S. Census Bureau, "American Community Survey," 2009.

240n *The opponents' various claims*: "Bike Lanes," Memorandum, City of New York, Office of the Mayor, 2011.

240n *the poorest quarter of all Americans*: Pucher, John, and Ralph Buehler, "Analysis of Bicycling Trends and Policies in Large North American Cities: Lessons for New York," final report, University Transportation Research Center, Rutgers University/Virginia Tech, 2011.

241 *Older African Americans and Latinos*: Ibid.

241 *that go with obesity*: Robert Wood Johnson Foundation Fact Sheet, "Do All Children Have Places to Be Active?" *Active Living Research*, May 2012, www.activelivingresearch.org/files/Synthesis_Disparities_Factsheet_May2012.pdf (accessed October 12, 2012).

241 *less access to jobs*: "Where We Need to Go: A Civil Rights Roadmap for Transportation Equity," Leadership Conference Education Fund, 2011.

241 *less access to food*: Economic Research Service, *Access to Affordable and Nutritious Food: Measuring and Understanding Food Deserts and Their Consequences: Report to Congress* (Washington, DC: U.S. Department of Agriculture, 2009).

242 *worse access to supermarkets*: Leone, A. F., et al., "The Availability and Affordability of Healthy Food Items in Leon County, Florida," www.med.upenn.edu/nems/docs/Leone_et_al_Abstract.doc (accessed March 3, 2012).

242 *even to have sidewalks*: King, A. C., C. Castro, A. A. Eyler et al., "Personal and Environmental Factors Associated with Physical Inactivity Among Different Racial-Ethnic Groups of U.S. Middle-Aged and Older-Aged Women," *Health Psychology*, 2000: 354–64.

242 *New Economics Foundation*: New Economics Foundation, 2002.

242 *in the U.K. benefit*: Sustainable Development Commission, "Fairness in a Car-Dependent Society," London, 2011.

242n *Sidewalks in Los Angeles*: Bloomekatz, Ari, "Suits Could Force L.A. to Spend Huge Sums on Sidewalk Repair," *Los Angeles Times*, January 30, 2012, http://articles.latimes.com/2012/jan/30/local/la-me-sidewalks-20120131 (accessed October 11, 2012).

243 *The number crunchers*: Litman, Todd, *Whose Roads? Evaluating Bicyclists' and Pedestrians' Right to Use Public Roadways* (Victoria, BC: Victoria Transport Policy Institute, 2012), 10–13.

243n *In American cities*: Litman, Todd, *Affordable-Accessible Housing in a Dynamic City: Why and How to Increase Affordable Housing Development in Accessible Locations* (Victoria, BC: Victoria Transport Policy Institute, 2013).

244 *segregated by income class*: Fry, Richard, and Paul Taylor, "The Rise of Residential Segregation by Income," *Pew Research Center*, August 1, 2012. www.pew socialtrends.org/2012/08/01/the-rise-of-residential-segregation-by-income (accessed October 14, 2012).

245 *Seattle's Rainier Valley*: Greenwich, Howard, and Margaret Wykowski, "Transit Oriented Development That's Healthy, Green & Just," *Puget Sound Sage*, May 14, 2012. www.pugetsoundsage.org//downloads/TOD%20that%20is %20Healthy,%20Green%20and%20Just.pdf (accessed October 11, 2012).

245 *lightning-fast gentrification*: Moss, Jeremiah, "Disney World on the Hudson," *New York Times*, August 21, 2012, A25.

245 *colonizing inner cities*: Ehrenhalt, Alan, *The Great Inversion and the Future of the American City* (New York: Knopf, 2012).

246 *Montgomery, Maryland*: Montgomery County Department of Housing and Community Affairs. "History of the Moderately Priced Dwelling Unit (MPDU) Program in Montgomery County," *MontgomeryCountyMaryland*, April 22, 2005, www6.montgomerycountymd.gov/dhctmpl.asp?url=/content/dhca/hous ing/housing_P/mpdu/history.asp (accessed October 10, 2012).

246n *Vancouver and Melbourne*: Pavletich, Hugh, and Wendell Cox, "8th Annual Demographia International Housing Affordability Survey: 2012," *Demographia*, www.demographia.com/dhi.pdf (accessed October 11, 2012).

248 *cycling to work*: Ipsos Public Affairs, "Encuesta de Percepción Bogotá Cómo Vamos 2009," 2009.

249 *improvement in air quality*: Behrentz, Eduardo, "Concentraciones de material particulado respirable suspendido en el aire en inmediaciones de una vía de transporte público colectivo," final report, Departamento de Ingeniería Civil y Ambiental, Universidad de los Andes, Centro de Investigaciones en Ingeniería Ambiental, 2006.

249 *Bogotans got healthier*: "We think this may be because the TransMilenio is the fastest way across the city, so people will walk farther to take the bus," surmised researcher Olga Luise Sarmiento; study: Gomez, L. F., et al., "Built Environment Attributes and Walking Patterns Among the Elderly Population in Bogotá," *American Journal of Preventative Medicine*, 2010: 592–99.

11. Everything Is Connected to Everything Else

251 *Walter Benjamin*: Benjamin, Walter, *Understanding Brecht* (London: Verso and New Left Books, 1973), 87.

252 *"'hedonistic sustainability'"*: Discussion with Ingels at the BMW Guggenheim Lab in New York City in 2011. Additional information: Quirk, Vanessa, "BIG's Waste-to-Energy Plant Breaks Ground, Breaks Schemas," ArchDaily, March 5, 2013, www.archdaily.com/339893 (accessed April 30, 2013); Woodward, Richard B., "Building a Better Future," *Wall Street Journal Magazine*, October 28, 2011, http://online.wsj.com/article/SB10001424052970204644504576653421385657578.htmlixzz1kPqwl62S (accessed March 3, 2012).

254n *By nearly 250,000 tons*: "Bus Rapid Transit Systems Reduce Greenhouse Gas Emissions, Gain in Popularity," Worldwatch Institute/Eye on Earth, www.worldwatch.org/node/4660 (accessed January 11, 2011).

254n *After the charge was*: "Central London Congestion Charging: Impacts Monitoring," Transport for London, fifth annual report, July 2007.

255 *Paris Plages has seen*: Mairie de Paris, "Paris Climate Protection Plan," Paris, 2007.

255 *copied Bogotá's mobility system*: Secretaria del Medio Ambiente, "Plan Verde: Ciudad de Mexico," www.om.df.gob.mx/programas/plan_verde/plan_verde_vlarga.pdf (accessed April 29, 2013).

257 *City of New York*: "Sustainable Streets: Strategic Plan for the New York City Department of Transportation, 2008 and Beyond," New York City Department of Transportation, 2008.

257 *bringing down emissions*: Chan, Margaret, "Cutting Carbon, Improving Health," *The Lancet*, 2009: 1870–71.

257n *Mexico experiences*: Interview with Guillermo Peñalosa, 2009.

257n *When we walk or cycle*: "Calories in Coca-Cola Classic," Calorie Count, http://caloriecount.about.com/calories-coca-cola-classic-i98047 (accessed March 3, 2012).

257n *Proponents of electric cars*: Libeskind, Daniel, "17 Words of Architectural Inspiration," TED, July 2007, www.ted.com/talks/daniel_libeskind_s_17_words_of_architectural_inspiration.html (accessed January 21, 2011).

258 *tens of billions more*: U.S. Department of Transportation, Federal Highway Administration, "Addendum to the 1997 Federal Highway Cost Allocation Study Final Report U.S. Department of Transportation Federal Highway Administration May 2000," www.fhwa.dot.gov/policy/hcas/addendum.htm (accessed March 3, 2012), adjusted to 2008 dollars.

258 *$180 billion annually*: Cambridge Systematics, Inc., "Crashes vs. Congestion Report. What's the Cost to Society?" Bethesda, MD: American Automobile Association, 2011.

258 *distance people drive*: Litman, Todd, and Steven Fitzroy, *Safe Travels: Evaluating Mobility Management Traffic Safety Impacts* (Victoria, BC: Victoria Transport Policy Institute, 2012).

258n *This includes health-care costs*: "Overweight and Obesity Statistics," Weight-Control Information Network, and information service of the National Institute of Diabetes and Digestive and Kidney Diseases, http://win.niddk.nih.gov/statistics (accessed March 3, 2012).

258n *Society reaps*: "Evaluating Safety and Health Impacts: TDM Impacts on Traffic Safety, Personal Security and Public Health," TDM Encyclopedia, Victoria Transport Policy Institute, February 22, 2012, www.vtpi.org/tdm/tdm58.htm (accessed March 3, 2012).

260 *a quarter of the cost of servicing*: Condon, Patrick M., *Seven Rules for Sustainable Communities: Design Strategies for the Post Carbon World* (Washington, DC: Island Press, 2010), 4.

260 *$18.9 billion*: Safe Routes to School National Partnership, "National Statistics on School Transportation," www.saferoutespartnership.org/sites/default/files/pdf/school_bus_cuts_national_stats_FINAL.pdf (accessed March 3, 2012).

260 *broke city governments*: Su, Eleanor Yang, "School Bus Service Vanishing Amid Cuts," *California Watch*, September 2, 2011, http://californiawatch.org/dailyreport/school-bus-service-vanishing-amid-cuts-12438 (accessed March 3, 2012).

260 *$2 trillion*: American Society of Civil Engineers, "Failing Infrastructure Cannot Support a Healthy Economy: Civil Engineers' New Report Card Assesses Condition of Nation's Infrastructure," January 28, 2009, https://apps.asce.org/reportcard/2009/RC_2009_noembargo.pdf (accessed March 3, 2012).

263 *looked at job density*: Minicozzi, Joseph, "The Value of Downtown: A Profitable Investment for the Community," Public Interest Projects, 2011.

263 *Walmart depresses average wages*: Dube, Arindrajit, T. William Lester, and Barry Eidlin, "A Downward Push: The Impact of Wal-Mart Stores on Retail Wages and Benefits," *UC Berkeley Labor Center*, December 2007, http://laborcenter.berkeley.edu/retail/walmart_downward_push07.pdf (accessed October 18, 2012).

264 *"heart and soul of Asheville"*: Muller, Michael, "Open For Biz: A Passionate Legacy," *Mountain Xpress*, August 17, 2010, www.mountainx.com/article/31638/Open-For-Biz-A-passionate-legacy (accessed March 3, 2012).

264n *The productive richness*: Civic Economics, "San Francisco Real Estate Diversity Study," San Francisco Locally Owned Merchants Alliance, 2007; Goetz, S. J., and H. Swaminathan, "Walmart and County-Wide Poverty," *Social Science Quarterly*, 2006: 211–26.

266 *reversing the trend*: Statistical analysis from Greg Raisman, City of Portland, Office of Transportation.

266n *1.4 million tons*: Cortright, Joe, "Portland's Green Dividend," White Paper, Chicago: CEOs for Cities, 2007.

266n *About 73 percent*: Cortright, "Portland's Green Dividend."

267 *investment of $100 million*: Kooshian, Chuck, and Steve Winkelman, "Growing Wealthier: Smart Growth, Climate Change and Prosperity," Center for Clean Air Policy, 2011.

267 *saving citizens*: City of North Vancouver.

268 *carbon U-turn*: Ipsos Reid Public Affairs, "Quality of Life and Financial Planning in the City of North Vancouver," City of North Vancouver, 2008.

270 *emissions by three-quarters*: Vancouver Deputy City Manager Sadhu Johnston in conversation, April 2012.

12: Retrofitting Sprawl

271 *Arcade Fire*: Arcade Fire, "Wasted Hours," *The Suburbs*, Merge Records, 2010, compact disc.

271 *William H. Whyte*: Project for Public Spaces, "William H. Whyre," www.pps .org/reference/wwhyte (accessed March 6, 2012).

274 *about 10 percent of homes*: Christopher Leinberger estimates that walkable neighborhoods make up less than 10 percent for sprawling cities such as Atlanta and Phoenix; Litman, Todd, *Where We Want to Be: Home Location Preferences and Their Implications for Smart Growth*, Victoria Transport Policy Institute, 2010.

274 *one out of every five*: Atlanta Regional Commission, "Lifelong Communities, A Regional Approach to Aging: A Vision for the Region's Future," Atlanta: Area Agency on Aging, 2010.

275 *120 million by 2050*: U.S. Census Bureau, "National Population Projections Released 2008 (Based on Census 2000)," www.census.gov/population/projec tions/data/national/2008.html (accessed April 29, 2013).

275 *right up to 2030*: Nelson, Arthur C., *Reshaping Metropolitan America: Development Trends and Opportunities* (Washington, DC: Island Press, 2013).

276 *Lakewood, southwest of Denver*: Dunham-Jones, Ellen, and June Williamson, *Retrofitting Suburbia* (Hoboken, NJ: John Wiley & Sons, 2011), 154–71.

278 *in the real estate market*: Leinberger, Christopher, "Walkable Urbanism," *Urban Land*, September 1, 2010, http://urbanland.uli.org/articles/2010/septoct /leinberger.

280 *eight parking spaces for every car*: Chester, Mikhail, Arpad Horvath, and Samer Madanat, "Parking Infrastructure: Energy, Emissions, and Automobile Life-cycle Environmental Accounting," *Environmental Research Letters*, 2010.

281 *an entirely new code*: Duany Plater-Zyberk, "Projects Map, U.S.," www.dpz.com /projects.aspx (accessed January 27, 2011); Seaside, Florida, "History," www .seasidefl.com/communityHistory.asp (accessed January 27, 2011).

281 *Seaside was the most influential*: "Best of the Decade: Design," *Time*, January 1, 1990, www.time.com/time/magazine/article/0,9171,969072,00.html (accessed January 27, 2011).

287 *rate of home ownership*: McKenna, Barrie, "To Follow Canada's Example, U.S. Tax Reform Essential," *The Globe and Mail*, August 8, 2011, www.theglobeand mail.com/report-on-business/commentary/barrie-mckenna/to-follow-canadas -example-us-tax-reform-essential/article2122284 (accessed March 3, 2012).

287 *gas taxes in 2012*: Randolph, Eleanor, "The Recession Squeeze on Buses and Trains," *New York Times*, December 31, 2011, www.nytimes.com/2012/01/01 /opinion/sunday/the-recession-squeeze-on-buses-and-trains.html (accessed March 3, 2012).

287 *approved by state governments*: Emerson, Chad, "All Sprawled Out: How the Federal Regulatory System Has Driven Unsustainable Growth," *Tennessee Law Review*, Tennessee Law Review Association, spring 2008.

288 *Commercial Center Revitalization Act*: Congress for the New Urbanism, "Sprawl Retrofit," www.cnu.org/sprawlretrofit (accessed March 3, 2012); South Carolina General Assembly, Reps. Smith, J. E., Brady, Agnew, R. L. Brown, and Whipper, "H 3604 Concurrent Resolution," 2011–2012, www.scstatehouse.gov /cgi-bin/web_bh10.exe?bill1=3604&session=119 (accessed March 3, 2012).

288 *writes Leinberger*: Leinberger, Christopher, *The Option of Urbanism: Investing in a New American Dream* (Washington, DC: Island Press), 50.

289n *Sociologists have found*: Sadalla, Edward K., and Virgil L. Sheets, "Symbolism in Building Materials: Self-Presentational and Cognitive Components," *Environment and Behavior*, 1993: 155–79.

291 *cut the tax rate by 30 percent*: *Mixed-Use Development*, 2nd ed. (Washington, DC: Urban Land Institute, 2003), 164.

291 *It usually takes eight hundred*: McPherson, Simon, and Adam Haddow, "Shall We Dense?: Policy Potentials," SJB Australia, 2011, www.sjb.com.au/docs/shall -we-dense_policy-potentials.pdf (accessed August 13, 2013).

292 *Warren Pledger*: Pledger, Warren, "Tampa Light Rail and the United Nations," *Examiner.com*, August 31, 2010, www.examiner.com/article/tampa-light-rail -and-the-united-nations (accessed March 3, 2012).

292n *As proof of a high-level conspiracy*: Mencimer, Stephanie, "'We Don't Need None of That Smart-Growth Communism,'" *Mother Jones*, November 18, 2010, www.motherjones.com/politics/2010/11/tea-party-agenda-21-un-sustainable-de velopment (accessed March 3, 2012); Morris, Nathan, "Playing Tea Party: Planning and Agenda 21," PlaceShakers and NewsMakers, January 6, 2012, www .placemakers.com/2012/01/06/playing-tea-party-planning-and-agenda-21 (accessed April 29, 2013).

294 *In 2008, for example*: Hawthorne, Christopher, "Atlantic on the Move," *Los Angeles Times*, May 13, 2012, www.latimes.com/entertainment/news/arts /boulevards/la-ca-atlantic-boulevard-los-angeles-index,0,378106.htmlstory (accessed October 22, 2012).

294 *More than three hundred cities*: Borys, Hazel, and Emily Talen, "Form-Based Codes? You're Not Alone," PlaceShakers and NewsMakers, www.placemakers .com/how-we-teach/codes-study (accessed April 29, 2013).

13. Save Your City, Save Yourself

295 *Jane Jacobs*: Jacobs, Jane, *The Death and Life of Great American Cities* (New York: Random House, 1961).

Acknowledgments

This project began with an idea, found early life as a series of magazine and newspaper stories, and grew into a book through the kindness and assistance of dozens of people over the course of five years.

I am grateful to the many people who shared their ideas with me. First among them is Enrique Peñalosa, who sparked the journey. The fire was stoked by many passionate minds. Among the many whose ideas and research I have borrowed or expanded upon are: Eric Britton, John Helliwell, Chris Barrington-Leigh, Patrick Condon, Gordon Price, Trevor Boddy, Lon Laclaire, Silas Archambault, Carlosfelipe Pardo, Elizabeth Dunn, Matt Hern, Emily Talen, Galina Tachieva, Frances Bula, Peter Norton, Larry Beasley, Larry Frank, Paul Zak, Nicholas Humphrey, Gil Peñalosa, Ricardo Montezuma, Jarrett Walker, June Williamson, Ellen Dunham-Jones, Todd Litman and the Victoria Transportation Policy Institute, Geoff Manaugh, Alan Durning and the Sightline Institute, Armando Roa, Felipe Zuleta, Alexandra Bolinder-Gibson, Colin Ellard, and ZUS. Edward Bergman was a constant source of ideas and *New York Times* stories.

I am grateful for the kindness of friends, family, and strangers who shared their homes and their time with me along the way. Big thanks to Sarah Minter, Arturo García, Branco, Mauricio Espinosa, Lorenia Parada, Mariel Loaiza, and la familia Domínguez-Flores in Mexico City. Thanks to Jaime Correa in Bogotá, Katherine Ball and Alec Neal in Portland, Byron Fast and Michael Prokopow in Toronto, Olivier Georger in Paris, Sarah Pascoe and Janet Fernau in London, Adam Fink, Adam Karsten Pedersen, and Henrik Lyng in Copenhagen, Doris Müller and Petra Marqua in Vauban, Steve Filmanowitz and Ben Brown in Atlanta, Kevin Wolf and Linda Cloud in Davis, Guillermo Jaimes in Los Angeles, Chris Tenove in Berkeley, Nancy, Randy, and Kim Strausser in San Joaquin County, Elizabeth Borne, Edward Bergman, and Dan Planko in New York, and the wonderful team at the BMW Guggenheim Labs in New York City and Berlin.

Erick Villagómez and Dan Planko generously donated infographics. Galina Tachieva, Jan Gehl, Lars Gemzøe, Bryn Davidson, Mike Sizemore, and Ethan Kent donated images. Scotty Keck translated ideas into more beautiful diagrams. Jan Semenza and Carlosfelipe Pardo helped with image sourcing. Cole Robertson wrangled images, permissions, and facts. Spanish translation came from Karla Cuervo Parada, and German from Michael Leukert.

Early research was supported by assignments from Jerry Johnson and Carol Toller at *The Globe and Mail*, Arjun Basu and Ilana Weitzman at *enRoute*, Anne Rose at *Westworld*, James Little at *explore*, Geoff Manaugh at *dwell*, Gary Ross and John Burns at *Vancouver* magazine, Rick Boychuk at *Canadian Geographic*, Dave Beers at *The Tyee*, and Amy Macfarlane and Jeremy Keehn at *The Walrus*.

The *Happy City* project would never have amounted to more than a collage of magazine stories without the cunning and charm of my agent and friend, Anne McDermid, and her fantastic team. The project received generous early support from the British Columbia Arts Council and the Canada Council for the Arts.

Any errors in these pages are my own. But the book would have been a shambling mess without the critical feedback of its early readers—Omar Domínguez and Michael Prokopow—and my editors in three offices: Tim Rostron at Doubleday, Helen Conford at Penguin, and Courtney Hodell, Mark Krotov, and Taylor Sperry at Farrar, Straus and Giroux. (Special thanks to Mark for giving the manuscript an urbanist's keen eye.) I am hugely grateful to Christine McLaren, whose hard work, reportage, and keen analysis infuse these pages. Christine came on board as a research assistant but left as a collaborator, dear friend, and fellow traveler on the road to the good city.

I am grateful for the cities that have nurtured me, especially Mexico, D.F., and East Vancouver. But if I have learned anything on this journey, it is that absolutely nothing contributes to happiness like our relationships with other people. I would not have survived intact without the love and support of my family, members of the Rose House, the Dommies, the Vancouver FCC, and my community of urban nerds and mountain pals, and, most of all, the heroically patient, loving, and forgiving Omar Domínguez. Thank you.

299 *writing haiku*: Naparstek, Aaron, *Honku: The Zen Antidote to Road Rage* (New York: Random House, 2003).

301n *Jon Orcutt*: Gleaned from Naparstek, Streetsblog, and DOT bios and press releases.

303 *Chan K'in Viejo*: "Chan K'in Viejo, 104; Led Mexican Tribe," *New York Times*, January 2, 1997, www.nytimes.com/1997/01/02/world/chan-k-in-viejo-104-led-mexican-tribe.html (accessed July 1, 2009).

304 *The Assyrians*: Moholy-Nagy, Sibyl, *Matrix of Man* (New York: Frederick A. Praeger, 1968), 161.

304 *national Land Ordinance*: Moholy-Nagy, *Matrix of Man*, 193–95 and John Reps, *The Making of Urban America: A History of City Planning in the United States* (Princeton, NJ: Princeton University Press, 1965), 214–17.

305 *public parks and plazas*: Reps, *The Making of Urban America*, 222.

309 *unprecedented heat wave*: Interviews with Jan Semenza; "Dying Alone: An Interview with Eric Klinenberg, Author of *Heat Wave: A Social Autopsy of Disaster in Chicago*," www.press.uchicago.edu/Misc/Chicago/443213in.html (accessed January 27, 2011); Semenza, Jan C., et al., "Heat-Related Deaths During the July 1995 Heat Wave in Chicago," *New England Journal of Medicine*, 1996: 84–90.

Epilogue: The Beginning

315 *David Harvey*: Harvey, David, "The Right to the City." *New Left Review*, September-October 2008, http://newleftreview.org/II/53/david-harvey-the-right-to-the-city (accessed November 1, 2012).

316 *"fear of exposure"*: Sennett, Richard, *The Conscience of the Eye: The Design and Social Life of Cities* (New York: W. W. Norton, 1990), xii.